# Industrial Applications of Big Data, AI, and Blockchain

Mahmoud El Samad
*Lebanese International University, Lebanon*

Ghalia Nassreddine
*Rafik Hariri University, Lebanon*

Hani El-Chaarani
*Beirut Arab University, Lebanon*

Sam El Nemar
*AZM University, Lebanon*

A volume in the Advances in Computational Intelligence and Robotics (ACIR) Book Series

IGI Global
PUBLISHER of TIMELY KNOWLEDGE

Published in the United States of America by
IGI Global
Engineering Science Reference (an imprint of IGI Global)
701 E. Chocolate Avenue
Hershey PA, USA 17033
Tel: 717-533-8845
Fax: 717-533-8661
E-mail: cust@igi-global.com
Web site: http://www.igi-global.com



Library of Congress Cataloging-in-Publication Data

CIP PENDING
ISBN: 9798369310465
eISBN: 9798369310472

This book is published in the IGI Global book series Advances in Computational Intelligence and Robotics (ACIR) (ISSN: 2327-0411; eISSN: 2327-042X)

British Cataloguing in Publication Data
A Cataloguing in Publication record for this book is available from the British Library.



For electronic access to this publication, please contact: eresources@igi-global.com.

# Advances in Computational Intelligence and Robotics (ACIR) Book Series

ISSN:2327-0411
EISSN:2327-042X

Editor-in-Chief: Ivan Giannoccaro, University of Salento, Italy

## MISSION

While intelligence is traditionally a term applied to humans and human cognition, technology has progressed in such a way to allow for the development of intelligent systems able to simulate many human traits. With this new era of simulated and artificial intelligence, much research is needed in order to continue to advance the field and also to evaluate the ethical and societal concerns of the existence of artificial life and machine learning.

The **Advances in Computational Intelligence and Robotics (ACIR) Book Series** encourages scholarly discourse on all topics pertaining to evolutionary computing, artificial life, computational intelligence, machine learning, and robotics. ACIR presents the latest research being conducted on diverse topics in intelligence technologies with the goal of advancing knowledge and applications in this rapidly evolving field.

## COVERAGE

- Computational Logic
- Pattern Recognition
- Computer Vision
- Cognitive Informatics
- Synthetic Emotions
- Robotics
- Cyborgs
- Natural Language Processing
- Computational Intelligence
- Brain Simulation

IGI Global is currently accepting manuscripts for publication within this series. To submit a proposal for a volume in this series, please contact our Acquisition Editors at Acquisitions@igi-global.com or visit: http://www.igi-global.com/publish/.

The Advances in Computational Intelligence and Robotics (ACIR) Book Series (ISSN 2327-0411) is published by IGI Global, 701 E. Chocolate Avenue, Hershey, PA 17033-1240, USA, www.igi-global.com. This series is composed of titles available for purchase individually; each title is edited to be contextually exclusive from any other title within the series. For pricing and ordering information please visit http://www.igi-global.com/book-series/advances-computational-intelligence-robotics/73674. Postmaster: Send all address changes to above address. 

## Titles in this Series

*For a list of additional titles in this series, please visit:*
*www.igi-global.com/book-series/advances-computational-intelligence-robotics/73674*

*Applications of Machine Learning in UAV Networks*
Jahan Hassan (Central Queensland University, Australia) and Saeed Alsamhi (Insight Centre for Data Analytics, University of Galway, Ireland)
Engineering Science Reference • copyright 2024 • 406pp • H/C (ISBN: 9798369305782) • US $285.00 (our price)

*Principles and Applications of Adaptive Artificial Intelligence*
Zhihan Lv (Uppsala University, Sweden)
Engineering Science Reference • copyright 2024 • 300pp • H/C (ISBN: 9798369302309) • US $325.00 (our price)

*AI and Blockchain Applications in Industrial Robotics*
Rajashekhar C. Biradar (Reva University, India) Geetha D. (Reva University, India) Nikhath Tabassum (Reva University, India) Nayana Hegde (Reva University, India) and Mihai Lazarescu (Politecnico di Torino, Italy)
Engineering Science Reference • copyright 2024 • 414pp • H/C (ISBN: 9798369306598) • US $300.00 (our price)

*Emerging Advancements in AI and Big Data Technologies in Business and Society*
Jingyuan Zhao (University of Toronto, Canada) Joseph Richards (California State University, Sacramento, USA) and V. Vinoth Kumar (Vellore Institute of Technology, India)
Engineering Science Reference • copyright 2024 • 320pp • H/C (ISBN: 9798369306833) • US $270.00 (our price)

*Advanced Applications of Generative AI and Natural Language Processing Models*
Ahmed J. Obaid (University of Kufa, Iraq) Bharat Bhushan (School of Engineering and Technology, Sharda University, India) Muthmainnah S. (Universitas Al Asyariah Mandar, Indonesia) and S. Suman Rajest (Dhaanish Ahmed College of Engineering, India)
Engineering Science Reference • copyright 2024 • 481pp • H/C (ISBN: 9798369305027) • US $270.00 (our price)

*For an entire list of titles in this series, please visit:*
*www.igi-global.com/book-series/advances-computational-intelligence-robotics/73674*

# Table of Contents


**Preface** ............ xiv

**Chapter 1**
Artificial Intelligence and Big Data Analytics in Green Supply Chain Management: Critical Analysis ............ 1
*Majida Jrad, Lebanese International University, Lebanon*

**Chapter 2**
Artificial Intelligence Applications in Renewable Power Systems ............ 26
*Mohamed Nassereddine, University of Wollongong in Dubai, UAE*
*Ghalia Nassreddine, Rafik Hariri University, Lebanon*
*Amal El Arid, Rafik Hariri University, Lebanon*
*Mahmoud Samad, Lebanese International University, Lebanon*

**Chapter 3**
Artificial Intelligence for Money Laundering Detection ............ 58
*Fouad M. Ziade, Lebanese University, Lebanon*
*Malak Mohamad Daher, Jinan University, Lebanon*
*Abdallah M. Ziade, Lebanese University, Lebanon*

**Chapter 4**
Artificial Intelligence in Central Banking: Benefits and Risks of AI for Central Banks ............ 70
*Peterson K. Ozili, Central Bank of Nigeria, Nigeria*

**Chapter 5**
Blockchain in Healthcare ............ 83
*Fouad M. Ziade, Lebanese University, Lebanon*
*Malak Mohamad Daher, Jinan University, Lebanon*
*Mustapha F. Ziade, HHL Leipzig Graduate School of Management, Germany*

**Chapter 6**
Blockchain Integration in Upstream Oil and Gas: Enhancing Performance Through Innovation ........ 97
*Kaustubh Laturkar, Michigan State University, USA*
*Kasturi Laturkar, Validation Associates LLC, USA*

**Chapter 7**
Blockchain Technology Through Bitcoin and Ethereum: A Comprehensive Review of Their Interdependent Relationship ........ 130
*Najib Saab, Lebanese International University, Lebanon*
*Mahmoud El Samad, Lebanese International University, Lebanon*

**Chapter 8**
Blockchain-Based Smart Contracts: Technical and Usage Aspects ........ 183
*Gulbir Singh, MMICT & BM, India*

**Chapter 9**
Cotton Health-Guard: AI-Enhanced Crop Health Assessment Through Image Classification ........ 204
*Manohar Kapse, Symbiosis Centre for Management and Human Resource Development, Symbiosis International University, India*
*Vinod Sharma, Symbiosis Centre for Management and Human Resource Development, Symbiosis International University, India*
*Jeanne Poulose, School of Business and Management, Christ University, India*
*N. Elangovan, Christ University, India*
*Yogesh Mahajan, Symbiosis Centre for Management and Human Resource Development, Symbiosis International University, India*

**Chapter 10**
The Role of Social Media Presence, Technology, and Personalization in Increasing Sales and Achieving Sustainable Business Growth ........ 220
*Lilian Shmait, University of Balamand, Lebanon*
*Lea Hamati, University of Balamand, Lebanon*
*Barbara Remlaoui, University of Balamand, Lebanon*
*Nour Khalil, University of Balamand, Lebanon*
*Christine Ghassan Haidar, University of Balamand, Lebanon*
*Sana Nasr, University of Balamand, Lebanon*
*Rita Nasr, University of Balamand, Lebanon*
*Sam El Nemar, University of Balamand, Lebanon*

**Chapter 11**
Transforming Human Resources With AI: Empowering Talent Management and Workforce Productivity ....... 254
*Mazen Fawaz Massoud, Jinan University, Lebanon*
*Bassel Maaliky, Luna Space Holding Company, Saudi Arabia*
*Abir Fawal, Beirut Arab University, Lebanon*
*Allam Mawllawi, Jinan University, Lebanon*
*Fadlallah Yahkni, Jinan University, Lebanon*

**Compilation of References** ....... 300

**About the Contributors** ....... 341

**Index** ....... 345

# Detailed Table of Contents

**Preface** .......... xiv

**Chapter 1**
Artificial Intelligence and Big Data Analytics in Green Supply Chain Management: Critical Analysis .......... 1
*Majida Jrad, Lebanese International University, Lebanon*

Technological advancement has led to a surge in their integration into various organizations spread across different economic sectors. Advanced technologies—BDA, IoT, machine learning, and AI—have been explored in terms of their benefits to the development of supply chain management (SCM), primarily environmental (green) practices. This research aims to generate existing evidence to comprehend how BDA and AI influence the development of GSCM. A systematic search strategy was developed using Google Scholar, Frontiers, and Science Direct databases. Ten quantitative studies identified various ways BDA and AI could be used in the supply chain, which foster GSCM development and competitive advantage maintenance in the long run. Results showed that by using the demonstrated medium, supply chain practitioners and supply chain managers will reduce cost overruns and waste, thus improving the effectiveness and efficiencies of the supply chain. GSCM development may lead to the recurrent use of recycling, renewing, and reusing resources within the chain network.

**Chapter 2**
Artificial Intelligence Applications in Renewable Power Systems .......... 26
*Mohamed Nassereddine, University of Wollongong in Dubai, UAE*
*Ghalia Nassreddine, Rafik Hariri University, Lebanon*
*Amal El Arid, Rafik Hariri University, Lebanon*
*Mahmoud Samad, Lebanese International University, Lebanon*

The field of power engineering has experienced significant advancements as a result of the integration of artificial intelligence methodologies, such as expert systems machine learning and artificial neural networks. In contemporary renewable energy systems, these approaches provide robust resources for the purposes of design, simulation, estimate, fault diagnostics, and fault-tolerant control. Over the course of recent decades, there has been rapid progress in the field of artificial intelligence technology, leading to a substantial increase in the utilization of AI applications inside modern industrial systems. This chapter provides an overview of the function of artificial intelligence in renewable energy systems. Three different types of renewable energy systems have been introduced in this discussion, including solar photovoltaic systems, wind turbine systems, and geothermal energy plants. Following the presentation of these systems, the authors proceed to critically examine the role of artificial intelligence in power prediction and defect detection within those systems.

**Chapter 3**
Artificial Intelligence for Money Laundering Detection ....................................58
*Fouad M. Ziade, Lebanese University, Lebanon*
*Malak Mohamad Daher, Jinan University, Lebanon*
*Abdallah M. Ziade, Lebanese University, Lebanon*

This chapter provides an overview of artificial intelligence (AI) methods for anti-money laundering (AML) and discusses challenges. The increasing complexity of financial crime has exposed the limitations of traditional rule-based AML approaches. AI technologies like machine learning, natural language processing, and computer vision show promise for improving AML effectiveness and efficiency. However, AI also faces hurdles around data quality, model interpretability, ethics, and proper human-AI collaboration. The chapter reviews the state-of-the-art AI techniques being applied across AML domains including customer due diligence, transaction monitoring, risk scoring, and investigations. Key recommendations for implementing AI in practice involve extensive testing, explainable models, strong governance, and human-centered design focused on trust and transparency. While AI has limitations, thoughtful deployment focused on fairness, accountability, and empowering human expertise can allow financial institutions and regulators to realize its benefits for combating money laundering.

**Chapter 4**
Artificial Intelligence in Central Banking: Benefits and Risks of AI for Central Banks.........................................................................................70
*Peterson K. Ozili, Central Bank of Nigeria, Nigeria*

This chapter identifies the benefit and risks of artificial intelligence in central banking. The benefit of artificial intelligence for central banks is that deploying artificial intelligence systems will encourage central banks to develop information technology (IT) and data science capabilities, it will assist central banks in detecting financial stability risks, it will aid the search for granular micro economic/non-economic data from the internet so that the data can support central banks in making policy decisions, it enables the use of AI-generated synthetic data, and it enables task automation in central banking operations. However, the use of artificial intelligence in central banking poses some risks which include data privacy risk, the risk that using synthetic data could lead to false positives, high risk of embedded bias, difficulty in explaining AI-based central bank policy decisions, and cybersecurity risk.

**Chapter 5**
Blockchain in Healthcare ........................................................................... 83
*Fouad M. Ziade, Lebanese University, Lebanon*
*Malak Mohamad Daher, Jinan University, Lebanon*
*Mustapha F. Ziade, HHL Leipzig Graduate School of Management, Germany*

Blockchain technology has emerged as a solution to tackle challenges in the healthcare sector, such as fragmented data vulnerabilities in security and a lack of transparency. In this chapter, the authors provide an overview of blockchain and its potential benefits for the healthcare industry. These include collaboration, improved integrity and security of data, enhanced efficiency, empowerment of patients, and advancements in supply chain management. However, implementing blockchain faces obstacles like scalability issues, the absence of interoperability standards uncertainties regarding regulatory aspects, and usability concerns. To ensure the adoption of technology in healthcare, the authors propose a strategic roadmap for both short-term implementation at individual hospitals and long-term transformation of insurance and billing processes through smart contract automation. This requires integrating with existing IT systems training for staff members addressing ethical considerations effectively and customizing approaches based on regional requirements.

**Chapter 6**
Blockchain Integration in Upstream Oil and Gas: Enhancing Performance Through Innovation.............................................................................. 97
*Kaustubh Laturkar, Michigan State University, USA*
*Kasturi Laturkar, Validation Associates LLC, USA*

With its complex exploration and production processes, extensive information exchange and stringent safety standards, the upstream oil and gas industry is embracing cutting-edge technologies to maximize operational efficiency and improve data reliability. Blockchain technology has risen to prominence as an appealing solution offering decentralized, trustworthy, and immutable information management capabilities. An outline of the upstream oil and gas industry is provided to demonstrate its role and impact on societal development. The fundamental principles of blockchain are then discussed, emphasizing its potential to revolutionize data handling, transactions, and smart contracts. The chapter also provides examples of some of the current operational projects in the upstream oil and gas industry that are exploring its potential uses and the challenges associated with its implementation. Through the insights presented in this chapter, oil and gas companies and key stakeholders can utilize blockchain technology to boost business performance and enhance efficiency.

**Chapter 7**
Blockchain Technology Through Bitcoin and Ethereum: A Comprehensive Review of Their Interdependent Relationship .................................................. 130
*Najib Saab, Lebanese International University, Lebanon*
*Mahmoud El Samad, Lebanese International University, Lebanon*

With a focus on the two most important cryptocurrencies, Bitcoin and Ethereum, this chapter explains the significance of blockchain in today's environment and analyzes its implementation in both networks as well as investigates how they work, describing their transactions, unique characteristics, benefits, and necessities, noting how Ethereum addressed some of Bitcoin's shortcomings with the introduction of smart contracts. They both depended on the proof of work (PoW) consensus mechanism at first, which Ethereum has moved to proof of stake (PoS) in its new upgrade as Ethereum 2.0. They examine the benefits and differences of these consensus protocols and other ones that deserve consideration and shed light on how they both have dealt with their challenges and drawbacks. Moreover, they analyze the prospects and likely improvements in blockchain technology, as they hope to illustrate the potential of blockchain along with Bitcoin and Ethereum to spark future innovation and address contemporary difficulties through their capabilities and network applications.

**Chapter 8**
Blockchain-Based Smart Contracts: Technical and Usage Aspects .................. 183
*Gulbir Singh, MMICT & BM, India*

Blockchains are decentralized, distributed, and immutable ledgers that can execute contracts on the blockchain, called smart contracts. Blockchain-based smart contracts have different challenges, opportunities, and applications in various fields like cryptocurrency systems, real estate, agriculture, logistics, and fire industry. The codes that can be executed and which operate on top of a blockchain to facilitate, implement, and enforce agreements between numerous parties in the absence of a trusted third party are called smart contracts. This chapter uses a taxonomy to classify different processes, such as comparing and contrasting the strengths and weaknesses of various methods and identifying research gaps and unanswered questions. The chapter also outlines some promising research guidelines for blockchain-based smart contracts and discusses the benefits and challenges. Researchers and practitioners in the field of blockchain-based smart contracts may find this chapter useful because it offers an overview of current and emerging developments in the field.

**Chapter 9**
Cotton Health-Guard: AI-Enhanced Crop Health Assessment Through Image Classification ........................................ 204
*Manohar Kapse, Symbiosis Centre for Management and Human Resource Development, Symbiosis International University, India*
*Vinod Sharma, Symbiosis Centre for Management and Human Resource Development, Symbiosis International University, India*
*Jeanne Poulose, School of Business and Management, Christ University, India*
*N. Elangovan, Christ University, India*
*Yogesh Mahajan, Symbiosis Centre for Management and Human Resource Development, Symbiosis International University, India*

Crop loss due to illness is the main issue that farmers deal with. The second issue is the delay in identifying which disorders to treat. Thus, the purpose of this study is to use the image classification technique to determine if the crop is healthy or sick. R software was used to implement picture categorization and machine learning techniques. The diseased leaf has been identified by the process of picture classification. In order to accomplish this, images of both healthy and diseased cotton crops were gathered from the fields. According to the study, the support vector machine algorithm is more accurate than other machine learning algorithms, which makes it suitable for real-time disease diagnosis and categorization.

**Chapter 10**
The Role of Social Media Presence, Technology, and Personalization in Increasing Sales and Achieving Sustainable Business Growth ......................... 220
*Lilian Shmait, University of Balamand, Lebanon*
*Lea Hamati, University of Balamand, Lebanon*
*Barbara Remlaoui, University of Balamand, Lebanon*
*Nour Khalil, University of Balamand, Lebanon*
*Christine Ghassan Haidar, University of Balamand, Lebanon*
*Sana Nasr, University of Balamand, Lebanon*
*Rita Nasr, University of Balamand, Lebanon*
*Sam El Nemar, University of Balamand, Lebanon*

While most businesses are now aware of the importance of focusing their marketing efforts on online advertising, many still struggle to effectively target their audience and convert online users to loyal customers. Nowadays, one of the main challenges faced by businesses is achieving sustainable growth and making profit in the long run while meeting the constantly changing demands of customers. Taking into consideration the psychology of consumer behaviour, the marketing strategies implemented, and the external factors that influence individuals, a comprehensive understanding of all those factors combined is necessary to plan and execute well-defined strategies for marketing professionals to follow. For that reason, a conceptual framework was designed to display all elements that contribute to increasing sales and achieving sustainable business growth by utilizing social media and technology strategically. Those factors were grouped into four main themes that cover effective marketing strategies, good customer relationships, personalization, and data collection.

**Chapter 11**
Transforming Human Resources With AI: Empowering Talent Management and Workforce Productivity ............................................................ 254
*Mazen Fawaz Massoud, Jinan University, Lebanon*
*Bassel Maaliky, Luna Space Holding Company, Saudi Arabia*
*Abir Fawal, Beirut Arab University, Lebanon*
*Allam Mawllawi, Jinan University, Lebanon*
*Fadlallah Yahkni, Jinan University, Lebanon*

AI is an irreplaceable human resources technological tool in the era of new technologies. AI allows recruiters to face tense talent shortages and resignation peril. AI benefits include talent identification, working time optimization, productivity elevation, and empowerment. Machine learning and profound learning advances imply faster processing speeds for applications and efficient solutions endorsed by human-artificial intelligence collaboration. Artificial intelligence experts in artificial intelligence concluded that AI will never replace employees but will act as an intelligent assistant supporting them to attain the organization's mission. Therefore, the biggest challenge for AI adoption is not technical but human. Innovative technologies depend on experts to train employees to use these intelligent machinery and systems intelligently. AI and talented workforces are partners in supporting the human resources transformation. Ultimately, employees gain in productivity and use their expertise for strategic decisions.

**Compilation of References** ............................................................ 300

**About the Contributors** ............................................................ 341

**Index** ............................................................ 345

# Preface

Welcome to *Industrial Applications of Big Data, AI, and Blockchain*. In the ever-evolving landscape of technology, these domains—Big Data, Artificial Intelligence (AI), and Blockchain—have emerged as transformative forces, shaping industries and revolutionizing conventional practices.

This book is a collaborative effort aimed at exploring and elucidating the multifaceted dimensions of these cutting-edge technologies. Edited by Mahmoud El Samad, Ghalia Nassreddine, Hani El-Chaarani, and Sam El Nemar, this compilation delves into the realms of Big Data, AI, and Blockchain, offering comprehensive insights, critical analyses, and innovative contributions.

The interconnectedness of Big Data, with its capacity to efficiently manage vast and diverse datasets, forms the bedrock of modern data-driven systems. Its attributes—velocity, volume, value, variety, and veracity—empower developers to create robust infrastructures, providing services ranging from data cleaning to sophisticated analysis.

The integration of AI across sectors—Business, Finance, Healthcare, Marketing, and Governance—has revolutionized operational paradigms. From automating tasks to enhancing decision-making accuracy, AI, bolstered by intelligent algorithms and Natural Language Processing, has become instrumental in predictive analysis and task optimization.

Blockchain, initially introduced for cryptocurrencies, has transcended its origins to become a decentralized technology applicable across diverse domains such as finance, healthcare, and governance. Its peer-to-peer approach fosters collaboration among nodes, eliminating the need for central authority and ensuring secure, transparent transactions.

This comprehensive volume caters to a diverse readership—researchers, industry professionals, technology enthusiasts, students, educators, and curious minds eager to grasp the transformative potential of these technologies across various sectors.

The chapters span an extensive spectrum, covering topics like AI-powered money laundering detection, Big Data analytics in healthcare, Blockchain in fintech, and the convergence of AI and Big Data in financial markets. These topics not only reflect the current landscape but also offer insights into future trends and challenges.

We extend our gratitude to the contributors whose expertise and dedication have enriched this compilation, making it a valuable resource for understanding the practical applications and implications of Big Data, AI, and Blockchain in the industrial landscape.

We invite you on a journey through the realms of innovation, exploration, and transformative technology encapsulated within the pages of this reference book.

## ORGANIZATION OF THE BOOK

### Chapter 1: "Artificial Intelligence and Big Data Analytics in Green Supply Chain Management: Critical Analysis" by Majida Jrad

This chapter investigates the influence of Big Data Analytics (BDA) and Artificial Intelligence (AI) on Green Supply Chain Management (GSCM). It identifies ten quantitative studies that reveal how the integration of BDA and AI can reduce costs, minimize waste, and enhance supply chain efficiencies, thereby promoting GSCM development.

### Chapter 2: "Artificial Intelligence Applications in Renewable Power Systems" by Mohamed Nassereddine, Ghalia Nassreddine, Amal El Arid, Mahmoud Samad

Focused on power engineering, this chapter provides an overview of AI's role in renewable energy systems. It delves into solar photovoltaic systems, wind turbine systems, and geothermal energy plants, emphasizing AI's contributions to design, fault diagnostics, and control within these systems.

### Chapter 3: "Artificial Intelligence for Money Laundering Detection" by Fouad Ziade, Malak Daher, Abdallah Ziade

Exploring AI methods in anti-money laundering, this chapter reviews machine learning and natural language processing techniques for enhanced AML effectiveness. It outlines challenges around data quality, model interpretability, ethics, and human-AI collaboration, recommending governance and transparent models for effective implementation.

### Chapter 4: "Artificial Intelligence in Central Banking: Benefits and Risks of AI for Central Banks" by Peterson Ozili

This article outlines AI's benefits (e.g., aiding in financial stability risk detection) and risks (e.g., data privacy concerns, bias, and explainability challenges) in central banking. It highlights the potential for IT and data science capabilities and the risks related to decision-making and data usage.

### Chapter 5: "Blockchain in Healthcare" by Fouad Ziade, Malak Daher, Mustapha Ziade

Focusing on blockchain's potential in healthcare, this chapter discusses benefits such as data integrity, security enhancements, and supply chain improvements. It also addresses scalability, interoperability, regulatory uncertainties, and usability concerns in implementing blockchain technology.

### Chapter 6: "Blockchain Integration in Upstream Oil and Gas: Enhancing Performance Through Innovation" by Kaustubh Laturkar, Kasturi Laturkar

This chapter explores blockchain's role in the upstream oil and gas industry, emphasizing its potential for decentralized, trustworthy data management. It discusses examples of ongoing projects and the associated challenges in implementing blockchain for enhanced efficiency.

### Chapter 7: "Blockchain Technology Through Bitcoin and Ethereum: A Comprehensive Review of Their Interdependent Relationship" by Najib Saab, Mahmoud El Samad

This chapter focuses on Bitcoin and Ethereum, exploring blockchain's significance and the evolution of their networks. It details their transactions, characteristics, consensus mechanisms, and improvements, shedding light on their capabilities and potential innovations.

### Chapter 8: "Blockchain-Based Smart Contracts: Technical and Usage Aspects" by Gulbir Singh

Examining blockchain-based smart contracts, this chapter categorizes methods, strengths, weaknesses, and research gaps. It discusses challenges, benefits, and emerging developments in blockchain-based smart contracts, offering insights for practitioners and researchers.

### Chapter 9: "Cotton Health-Guard: AI-Enhanced Crop Health Assessment Through Image Classification" by Manohar Kapse, Vinod Sharma, Jeanne Poulose, Elangovan N., Yogesh Mahajan

This chapter utilizes image classification techniques to identify healthy and diseased cotton crops, highlighting the support vector machine algorithm's efficacy. It emphasizes real-time disease diagnosis and categorization for improved crop health assessment.

### Chapter 10: "The Role of Social Media Presence, Technology, and Personalization in Increasing Sales and Achieving Sustainable Business Growth" by Lilian Shmait, Lea Hamati, Barbara Remlaoui, Nour Khalil, Christine Haidar, Sana Nasr, Rita Nasr, Sam El Nemar

Focusing on effective marketing strategies, customer relationships, personalization, and data collection, this chapter presents a framework to achieve sustainable business growth through social media and technology. It addresses consumer behavior and adaptable marketing strategies.

### Chapter 11: "Transforming Human Resources With AI: Empowering Talent Management and Workforce Productivity" by Mazen Massoud, Bassel Maaliky, Abir Fawal, Allam Mawllawi, Fadlallah Yahkni

Highlighting AI's role in HR, this chapter discusses its benefits in talent identification, productivity, and workforce empowerment. It emphasizes AI's support as an assistant rather than a replacement, outlining the need for expert training and human-AI collaboration in achieving organizational goals.

## IN SUMMARY

As editors of *Industrial Applications of Big Data, AI, and Blockchain*, we've embarked on a journey through the transformative landscapes of these cutting-edge technologies. The chapters within this reference book have provided a panoramic view of the myriad applications, challenges, and potentials encapsulated within Big Data, Artificial Intelligence (AI), and Blockchain.

From the critical analysis of AI and Big Data Analytics in Green Supply Chain Management to the exploration of Blockchain in Healthcare and the intricate role of AI in central banking, each chapter unveils a tapestry of innovation and practical insights.

The amalgamation of research efforts by esteemed contributors has laid bare the multifaceted dimensions of these technologies, revealing their potential to revolutionize industries, reshape decision-making, and enhance operational efficiencies.

Our journey encompassed the examination of AI applications in renewable power systems, the intricate details of Blockchain's integration in various sectors like oil and gas, the comprehensive review of Bitcoin and Ethereum's interdependent relationship, and the significance of social media and personalization in business growth.

Moreover, the exploration of AI-enhanced crop health assessment and the transformation of Human Resources through AI-powered talent management signify the breadth and depth of these technologies' impact across diverse domains.

As we conclude this compendium, it's evident that while these technologies offer immense promise, they are not without challenges. Issues of data privacy, scalability, ethical considerations, and human-AI collaboration are critical facets that demand attention in their implementation.

Yet, with careful consideration, governance, and collaboration, the transformative potential of Big Data, AI, and Blockchain remains profound. We extend our gratitude to the contributors whose expertise has enriched this collection and hope that this compendium serves as a guiding beacon for researchers, industry professionals, students, and technology enthusiasts navigating the ever-evolving landscape of these revolutionary technologies.

With optimism for the future and an unwavering commitment to exploring the frontiers of technological innovation, we bid you farewell from the captivating world of "Industrial Applications of Big Data, AI, and Blockchain."

*Mahmoud El Samad*
*Lebanese International University, Lebanon*

*Ghalia Nassreddine*
*Rafik Hariri University, Lebanon*

*Hani El-Chaarani*
*Beirut Arab University, Lebanon*

*Sam El Nemar*
*AZM University, Lebanon*

# Chapter 1
# Artificial Intelligence and Big Data Analytics in Green Supply Chain Management:
## Critical Analysis

**Majida Jrad**
*Lebanese International University, Lebanon*

## ABSTRACT

*Technological advancement has led to a surge in their integration into various organizations spread across different economic sectors. Advanced technologies—BDA, IoT, machine learning, and AI—have been explored in terms of their benefits to the development of supply chain management (SCM), primarily environmental (green) practices. This research aims to generate existing evidence to comprehend how BDA and AI influence the development of GSCM. A systematic search strategy was developed using Google Scholar, Frontiers, and Science Direct databases. Ten quantitative studies identified various ways BDA and AI could be used in the supply chain, which foster GSCM development and competitive advantage maintenance in the long run. Results showed that by using the demonstrated medium, supply chain practitioners and supply chain managers will reduce cost overruns and waste, thus improving the effectiveness and efficiencies of the supply chain. GSCM development may lead to the recurrent use of recycling, renewing, and reusing resources within the chain network.*

DOI: 10.4018/979-8-3693-1046-5.ch001

## 1. INTRODUCTION

The exploration of "Artificial Intelligence and Big Data Analytics in Green Supply Chain Management: Critical Analysis" commences with a profound examination of Green Supply Chain Management (GSCM). This chapter serves as a foundational backdrop, delving into the origins and evolution of GSCM, a discipline that transcends traditional supply chain practices to embrace environmental and social responsibility. GSCM represents a holistic approach to business operations, intertwining principles of environmental stewardship, ethical considerations, and economic viability. As businesses increasingly recognize the imperative for sustainable practices, GSCM emerges as a strategic response to this global mandate. In this chapter, our objective is to navigate the foundational principles of GSCM, shedding light on its historical development and its current role as a catalyst for environmentally conscious supply chain practices.

This exploration commences by establishing the contextual imperative for sustainable supply chains. The global landscape bears witness to a rising awareness of environmental concerns, coupled with a growing acknowledgment of businesses' pivotal role in shaping a sustainable future. This section elucidates the evolution of the green supply chain paradigm, probing into historical shifts, regulatory influences, and market dynamics that have propelled sustainability to the forefront of corporate agendas.

As the exploration traverses this historical backdrop, it becomes evident that Green Supply Chain Management (GSCM) is more than a fleeting trend; it represents a strategic response to our time's ecological and social challenges. Businesses are no longer evaluated solely on economic performance but are scrutinized for their commitment to responsible and sustainable practices. Against this backdrop, our exploration unfolds, aiming to comprehend how AI and Big Data Analytics function as transformative agents within the framework of GSCM.

In the subsequent chapters, our journey unveils the symbiotic relationship between AI, Big Data Analytics, and Green Supply Chain Management. Through a critical analysis of their integration, the exploration aims to navigate challenges, unearth opportunities, and contribute to the ongoing dialogue shaping the future of sustainable business practices. Together, let us embark on this exploration where innovation and sustainability converge to chart a course toward responsible and resilient supply chains.

## 2. GREEN SUPPLY CHAIN MANAGEMENT

The foundation of our exploration lies in understanding the relationship between supply chain management and the overarching concept of 'green.' Stadtler (2014) defines supply chain management (SCM) as the strategic coordination of business functions within and across its supply chain to enhance long-term performance. As environmental concerns gained prominence, Green Supply Chain Management (GSCM) emerged, encompassing sustainability considerations across all supply chain functions (Tseng et al., 2019). Environmental concerns within GSCM extend beyond the traditional supply chain, containing reductions in environmental implications, recycling, remanufacturing, and reusing (Seman et al., 2012). GSCM is not only about minimizing ecological impacts but also entails practices that enhance environmental and economic performance by fostering strong relationships with stakeholders such as customers, suppliers, and investors (Teixeira et al., 2018).

Green manufacturing, green purchasing, and reverse logistics are among the practices contributing to simultaneous environmental and economic performance enhancement.

Borrowing from diffusion theory arguments (Yang et al., 2023), GSCM activities involve disseminating environmental management knowledge throughout the supply chain. Organizations committed to social and ecological factors, in addition to economic gains, tend to attract more stakeholders, resulting in a competitive advantage (Laari et al., 2018). The theoretical perspective parallels the diffusion theory, emphasizing that companies integrating new practices, such as green approaches, strategically enhance their value proposition and competitive advantage.

In summary, 'green' in SCM involves integrating environmental concerns throughout the supply chain, leading to a competitive advantage. The subsequent sections explore how AI and BDA technologies can influence and further enhance the development of environmental initiatives in supply chain management.

### 2.1. The Impact of Big Data Analytics on Green Supply Chain Management Development

Big Data Analytics (BDA) emerges as a pivotal player in enabling the development of Green Supply Chain Management (GSCM) within organizations. Das et al. (2023) highlight that BDA creates a data mining environment throughout the supply chain, providing valuable insights to improve GSCM. For instance, manufacturing companies can use BDA technologies to assess the environmental impact of their processes, enabling them to incorporate sustainable technologies that reduce lead times and improve production efficiency.

The dynamic capabilities of BDA, as conceptualized by Oesterreich et al. (2022), contribute positively to supply chain performance measures and adaptability. Drawing from the Resource-Based View (RBV) theory proposed by Barney (1991), BDA is considered a strategic resource that positively impacts a company's competitive advantage. By integrating BDA into daily operational activities, supply chain managers can accurately assess costs incurred within the supply chain. Predictive technology combined with past sales trends allows managers to identify opportunities for green practices, such as reusing and recycling, to reduce costs and gain a competitive advantage strategically.

GSCM, driven by increasing environmental awareness, integrates BDA as a control environmental measure within and between companies. Ikram et al. (2021) use BDA in Jiangsu Province, China, for real-time ecological data analysis. This technology optimizes manufacturing processes, reducing emissions (Dubey et al., 2020). Similar findings by Agbehadji et al. (2020) emphasize using real-time monitoring through BDA to control energy consumption in companies, subsequently improving efficiency and supply chain effectiveness.

Technological progress has elevated the importance of BDA in decision-making processes, covering analytical fields like descriptive, predictive, and normative analysis (Elgendy et al., 2022). The relationship between BDA and GSCM development is explored through the Organizational Information Processing Theory (OIPT) by Doss et al. (2022). This theory, rooted in Thompson's (1967) work, posits that companies evolve into systems encapsulating various external and internal processes marked by uncertainty and complexity. The theory offers grounds for exploring organizational behavior through information processing mechanisms. In modern times, the rapid rise of data volume to be managed by companies leads to higher integration of information processing, which mandates the involvement of external and internal entities.

BDA is positioned by Doss et al. (2022) as enhancing organizational information processing capabilities and strengthening the collaborative environment. The information acquired can be used to make external supply chain decisions like integrating green purchasing practices to improve efficiency. Therefore, companies' use of BDA information processing capabilities to strengthen SCM efficiencies through assimilating green practices builds on OIPT approaches. BDA enhances organizational information processing capabilities, supporting collaborative environments and aiding external supply chain decisions, such as integrating green purchasing practices to improve efficiency. The discussions presented lead to the proposed assumption: Big Data analytics positively impacts GSCM development in organizations and may positively influence an organization's competitive advantage.

## 2.2. The Impacts of Artificial Intelligence in GSCM Development

Artificial Intelligence (AI) is defined as machines imitating and communicating capabilities, leading to enhanced problem-solving accuracy (McCarthy, 2007). Saad and Khamkham (2022) emphasize that AI adoption enhances collaboration in supply chain processes through accurate information distribution and transfer. AI technologies, utilizing intelligent equipment like wireless sensor networks and cloud computing, contribute to creating virtual infrastructures that facilitate GSCM development.

Cloud computing, a significant contributor to GSCM (Končar et al., 2020), aids decision-makers in reducing uncertainty in processing, demand, and supply (Nozari et al., 2021). Through cloud computing, AI technology provides infrastructure services, software, and platforms accessible via the Internet, allowing supply chain managers to monitor information flow within the supply chain. By creating the Internet of Things (IoT) and cloud computing, AI offers accessibility to Data Environment Analysis technology, aiding in green supplier selection (Dutta et al., 2021). The right choice of suppliers significantly impacts supply chain performance by improving efficiency and reducing environmental impacts through waste mitigation.

AI technologies support demand forecasting, which is applicable in transportation and logistics optimization within the supply chain (Hu et al., 2020). Organizations utilizing AI's demand forecasting capabilities can analyze traffic patterns and fuel consumption data, identifying efficient transportation routes. This reduces fuel and time consumption, facilitating green distribution and lowering supply chain carbon footprints. The operational performance optimization offered by AI algorithms maximizes profits and provides a competitive advantage through customer behavior optimization and competitor pricing based on market conditions.

## 2.3. Integration of AI and Big Data in GSCM

The synthesis of AI and Big Data Analytics within the Green Supply Chain Management framework marks a transformative phase in the evolution of sustainable supply chain practices. As established in the preceding sections, both AI and BDA independently contribute to GSCM development, optimizing efficiency, reducing costs, and improving environmental sustainability. The intersection of AI and BDA promises a new era of enhanced decision-making, holistic insights, and adaptive strategies for sustainable supply chains. By leveraging the complementary strengths of AI in intelligent processing and decision-making and understanding their environmental impact, uncover opportunities for green practices and strengthen their overall GSCM performance.

## 3. EMPIRICAL ANALYSIS

A quantitative review approach was employed to address the outlined research objectives. In contrast to the qualitative method, the quantitative review approach facilitates the testing of hypotheses and establishing cause-and-effect relationships (Yusup et al., 2018). Furthermore, the objective nature of the quantitative review approach, as Kandel (2020) highlighted in this context, assisted the researcher in grasping various assumptions related to optimistic AI and BDA implications in Supply Chain Management (SCM). Using the quantitative reviews approach, the researcher, leveraging gathered data, could cultivate a new understanding based on existing knowledge regarding whether BDA and AI contribute positively or negatively to GSCM development.

### 3.1. Data Collection Method

This research used a systematic literature review approach as the primary data-gathering medium. According to Flinn et al. (2015), systematic literature reviews are perceived as credible sources emerging from thorough outcome statements. More and more researchers are using systematic literature reviews. Van Dinter et al. (2021) cited accuracy, whereas risk replicability advantages were cited by Boell and Cecez-Kecmanovic (2015) as the main reasons for using a systematic literature review in their research. In this context, systematic reviews addressed the main research question: What are the implications of BDA and AI in GSCM development? An advantage highlighted in Rother's (2007) research is that systematic reviews help answer a defined research question.

### 3.2. Search Strategy

According to Nightingale (2009), a search strategy combines organized phrases, keywords, and subject headings used during database searches. The search strategy aims to facilitate the identification of relevant studies. Considering the central research question, the PICo (problem, interest, and context) strategy, as opposed to PICO (population, intervention, comparison, and outcome), was incorporated during the research activity. The PICo search strategy used is summarized in Table 1.

### 3.3. Inclusion and Exclusion Criteria

An inclusion criterion is defined by Hornberger and Rangu (2020) as a process of identifying the study population in a uniform and objective approach. Exclusion criteria, on the other hand, encompass traits that can result in a recruited population

*Table 1. Summary of PICO search strategy used during research activity*

| | Key Terms | Search Terms |
|---|---|---|
| Problem | Artificial Intelligence and Big Data | *Big Data Analytics* OR * Artificial Intelligence* |
| Interest | Green supply chain management development | *Green supply chain management* OR *Green supply chain* |
| Context | Artificial Intelligence and Big Data Analytics Implications AND green supply chain management development | *Artificial Intelligence impacts* OR *Big Data Analytics impacts* OR *Green supply chain management development* |

*Table 2. Inclusion and exclusion criteria used during the research activity*

| Inclusion | Exclusion |
|---|---|
| The article explores the implications of big data analytics on green supply chain management development. | Only explores the implications of big data analytics on supply chain management development. |
| The study explores the implications of artificial intelligence on green supply chain management development. | Only explores artificial intelligence implications on the development of supply chain management without considering environmental initiatives. |
| The article is written in the English language | The report is written in languages other than English. |
| Explores green supply chain management development from big data analytics and artificial intelligence impacts | Explores green supply chain management development from advanced technologies other than big data analytics and artificial intelligence. |

or articles ineligible for the research (Hornberger and Rangu, 2020). The inclusion and exclusion criteria used during the research activity are summarized in Table 2.

## 3.4. Databases

The literature search was carried out in August 2023; among the searched databases was Science Direct, which offers book chapters and journal articles from more than 12,000 books and 3,500 peer-reviewed journals. This provided the researcher with a broader scope of necessary research materials. ResearchGate database was equally used, attributed to being a hub facilitating academic publication sharing, which increased the researcher's access to broad academic publications related to the phenomenon under investigation. Other databases used during the research period include JSTOR, Frontiers, Emerald Insights, and Google Scholar. The search databases provided the researcher with platforms for narrowing results, quickly finding needed articles pertinent to testing the hypotheses to satisfy the research objectives. Ten articles were included in this research.

*Figure 1. Summary of the PRISMA flow diagram*

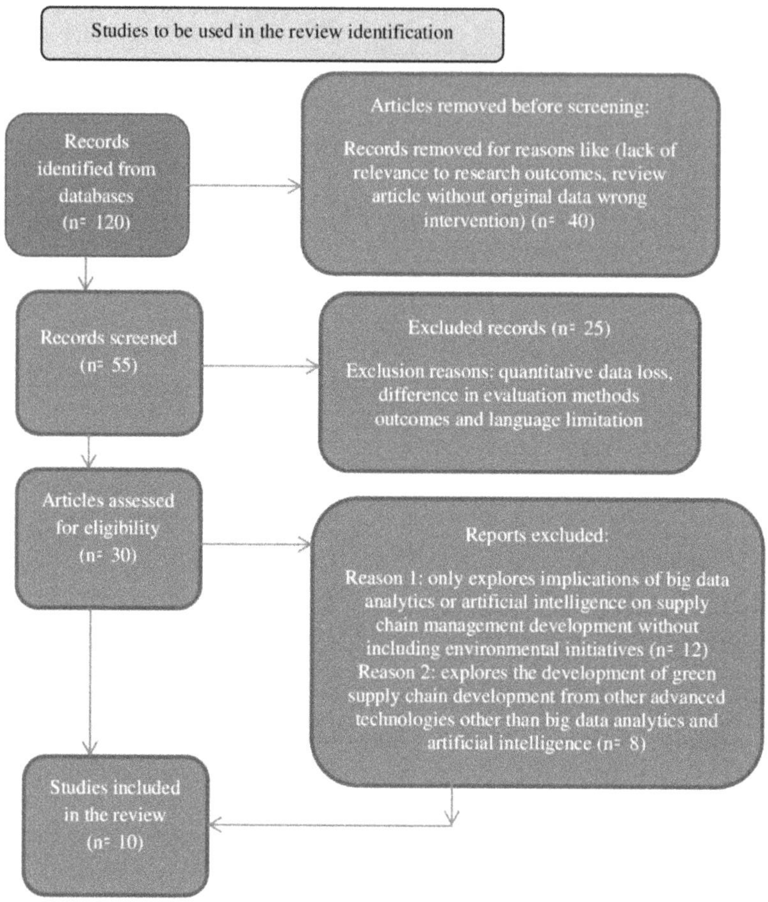


## 3.5. Further Searching

In conducting further research, this research incorporated PRISMA 2020 guidelines presented by Page et al. (2021) and is illustrated in flow chart 1.

## 3.6. Conducting and Documenting the Search and Selection Process

A detailed account of the data-gathering procedure was maintained during the research activity to keep track of all searches. Among the funds saved included

(a) the searched search engines, (b) periods the search was conducted, and (c) the used databases. The studies used in this review were primarily located using the institutional library system and saved in an electronic folder. Where no electronic versions of the literature were available, the researcher created hard copies, which were stored in a designated drawer only accessible by the researcher.

## 4. EMPIRICAL RESULTS AND FINDINGS

This review section encapsulates a thorough appraisal of the literature and results summary. This section starts with demonstrating relevant publications by year and percentage in the number of cited documents per year (2019-2022) generated from SCOPUS journals search. This is followed by a summary of the literature that starts this research and a detailed appraisal of the papers and subsequent analysis.

### 4.1. Publication by Year

Figure 2 shows the pattern of citations of relevant publications on BDA and AI (2019-2022) concerning green supply chain management. The chart demonstrates fluctuations in quotations with high records in journals like Engineering Applications and the International Journal of Robotics Research. Overall, the graph reflects increased research on the implications of artificial intelligence and big data analytics regarding green supply chain management development in recent years (2019-2022). As demonstrated in the figure above, the high to medium citations could be attributed to the growth in the application of AI and BDA in the supply chain of different industrial sectors. Moreover, the development of 'green initiatives' within the supply chain to minimize costs and improve efficiency could also be regarded as among the supporting reasons for the high to medium trends in citations in the recent past. Figure 3 below further supports the above arguments, demonstrating the citation percentage of publications about BDA, AI, and GSCM development (2019-2022).

The figure demonstrates low to high citation percentages at the beginning. Nonetheless, the fall in citation percentages in relevant documents (i.e., those investigating BDA and AI implications on GSCM development) could be correlated with ongoing research skewed to discover ways that the technologies can be used to aid in GSCM development in various sectors on a broader scale than what is already found (similar trends are also evident in figure 3 below representing the trend of BDA-AI technologies implications on GSCM development).

*Figure 2. Bar chart representing the number of relevant AI and BDA journals cited (2019-2022)*

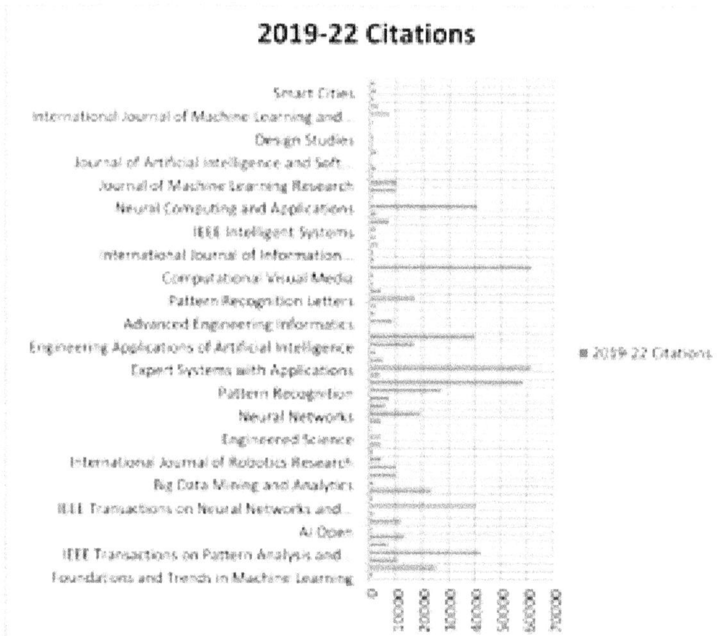


*Figure 3. Percentage of citations of (2019-2022) documents on AI, BDA, and GSCM development*

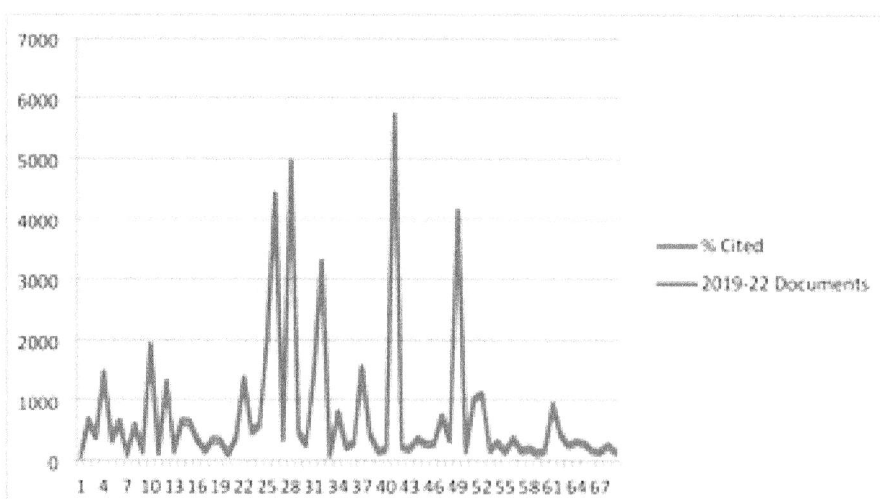

*Figure 4. Bar-chart representation of the trend in BDA-AI documents focusing on how the technologies influence GSCM development*

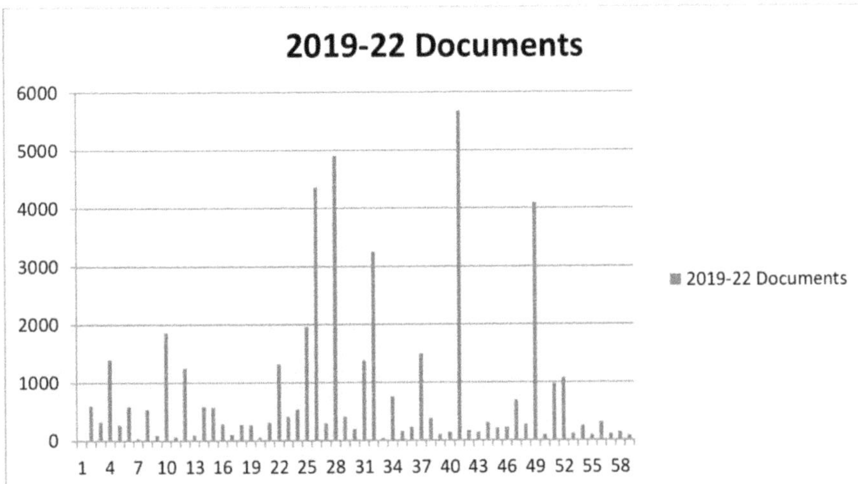


## 4.2. Systematic Literature

Table 3 includes the literature considered relevant for the systematic review.

## 4.3. Appraisal of the Quantitative Papers

Deriving information presented in Table 3 above, all the papers identified through the literature research used quantitative methods. The nature of the research phenomenon, the impacts of BDA and AI in GSCM development, is a broad topic due to factors like disparities in sectors and technological advancement in different regions of the world. For this reason, coupled with the characteristic of the quantitative method presented by Rahman (2020) using quantitative data compared to qualitative, it provides more generalizability and width across a larger population. To increase the breadth of study on the influences of GSCM development stemming from BDA and AI in most searched literature, translated to quantitative methods compared to qualitative and mixed approaches.

The above notwithstanding, the papers used various quantitative methods, with surveys and systematic literature reviews being the most frequently utilized as they accounted for four of the ten incorporated literature each. Other quantitative methods include a case study by Shokouhyar et al. (2020) and green supply chain management model development by Guan et al. (2022). Appraisal of the papers used in the survey

*Table 3. Summary of articles used in the systematic literature review*

| Number | Author, Year | Study Design | Industry | Main Findings |
|---|---|---|---|---|
| **1** | Gallo et al. (2023) | Quantitative: A survey of 402 participants | Manufacturing sector (Turkey) | There was a strong positive relationship between BDA-AI technology and GSCM. Application of BDA-AI technologies by top management enabled supply chain and logistics managers to support environmental performance through green activities like recycling in manufacturing. Little commitment by top management to applying BDA-AI technologies dampened GSCM development in the companies. |
| **2** | Al-Khatib and Shuhaiber (2022) | Quantitative method: survey method.<br>438 participants | Manufacturing sector (Jordan) | There was a positive relationship between the effects of big data analytics and artificial intelligence in green supply chain management performance. The relationship was analyzed through green human capital paradigms where BDA-AI technologies enhance skills and experience (through training) related to environmental aspects viable in improving supply chain activities. As an intangible asset, green human capital plays a fundamental role in creating new ideas and knowledge related to environmental aspects, thus solving environmental challenges faced by the supply chain and supporting GSCM development in the long run.<br>BDA-AI led to the sustainable performance of GSCM by optimizing the utilization of resources like human resources, especially when including environmental elements. |
| **3** | Benzidia et al. (2021) | Quantitative: systematic literature review of 168 hospital articles | Healthcare sector (France) | Findings showed that BDA-AI technologies have significant environmental process integration to supply chain management effect. The embedded capabilities in BDA-AI technologies contributed to improving information processes and internal hospital processes capacities. Enforcing these technologies helped in mitigating uncertainties resulting from unit interdependence. BDA-AI is observed to improve environmental process integration in the supply chain through enhancing collaboration between supply chain stakeholders. Aligning information capacities at external and internal levels of the hospital supply chain facilitates stakeholder collaboration. This translates to stakeholder consensus to ensure circular economic philosophy integration, strengthening environmental performance within the supply chain management. |
| **4** | Naz et al. (2022) | Quantitative research: Systematic literature review, 353 articles acquired from Scopus database and meta-analysis focused on BDA and AI implications.<br>The majority focused on BDA.<br>Substantial number of articles focused on AI implications. | General sector | A positive relationship exists between BDA-AI and GSCM through reducing carbon emission levels. BDA-AI adoption through technologies like meta-heuristic algorithms helps supply chain managers optimize significant scale supply chain management problems, hence reducing carbon emissions by including renewable materials, fostering GSCM development in the long run.<br>It was noted that using analytic hierarchy (AHP) in companies optimizes transportation systems. This reduces resource utilization, leading to less pollution. Ultimately, this improves the SCM efficiencies and development of GSCM. |

*continued on the following page*

*Table 3. Continued*

| Number | Author, Year | Study Design | Industry | Main Findings |
|---|---|---|---|---|
| 5 | Shahzad et al. (2022) | Quantitative method: Surveys; 347 supply chain personnel | General sector | It was observed that most of the respondents reported a positive relationship between organizational performance, BDA-AI integration, and GSCM development. AI algorithms can be used by Supply chain personnel like inventory, logistics, and supply chain managers to identify recyclable materials in the cause of product cycle. This reduces costs and waste within the supply chain. On the other hand, BDA was noted to gather substantial data amounts whose analysis draws insights into sustainable transport and supply chains. |
| 6 | Lerman et al. (2022) | Quantitative method: Survey 1,500 executives, managers, and directors in the supply chain | Small-and-medium companies (Brazil) | Intelligent supply chain (digital transformation strategy including technologies like BDA-AI) facilitates green performance in the supply chain. As indicated in the literature, incorporating green purchasing activities leads to higher GSCM through green relationships (internal and external GSCM activities). However, BDA-AI alone was observed to be insufficient in stimulating GSCM development, which calls for GSCM configuration. |
| 7 | Lee and Mangalaraj (2022) | Quantitative method: Systematic literature review encompassing 60 articles and meta-analysis, where the majority focused on BDA implications on GSCM development | Construction sector | It was concluded that predictive analytics capabilities of BDA are resourceful in optimizing resource like time and transportation cost allocation within the supply chain. By combining AI algorithms, enhance the supply chain management optimization capabilities. This reduces waste, an aspect besides facilitating GSCM development, promotes competitive advantage maintenance through supply chain efficiencies. |
| 8 | Shokouhyar et al. (2020) | Quantitative: Case study on 180 companies narrowing to the supply chain management. | 180 Pharmaceutical companies (Iran) | The results demonstrated that BDA-AI have strong implications on the GSCM in the pharmaceutical industry. The strong implications from the technologies results from their contribution to planning and supplementing technical knowledge. This translates to positive impacts on personal expertise and management capabilities. Green HRM (management capabilities) implements practices like development and training. Green HRM supports GSCM development as through training, employees are made aware of environmental management intricacies. |
| 9 | Wang et al. (2023) | Quantitative method: systematic literature review, 144 articles | General | There was an observed positive relationship between BDA-AI, organizational performance and GSCM development. BDA study of large volume of data: long-term consumption can aid in mitigating oversupply (waste reduction). This contributes to competitive advantage (organizational performance) by meeting consumer's needs and simultaneously contributing to the realization of green operations (green initiatives) in the SCM. Artificial intelligence through robotics, can impact GSCM development through optimizing production practices.<br>It was also noted that in BDA-AI, in company processes like manufacturing and processing, the need for precise control of the overall production process limits the effective use of the technologies, hence limiting GSCM development in the long run. |
| 10. | Guan et al. (2022) | Quantitative: construction of green supply chain management model | General | BDA-AI was found to positively impact GSCM development by stimulating inventory management. Combining IPSO and BPNN-AI algorithms improves neural network generalized performance, reducing stock-outs, improving supply chain management efficiency health, and promoting green initiatives (inventory waste reduction). |

will follow the Roever (2015) questionnaire checklist. All the documents that used survey methods included Shahzad et al. (2022), Al-Khatib and Shuhaiber (2022), Gallo et al. (2023), and Lerman et al. (2022), all used large participant numbers. This helped enhance supply chain management personnel representation, thus providing more accurate results. Nonetheless, Queirós et al. (2017) state that the accuracy increment from using large samples is relatively small, leading researchers to incur expenses in recruiting extra supply chain management personnel.

Four identified studies used systematic literature reviews, all apprised using the AMSTAR checklist. Wang et al. (2023) literature review did not contain PICO and PRISMA guidelines. The lack of PICO strategy components in the study presents potential implications, like the lack of a developed research question, thus limiting the literature search of relevant reports (Eriksen and Frandsen, 2018). On the other hand, according to Eriksen and Frandsen (2018), a lack of PRISMA guidelines may result in inefficiency in transparency and scientific merit of the reported systematic review. Nonetheless, the included literature answered the research aims on how big data analytics fosters the development of GSCM.

Meta-analysis was included in reviews presented by Lee and Mangalaraj (2022) and Naz et al. (2022), where PRISMA guidelines were used in both papers alongside that given by Benzidia et al. (2021) (despite not using meta-analysis). Using PRISMA guidelines in a systematic literature review is advantageous as it demonstrates its quality and allows readers to assess embedded weaknesses and strengths. Nonetheless, PRISMA guidelines also present notable challenges, for example, article heterogeneity presented by Jackson et al. (2016), which reduces the comparability of results across populations.

## 4.4. Findings

Quantitative studies in the literature search add to the existing knowledge body on big data analytics and artificial intelligence implications in green supply chain management development. Despite underlying challenges like the incapability of BDA-AI alone stimulating GSCM development in Lerman et al. (2022) literature findings, all studies reported a positive relationship between BDA AI on GSCM development and competitive advantage (organizational performance). BDA technologies in supporting GSCM development, as argued by Lee and Mangalaraj (2022) and Naz et al. (2022), result from optimization of problems within the supply chain management, including renewable resources to sectors within the supply chain with observed waste, an approach that reduces carbon emissions. Reducing carbon emissions through renewable resources improves production efficiency, thus fostering long-term competitive advantage and growth of using green practices in the supply chain.

AI algorithms have been observed by Shahzad et al. (2022) and Guan et al. (2022) to support GSCM development in organizations. Guan et al. (2022) use a green supply chain management model; AI algorithms like IPSO improve supply chain efficiency by facilitating operations like stockout reduction. Efficiency is promoted through waste reduction (from stockout reduction), which summarizes the use of green initiatives in supply chain management. BDA-AI is noted by Shokouhyar et al. (2020) and Al-Khatib and Shuhaiber (2022) as supporting GSCM development through green human capital. Green HRM practices like training and development have been presented by Al-Khatib and Shuhaiber (2022), fostering green human capital as a key player in new ideas and knowledge development concerning environmental issues the SCM faces.

Shokouhyar et al. (2020) echo similar thoughts, whereby incorporating BDA-AI technologies in the supply chain supplements technical knowledge. Training and development, besides technical knowledge acquired through green training, increases the employees' awareness of environmental management tactics. According to Casey and Sieber (2016), ecological commitment by organizations potentially improves employee motivation (i.e., stimulating their creative involvement in birthing new but practical ideas applicable to reducing energy consumption during processing). In the long run, employee commitment supports competitive advantage, subsequently leading to the growth of GSCM (i.e., integration of energy consumption approaches).

Negative implications on BDA-AI on the development of GSCM are observed by Wang et al. (2023), whereby despite the reduction of waste initiatives included in the SCM of a company, the requirement of precise control over the technologies may ultimately limit GSCM. Constructing and analyzing AI algorithms needs an individual with enough knowledge of operating the machine. Typically, these technologies have broad languages that are challenging to learn. This limits knowledge and skills acquisition by most individuals, reducing the margin of those specialized in the technologies. Comparing the number of organizations assimilating BDA-AI in their operations compared to the available experts, the former outweighs the former. In the long run, this limits the use of BDA-AI in some companies, subsequently reducing the development of GSCM.

## 5. DISCOURSES RELATED TO THE TESTING THE HYPOTHESIS

A strong correlation exists between the connectedness of BDA and GSCM development. With the proliferation of social media and technological advancement, Zhou et al. (2019) state influenced organizational performance due to a parallel rise in competition in different markets. GSCM is defined by Jemai et al. (2020) as a sustainable supply chain with coordination in business processes within a resource-wasteful supply chain. Improving its sustainability through implementing recycling lowers the whole business cost, stimulating production efficiency. BDA-AI technologies help in transforming data into relevant information. This information is sequentially used in decision-making processes, potentially supporting the supply chain. Zhang et al. (2022) state that GSCM is potentially properly managed when BDA-AI is in the organization, which fosters environmental management systems (EMS). EMS is defined as an adequately recognized tool by the European Commission (EC), which potentially leads to a shift towards a more circular economy (Bravi et al., 2020).

BDA-AI is characterized by analyzing large data volumes, which may give valuable insights to supply chain managers on the best ways of incorporating environmental initiatives. Managers may learn better ways to reduce air pollution in logistics. The availability of BDA-AI provides new insights concerning ecological initiatives based on the dynamics of market trends and consumer preferences. In the long run, this leads to the development of EMS, which primarily aims to facilitate organizations in achieving set environmental objectives. For a construction company that intends to use recyclable plastics during construction, EMS may enable the management to utilize cross-function resources to help manage environmental issues resulting in waste during construction.

The literature review section has vastly discussed the implication of BDA in GSCM development and competitive advantage maintenance. Agbehadji et al. (2022) research demonstrates the use of technology in real-time monitoring of electricity consumption (measuring electricity consumed in production processes) may allow the supply chain managers to make changes in consumption habits by integrating renewable energy sources like solar energy to power up procedures that require a high quantity of electricity. In this light, BDA deploys GSCM practices like reduction and cost reduction. Progressively, this translates to enhanced supply chain management and overall organizational effectiveness. In terms of competitive advantage, organizations, by using BDA technologies, may produce a product at lower costs than existing competitors, improving their competitive advantage.

Positive influences of BDA-AI in competitive advantage and stimulating GSCM development are also observed from the used searched literature of Wang et al. (2023), Naz et al. (2022), and Gallo et al. (2023). Meta-heuristics algorithms are AI technologies cited by Naz et al. (2022) that influence the optimization of large-scale management issues like long routes during delivery. Optimization, i.e., reducing delivery time by identifying possible short ways, may decrease carbon emission (due to shorter periods during delivery). In the long run, BDA supports GSCM development by reducing carbon emissions. Similar arguments are echoed by Hu et al.'s (2020) research in the literature review section, whereby traffic pattern analysis using AI forecasting capabilities can quickly identify efficient routes, fostering green distribution. Improving supply chain efficiencies in this light addresses the lateness of delivery challenge, hence nurturing customer satisfaction and loyalty (paradigms of competitive advantage).

BDA-AI is presented by Benzidia et al. (2021) as positively influencing competitive advantage and GSCM development through streamlining information processing. Integrating OIPT theory (organizational information processing theory) cited by Doss et al. (2022) in the literature review information processing mechanisms by BDA-AI, considering the large volume of data needed to be processed by organizations, can be used in decision-making processes of implementing green purchasing practices in the external supply chain. Benzidia et al. (2022) posit that aligning information capacities using BDA-AI technologies facilitates stakeholder collaboration in consensus in foreseeing the inclusion of green activities and strengthening supply chain management's environmental performance.

## 5.1. Limitations and Strengths

Improving GSCM development in organizations using BDA and AI technologies was a strength of this review as it allowed consideration of different ways the technologies foster GSCM development. The study also included various kinds of literature, which is a strength due to the providence of an independent literature review. Again, the lack of narrowing to a specific sector broadened the spectrum through which BDA and AI technologies have been accessed in promoting GSCM development.

Nevertheless, there are several limitations to this review. This research focused on AI and BDA technological impacts on GSCM development. This is a limitation as there are different technological advances, like Blockchain and machine learning, which promote GSCM development in organizations. This reduces comprehension of a broader perspective as to how other technologies apart from BDA and AI may limit or stimulate the development of GSCM. Moreover, another limitation is the lack of individual identification of relevant studies to the research subject. This reduces the scope of comprehension of other ways BDA and AI influence GSCM development. Also, there is a potential bias in estimating the implications of BDA and AI in GSCM development. This results from the lack of all studies being RCTs (Randomized Controlled Trials), whereby bias in this context links to publications that majorly showed positive effects. As a result, this led to limitations in including studies that showed challenges resulting from BDA and AI in organizations that may negatively reduce GSCM development.

## 6. CONCLUSION

In conclusion, the included literature for this systematic literature review reveals a positive relationship between GSCM development and BDA and AI, where the latter influences the former. The literature has highlighted these technological capabilities as platforms fostering GSCM development. Ideally, 'green,' as explained in the literature review section of this research, encompasses environmental practices like green purchasing, green marketing, distribution, and reverse logistics into SCM (the decentralized flow of services and goods management).

Improvement of competitive advantage has resulted from BDA-AI supporting the effective assimilation of green practices into organizational SCM. The use of AI algorithms and different analytical methods of BDA exposes supply chain management personnel like supply chain and logistic managers to broad data like air and carbon emission production rates during the transportation of products to the consumer. Therefore, using the capabilities of the technologies to analyze traffic reduces the time taken for delivery. This aspect leads to consumer satisfaction and potential re-purchasing from the company, stimulating competitive advantage. Subsequently, analyzing the traffic data fosters the incorporation of green initiatives, i.e., reducing carbon emissions and air pollution through short delivery routes. Repetitive utilization of the short courses supports GSCM development in the long run.

Cost reduction is another factor that results from the relationship between GSCM development and BDA-AI. As already established, BDA-AI is an advanced technology with superior capabilities like analyzing large data amounts in different formats (for BDA) and making inferences from the data (AI). In so doing, supply chain managers are offered an optimized depiction of the overall supply chain, including operating expenses and inventory returns. From this, the manager can quickly identify areas for waste reduction. Suppose operating fees in a construction project cycle are higher due to cost overruns emerging from building materials waste. In that case, a manager can integrate measures like green purchasing (buying from suppliers who provide sustainable construction materials like bamboo). Over time, using renewable materials will reduce costs associated with purchasing building materials, improving supply chain efficiency. It is argued that this factor replicates positive impacts on competitive advantage. Again, the repetitive use of renewable materials for construction integrates environmental concerns in the supply chain, fostering GSCM development.

### 6.1. Recommendations

It is suggested that future systematic research should focus on other technologies like Blockchain, cloud computing, and IoT, among others, to increase the scope of understanding how they impact GSCM development. This will also aid in answering questions like how digital technologies influence GSCM development.

## 6.2. Practical Implications

The findings presented in this research emerge effective for personnel in supply chain management, like inventory, logistics, and supply chain managers, as they can adopt the various ways of using BDA and AI to promote GSCM development. This research has highlighted the AI capabilities of algorithms and various analytical measures of BDA. Supply chain management personnel can use these capabilities to analyze supply chain optimization factors, i.e., measuring electricity consumption emissions during transportation. As a result, they can implement needed green initiatives of green distribution (by locating the shortest delivery routes) and green purchasing (buying from green suppliers). Practicing such findings within the various supply chain networks will reduce costs and waste production, thus improving the supply chain efficiencies, agility, and effectiveness, factors that will positively contribute to competitive advantage maintenance. Also, repetitive use of the green practices highlighted in this research will allow supply chain practitioners to develop GSCM in the long run.

## REFERENCES

Agbehadji, I. E., Awuzie, B. O., Ngowi, A. B., & Millham, R. C. (2020). Review of big data analytics, artificial intelligence, and nature-inspired computing models towards accurate detection of COVID-19 pandemic cases and contact tracing. *International Journal of Environmental Research and Public Health, 17*(15), 5330. doi:10.3390/ijerph17155330 PMID:32722154

AL-Khatib, A., & Shuhaiber, A. (2022). Green intellectual capital and green supply chain performance: Does big data analytics capabilities matter? *Sustainability (Basel), 14*(16), 10054. doi:10.3390/su141610054

Barney, J. (1991). Firm resources and sustained competitive advantage. *Journal of Management, 17*(1), 99–120. doi:10.1177/014920639101700108

Benzidia, S., Makaoui, N., & Bentahar, O. (2021). The impact of big data analytics and artificial intelligence on green supply chain process integration and hospital environmental performance. *Technological Forecasting and Social Change, 165*, 120557. doi:10.1016/j.techfore.2020.120557

Boell, S. K., & Cecez-Kecmanovic, D. (2015). On being 'systematic'in literature reviews. *Formulating Research Methods for Information Systems*, *2*, 48–78. doi:10.1057/9781137509888_3

Bravi, L., Santos, G., Pagano, A., & Murmura, F. (2020). Environmental management system according to ISO 14001: 2015 as a driver to sustainable development. *Corporate Social Responsibility and Environmental Management*, *27*(6), 2599–2614. doi:10.1002/csr.1985

Casey, D., & Sieber, S. (2016). Employees, sustainability, and motivation: Increasing employee engagement by addressing sustainability and corporate social responsibility. *Research in Hospitality Management*, *6*(1), 69–76. doi:10.2989/RHM.2016.6.1.9.1297

Chen, D. Q., Preston, D. S., & Swink, M. (2021). How big data analytics affects supply chain decision-making: An empirical analysis. *Journal of the Association for Information Systems*, *22*(5), 1224–1244. doi:10.17705/1jais.00713

Christensen, L.B., Johnson, B., Turner, L.A., & Christensen, L.B. (2011). *Research methods, design, and analysis*. Academic Press.

Das, G., Li, S., Tunio, R. A., Jamali, R. H., Ullah, I., & Fernando, K. W. T. M. (2023). The implementation of green supply chain management (GSCM) and environmental management system (EMS) practices and its impact on market competitiveness during COVID-19. *Environmental Science and Pollution Research International*, *30*(26), 1–16. doi:10.1007/s11356-023-27077-z PMID:37121948

Doss, A. N., Maurya, N., Guru, K., Masood, G., Jaiswal, S., & Naved, M. 2022, June. The Impact of Data Mining and Artificial Intelligence on Supply Chain Management and Environmental Performance. In *Proceedings of Second International Conference in Mechanical and Energy Technology: ICMET 2021, India* (pp. 503-511). Singapore: Springer Nature Singapore.

Dubey, R., Gunasekaran, A., Childe, S. J., Bryde, D. J., Giannakis, M., Foropon, C., Roubaud, D., & Hazen, B. T. (2020). Big data analytics and artificial intelligence pathway to operational performance under the effects of entrepreneurial orientation and environmental dynamism: A study of manufacturing organisations. *International Journal of Production Economics*, *226*, 107599. doi:10.1016/j.ijpe.2019.107599

Dutta, P., Jaikumar, B., & Arora, M. S. (2021). Applications of data envelopment analysis in supplier selection between 2000 and 2020: A literature review. *Annals of Operations Research*, 1–56.

Elgendy, N., Elragal, A., & Päivärinta, T. (2022). DECAS: A modern data-driven decision theory for big data and analytics. *Journal of Decision Systems, 31*(4), 337–373. doi:10.1080/12460125.2021.1894674

Eriksen, M. B., & Frandsen, T. F. (2018). The impact of patient, intervention, comparison, outcome (PICO) as a search strategy tool on literature search quality: A systematic review. *Journal of the Medical Library Association: JMLA, 106*(4), 420. doi:10.5195/jmla.2018.345 PMID:30271283

Flinn, L., Braham, L., & das Nair, R. (2015). How reliable are case formulations? A systematic literature review. *British Journal of Clinical Psychology, 54*(3), 266–290. doi:10.1111/bjc.12073 PMID:25515566

Gallo, H., Khadem, A., & Alzubi, A. (2023). The Relationship between Big Data AnalyticArtificial Intelligence and Environmental Performance: A Moderated Mediated Model of Green Supply Chain Collaboration (GSCC) and Top Management Commitment (TMC). *Discrete Dynamics in Nature and Society.*

Grover, V., Chiang, R. H., Liang, T. P., & Zhang, D. (2018). Creating strategic business value from big data analytics: A research framework. *Journal of Management Information Systems, 35*(2), 388–423. doi:10.1080/07421222.2018.1451951

Guan, Y., Huang, Y., & Qin, H. (2022). Inventory management optimization of green supply chain using ipso-bpnn algorithm under the artificial intelligence. *Wireless Communications and Mobile Computing, 2022*, 2022. doi:10.1155/2022/8428964

Hasan, R., Kamal, M. M., Daowd, A., Eldabi, T., Koliousis, I., & Papadopoulos, T. (2022). Critical analysis of the impact of big data analytics on supply chain operations. *Production Planning and Control*, 1–25.

Helo, P., & Hao, Y. (2022). Artificial intelligence in operations management and supply chain management: An exploratory case study. *Production Planning and Control, 33*(16), 1573–1590. doi:10.1080/09537287.2021.1882690

Hornberger, B., & Rangu, S. (2020). *Designing inclusion and exclusion criteria.* Academic Press.

Hu, W. C., Wu, H. T., Cho, H. H., & Tseng, F. H. (2020). Optimal route planning system for logistics vehicles based on artificial intelligence. *Journal of Internet Technology, 21*(3), 757–764.

Ikram, M., Zhang, Q., & Sroufe, R. (2021). Future of quality management system (ISO 9001) certification: Novel grey forecasting approach. *Total Quality Management & Business Excellence, 32*(15-16), 1666–1693. doi:10.1080/14783363.2020.1768062

Jackson, T., Thomas, S., Stabile, V., Shotwell, M., Han, X., & McQueen, K. (2016). A systematic review and metaanalysis of the global burden of chronic pain without clear etiology in low-and middle-income countries: Trends in heterogeneous data and a proposal for new assessment methods. *Anesthesia and Analgesia, 123*(3), 739–748. doi:10.1213/ANE.0000000000001389 PMID:27537761

Jemai, J., Do Chung, B., & Sarkar, B. (2020). Environmental effect for a complex green supplychain management to control waste: A sustainable approach. *Journal of Cleaner Production, 277*, 122919. doi:10.1016/j.jclepro.2020.122919

Kandel, B. (2020). Qualitative Versus Quantitative Research. *Journal of Product Innovation Management, 32*(5), 658.

Kazancoglu, Y., Kazancoglu, I., & Sagnak, M. (2018). A new holistic conceptual framework for green supply chain management performance assessment based on circular economy. *Journal of Cleaner Production, 195*, 1282–1299. doi:10.1016/j.jclepro.2018.06.015

Končar, J., Vučenović, S., & Marić, R. (2020). Green supply chain management in retailing based on Internet of things. *Integration of Information Flow for Greening Supply Chain Management*, 181-202.

Laari, S., Töyli, J., & Ojala, L. (2018). The effect of a competitive strategy and green supply chain management on the financial and environmental performance of logistics service providers. *Business Strategy and the Environment, 27*(7), 872–883. doi:10.1002/bse.2038

Lee, I., & Mangalaraj, G. (2022). Big data analytics in supply chain management: A systematic literature review and research directions. *Big Data and Cognitive Computing, 6*(1), 17.

Lerman, L. V., Benitez, G. B., Müller, J. M., de Sousa, P. R., & Frank, A. G. (2022). Smart green supply chain management: A configurational approach to enhance green performance through digital transformation. *Supply Chain Management, 27*(7), 147–176. doi:10.1108/SCM-02-2022-0059

McCarthy, J. (2007). *What is artificial intelligence*. Academic Press.

Naz, F., Agrawal, R., Kumar, A., Gunasekaran, A., Majumdar, A., & Luthra, S. (2022). Reviewing the applications of artificial intelligence in sustainable supply chains: Exploring research propositions for future directions. *Business Strategy and the Environment, 31*(5), 24002423. doi:10.1002/bse.3034

Nekmahmud, M. D., Rahman, S., Sobhani, F. A., Olejniczak-Szuster, K., & Fekete-Farkas, M. (2020). A systematic literature review on development of green supply chain management. *Polish Journal of Management Studies, 22*(1), 351–370. doi:10.17512/pjms.2020.22.1.23

Nightingale, A. (2009). A guide to systematic literature reviews. *Surgery (Oxford), 27*(9), 381384. doi:10.1016/j.mpsur.2009.07.005

Nozari, H., Fallah, M., & Szmelter-Jarosz, A. (2021). A conceptual framework of green smart IoTbased supply chain management. *International Journal of Research in Industrial Engineering, 10*(1), 22-34.

Oesterreich, T. D., Anton, E., & Teuteberg, F. (2022). What translates big data into business value? A metaanalysis of the impacts of business analytics on firm performance. *Information & Management, 59*(6), 103685. doi:10.1016/j.im.2022.103685

Page, M. J., McKenzie, J. E., Bossuyt, P. M., Boutron, I., Hoffmann, T. C., Mulrow, C. D., Shamseer, L., Tetzlaff, J. M., Akl, E. A., Brennan, S. E., Chou, R., Glanville, J., Grimshaw, J. M., Hróbjartsson, A., Lalu, M. M., Li, T., Loder, E. W., Mayo-Wilson, E., McDonald, S., ... Moher, D. (2021). The PRISMA 2020 statement: An updated guideline for reporting systematic reviews. *International Journal of Surgery, 88*, 105906. doi:10.1016/j.ijsu.2021.105906 PMID:33789826

Pournader, M., Ghaderi, H., Hassanzadegan, A., & Fahimnia, B. (2021). Artificial intelligence applications in supply chain management. *International Journal of Production Economics, 241*, 108250. doi:10.1016/j.ijpe.2021.108250

Qader, G., Junaid, M., Abbas, Q., & Mubarik, M. S. (2022). Industry 4.0 enables supply chain resilience and supply chain performance. *Technological Forecasting and Social Change, 185*, 122026. doi:10.1016/j.techfore.2022.122026

Queirós, A., Faria, D., & Almeida, F. (2017). Strengths and limitations of qualitative and quantitative research methods. *European Journal of Education Studies.*

Rahman, M.S. (2020). *The advantages and disadvantages of using qualitative and quantitative approaches and methods in language "testing and assessment" research: A literature review.* Academic Press.

Raman, S., Patwa, N., Niranjan, I., Ranjan, U., Moorthy, K., & Mehta, A. (2018). Impact of big data on supply chain management. *International Journal of Logistics, 21*(6), 579–596. doi:10.1080/13675567.2018.1459523

Roever, L. (2015). Critical appraisal of a questionnaire study. *Evid Based Med Pract, 1*(2), 1–2.

Rother, E. T. (2007). Systematic literature review X narrative review. *Acta Paulista de Enfermagem, 20*, v–vi. doi:10.1590/S0103-21002007000200001

Saad, S. M., & Khamkham, M. (2022). The Applications of AI in GSCM–A Systematic Literature Review. *Advances in Manufacturing Technology, 35*, 348–353. doi:10.3233/ATDE220615

Seman, N. A. A., Zakuan, N., Jusoh, A., Arif, M. S. M., & Saman, M. Z. M. (2012). Green supply chain management: A review and research direction. *International Journal of Managing Value and Supply Chains, 3*(1), 1–18. doi:10.5121/ijmvsc.2012.3101

Shahzad, F., Du, J., Khan, I., & Wang, J. (2022). Decoupling institutional pressure on green supply chain management efforts to boost organizational performance: Moderating impact of big data analytics capabilities. *Frontiers in Environmental Science, 10*, 911392. doi:10.3389/fenvs.2022.911392

Shokouhyar, S., Seddigh, M. R., & Panahifar, F. (2020). Impact of big data analytics capabilities on supply chain sustainability. *Development, 17*(1), 33–57.

Stadtler, H. (2014). Supply chain management: An overview. *Supply chain management and advanced planning: Concepts, models, software, and case studies*, 3-28.

Teixeira, C. R. B., Assumpção, A. L., Correa, A. L., Savi, A. F., & Prates, G. A. (2018). The contribution of green logistics and sustainable purchasing for green supply chain management. *Independent Journal of Management & Production, 9*(3), 1002–1026. doi:10.14807/ijmp.v9i3.789

Toorajipour, R., Sohrabpour, V., Nazarpour, A., Oghazi, P., & Fischl, M. (2021). Artificial intelligence in supply chain management: A systematic literature review. *Journal of Business Research, 122*, 502–517. doi:10.1016/j.jbusres.2020.09.009

Tseng, M. L., Islam, M. S., Karia, N., Fauzi, F. A., & Afrin, S. (2019). A literature review on green supply chain management: Trends and future challenges. *Resources, Conservation and Recycling, 141*, 145–162. doi:10.1016/j.resconrec.2018.10.009

van Dinter, R., Tekinerdogan, B., & Catal, C. (2021). Automation of systematic literature reviews: A systematic literature review. *Information and Software Technology, 136*, 106589. doi:10.1016/j.infsof.2021.106589

Wang, Y., Yang, Y., Qin, Z., Yang, Y., & Li, J. (2023). A Literature Review on the Application of Digital Technology in Achieving Green Supply Chain Management. *Sustainability (Basel)*, *15*(11), 8564. doi:10.3390/su15118564

Yang, Y., Chen, J., Lee, P. K., & Cheng, T. C. E. (2023). How to enhance the effects of the green supply chain management strategy in the organization: A diffusion process perspective. *Transportation Research Part E, Logistics and Transportation Review*, *175*, 103148. doi:10.1016/j.tre.2023.103148

Yusup, M., Naufal, R. S., & Hardini, M. (2018). Management of utilizing data analysis and hypothesis testing in improving the quality of research reports. *Aptisi Transactions on Management*, *2*(2), 159–167.

Zhang, Q., Gao, B., & Luqman, A. (2022). Linking green supply chain management practices with competitiveness during covid 19: The role of big data analytics. *Technology in Society*, *70*, 102021. doi:10.1016/j.techsoc.2022.102021 PMID:36090699

Zhou, S. S., Zhou, A. J., Feng, J., & Jiang, S. (2019). Dynamic capabilities and organizational performance: The mediating role of innovation. *Journal of Management & Organization*, *25*(5), 731–747. doi:10.1017/jmo.2017.20

# Chapter 2
# Artificial Intelligence Applications in Renewable Power Systems

**Mohamed Nassereddine**
*University of Wollongong in Dubai, UAE*

**Amal El Arid**
https://orcid.org/0000-0001-5712-2138
*Rafik Hariri University, Lebanon*

**Ghalia Nassreddine**
https://orcid.org/0000-0001-9434-2914
*Rafik Hariri University, Lebanon*

**Mahmoud Samad**
https://orcid.org/0000-0002-6396-1509
*Lebanese International University, Lebanon*

## ABSTRACT

*The field of power engineering has experienced significant advancements as a result of the integration of artificial intelligence methodologies, such as expert systems machine learning and artificial neural networks. In contemporary renewable energy systems, these approaches provide robust resources for the purposes of design, simulation, estimate, fault diagnostics, and fault-tolerant control. Over the course of recent decades, there has been rapid progress in the field of artificial intelligence technology, leading to a substantial increase in the utilization of AI applications inside modern industrial systems. This chapter provides an overview of the function of artificial intelligence in renewable energy systems. Three different types of renewable energy systems have been introduced in this discussion, including solar photovoltaic systems, wind turbine systems, and geothermal energy plants. Following the presentation of these systems, the authors proceed to critically examine the role of artificial intelligence in power prediction and defect detection within those systems.*

DOI: 10.4018/979-8-3693-1046-5.ch002

## INTRODUCTION

Over the past decade, there has been a noticeable increase in power usage worldwide, primarily attributed to the technology revolution. In the present era, electronic devices and power systems are integral elements that comprise the fundamental aspects of modern human existence. Electricity is deemed indispensable for numerous critical activities at both organizational and individual levels. Furthermore, the escalating global population and the advancement of smart cities will contribute to a substantial surge in the need for power in the forthcoming years.

Power generation systems primarily rely on three main energy sources: nuclear power, fossil fuels, and renewable sources. Currently, the predominant source of power generation relies on steam turbines, which are fueled by fossil fuels, nuclear energy, biomass, or geothermal resources. However, it is important to note that these turbines have the potential to generate a significant amount of carbon emissions, which can have adverse effects on the Earth's ecosystem, the environment, and human well-being. The U.S. Environmental Protection Agency (EPA) (2003) states that the creation of energy from fossil fuels results in the production of the following elements:

- Carbon dioxide ($CO_2$) has the potential to exert a significant influence on climate change. Undoubtedly, the combustion of fuels results in the release of carbon dioxide into the surrounding environment. The emission of $CO_2$ and its subsequent pollution pose a significant environmental hazard, potentially resulting in adverse consequences such as coastal flooding, heightened frequency and intensity of heat waves, exacerbated drought conditions, an upsurge in severe storms, and an amplified propagation of infectious diseases (Islam, et al., 2021).
- The amalgamation of sulfur dioxide ($SO_2$) with rainwater results in the formation of acid rain, which has the potential to cause detrimental effects on flora in forests and fruit crops. Undoubtedly, this particular combination has the potential to be lethal to plant life. Furthermore, the emission of $SO_2$ has the potential to cause the acidification of rivers, resulting in the creation of biologically inert environments, as well as altering the chemical composition of soil. Sulfur dioxide has been observed to expedite the degradation of rock and paint, resulting in detrimental effects on numerous architectural structures and historical landmarks (Xu, et al., 2021).
- The chemical element Mercury has the ability to remain suspended in the atmosphere for duration of approximately one year, thereby posing a significant risk of pollution to both terrestrial and aquatic environments. Furthermore, it has the capability to be transported over vast distances

spanning thousands of kilometers from its initial location. Exposure to this substance has the potential to adversely affect the central nervous system and result in congenital abnormalities (Gworek, et al., 2020).

- Nitrogen oxides ($NO_x$) have the potential to generate ground-level ozone and smog upon exposure to sunlight. Additionally, it leads to a rise in algal growth inside freshwater bodies such as lakes and rivers. Consequently, the reduction in oxygen levels in the water exerts an impact on aquatic fauna, including fish and various other creatures. Nitrogen dioxide has the potential to induce respiratory ailments in animals. (Oruc & Dincer, 2019).

Consequently, numerous nations initiated efforts to explore alternative energy sources in order to safeguard the environment and human well-being, while mitigating pollution levels. In recent times, a number of countries including China, the United States, France, and many European nations have adopted the utilization of renewable energy sources, such as solar and wind power, as a means to generate electricity while minimizing the release of harmful substances such as sulfur dioxide ($SO_2$), carbon dioxide ($CO_2$), and other pollutants. In recent times, a growing number of multinational corporations and industrial sectors have been embracing innovative methodologies rooted in renewable resources in order to provide environmentally sustainable forms of energy (Gonzalo, et al., 2019; Hamilton, et al., 2021).

One of the primary challenges associated with the utilization of renewable energy sources pertains to their inherent volatility. The utilization of diverse energy sources may also lead to substantial integration expenses (Boza & Evgeniou, 2021). The aforementioned challenges can be addressed by the utilization of contemporary technology such as Artificial Intelligence (Nassereddine, 2020).

Artificial intelligence (AI) is a field within the discipline of computer science that involves the development and construction of computer systems capable of emulating human intelligence (ElSamad et al., 2023). Artificial intelligence (AI) has seen extensive utilization in various domains, encompassing expert systems, natural language processing, speech recognition, and machine vision (Zhang & Lu, 2021). In contemporary times, artificial intelligence (AI) systems have been widely incorporated across various domains, including but not limited to medicine, media, finance, and education (Pandian, 2019; Zawacki-Richter, et al., 2019).

Regarding renewable systems, artificial intelligence (AI) can potentially be employed to address several challenges as expressed in Table 1.

This chapter comprises five sections. The following section provides a description of several forms of renewable energy systems. Subsequently, the topic of AI will be succinctly introduced. Afterwards, the utilization of AI for the enhancement of renewable energy systems is expounded. This chapter concludes by emphasizing the

*Table 1. Artificial intelligence challenges that are addressed in renewable systems*

| Challenge | Reference Paper |
|---|---|
| Optimization | He et al. (2022) |
| Fault Detection | Zhao et al. (2019) |
| Power Prediction | Wang et al. (2020) |
| Diagnosis | Wang (2021) |
| Power Quality Problems | Machlev et al. (2022) |
| Reliability and Resilience Topics | Wang et al. (2019) |

significance of employing artificial intelligence (AI) based systems in renewable energy systems.

## RENEWABLE ENERGY SYSTEMS

Renewable energy sources such as solar, wind, hydropower, biofuels, and others are playing a prominent role in the ongoing transition aimed at reducing carbon-intensive emissions. Urban areas play a crucial role in the development of sustainable cities. Over the past ten years, there has been a notable surge in the capacity for electricity generation, primarily attributed to legislative backing and rapid cost reductions in renewable energy sources such as wind and solar photovoltaics (Khaleel, et al., 2022).

The utilization of renewable sources in the domains of power generation, heating, and transportation is a key strategy in mitigating the rise in mean world temperatures to a maximum of 1.5°C. The utilization of Renewable energy sources enables electricity generation to achieve a state of near-zero carbon emissions under the envisioned scenario of achieving Net Zero Emissions by the year 2050. Furthermore, the utilization of renewable transport fuels and renewable heat technologies results in a reduction in emissions in various sectors such as buildings, industries, and transportation. The deployment of solar photovoltaic (PV) and wind power has experienced significant growth in the recent years due to robust policy impetus, escalating fossil fuel prices, and mounting apprehensions over energy security. Solar photovoltaic (PV) systems are projected to account for approximately 75% of the anticipated growth in global renewable energy capacity for the recent years. The solar photovoltaic (PV) capacity encompasses both large-scale utility installations and smaller dispersed systems. According to the findings of Azeyedo et al. (2022), it is projected that the global capacity of renewable energy will reach 4,500 gigawatts (GW) by the conclusion of the recent years. The aforementioned capacity exhibits a

*Figure 1. The electricity generated by renewable energy systems throughout the period spanning from 2017 to 2023*

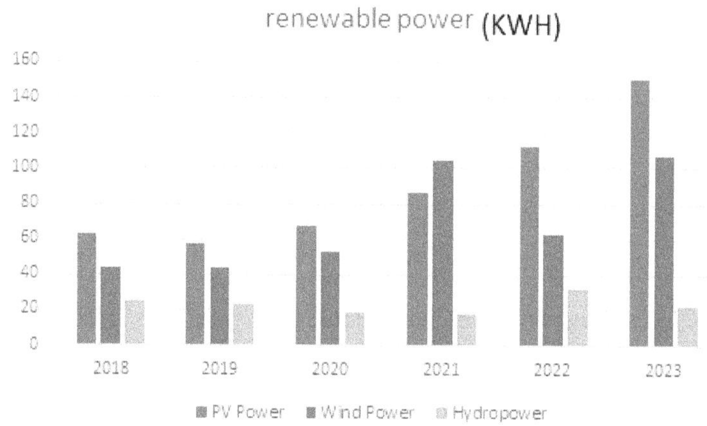


level of equivalence to the combined power output of China and the United States, as depicted in Figure 1.

This section will provide an illustration of three renewable power systems: Solar Photovoltaic (PV) system, Wind Systems, and Geothermal systems.

## Solar Photovoltaic Systems

The primary constituent of a photovoltaic (PV) system is comprised of solid-state semiconductor components that generate electrical energy upon exposure to light. Solar cells serve as the fundamental components of solar panels. A photovoltaic module consists of many solar cells that are interconnected in both parallel and series configurations. In order to optimize the electrical characteristics of photovoltaic (PV) modules, a parallel connection is employed to maximize the output current, while a series connection is utilized to maximize the output voltage. Solar photovoltaic (PV) power systems have gained commercial traction in several countries due to its advantageous characteristics, such as long-term benefits and minimal maintenance demands (Pakkiraiah & Sukumar, 2016). Sunlight consists of discrete units of energy known as photons. The phenomenon known as the photovoltaic effect involves the interaction between a photon and a solar panel, resulting in the generation of an electric current. Despite the individual panels yielding a little quantity of power in isolation, their collective integration enables the formation of a solar array capable of generating substantial quantities of energy. The current produced by a solar panel is a direct current (DC). Although computers, phones, and other electronic devices operate on direct current (DC) power, they are designed to function with the electrical utility grid, which predominantly provides and requires alternating current (AC). Hence, the utilization of an inverter is imperative in order to transform the direct current (DC) solar electricity into alternating current (AC), thereby enabling its practical application in residential and industrial settings. The AC electricity produced by the inverter can be employed to power local electronic devices or transmitted to the electrical grid for utilization in other locations.

Currently, there are two primary classifications of Solar Photovoltaic (PV) systems in existence. The two types of photovoltaic (PV) systems that will be discussed in this analysis are on-grid PV systems and off-grid PV systems. As depicted in Figure 2, an on-grid solar system refers to a system that is directly interconnected with the electrical grid of the utility. By employing this particular Solar Photovoltaic (PV) system, individuals can attain a continuous supply of electrical power. This particular form of system guarantees that the user will consistently have access to the necessary electricity to fulfill their requirements, regardless of the sun conditions. One primary benefit of this approach is the elimination of the necessity for individuals to invest in costly battery backups for the purpose of storing surplus energy. This observation highlights the increasing prevalence of on-grid systems in residential environments. Moreover, corporations may employ this system to fulfill their daily requirements and capitalize on the surplus electricity it produces. The off-grid solar system is a self-sustaining system that operates independently from the utility's power grid. This particular category necessitates the utilization of a storage battery that must be interconnected with a solar energy system. In periods of clear weather, the solar

*Figure 2. Various types of PV solar systems in use: (a) off-grid solar system refers to a self-sufficient energy system that operates independently from the main electrical grid and (b) on-grid solar system connected to the main electrical grid*
*Source: Awasthi et al. (2020)*

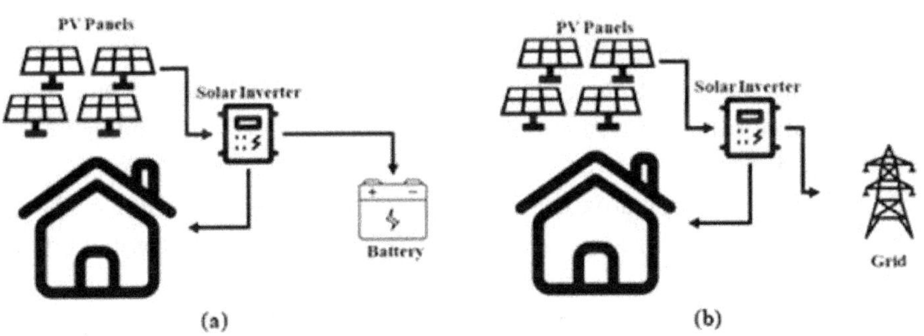

system has the capacity to generate electrical energy, which can be subsequently stored in a battery for further utilization during periods of low solar irradiance, such as nighttime or inclement weather conditions. One primary drawback associated with this system is the potential for users to experience reduced or nonexistent access to energy during periods of limited sunlight, particularly if they possess an inadequate storage mechanism. The utilization of this system is very suitable for deployment in rural and remote regions, characterized by frequent occurrences of power interruptions (Karthikeyan, et al., 2017).

One of the main limitations associated with solar photovoltaic (PV) systems is their diminished efficiency, which can be attributed to the panels' significant reliance on meteorological conditions that exhibit great variability, including temperature and sun radiation (Varshney & Tariq, 2014).

## Wind Systems

Wind energy refers to the utilization of the force generated by the wind to generate power. The conversion of wind current into electrical energy is achieved by the utilization of a wind turbine, as depicted in Figure 3. This process involves the rotor, which effectively transfers the kinetic energy of the wind into mechanical energy. Subsequently, the generator undergoes a conversion process wherein the mechanical energy generated is transformed into electrical energy. The rotor and generator are well recognized as fundamental devices utilized for the extraction of energy.

The blades of wind turbines are employed to harness the kinetic energy present in the wind. Undoubtedly, the blades experience the passage of wind, resulting in the generation of lift akin to the aerodynamic principles observed in the wings of an airplane. Consequently, this lift induces a rotational motion in the blades. The blades that are affixed to an electric generator provide a rotational motion that results in the production of energy.

Over the past decade, wind power has emerged as a highly regarded renewable energy source, gaining prominence in both technical and commercial spheres. Wind energy offers significant advantages, encompassing a wide range of capabilities spanning from a few kilowatts to multiple megawatts. Wind energy can serve as the foundation for the construction of both small off-grid systems and huge grid-connected wind farms. The whole capacity experienced an annual growth rate of 13.5%, resulting in a cumulative capacity exceeding 845 GW. According to Hannan et al. (2023), China emerged as the dominant player in the industry, holding the most market share. Subsequently, the United States, the United Kingdom, Brazil, and Vietnam followed suit in terms of market presence. Based on the findings of

*Figure 3. The primary constituents of a wind turbine*

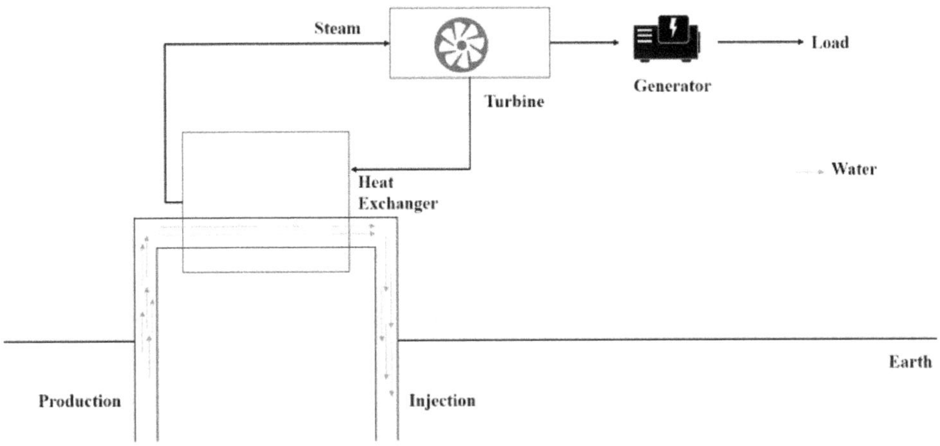


the Global Wind Energy Council (GWEC[1]), it is projected that the capacity of wind power would surpass the significant milestone of 1 terawatt by the end of 2023.

Moreover, as illustrated in Figure 4[1], the turbine wind power generation cover more than 10% of American power need in 2022. Figure 4-a shows the wind turbine produced power in US between 1990 and 2022. However, figure 4-b shows the percentage of wind turbine power produced from the total power production in US between 1990 and 2022.

*Figure 4. (a) The trends in wind turbine electricity generation in the United States from 1990 to 2022, (b) the proportion of wind power generation in the United States relative to the total electricity generated*

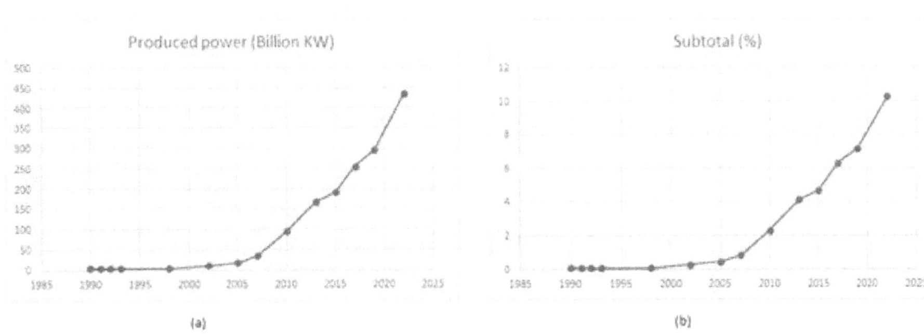

## Geothermal Power Systems

Geothermal energy, often known as the thermal energy contained inside the Earth, is harnessed in geothermal power plants for the purpose of electricity generation. The primary distinction between them and a coal or nuclear power plant lies in the nature of the heat source. The utilization of geothermal energy involves harnessing the Earth's heat as a viable alternative to nuclear or coal plant reactors or boilers. Undoubtedly, the temperature of the Earth increases as one descends deeper into its layers. The phenomenon being referred to as the geothermal gradient. It is seen that thermal energy ascends towards the Earth's surface from its heated interior. On average, there is an increase in temperature of approximately 25°C for every kilometer of depth. Geothermal energy is driven by the temperature gradient, facilitating its utilization for power generation and heating purposes.

Geothermal power plants use the thermal energy present in the Earth's subsurface by extracting hot water or steam through an interconnected system of wells. The majority of geothermal power facilities typically reintroduce the water they harvest from under the Earth's surface back into the subsurface. The need for make-up water supplies arises due to the often occurrence of water consumption rates exceeding water recovery rates. The steam derived from the Earth's natural sources is directed through a turbine. The turbine is linked to a generator that generates electrical power (refer to Figure 5).

*Figure 5. The fundamental framework of a geothermal power plant*

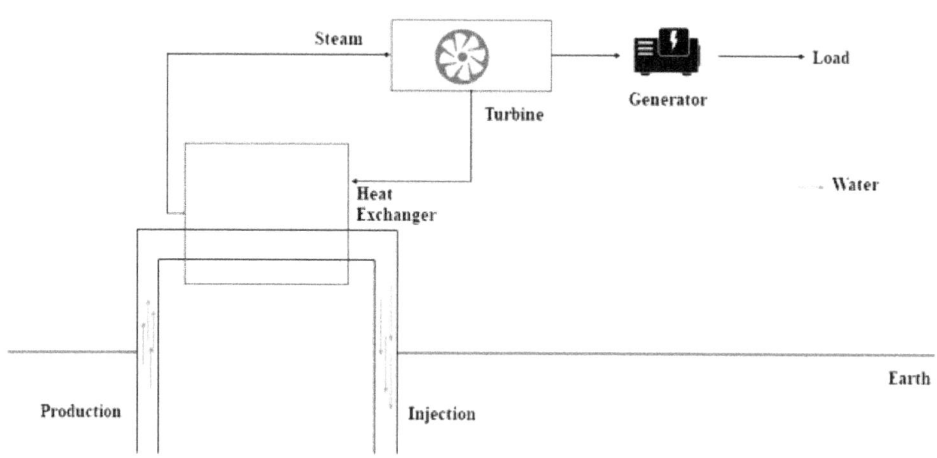

*Table 2. Several advantages that are related with the exploitation of geothermal power systems*

| Advantage | Description |
|---|---|
| Renewable | Over the course of billions of years, the ongoing decay of naturally existing radioactive elements will continuously replenish the thermal energy emitted from the Earth's interior. |
| Base load | Irrespective of meteorological conditions, geothermal power plants have the capability to generate electricity in a continuous manner, operating nearly around the clock, throughout the week. |
| Fuel Independency | Household geothermal resources have the potential to be utilized for various purposes such as power generating, heating, and cooling. |
| Compact Design | Geothermal heat pumps and power plants exhibit a relatively compact footprint, similar to that of other renewable energy sources such as wind turbines and solar photovoltaic (PV) power plants.Household geothermal resources possess the potential to be utilized for the purposes of electricity generation, heating, and cooling. |
| Cleanliness | Modern geothermal power plants exhibit life cycle emissions that are four times lower than those of solar photovoltaics and six to twenty times lower than those of natural gas. Furthermore, this particular renewable system is characterized by the absence of greenhouse gas emissions. Geothermal power plants exhibit a lower average water use during their production cycle in comparison to conventional electricity-generation methods. |

Table 2 illustrates some advantages associated with the utilization of geothermal power systems (Zarrouk & Moon, 2014).

## ARTIFICIAL INTELLIGENCE

Artificial intelligence (AI) has become a prominent and advanced technology utilized across several sectors in the contemporary era. Artificial intelligence (AI) is a subfield within the discipline of computer science that involves the development of intelligent computer systems designed to replicate and simulate human cognitive processes. The impact of artificial intelligence (AI) is increasingly being observed across a diverse range of businesses. Currently, artificial intelligence (AI)-based systems are extensively utilized across several domains, as illustrated in Table 3.

Artificial intelligence encompasses various categories, as depicted in Figure 6 (Regona, et al., 2022). In the subsequent section, the authors will provide a concise examination of these various categories.

*Table 3. Various sectors that utilize artificial intelligence (AI) in its technological applications*

| Sector | Reference | Description |
|---|---|---|
| Healthcare | Shaheen (2021) | Artificial intelligence is utilized to support medical professionals in the tasks of disease diagnosis, prediction of patient outcomes, and the development of treatment procedures. |
| Transportation Systems | Nasserddine & Arid (2023) | Artificial intelligence is being employed to enhance transportation systems through several applications, including accident prevention, autonomous vehicles, and predictive maintenance. |
| Education | Zhai et al. (2021) | Artificial intelligence has emerged as a modern tool in the field of education, enabling teachers to receive feedback, identify areas requiring further improvement, and personalize learning experiences for students. |
| Finance | Cao (2022) | Artificial intelligence is employed within the finance industry to enhance customer service, automate investment management, and detect instances of fraudulent behavior. |
| Marketing | Conick (2017) | Artificial intelligence is extensively employed within the field of marketing to evaluate customer data, tailor promotional strategies, and enhance consumer engagement. |

*Figure 6. Different types of AI*

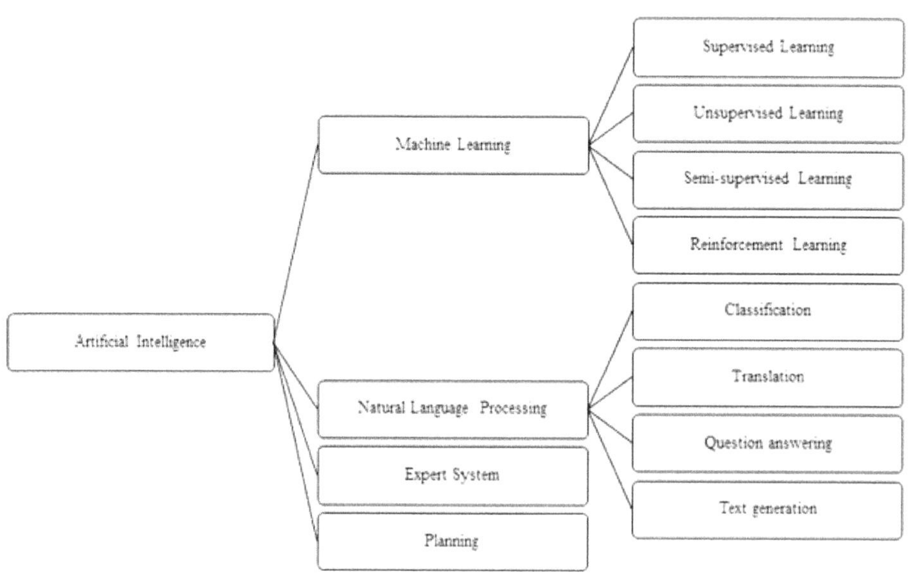

## Machine Learning

Machine Learning (ML) is a distinct field within the broader domain of Artificial Intelligence (AI) that centers on the application of data and algorithms to emulate the cognitive mechanisms of human learning. Its primary objective is to improve predictive accuracy by incorporating historical data and experiential knowledge. There are four discrete classifications of machine learning, as identified by Mahesh (2020).

1. Supervised learning involves the utilization of labeled input data to train a model.
2. Unsupervised learning is a machine learning approach that leverages unlabeled or unprocessed data.
3. Semi-supervised learning refers to a machine learning approach wherein a predictive model is trained by utilizing a substantial quantity of unlabeled data alongside a limited quantity of labeled data.
4. Reinforcement learning is a subfield within the broader discipline of machine learning. The task involves constructing a system that exhibits optimal behavior to maximize reward within a specific context. The utilization of this approach is prevalent among a diverse range of software and devices in order to ascertain the most advantageous course of action or behavior in a specific situation.

### Machine Learning Techniques

This section will exclusively focus on four machine learning approaches.

1. Regression analysis is a statistical approach utilized to investigate the association between independent variables and a dependent variable or outcome (Rong & Bao-Wen, 2018). The aforementioned approach is commonly employed as a method for forecasting continuous outcomes within the context of a machine learning challenge. It falls under the heading of guided learning. There exist three primary categories of regression analysis, namely Simple Linear Regression, Multiple Linear Regression, and Logistic Regression.
2. Classification is a supervised learning technique that involves the prediction of the correct label for a given input dataset. Prior to making predictions, it is necessary to train the classification model using a designated training set and subsequently evaluate its performance using test data. Various techniques are employed in the field of classification, including nearest neighbors, decision trees, support vector machines, and neural networks (Soofi & Awan, 2017).
3. Clustering is classified as an unsupervised machine learning technique. This technique enables the identification and categorization of analogous data points

within larger datasets, alleviating concerns regarding the outcome. Data is commonly classified by a process called clustering, which is also referred to as cluster analysis. This technique is employed to organize data into structures that are easier to handle and understand.

4. Association is a technique utilized to identify concealed relationships among variables within extensive datasets. The technique is widely utilized in the fields of machine learning and data mining, finding application in several domains such as fraud detection, market basket analysis, and customer segmentation.

## Natural Language Processing

Natural Language Processing (NLP) is a component of Artificial Intelligence (AI) that enables machine or computer-based systems to process and comprehend human language. NLP facilitates the automation of repetitive tasks by machines. Several examples of NLP systems include machine translation, summarization, ticket classification, and spell checking. (Chowdhary & Chowdhary, 2020):

1. Text classification is a computational technique employed to automatically categorize unstructured textual data into a predetermined set of classes. Text classifiers possess the ability to effectively arrange, systematize, and categorize a wide range of textual content, encompassing web resources, published materials, scientific research, and customer support inquiries.
2. One significant advancement in the field of artificial intelligence (AI) is the integration of natural language processing (NLP) techniques within machine translation systems. The advent of natural language processing (NLP) has enabled computers to comprehend, interpret, and generate language in a manner that is more akin to human understanding and contextual awareness. The inclusion of sentiment analysis, part-of-speech tagging, named entity recognition, and other related subtasks are observed. Various tools are employed at different stages of the translation process to enhance the quality of both the target language production and the source language understanding.
3. The objective of question answering research and development in the field of natural language processing (NLP) is to provide responses to inquiries in natural language that closely resemble human-like answers.
4. Text generation is widely recognized as a crucial and challenging undertaking within the field of NLP (Iqbal & Qureshi, 2020). The process is commonly referred to as natural language generation (NLG). Natural Language Generation (NLG) is a computational approach that leverages both linguistic and non-linguistic input in many formats, including text, numerical data, images, and graphs, to generate coherent and understandable writing in a human language.

One of the most significant techniques among them is text-to-text generation, commonly referred to as "text generation" for brevity. To fulfill this objective, scholars have developed a wide array of technologies. Text generation is a process that takes input text, such as a collection of keywords or a sequence, and transforms it into semantic representations in order to generate the corresponding output text.

## Expert System

An expert system refers to a computer program designed to replicate the decision-making processes and activities of individuals or a collective group with extensive knowledge and expertise within a certain domain. Expert systems utilize artificial intelligence (AI) technologies (Tripathi, 2011). The primary objective is to provide support and assistance to human experts, rather than seeking to supplant them. The concept of expert systems was first introduced by Edward Feigenbaum in the year 1970. In his essay published in 1984, Feigenbaum asserted that the paradigm of "knowledge processing" was superseding that of data processing in the global context. This statement suggests that computers possess greater computational capabilities compared to basic calculators and are capable of effectively solving complex issues.

Expert systems are a type of computational system that utilizes both experiential data and factual information to construct a repository of knowledge. This knowledge base is then integrated with an inference engine, which is also referred to as a rules engine. A rules engine refers to a collection of guidelines that are utilized to apply the knowledge base to various scenarios presented to the computer.

The inference engine retrieves data from the knowledge base by one of two methods:

1. By employing the technique of forward chaining, it is possible to make logical predictions about future events by carefully examining and analyzing a series of factual statements.
2. By employing the technique of backward chaining, it is possible to determine the origin of an occurrence in a logical manner through the examination and analysis of a series of factual information. A medical diagnosis is often established by the examination and analysis of a set of symptoms. The provided instance exemplifies the utilization of backward chaining.

Typically, an expert system comprises three fundamental components, as listed below (Liebowitz, 2019):

1. A knowledge repository is a centralized platform or system that stores and organizes information, allowing for easy access and retrieval of knowledge. The following component is designated for the purpose of storing information within the expert system. The expert system's knowledge base is populated by domain-specific information provided by human specialists. The inclusion of a knowledge acquisition module in the knowledge base is a common practice, as it allows the system to gather information from external sources and subsequently store it within the knowledge base.
2. The inference engine is responsible for retrieving relevant material from the knowledge base in order to resolve a user's issue. The system operates based on a set of rules, wherein it transforms existing data from the knowledge base into a series of rules. Subsequently, these rules are utilized to make informed decisions. Inclusion of an explanation module within inference engines is a common practice, wherein the module elucidates the process by which the algorithm has reached its conclusion for the benefit of users.
3. The user interface of the expert system serves as the medium via which end users interact with the system in order to seek resolutions to their inquiries or problems.

## Planning

The field of AI planning investigates the utilization of autonomous techniques for the purpose of resolving challenges related to scheduling and planning. Undoubtedly, the task of planning presents itself as a formidable problem when one seeks to attain a desired objective starting from an initial state. Artificial intelligence (AI) has the potential to provide assistance in addressing this particular issue. Planning is a systematic approach used to determine the most optimal procedural course of action for achieving the objectives of a declaratively defined system, with the aim of maximizing overall performance metrics. Automated planners ascertain the appropriate transformations to incorporate in a given state from the pool of accessible transformations. In contrast to the categorization issue, planners offer a means of ensuring the quality of the solution (Chakraborti, et al., 2020).

Planning is a well-established subfield within the domain of AI. Planning involves the identification of a systematic sequence of actions for a system that is stated in a declarative manner, with the aim of achieving its objectives while maximizing overall performance metrics. Automated planners determine the appropriate transformations to be implemented in a given state from the available set of transformations for that state. In contrast to the categorization problem, planners offer assurances regarding the quality of the solution.

The utilization of AI planning approaches offers several advantages, as outlined below:

1. The concept of ability refers to an individual's capacity or potential to perform a particular task or achieve a specific outcome.
2. Process automation, such as autonomous driving and medical expert systems, necessitates the attribution of responsibility.
3. Rapid prototyping: expedited problem-solving
4. There is a wide range of readily available planners, including both open-source options and those developed by IBM.
5. The phenomenon under consideration exhibits a perpetual state of transformation, albeit in subtle manners.

## ARTIFICIAL INTELLIGENCE IN RENEWABLE SYSTEMS

The field of power electronics and power engineering has experienced significant advancements as a result of the integration of artificial intelligence (AI) methodologies such as expert systems (ESs), fuzzy logic (FL), and artificial neural networks (ANNs). In the present day, artificial intelligence (AI) provides robust capabilities in the areas of design, modeling, control, estimation, fault diagnostics, and fault-tolerant control for smart grid (SG) and renewable energy systems (RESs). Over the course of recent decades, there has been rapid progress in the field of artificial intelligence (AI) technology, leading to a substantial increase in the range of applications inside modern industrial systems. This section will show and debate the application of AI in RESs.

### Artificial Intelligence in Solar Photovoltaic Systems

One significant limitation associated with the utilization of a solar photovoltaic (PV) system is to the inherent unpredictability of the generated power. Hence, it is imperative to develop a system that can effectively forecast the generated power with precision. Undoubtedly, the utilization of a precise prediction system for photovoltaic (PV) systems enables users to implement contingency strategies for conventional power sources. Nevertheless, this undertaking can prove to be quite arduous because to its heavy dependence on external factors, including weather conditions and sun radiation. Over the past decade, there has been a discernible rise in the utilization of data-driven models for forecasting solar radiation. This trend can be attributed to significant advancements in high-performance computing technology and the increased availability of mass storage memory devices. In the preceding decade, numerous methodologies have been devised for the purpose of forecasting the power generation of photovoltaic (PV) systems. This prediction can be conducted via insolation, which is widely regarded as the most efficacious factor in practical implementations.

Nevertheless, the utilization of this methodology necessitates a substantial amount of meteorological data for the purpose of deciphering differential equations, hence resulting in significant implementation expenses (Mandal, et al., 2012). The utilization of artificial intelligence (AI) methodologies provide a viable solution for addressing these challenges. Numerous research have been conducted to evaluate the efficacy of these models. However, enhancing the predictive precision of these data-driven techniques remains challenging in order to effectively facilitate sophisticated controls inside building systems, such as model predictive control (MPC) in smart buildings.

The optimization of energy harvest in PV panels is a crucial factor in enhancing the power output of solar photovoltaic systems. In their study, Jyothy and Sindhu (2018) utilized the Artificial Neural Network (ANN) technique to develop a controller for Maximum Power Point Tracking (MPPT) in solar photovoltaic systems. Furthermore, a comparison was made between the efficacy of conventional Maximum Power Point Tracking (MPPT) methods and an MPPT controller based on Artificial Neural Networks (ANN). The three methods under consideration are the fractional open circuit voltage method, the incremental conductance approach, and the hill climbing method, sometimes known as the perturb and watch method. The simulations were conducted using MATLAB/SIMULINK, and subsequent analysis was performed on the obtained data.

The study conducted by Pang et al. (2020) introduced an artificial neural network (ANN) model and a recurrent neural network (RNN) model for the purpose of evaluating the efficacy of deep learning algorithms in predicting solar radiation. The meteorological data obtained from a weather station located in Alabama was utilized as the fundamental dataset for the training procedure. A complete study of the accuracies and efficiency was conducted, encompassing many scenarios that used variable sample frequencies and moving window techniques. The findings of the study demonstrate that the RNN model outperforms the ANN model in predicting solar radiation. Specifically, the RNN model exhibits a much higher level of prediction accuracy, with a notable 47% enhancement in Normalized Mean Bias Error (NMBE) and a 26% improvement in Root-Mean-Squared Error (RMSE) compared to the ANN model. Furthermore, the potential for enhancing the accuracy of forecasting can be further explored by the incorporation of more detailed data or the implementation of a moving-window technique inside the prediction model. The augmentation of the sample frequency of the training data from 1 hour to 10 minutes resulted in a reduction of the Root-Coefficient of Variation Mean-Squared Error (CV(RMSE)) for the Artificial Neural Network (ANN) model from 30.9% to

9.41%. Similarly, the CV(RMSE) for the Recurrent Neural Network (RNN) model decreased from 9.83% to 7.64%. The introduction of the moving-window approach resulted in a notable enhancement of the NMBE for the RNN model, with a decrease from 0.9% to 0.2%. Moreover, it has been discovered that the presence of cloud cover can exert a substantial influence on the accuracy of predictions.

In their study, Sujatha et al. (2016) put forth a solar tracking system that utilizes Artificial Neural Network (ANN) based Image Processing (IPT) techniques to estimate the azimuth angle of the sun. This estimation is achieved by integrating data from an image sensor and the Global Positioning System (GPS). The determination of whether the prevailing weather conditions are characterized by sunshine or cloudiness was achieved by integrating features derived from image processing techniques with an artificial intelligence-based decision-making mechanism. The sun tracking system utilized astronomical computations to estimate its operational parameters, as inferred from the acquired outcomes. The experimental outcomes were employed to assess and authenticate the proposed advanced configuration, and they have been made accessible on the cloud platform for coordination purposes.

Solar power plants have been widely deployed throughout many regions globally. To ensure their reliability and safety, continuous monitoring and security measures are needed. Fault detection technology is utilized to safeguard and segregate solar plants, which are susceptible to a range of flaws and malfunctions. Despite the existence of several international standards, the presence of imperceptible photovoltaic flaws continues to pose significant challenges. As a result, there is a growing development of advanced technologies, including artificial intelligence (AI) and the internet of things (IoT), in the field of photovoltaic system diagnosis, remote sensing, and problem detection. Solar plants not only provide renewable energy but also yield substantial amounts of data, encompassing power production among other metrics. The attainment of a precise depiction of power yields should be feasible with the utilization of artificial intelligence (AI). The whole energy production of solar parks may be monitored and analyzed. The research revealed that the artificial intelligence (AI) system exhibited the capability to detect and identify potential problems within a solar park. This would potentially streamline and accelerate maintenance tasks. This study delves into the examination of the potential applications of Internet of Things (IoT) and deep learning (DL) techniques in the context of solar power plants. The discussion revolves around the accuracy and precision of advanced techniques, such as Deep Learning (DL). The integration of deep learning (DL) and Internet of Things (IoT) techniques for defect detection and diagnosis in solar facilities located in remote places can be considered as a financially and technically viable option by incorporating these capabilities into low-cost hardware components such as inexpensive chips.

In their recent study, Hammoudi et al. (2022) conducted a comprehensive evaluation of the current maintenance procedures employed in photovoltaic (PV) solar systems, with a specific focus on the utilization of deep learning and Internet of Things (IoT) technologies. Based on the analysis conducted, it was observed that a significant majority of the studies employed the widely recognized CNN or LSTM algorithms. Additionally, as a precautionary measure, certain researchers endeavored to devise a model capable of identifying defaults that arise during the operation of solar plants, with a predominant focus on detecting physical irregularities. While the proposed solutions demonstrate competence in addressing individual defaults, their efficacy may not be compelling enough to convince the maintenance industry to embrace them. In this context, it is imperative that forthcoming research focuses on employing the identical model to address many defaults simultaneously.

## Artificial Intelligence in Wind Turbine Systems

The growing incorporation of wind power in various urban areas worldwide presents significant issues attributed to its intermittent and variable characteristics. Improving the precision of short-term wind power forecasts is crucial for ensuring the economic and secure operation of the energy grid in this context. In their study, Liu et al. (2017) introduced an innovative hybrid methodology aimed at enhancing short-term wind power prediction. The proposed methodology utilizes an adaptive neuro-fuzzy inference system (ANFIS) that combines three distinct forecasting models. The three distinct inference models are the least squares support vector machine (LSSVM), the radial basis function neural network (RBFNN), and the backpropagation neural network (BPNN). Furthermore, the selection of suitable inputs for each of the three unique models was made using a novel data preparation method that utilizes the Pearson correlation coefficient (PCC). The assembled findings demonstrated the advancements achieved through the utilization of the PCC-based data preparation approach. Moreover, the comparison evaluations revealed that the proposed hybrid methodology exhibits a significant improvement in accuracy when compared to three distinct models.

Zheng et al. (2018) introduced a novel approach for forecasting short-term wind power generation in microgrids. The approach utilized in this study involved the integration of three distinct computational techniques: genetic algorithm (GA), particle swarm optimization (PSO), and adaptive neuro-fuzzy inference systems (ANFIS). The efficacy of the proposed methodology was assessed by employing authentic meteorological data and wind power generation statistics obtained from a case study microgrid system in Beijing. The performance of four alternative prediction approaches was evaluated through testing. The proposed solution demonstrated superior accuracy and reliability compared to alternative approaches, surpassing their performance.

Wang et al. (2020) proposed the utilization of three artificial intelligence (AI) approaches, including swarm optimization algorithms (SOA), Support Vector Machine, and artificial neural networks (ANN), in the context of wind turbine applications. Artificial neural networks (ANNs) are extensively utilized in the field of wind energy for the purpose of forecasting wind density, speed, and power generation. The aforementioned entities demonstrate a high level of precision in their prognostications, possess the ability to adjust to changing circumstances, have self-regulatory capabilities, exhibit resilience in the face of errors or malfunctions, and are characterized by ease of operation.

The authors of the study (Hong & Rioflorido, 2019) introduced a hybrid deep learning neural network model designed for the purpose of predicting wind power generation with a 24-hour lead time. The proposed solution utilized a combination of a Convolutional Neural Network (CNN), a cascaded Radial Basis Function Neural Network (RBFNN), and a double Gaussian function (DGF). The utilization of convolution, kernel, and pooling techniques enables the convolutional neural network (CNN) to extract pertinent features related to wind power. The supervised Radial Basis Function Neural Network (RBFNN) addresses the issue of unknown characteristics by using a Dynamic Growth Function (DGF). The simulations were conducted utilizing authentic wind power generation data obtained from a wind farm. The suggested technique is implemented using the TensorFlow and Keras libraries. The present study presents a comparative analysis of multiple techniques. Based on the simulation results, it was determined that the proposed methodology exhibited greater accuracy in 24-hour wind power forecasting compared to existing methodologies.

The study conducted by Yang (2019) utilized the least squares support vector machine (LSSVM) to forecast wind speed and the corresponding generated power. Furthermore, the researchers utilized an enhanced ant colony optimization (IACO) approach to optimize the key parameters that possess a significant impact on the least squares support vector machine (LSSVM) regression model. The efficacy of this approach was evaluated within a wind farm located in Gansu province. The findings of the predictive study illustrate that the IACO-LSSVM model may attain higher levels of prediction accuracy, hence validating the effectiveness and feasibility of this approach.

The ability to estimate wind turbine power output allows operators to proactively address potential concerns and prevent unexpected failures and financial losses by spotting irregularities in turbine performance in advance. The research conducted by Morshedizadeh et al. (2017) examined the SCADA data of 21 pitch regulated 2.3 MW turbines for a duration of 20 months. In order to ascertain the most prominent characteristic of the power generation process across more than 150 signals in the SCADA collected data, the researchers employed a correlation coefficient analysis. Furthermore, a proposed technique is recommended as a means to address the issue of missing and outlier values. The findings of the study indicate that the effectiveness of data analysis and prediction can be improved by carefully selecting appropriate decision tree models and mean value combinations for imputation. Hence, the integration of these factors could prove to be a beneficial asset in forecasting turbine power generation. Consequently, the amalgamation could serve as a valuable instrument for predicting turbine power generation.

Zhang et al. (2021) proposed a novel approach that utilizes spatiotemporal correlations to improve the accuracy of power prediction in wind farm clusters. Initially, the spatiotemporal correlation characteristics of wind farms situated within a wind cluster were quantified by employing three correlation coefficients. The coefficients were weighted utilizing the Shapley value methodology, and the determination of a standard wind farm is achieved by aggregating the nominal capacities of the individual wind farms. Subsequently, a matrix was constructed to represent the characteristic features of the wind farm cluster, including the spatial and temporal factors that influence the generation of wind power. In this study, a convolutional neural network (CNN) was employed to extract the primary features from the matrix. In this study, a Long Short-Term Memory (LSTM) neural network was employed to establish the relationship between significant attributes and power generation. Additionally, the LSTM model was utilized to forecast the power output of a cluster of wind farms, considering the temporal patterns inherent in wind power generation. The confirmation of the recommended approach's viability and performance was ultimately achieved by utilizing real operating data from wind farm clusters in North China as a representative case study. The recommended strategy has facilitated the development of a novel and precise methodology for forecasting the future power output of wind farm clusters.

Researchers globally have been confronted with the challenge of optimizing wind power generation and reducing operational interruptions as grid-connected wind farms become increasingly prevalent in contemporary power systems. Artificial intelligence (AI) and machine learning (ML) algorithms have become indispensable tools for the design of controllers and control schemes, owing to the intricate nature of wind turbine systems and the inherent difficulty in accurately forecasting variable wind speeds. Despite the existence of several review papers published in recent years, there is a noticeable dearth of comprehensive literature reviews that encompass both artificial intelligence (AI) and machine learning (ML) in the context of wind turbine control systems. This gap is particularly evident when it comes to the latest control techniques. In the study conducted by Farrar et al. (2023), a comprehensive examination of machine learning (ML) and artificial intelligence (AI) in wind turbine systems was provided.

This research performs a literature review by encompassing the following aspects:

1. Rationale for the significance of optimizing wind farm power generation;
2. Challenges associated with devising an efficient control scheme for wind farms;
3. Elucidation of the diverse types of artificial intelligence (AI) and machine learning (ML) algorithms employed in wind farm controllers and control schemes;
4. Application of AI and ML techniques for wind speed prediction;
5. Application of AI and ML techniques for wind power prediction;
6. Application of AI and ML techniques for monitoring mechanical components and detecting faults;
7. Application of AI and ML techniques for preventing and detecting electrical faults.

## Artificial Intelligence in Geothermal Power Plants

Geothermal power plants are considered to be very dependable and environmentally friendly methods of electricity generation with low carbon emissions. Nevertheless, the integration of advanced modeling software has the potential to significantly improve operational efficiency across several geothermal power facilities. The integration of digital twins into geothermal operations has become more feasible due to recent advancements in artificial intelligence (AI) and machine learning (ML) tools. This integration offers engineers a deeper understanding of the complex interactions among components within larger systems. Additionally, it facilitates improved exploration of the operational space. Several challenges have hindered the progress of geothermal operational analysis, with the primary impediment being the complexity of applying idealized thermodynamic models to real-world systems that experience continual performance degradation over time.

In their publication, Buster et al. (2021) introduced the concept of GOOML (Geothermal Operational Optimization with Machine Learning). This is a novel machine learning framework designed specifically for the purpose of optimizing geothermal operations. The hybrid data-driven thermodynamics technique employed by GOOML enables the accurate modeling of the real-world performance characteristics of as-built geothermal systems. Moreover, in order to achieve cutting-edge optimization, the integration of GOOML with the broader AI and ML ecosystem may be accomplished with ease. This modeling approach has been employed by a significant number of geothermal power plants, with consistently reliable outcomes. Therefore, the authors expect that the GOOML framework will have broad applicability to geothermal power plants worldwide.

The development of an artificial intelligence (AI) technique for the simulation of the geothermal organic Rankin cycle (GORC) equipped with a solar thermal unit was documented in a study conducted by Khosravi et al. in 2019. The authors have effectively illustrated the ability of artificial intelligence tools to faithfully replicate the operational dynamics of a sophisticated renewable energy system. The intelligent methods proposed in this study include the multilayer perceptron (MLP) neural network optimized with the particle swarm optimization (PSO) algorithm, referred to as MLP-PSO, and the adaptive neuro-fuzzy inference system (ANFIS) optimized with the PSO algorithm, referred to as ANFIS-PSO. The models were developed by considering the key design characteristics of the geothermal system, including solar radiation, well temperature, working fluid mass flow rate, turbine output pressure, solar collector surface area, and preheater inlet pressure. The intelligent models utilized the specified input variables to make predictions regarding the levelized cost of energy (LCOE), energy efficiency, net power production, and energy efficiency of the GORC. An investigation was conducted to analyze the economic aspects, as well as the energy and energy-related factors, of refrigerants characterized by low global warming potential (GWP). The findings indicate that intelligent models possess the ability to accurately forecast targets. However, it was shown that ANFIS-PSO exhibits superior performance compared to MLP-PSO while modeling the GORC with a solar system.

In their study, Olabi et al. (2023) employed several artificial intelligence methodologies to elucidate the categorizations, functionalities, and efficacious design optimization of energy systems across a range of applications. This study examined the utilization of artificial intelligence and its various subcategories in the context of forecasting, controlling, and optimizing the functioning of energy systems that incorporate thermal energy storage facilities. Moreover, a comprehensive examination of the performance of these technologies was presented, highlighting their remarkable precision in attaining diverse objectives.

The study conducted by Pandey and Singh (2021) focuses on the utilization of artificial neural network (ANN) for the purpose of predicting the thermal drawdown of an improved geothermal system (EGS). A numerical model of Enhanced Geothermal Systems (EGS) was built in three dimensions in order to generate the data sets used for training and testing an ANN. A quantitative investigation was conducted to analyze the production of geothermal energy under different injection operation circumstances and reservoir crack apertures. The input parameters for an Artificial Neural Network (ANN) encompass temperature, mass flux, pressure, and fracture transmissivity, whilst the output parameter is the temperature of the production well. The optimization of the artificial neural network (ANN) involved the utilization of the Levenberg–Marquardt back-propagation learning technique, as well as the tan-sigmoid and linear transfer functions. The optimal outcomes were achieved using an artificial neural network (ANN) structure comprising of eight concealed layers and 20 neurons within each hidden layer. This configuration successfully facilitated the accurate prediction of production temperature within a desirable range, as evidenced by a coefficient of determination (R2) exceeding 0.99. The artificial neural network (ANN) model achieved a satisfactory level of accuracy, as indicated by a percentage error below (± 4.5). The findings derived from the numerical simulations indicate that the impact of fracture transmissivity on thermal drawdown is comparatively less significant when compared to the injection mass flux and temperature. Based on the findings, the authors have verified that artificial neural network (ANN) modeling has the capability to accurately estimate the thermal decline of an enhanced geothermal system (EGS).

## FUTURE RESEARCH DIRECTIONS

Further investigation is necessary to address the suboptimal efficacy of certain components inside hybrid systems. Hence, it is imperative to do additional study in order to enhance the effectiveness of the system through the utilization of contemporary AI techniques. Furthermore, the current artificial intelligence methodology employed in energy system management can be further improved through the utilization of big data.

The integration of the Internet of Things with AI-based systems enables the monitoring and diagnosis of system issues. Natural Language Processing techniques, such as the utilization of chatbots, can also be employed for the purpose of controlling hybrid energy systems.

## CONCLUSION

In recent years, there has been a notable increase in global power consumption due to the advent of the technological revolution. In contemporary society, electronics and electricity devices have emerged as the fundamental constituents of human existence. The absence of electricity is often believed to render certain essential jobs unachievable, both within corporate environments and on an individual basis. Furthermore, with the ongoing development of smart cities and the projected increase in global population, there will be an escalating demand for energy in the foreseeable future. Therefore, the acquisition of a sustainable and environmentally friendly source of electricity has become a crucial necessity.

In recent years, numerous nations and sectors have adopted the utilization of renewable energy systems. Nevertheless, the power generated by these systems has a degree of unpredictability. Emerging technologies such as Artificial Intelligence (AI), Machine Learning (ML), and others have the potential to address this issue. This chapter provides an overview of the function that artificial intelligence (AI) plays in renewable energy systems. Initially, the presentation introduced three primary forms of renewable energy systems, including solar photovoltaic (PV) systems, wind turbine plants, and geothermal power plants. Subsequently, artificial intelligence (AI) was explicated. Subsequently, the presentation focused on the involvement of artificial intelligence (AI) in renewable energy systems.

The authors' primary objective was to provide a comprehensive analysis of the utilization of artificial intelligence (AI) inside several energy systems, namely solar photovoltaic (PV) systems, wind turbine plants, and geothermal power plants. The researchers directed their attention towards examining the significance of artificial intelligence (AI) in the context of power forecasting and problem detection within renewable energy systems. Numerous artificial intelligence (AI) systems have been proposed and evaluated in recent years. However, it is necessary to compare various models in order to conduct a more comprehensive study.

## REFERENCES

Awasthi, A., & Shukla, A. K., M. M., Dondariya, C., Shukla, K. N., Porwal, D., & Richhariya, G. (2020). Review on sun tracking technology in solar PV system. *Energy Reports*, *6*, 392–405. doi:10.1016/j.egyr.2020.02.004

Azevedo, M., Baczyńska, M., Hoffman, K., & Krauze, A. (2022). *Lithium mining: How new production technologies could fuel the global EV revolution.* McKinsey & Company. https://www. mckinsey. com/~/media/mckinsey/industries/metal s%20and% 20mining/our% 20in sights/lithium% 20mining% 20how% 20new% 20production% 20technologies% 20could% 20fuel

Boza, P., & Evgeniou, T. (2021). Artificial intelligence to support the integration of variable renewable energy sources to the power system. *Applied Energy*, *290*, 116754. doi:10.1016/j.apenergy.2021.116754

Buster, G., Siratovich, P., Taverna, N., Rossol, M., Weers, J., Blair, A., Huggins, J., Siega, C., Mannington, W., Urgel, A., Cen, J., Quinao, J., Watt, R., & Akerley, J. (2021). A new modeling framework for Geothermal Operational Optimization with Machine Learning (GOOML). *Energies*, *14*(20), 6852. doi:10.3390/en14206852

Cao, L. (2022). Ai in finance: Challenges, techniques, and opportunities. *ACM Computing Surveys*, *55*(3), 1–38. doi:10.1145/3502289

Chakraborti, T., Sreedharan, S., & Kambhampati, S. (2020). The emerging landscape of explainable ai planning and decision making. *arXiv preprint arXiv:2002.11697.*

Chowdhary, K., & Chowdhary, K. R. (2020). Natural language processing. *Fundamentals of artificial intelligence*, 603-649.

Conick, H. (2017). The past, present and future of AI in marketing. *Marketing News*, *51*(1), 26–35.

El Samad, M., Nasserddine, G., & Kheir, A. (2023). Introduction to Artificial Intelligence. In *Artificial Intelligence and Knowledge Processing* (pp. 1–14). CRC Press. doi:10.1201/9781003328414-1

Farrar, N. O., Ali, M. H., & Dasgupta, D. (2023). Artificial intelligence and machine learning in grid connected wind turbine control systems: A comprehensive review. *Energies*, *16*(3), 1530. doi:10.3390/en16031530

Gonzalo, A. P., Marugán, A. P., & Márquez, F. P. G. (2019). A review of the application performances of concentrated solar power systems. *Applied Energy*, *255*, 113893. doi:10.1016/j.apenergy.2019.113893

Gworek, B., Dmuchowski, W., & Baczewska-Dąbrowska, A. H. (2020). Mercury in the terrestrial environment: A review. *Environmental Sciences Europe*, *32*(1), 1–19. doi:10.1186/s12302-020-00401-x

Hamilton, I., Kennard, H. A., Höglund-Isaksso, L., Kiesewetter, G., Lott, M., & Watts, N. (2021). The public health implications of the Paris Agreement: A modelling study. *The Lancet. Planetary Health*, *5*(2), 5. doi:10.1016/S2542-5196(20)30249-7 PMID:33581069

Hammoudi, Y., Idrissi, I., Boukabous, M., Zerguit, Y., & Bouali, H. (2022). Review on maintenance of photovoltaic systems based on deep learning and internet of things. *Indonesian Journal of Electrical Engineering and Computer Science*, *26*(2), 1060–1072. doi:10.11591/ijeecs.v26.i2.pp1060-1072

Hannan, M. A., Al-Shetwi, A. Q., Mollik, M. S., Ker, P. J., Mannan, M., Mansor, M., Al-Masri, H. M. K., & Mahlia, T. I. (2023). Wind Energy Conversions, Controls, and Applications: A Review for Sustainable Technologies and Directions. *Sustainability (Basel)*, *15*(5), 3986. doi:10.3390/su15053986

He, Q., Zheng, H., Ma, X., Wang, L., Kong, H., & Zhu, Z. (2022). Artificial intelligence application in a renewable energy-driven desalination system: A critical review. *Energy and AI*, *7*, 100123. doi:10.1016/j.egyai.2021.100123

Hong, Y. Y., & Rioflorido, C. L. P. P. (2019). A hybrid deep learning-based neural network for 24-h ahead wind power forecasting. *Applied Energy*, *250*, 530–539. doi:10.1016/j.apenergy.2019.05.044

Iqbal, T., & Qureshi, S. (2022). The survey: Text generation models in deep learning. *Journal of King Saud University. Computer and Information Sciences*, *34*(6), 2515–2528. doi:10.1016/j.jksuci.2020.04.001

Islam, M. M., Khan, M. K., Tareque, M., Jehan, N., & Dagar, V. (2021). Impact of globalization, foreign direct investment, and energy consumption on CO2 emissions in Bangladesh: Does institutional quality matter? *Environmental Science and Pollution Research International*, *28*(35), 48851–48871. doi:10.1007/s11356-021-13441-4 PMID:33929670

Jyothy, L. P., & Sindhu, M. R. (2018, February). An artificial neural network based MPPT algorithm for solar PV system. In *2018 4th International Conference on Electrical Energy Systems (ICEES)* (pp. 375-380). IEEE. 10.1109/ICEES.2018.8443277

Karthikeyan, V., Rajasekar, S., Das, V., Karuppanan, P., & Singh, A. K. (2017). Grid-connected and off-grid solar photovoltaic system. *Smart Energy Grid Design for Island Countries: Challenges and Opportunities*, 125-157.

Khaleel, M. M., Alsharif, A., & Imbayah, I. I. K. (2022). Renewable energy technologies: Recent advances and future predictions. *African Journal of Advanced Pure and Applied Sciences*, 58-64.

Khosravi, A., Syri, S., Zhao, X., & Assad, M. E. H. (2019). An artificial intelligence approach for thermodynamic modeling of geothermal based-organic Rankine cycle equipped with solar system. *Geothermics*, *80*, 138–154. doi:10.1016/j.geothermics.2019.03.003

Liebowitz, J. (Ed.). (2019). *The handbook of applied expert systems.* CRC Press. doi:10.1201/9780138736654

Liu, J., Wang, X., & Lu, Y. (2017). A novel hybrid methodology for short-term wind power forecasting based on adaptive neuro-fuzzy inference system. *Renewable Energy*, *103*, 620–629. doi:10.1016/j.renene.2016.10.074

Machlev, R., Heistrene, L., Perl, M., Levy, K. Y., Belikov, J., Mannor, S., & Levron, Y. (2022). Explainable Artificial Intelligence (XAI) techniques for energy and power systems: Review, challenges and opportunities. *Energy and AI, 9*, 100169. doi:10.1016/j.egyai.2022.100169

Mahesh, B. (2020). Machine learning algorithms-a review. *International Journal of Science and Research, 9*(1), 381-386.

Mandal, P., Madhira, S. T. S., Meng, J., & Pineda, R. L. (2012). Forecasting power output of solar photovoltaic system using wavelet transform and artificial intelligence techniques. *Procedia Computer Science, 12*, 332–337. doi:10.1016/j.procs.2012.09.080

Morshedizadeh, M., Kordestani, M., Carriveau, R., Ting, D. S. K., & Saif, M. (2017). Application of imputation techniques and adaptive neuro-fuzzy inference system to predict wind turbine power production. *Energy, 138*, 394–404. doi:10.1016/j.energy.2017.07.034

Nasserddine, G., & Arid, A. E. (2023). Artificial Intelligence in Navigation Systems. In *Handbook of Research on AI Methods and Applications in Computer Engineering* (pp. 86–107). IGI Global. doi:10.4018/978-1-6684-6937-8.ch005

Nassereddine, M. (2020). Machine learning roles in advancing the power network stability due to deployments of renewable energies and electric vehicles. *International Journal of Emerging Electric Power Systems, 21*(3), 20190270. doi:10.1515/ijeeps-2019-0270

Olabi, A. G., Abdelghafar, A. A., Maghrabie, H. M., Sayed, E. T., Rezk, H., Al Radi, M., ... Abdelkareem, M. A. (2023). Application of artificial intelligence for prediction, optimization, and control of thermal energy storage systems. *Thermal Science and Engineering Progress, 39*, 101730. doi:10.1016/j.tsep.2023.101730

Oruc, O., & Dincer, I. (2019). Environmental impact assessment of using various fuels in a thermal power plant. *International Journal of Global Warming, 18*(3-4), 191–205. doi:10.1504/IJGW.2019.101082

Pakkiraiah, B., & Sukumar, G. D. (2016). *Research survey on various MPPT performance issues to improve the solar PV system efficiency*. Academic Press.

Pandey, S. N., & Singh, M. (2021). Artificial neural network to predict the thermal drawdown of enhanced geothermal system. *Journal of Energy Resources Technology, 143*(1), 010901. doi:10.1115/1.4048067

Pandian, D. A. P. (2019). Artificial intelligence application in smart warehousing environment for automated logistics. *Journal of Artificial Intelligence and Capsule Networks*, *1*(2), 63–72. doi:10.36548/jaicn.2019.2.002

Pang, Z., Niu, F., & O'Neill, Z. (2020). Solar radiation prediction using recurrent neural network and artificial neural network: A case study with comparisons. *Renewable Energy*, *156*, 279–289. doi:10.1016/j.renene.2020.04.042

Regona, M., Yigitcanlar, T., Xia, B., & Li, R. Y. M. (2022). Opportunities and adoption challenges of AI in the construction industry: A PRISMA review. *Journal of Open Innovation*, *8*(1), 45. doi:10.3390/joitmc8010045

Rong, S., & Bao-Wen, Z. (2018). The research of regression model in machine learning field. In *MATEC Web of Conferences* (Vol. 176, p. 01033). EDP Sciences. 10.1051/matecconf/201817601033

ShaheenM. Y. (2021). Applications of Artificial Intelligence (AI) in healthcare: A review. *ScienceOpen* Preprints.

Soofi, A. A., & Awan, A. (2017). Classification techniques in machine learning: Applications and issues. *Journal of Basic and Applied Sciences*, *13*(1), 459–465. doi:10.6000/1927-5129.2017.13.76

Sujatha, K., Ponmagal, R. S., Godhavari, T., & Kumar, K. R. (2016, December). Automation of solar system for maximum power point tracking using artificial neural networks and IoT. In *2016 IEEE Uttar Pradesh Section International Conference on Electrical, Computer and Electronics Engineering (UPCON)* (pp. 61-66). IEEE. 10.1109/UPCON.2016.7894625

Tripathi, K. P. (2011). A review on knowledge-based expert system: Concept and architecture. *IJCA Special Issue on Artificial Intelligence Techniques-Novel Approaches & Practical Applications*, *4*, 19–23.

Varshney, A., & Tariq, A. (2014). Simulink model of solar array for photovoltaic power generation system. *Int J Electr Electr Eng*, *7*(2), 8.

Wang, H. (2021). Fault diagnosis in hybrid renewable energy sources with machine learning approach. *Journal of Trends in Computer Science and Smart Technology*, *3*(3), 222-237.

Wang, H., Lei, Z., Zhang, X., Zhou, B., & Peng, J. (2019). A review of deep learning for renewable energy forecasting. *Energy Conversion and Management*, *198*, 111799. doi:10.1016/j.enconman.2019.111799

Wang, H., Liu, Y., Zhou, B., Li, C., Cao, G., Voropai, N., & Barakhtenko, E. (2020). Taxonomy research of artificial intelligence for deterministic solar power forecasting. *Energy Conversion and Management*, *214*, 112909. doi:10.1016/j.enconman.2020.112909

Wang, Y., Yu, Y., Cao, S., Zhang, X., & Gao, S. (2020). A review of applications of artificial intelligent algorithms in wind farms. *Artificial Intelligence Review*, *53*(5), 3447–3500. doi:10.1007/s10462-019-09768-7

Xu, C., Zhao, W., Zhang, M., & Cheng, B. (2021). Pollution haven or halo? The role of the energy transition in the impact of FDI on SO2 emissions. *The Science of the Total Environment*, *763*, 143002. doi:10.1016/j.scitotenv.2020.143002 PMID:33187715

Yang, J. (2019). A novel short-term multi-input–multi-output prediction model of wind speed and wind power with LSSVM based on improved ant colony algorithm optimization. *Cluster Computing*, *22*(S2, Suppl 2), 3293–3300. doi:10.1007/s10586-018-2107-1

Zarrouk, S. J., & Moon, H. (2014). Efficiency of geothermal power plants: A worldwide review. *Geothermics*, *51*, 142–153. doi:10.1016/j.geothermics.2013.11.001

Zawacki-Richter, O., Marín, V. I., Bond, M., & Gouverneur, F. (2019). Systematic review of research on artificial intelligence applications in higher education–where are the educators? *International Journal of Educational Technology in Higher Education*, *16*(1), 1–27. doi:10.1186/s41239-019-0171-0

Zhai, X., Chu, X., Chai, C. S., Jong, M. S. Y., Istenic, A., Spector, M., Liu, J.-B., Yuan, J., & Li, Y. (2021). A Review of Artificial Intelligence (AI) in Education from 2010 to 2020. *Complexity*, *2021*, 1–18. doi:10.1155/2021/8812542

Zhang, C., & Lu, Y. (2021). Study on artificial intelligence: The state of the art and prospects. *Journal of Industrial Information Integration*, *23*, 100224. doi:10.1016/j.jii.2021.100224

Zhang, J., Liu, D., Li, Z., Han, X., Liu, H., Dong, C., Wang, J., Liu, C., & Xia, Y. (2021). Power prediction of a wind farm cluster based on spatiotemporal correlations. *Applied Energy*, *302*, 117568. doi:10.1016/j.apenergy.2021.117568

Zhao, Y., Li, T., Zhang, X., & Zhang, C. (2019). Artificial intelligence-based fault detection and diagnosis methods for building energy systems: Advantages, challenges and the future. *Renewable & Sustainable Energy Reviews*, *109*, 85–101. doi:10.1016/j.rser.2019.04.021

Zheng, D., Semero, Y. K., Zhang, J., & Wei, D. (2018). Short-term wind power prediction in microgrids using a hybrid approach integrating genetic algorithm, particle swarm optimization, and adaptive neuro-fuzzy inference systems. *IEEJ Transactions on Electrical and Electronic Engineering*, *13*(11), 1561–1567. doi:10.1002/tee.22720

## ADDITIONAL READING

Abualigah, L., Zitar, R. A., Almotairi, K. H., Hussein, A. M., Abd Elaziz, M., Nikoo, M. R., & Gandomi, A. H. (2022). Wind, solar, and photovoltaic renewable energy systems with and without energy storage optimization: A survey of advanced machine learning and deep learning techniques. *Energies*, *15*(2), 578. doi:10.3390/en15020578

Bose, B. K. (2017). Artificial intelligence techniques in smart grid and renewable energy systems—Some example applications. *Proceedings of the IEEE*, *105*(11), 2262–2273. doi:10.1109/JPROC.2017.2756596

Cheng, L., & Yu, T. (2019). A new generation of AI: A review and perspective on machine learning technologies applied to smart energy and electric power systems. *International Journal of Energy Research*, *43*(6), 1928–1973. doi:10.1002/er.4333

Hu, W., Wu, Q., Anvari-Moghaddam, A., Zhao, J., Xu, X., Abulanwar, S. M., & Cao, D. (2022). Applications of artificial intelligence in renewable energy systems. *IET Renewable Power Generation*, *16*(7), 1279–1282. doi:10.1049/rpg2.12479

Ibrahim, M. S., Dong, W., & Yang, Q. (2020). Machine learning driven smart electric power systems: Current trends and new perspectives. *Applied Energy*, *272*, 115237. doi:10.1016/j.apenergy.2020.115237

Ibrar, M., Hassan, M. A., Shaukat, K., Alam, T. M., Khurshid, K. S., Hameed, I. A., Aljuaid, H., & Luo, S. (2022). A machine learning-based model for stability prediction of decentralized power grid linked with renewable energy resources. *Wireless Communications and Mobile Computing*, *2022*, 1–15. doi:10.1155/2022/2697303

Perera, K. S., Aung, Z., & Woon, W. L. (2014). Machine learning techniques for supporting renewable energy generation and integration: a survey. In *Data Analytics for Renewable Energy Integration: Second ECML PKDD Workshop, DARE 2014, Nancy, France, September 19, 2014, Revised Selected Papers 2* (pp. 81-96). Springer International Publishing. 10.1007/978-3-319-13290-7_7

Rangel-Martinez, D., Nigam, K. D. P., & Ricardez-Sandoval, L. A. (2021). Machine learning on sustainable energy: A review and outlook on renewable energy systems, catalysis, smart grid and energy storage. *Chemical Engineering Research & Design*, *174*, 414–441. doi:10.1016/j.cherd.2021.08.013

Zhang, J., Cho, H., & Mago, P. J. (2021). Energy conversion systems and Energy storage systems. In *Energy Services Fundamentals and Financing* (pp. 155–179). Academic Press. doi:10.1016/B978-0-12-820592-1.00007-5

Zhou, Y. (2022). Artificial intelligence in renewable systems for transformation towards intelligent buildings. *Energy and AI*, 100182.

## KEY TERMS AND DEFINITIONS

**Artificial Intelligence:** The study and advancement of computer systems that are capable of conducting tasks that typically demand human intelligence, such as speech recognition, language translation, visual perception, and decision-making.

**Defect Detection:** The likelihood of detecting a discontinuity according to the parameter of the discontinuity in question.

**Geothermal Energy Plant:** Steam generation by drawing fluids from subterranean reservoirs to the surface. This steam subsequently turns turbines that produce electricity.

**Machine Learning:** The application and advancement of computer systems capable of learning and adapting autonomously through the utilization of statistical models and algorithms to analyze data patterns and derive conclusions.

**Power Prediction:** The capability of a scientific theory to produce predictions that can be tested.

**Renewable Power System:** Energy obtained from renewable natural sources that are replenished at a rate exceeding their consumption.

**Solar Photovoltaic System:** An electrical power infrastructure engineered to generate usable solar energy via photovoltaic processes.

**Wind Turbine:** An apparatus designed to convert the kinetic energy of the wind into electrical energy.

## ENDNOTE

1 https://balkangreenenergynews.com/wind-industry-set-for-record-growth-until-2025-but-bottlenecks-are-looming/

# Chapter 3
# Artificial Intelligence for Money Laundering Detection

**Fouad M. Ziade**
*Lebanese University, Lebanon*

**Malak Mohamad Daher**
https://orcid.org/0009-0002-9886-7763
*Jinan University, Lebanon*

**Abdallah M. Ziade**
https://orcid.org/0000-0001-5967-5027
*Lebanese University, Lebanon*

## ABSTRACT

*This chapter provides an overview of artificial intelligence (AI) methods for anti-money laundering (AML) and discusses challenges. The increasing complexity of financial crime has exposed the limitations of traditional rule-based AML approaches. AI technologies like machine learning, natural language processing, and computer vision show promise for improving AML effectiveness and efficiency. However, AI also faces hurdles around data quality, model interpretability, ethics, and proper human-AI collaboration. The chapter reviews the state-of-the-art AI techniques being applied across AML domains including customer due diligence, transaction monitoring, risk scoring, and investigations. Key recommendations for implementing AI in practice involve extensive testing, explainable models, strong governance, and human-centered design focused on trust and transparency. While AI has limitations, thoughtful deployment focused on fairness, accountability, and empowering human expertise can allow financial institutions and regulators to realize its benefits for combating money laundering.*

DOI: 10.4018/979-8-3693-1046-5.ch003

# 1. INTRODUCTION

## 1.1. Money Laundering and Its Impact on Society and Economy

Money laundering is the process of disguising the origins of money obtained through illegal activities by funneling it through legitimate businesses (Levi, 2021). It allows criminals to hide and accumulate wealth, avoid prosecution, and continue illicit operations (Masciandaro & Takats, 2007). Money laundering has become a global issue, with estimates that 2-5% of global GDP is laundered money annually (Schneider, 2010). This illicit financial activity has detrimental effects on economic growth, governance, and societal welfare.

Money laundering distorts asset and commodity prices and allows criminal enterprises to continue profitable operations (Reuter, 2013). It provides resources for terrorism, drug, and human trafficking, and public corruption (Ferwerda, 2013). The influx of dirty money creates unfair competition for legitimate businesses, misallocates resources, and decreases productivity (Unger et al., 2006). Money laundering also erodes public trust in financial institutions that are exploited and increases the costs of compliance and monitoring (Barone & Masciandaro, 2011).

Governments worldwide have enacted anti-money laundering regulations to detect, deter, and prevent this financial crime (Sharman, 2010). However, the increasing complexity and integration of the global financial system provide opportunities for laundering and make enforcement difficult (Ngai, 2011). More research is needed to understand evolving techniques and effects of money laundering to inform evidence-based policies. With vigilance and coordinated efforts across borders, the harm of this illicit activity can be mitigated.

## The Main Ideas Discussed in This Chapter

- To provide an overview of the current state-of-the-art artificial intelligence (AI) methods for anti-money laundering (AML) and their applications in different domains and contexts
- To discuss the main challenges and opportunities of using AI for AML, such as data quality and availability, explain ability and transparency, ethical and legal issues, and human-AI collaboration.
- To offer recommendations and best practices for implementing AI for AML in practice and to identify the key directions for future research and development in this field.

## 1.2. The Challenges and Limitations of Traditional Anti-Money Laundering (AML) Methods

Traditional anti-money laundering (AML) solutions face challenges and limits.

AML efforts seek to detect and restrict the movement of illegally obtained monies via financial institutions. Traditional AML approaches, on the other hand, confront a variety of obstacles and constraints in today's financial sector (Levi, Reuter, & Halliday, 2018). One of the most significant issues in the digital age is the increasing volume and speed of financial transactions. With billions of moneys moving across borders in real time, it is impossible for regulators to spot illicit transfers (Levi, 2022). Similarly, the growing usage of cryptocurrencies and decentralized finance platforms bypasses traditional financial regulation, producing "blind spots" for detecting money laundering activities (Foley, Karlsen, & Putnins, 2019).

Another drawback of traditional AML techniques is their reliance on rule-based systems. These rules are designed to detect unusual transaction patterns, such as big cash deposits or transfers to high-risk nations. Strict laws, on the other hand, are prone to abuse by clever money launderers who adapt their behavior to evade detection (Levy et al., 2018). Simultaneously, regulations can produce an excessive number of false positives, classifying many valid transactions as suspicious (Halliday, Levi, & Reuter, 2020). Regulators must constantly update rules in order to detect new money laundering schemes.

Anti-money laundering measures are further hampered by increased international regulatory complexity. Money launderers can take advantage of anomalies and shortcomings in national anti-money laundering systems (Halliday et al., 2020). Furthermore, money laundering networks can function across borders due to a lack of rapid information exchange between governments. To overcome these coordination issues, major investment in cross-border cooperation and technology integration is required (Levy, 2022).

Traditional rules-based AML techniques, while essential in preventing financial crime, struggle with the speed and complexity of modern finance. Despite these limits, advances in data analytics, machine learning, and worldwide collaboration may help authorities detect money laundering more successfully.

## 1.3. Introduce Artificial Intelligence (AI) and Its Potential to Improve AML Effectiveness and Efficiency

Introducing artificial intelligence (AI) and its potential to increase the effectiveness and efficiency of anti-money laundering efforts.

Anti-money laundering (AML) systems seek to detect illegal financial transactions, but they confront difficulties in managing big and complicated data sets. Machine learning and other artificial intelligence (AI) technology may increase the effectiveness and efficiency of anti-money laundering initiatives. AI algorithms can be trained to examine massive amounts of transaction data and spot patterns that signal money laundering (Weber, 2019). AI systems learn freely and upgrade their detecting capabilities when they are exposed to fresh data, rather than relying on pre-defined criteria. This enables for the ongoing improvement of money laundering classification algorithms (Kou, Chou, & Lou, 2020).

AI also makes it easier to analyze cross-border money flows and global entity interactions. AI can assist in the discovery of cross-border money laundering networks by exposing links between accounts, corporations, and jurisdictions (Nakashima, 2018). Furthermore, AI-powered surveillance can occur in real-time, allowing for the speedy reporting of suspect transfers before money are lost in the financial system. Weber (2019) claims that experimental machine-learning systems have demonstrated accuracy rates of more than 99% in identifying money laundering transactions based on samples of suspicious conduct.

However, efficient AI application necessitates large upfront development investments. Regulators should closely examine AI systems to verify that detection criteria are fair and detect money laundering without producing excessive false positives (Arner et al., 2020). AI competes with, but does not replace, human AML investigators, whose knowledge is still required when deciphering AI outputs. Artificial intelligence, when used wisely, has the potential to improve the efficiency, speed, and accuracy of anti-money laundering.

## 2. AI METHODS FOR AML

### 2.1. The State-of-the-Art AI Methods for AML, Such as Machine Learning, Natural Language Processing, Computer Vision, and Deep Learning

A range of artificial intelligence (AI) tools are emerging to help financial institutions and regulators improve their anti-money laundering (AML) operations.

Machine learning algorithms are being applied to enormous datasets of transactions in order to find trends and anomalies that could indicate money laundering or terrorist financing (Weber, 2019). Machine learning algorithms can detect probable laundering activities at rapid speeds by training on samples of questionable activity. Natural language processing is also being used to scan client conversations and documents for keywords and phrases relevant to laundering (Zhang et al., 2022).

Image recognition and other computer vision techniques enable scanning of client IDs, receipts, and other documents to extract structured data and verify identities

(Zhang et al., 2022). This can aid in the detection of fake documents used to launder money. Deep learning methods that integrate neural networks and powerful computing capabilities are being investigated in order to detect more complicated money laundering typologies across international criminal networks (Chen & Terzi, 2019).

However, the majority of current AML-focused AI is still in the research and development stage. Before full-scale adoption at financial institutions, real-world testing is essential to evaluate accuracy and avoid bias (Arner et al., 2020). While AI methods show potential for enhancing AML, well-designed algorithms, large training datasets, and the interpretability of AI conclusions will be required to assure success. To strategically employ AI in AML contexts, ongoing human expertise in financial crimes is still required.

## 2.2. Apply Methods to Different Stages of the Anti-Money Laundering Path, Such as Customer Due Diligence, Transaction Monitoring, Risk Assessment, and Investigation

Artificial intelligence (AI) can help with anti-money laundering (AML) operations at several stages:

Natural language processing systems can scan client conversations and documents to extract crucial data points for due diligence (Rahman, 2012). Identity can be verified using computer vision algorithms using government IDs and other customer documentation (Zhang et al., 2022). This automates elements of customer background screening in order to onboard new clients more efficiently.

Transaction Monitoring: Machine learning models trained on labeled datasets can automatically monitor transactions and report anomalies in real-time (Weber, 2019). This provides continuous automated oversight of an institution's transaction activities.

Risk Assessment: Network analysis algorithms can map relationships between consumers, accounts, transactions, locations, and other factors to uncover high-risk relational patterns (Chen & Terzi, 2019). This enables more comprehensive risk scoring of customers.

Investigation: Link analysis uses graph databases and network science to reveal laundering typologies and intricate criminal relationships buried inside an institution's transaction data (Wang et al., 2022). This can help in-depth investigations.

Integrating AI thoughtfully into AML procedures can improve efficiency, effectiveness, and insight. However, continual human expertise is required for strategic oversight and interpretation of AI systems. As algorithms examine fresh data, they must be checked to ensure correctness and fairness (Arner et al., 2020). AI can supplement AML personnel by combining human and machine intelligence.

## 2.3. Case Studies of Successful AI Applications for AML

### Case Study Number One: SAS and Nordea Bank

SAS's AI-powered anti-money laundering technology was adopted by Nordea Bank, a leading Nordic financial services organization. To detect suspicious behavior in consumer transactions and conversations, the software employs machine learning and natural language processing. It detects high-risk situations automatically while reducing false positives. When compared to legacy rules-based systems, AI-enhanced monitoring resulted in a 50% improvement in detection rates and a 60% drop in false positives after 18 months. The increased efficiency allowed investigators to focus on the most dangerous cases. Nordea proved the ability of AI to increase AML productivity at a large multinational bank (SAS, 2021).

### Feedzai and FTC Capital Case Study

Feedzai's machine-learning software was used by FTC Capital, a Brazilian financial firm, to monitor AML. To map risk linkages between clients and accounts, the system employs AI techniques such as topological data analysis. Feedzai assisted FTC Capital in reducing false positives by over 95% while increasing detections by 25% in its first year. The project demonstrated how to successfully use AI-powered transaction monitoring and risk rating in a difficult regulatory environment (Feedzai, 2018).

These examples demonstrate AI's usefulness in improving the accuracy and efficiency of traditional AML systems. AI-enabled solutions, when carefully applied, can result in increased detection rates, fewer false warnings, and better resource allocation for financial crime analysts. Human expertise, on the other hand, is still required for strategic monitoring and decision-making.

## 3. AI CHALLENGES FOR AML

### AI Opportunities for AML

AI has the potential to have a considerable impact on financial services, particularly anti-money laundering and counter-terrorist financing measures, by supporting financial institutions and regulators in more effectively identifying and preventing money laundering and terrorist financing (Arner et al., 2020). Machine learning and natural language processing AI approaches enable the examination of enormous datasets to find sophisticated laundering typologies and questionable transaction patterns (Rahman, 2022). However, employing AI in AML/CFT is fraught with difficulties. Legislative and regulatory hurdles to data sharing and AI adoption may exist. There are ethical concerns about data privacy and algorithmic bias. To reduce the danger of errors or unjust outcomes, thorough training data, security, and human monitoring are required (Arner et al., 2020).

The Financial Action Task Force (FATF), the worldwide standard-setting authority for AML/CFT, investigates how emerging technologies such as RegTech, SupTech, and AnaTech (analytics technology) might improve financial system safeguards (FATF, 2019). However, hurdles to innovation remain. The FATF aims to create awareness and facilitate discourse among stakeholders in the public and commercial sectors in order to overcome difficulties and limits. This can aid in the development of governance structures that allow for responsible AI use while mitigating associated risks (FATF, 2019). Overall, AI has the potential to improve the effectiveness and efficiency of financial crime enforcement. However, careful deployment and continued human skill will be required to fully realize its potential.

## 3.1. The Main Challenges and Limitations of AI for AML, Such as Data Quality and Availability, Explain Ability and Transparency, Ethical and Legal Issues, and Human-AI Collaboration

The primary AI problems and constraints for AML, including data quality and availability, explainability and transparency, ethical and regulatory issues, and human-AI collaboration.

Data Quality and Availability: The data used to train AI models is only as good as the data used to train them. Inadequate data volume, skewed data, or low-quality data with mistakes can all drastically impair model accuracy and result in erroneous judgements (Arner et al., 2020). It is challenging to obtain extensive, representative, and well-labeled AML training data.

Explain ability and transparency: Many advanced AI systems operate as black boxes, making it difficult to comprehend the reasoning behind model decisions. This lack of explain ability undermines AI trust and responsibility (Rahman, 2022). To ensure fairness, regulators need clarification on how models detect money laundering.

Ethical and legal concerns: Artificial intelligence must prevent unlawful discrimination or profiling. Due process concerns arise when judgments that have a significant influence on people's lives are automated (Rahman, 2022). While combating crime, AML systems must preserve privacy. To address these ethical quandaries, strict governance is essential.

Collaboration between humans and artificial intelligence (AI): AI cannot completely replace human intelligence and skill. Analysts with advanced skills are required to monitor model development, assess findings, research difficult instances, and make decisions (Arner et al., 2020). Getting the correct mix of human-AI collaboration is an ongoing problem.

Overall, AI has limitations, despite its promise. To mitigate dangers and use AI ethically and successfully, thoughtful implementation, thorough testing, responsible practices, and human oversight are required. AI adoption should be driven by fairness, accountability, and transparency.

## 3.2. The Key Opportunities and Directions for Future Research and Development of AI for AML, Such as Incorporating Unstructured Data, Enhancing Interpretability and Accountability, Ensuring Fairness and Privacy, and Empowering Human Experts

Incorporating Unstructured Data: A major opportunity is to incorporate unstructured data like clinical notes, pathology reports, and medical images alongside structured data to build more accurate and robust AML models. Natural language processing and computer vision techniques can help make sense of unstructured data. This provides a more holistic view of each patient.

Enhancing Interpretability and Accountability: Current AI models for AML are often black boxes, making it hard to understand their reasoning and build trust. Techniques like LIME, SHAP, and counterfactual explanations can enhance interpretability. Rigorous testing and auditing processes are needed to ensure model accountability and minimize risks.

Ensuring Fairness and Privacy: Fairness is critical as dataset biases can lead to inequitable model performance across patient subgroups. Techniques like adversarial debiasing and differential privacy can help ensure fairness and patient data privacy. Monitoring and transparency of model performance across subgroups is important.

Empowering Human Experts: The goal should be combining AI and human intelligence for optimal AML care. Interactive interfaces that provide explanations, justify recommendations, and incorporate human feedback can improve synergy. AI can empower rather than replace experts.

Overall, human-centered AI that incorporates multimodal data, provides transparency, minimizes bias, and seamlessly integrates with workflows has tremendous potential for advancing AML research and care. The keys are interpretability, accountability, fairness, and collaborative decision-making.

# 4. CONCLUSION

## 4.1. Summary of the Chapter

The text provides an overview of artificial intelligence (AI) methods for anti-money laundering (AML) and discusses challenges and future opportunities. It introduces money laundering and its harmful societal and economic impacts. Traditional AML methods have limitations in detecting complex and cross-border financial crimes. AI technologies like machine learning, natural language processing, and computer vision have the potential to improve AML efficiency and effectiveness. However, AI adoption faces challenges like data quality, model interpretability, ethics, and proper human-AI collaboration. Case studies demonstrate successful applications of AI for enhanced transaction monitoring and risk assessment. Key future AML research directions include incorporating unstructured data, enhancing model explain ability, ensuring fairness, and empowering human experts through human-centered AI design. Overall, the text covers the state of AI for AML, implementation challenges, successful examples, and recommendations for a measured approach that focuses on accountability, transparency, and human expertise.

## 4.2. The Benefits and Implications of AI for AML for Financial Institutions, Regulators, and Society

Benefits for financial institutions:

- Improved efficiency and accuracy in detecting suspicious transactions and money laundering typologies through automated monitoring and risk scoring powered by AI. This reduces compliance costs.
- Faster client onboarding and background checks enabled by AI-based identity verification and due diligence.
- Focus of human AML investigators on the highest risk cases rather than manual monitoring. This improves productivity.

Benefits for regulators:

- Better oversight over financial crimes by analyzing larger datasets of cross-border transactions and relational networks to uncover sophisticated money laundering schemes.
- Real-time monitoring capabilities and rapid information exchange across borders. This enhances enforcement.
- Guidance on governance frameworks for responsible AI use in AML to manage risks.

Benefits for society:

- Disruption of money laundering networks reduces resources available for terrorism, human trafficking, drug trade, and other criminal activities.
- A fairer and more secure financial system through the detection of illegal money flows. This promotes economic growth and stability.
- Protection of citizens from financial crimes by using advanced technology for public good.

Implications:

- Require significant upfront investments and change management to integrate AI into AML systems and workflows.
- Need for transparency, accountability, and ethics to build trust and address risks of AI systems.
- Continued importance of human expertise to provide oversight, investigate complex cases, make judgments, and collaborate with AI.

## 4.3. Recommendations and Best Practices for Implementing AI for AML in Practice

- Conduct extensive testing and validation using real-world data before full deployment to ensure models are accurate, unbiased, and compliant.
- Implement explainable AI methods to increase model interpretability and transparency. This builds trust and accountability.
- Establish rigorous model governance frameworks for continuous monitoring, auditing, and human oversight.
- Employ techniques like differential privacy, federated learning, and encryption to protect personal data privacy and security.
- Monitor AI model performance for unfair biases or discrimination across population subgroups. Mitigate any issues.
- Provide interactive interfaces and visualizations to help human experts understand AI outputs and collaborate effectively.
- Start small with well-defined pilot projects and measure outcomes before expanding to larger-scale implementations.
- Involve compliance, legal, and ethics advisors early in the AI deployment process to address regulatory and ethical risks.
- Clearly communicate changes, provide training, and get user feedback to gain organizational buy-in during the transition.
- Hire or develop in-house AI and data science expertise to implement solutions tailored to the organization's needs and data.
- Participate in industry knowledge-sharing networks to learn best practices and keep updated on the latest AI advances relevant to AML.

- Develop the capability to rapidly adapt AI systems to detect new typologies as financial crimes evolve. Maintain human-led oversight.

## REFERENCES

Arner, D. W., Narbel, P. A., & Buckley, R. P. (2020). *FinTech for financial inclusion: A framework for digital financial transformation*. World Bank.

Barone, R., & Masciandaro, D. (2011). Organized crime, money laundering and legal economy: Theory and simulations. *European Journal of Law and Economics*, *32*(1), 115–142. doi:10.1007/s10657-010-9203-x

ChenT.TerziE. (2019). Problems and solutions in developments of AI in anti-money laundering: A survey. ArXiv. https://arxiv.org/abs/1910.07450

Feedzai. (2018). *Feedzai helps FTC capital reduce false positives by over 95 percent.* https://feedzai.com/cases/ftc/

Ferwerda, J. (2013). The effects of money laundering. In M. D. Jesilow & S. S. Simpson (Eds.), *International handbook of financial crimes*. Edward Elgar Publishing.

Financial Action Task Force (FATF). (2019). *Guidance for a risk-based approach to virtual assets and virtual asset service providers*. https://www.fatf-gafi.org/media/fatf/documents/recommendatio ns/RBA-VA-VASPs.pdf

Foley, S., Karlsen, J. R., & Putniņš, T. J. (2019). Sex, drugs, and bitcoin: How much illegal activity is financed through cryptocurrencies? *Review of Financial Studies*, *32*(5), 1798–1853. doi:10.1093/rfs/hhz015

HallidayT. C.LeviM.ReuterP. (2020). Global surveillance of dirty money: Assessing assessments of regimes to control money-laundering and combat the financing of terrorism. American Bar Foundation. https://doi.org/ doi:10.2139/ssrn.3528830

Kou, Y., Chou, C., & Lou, J. (2020). Artificial intelligence and money laundering. *Asian Journal of Law and Economics*, *11*(2), 375–391.

Levi, M. (2022). Money for crime and money from crime: Financing crime and laundering crime proceeds. *Annual Review of Criminology*, *5*, 241–261. doi:10.1146/annurev-criminol-011419-041508

Levi, M., Reuter, P., & Halliday, T. (2018). Can the AML system be evaluated without better data? *Crime, Law, and Social Change*, *69*(2), 307–328. doi:10.1007/s10611-017-9757-4

Masciandaro, D., & Takats, E. (2007). The dark side of global finance: The black hole of illegal money laundering. *Economic Notes*, *36*(1), 1–37.

Nakashima, E. (2018, April 2). The algorithms that detect hate speech online are biased against blacks. *The Washington Post*. https://wapo.st/3OpYM7f

Ngai, V. (2011). Financial institutions and the anti-money laundering regulations: Cost-benefit study from anti-money laundering regulation perspective in the UK. *Journal of Money Laundering Control*, *14*(3), 217–234.

Opportunities and Challenges of New Technologies for AML/CFT. (n.d.). https://www.fatf-gafi.org/content/dam/fatf-gafi/guidance/Opportunities-Challenges-of-New-Technologies-for-AML-CFT.pdf

Rahman, A. (2022). Anti-money laundering: The promise and limitations of AI. *Journal of Investment Compliance*, *23*(1), 20–26.

Reuter, P. (2013). Are estimates of the volume of money laundering either feasible or useful? In B. Unger & D. van der Linde (Eds.), *Research handbook on money laundering* (pp. 224–233). Edward Elgar Publishing. doi:10.4337/9780857934000.00028

SAS. (2021). *AI-driven AML gives Nordea 50% detection boost*. https://www.sas.com/en_gb/customers/nordea.html

Schneider, F. (2010). Turnover of organized crime and money laundering: Some preliminary empirical findings. *Public Choice*, *144*(3), 473–486. doi:10.1007/s11127-010-9676-8

Sharman, J. C. (2010). Anti-money laundering systems in international banking. *New Political Economy*, *15*(3), 317–330.

Unger, B., Ferwerda, J., van den Broek, M., & Deleanu, I. (2006). *The economic and legal effectiveness of the European Union's anti-money laundering policy*. Edward Elgar Publishing. https://www.napier.ai/post/ai-aml-challenges

Wang, W., Chen, Y., Chen, T., & Terzi, E. (2022). Financial transaction graph analysis for anti-money laundering using deep learning. *Applied Network Science*, *7*(1).

Weber, V. (2019). The data science approaches used in anti-money laundering. *Journal of Tax Administration*, *5*(2), 120–133.

Zhang, J., Blaschke, T., Chen, Y., Chen, T., & Terzi, E. (2022). AI for anti-money laundering: A framework for representation learning. *Applied Sciences (Basel, Switzerland)*, *12*(2), 728.

# Chapter 4
# Artificial Intelligence in Central Banking:
## Benefits and Risks of AI for Central Banks

**Peterson K. Ozili**
https://orcid.org/0000-0001-6292-1161
*Central Bank of Nigeria, Nigeria*

## ABSTRACT

*This chapter identifies the benefit and risks of artificial intelligence in central banking. The benefit of artificial intelligence for central banks is that deploying artificial intelligence systems will encourage central banks to develop information technology (IT) and data science capabilities, it will assist central banks in detecting financial stability risks, it will aid the search for granular micro economic/non-economic data from the internet so that the data can support central banks in making policy decisions, it enables the use of AI-generated synthetic data, and it enables task automation in central banking operations. However, the use of artificial intelligence in central banking poses some risks which include data privacy risk, the risk that using synthetic data could lead to false positives, high risk of embedded bias, difficulty in explaining AI-based central bank policy decisions, and cybersecurity risk.*

## 1. INTRODUCTION

Artificial intelligence is the imitation of human intelligence by machines or the ability of machines to perform tasks using human intelligence (Lin, 2019; Ozili, 2023a). The use of artificial intelligence (AI) systems in the financial services industry is transforming the way financial institutions use data to acquire, use and

DOI: 10.4018/979-8-3693-1046-5.ch004

manage money, and it is changing how they serve their customers. The rise of artificial intelligence in the financial sector is also raising questions about the role of artificial intelligence for financial regulation and for central banking. This paper focuses on the latter – central banking.

Central banking is the activity performed by a central bank. A central bank is a public institution that manages the currency of a country and controls the amount of money in circulation (Goodhart, 1995). The core objectives of a central bank are price stability, financial stability, monetary stability, exchange rate management, lender of last resort, and banker to the government (Swinburne, 1991; Blinder, 2010; Ozili, 2020). Monetary stability means the provision of adequate money supply, price stability means achieving low inflation and financial stability means the absence of financial crisis or banking crisis.

Questions are emerging about how artificial intelligence would affect the operations and statutory objectives of a central bank. Some of the questions that have emerged are: Does artificial intelligence offer any benefits to central banks? Will artificial intelligence transform central banking? If so, will artificial intelligence usher in an era of modern central banking that is AI-led? Or are these questions the result of wishful thinking? The truth is: it is too early to know for sure whether and how AI would affect central banking. But what we know is that central banks are expected to respond to the pressure on financial institutions to use AI algorithm to serve their customers and to improve their operational efficiency. A central bank can participate in this process by developing a financial sector-wide AI regulatory framework. But this is not the only way in which central banks can get involved in the ongoing AI transformation of the financial sector. Apart from developing a financial sector-wide AI regulatory framework, central banks are expected to respond to the artificial intelligence transformation by using AI systems to improve central bank operational efficiency and to serve their institutional customers and the financial institutions they regulate or oversee. The decision of central banks to adopt artificial intelligence systems will be determined by the need to catch-up with technological advancement and the need to reinvent central banking to meet the modern reality of the digital world.

There is limited knowledge in the literature about the role of artificial intelligence in central banking. A lot of debates have emerged about the role, benefits, and risks of artificial intelligence for private financial institutions such as the potential for financial institutions to use artificial intelligence systems to offer customized services to customers, automate tasks, manage risks and to offer more targeted advertising to customers (Fernández, 2019; Hu and Chen, 2022). Much of these debates are focused on private financial institutions (Johnson, Pasquale, and Chapman, 2019; Königstorfer and Thalmann, 2020). However, such debates do not exist for central banks despite the fact that central banks are responsible for the soundness and stability of the financial system (Sinclair, 2000; Goodhart, 2011), and they play a significant role in financial sector development (Neyapti, 2003). Therefore, in this paper, we highlight the benefits and risks of artificial intelligence in central banking.

The discussion in this article contributes to the literature that identify the role of artificial intelligence in finance, but which have not considered the role of artificial intelligence in central banking. The discussion in the article also contributes to the literature that examine the digital transformation of central banks. Such studies have examined, extensively, how central banks have embraced digital innovations such as real-time gross settlement (RTGS)-based digital payment systems, central bank digital currency and cryptocurrency (Jackson and Manning, 2007; Nabilou and Prum, 2019; Keister and Sanches, 2023; Ozili, 2023b), but such studies have not considered the role of artificial intelligence in central banking. This article therefore contributes to this literature by focusing on the benefits and risks of artificial intelligence for central banks.

The rest of the paper is organised as follows. Section 2 presents the literature review. Section 3 presents the benefits of artificial intelligence in central banking. Section 4 presents the risks of artificial intelligence in central banking.

Section 5 highlights some technical difficulties in implementing artificial intelligence in central banking. Section 6 identifies some key considerations for central banks. Section 6 presents the conclusion.

## 2. LITERATURE REVIEW

Some studies examine the digital transformation of central banking. For instance, Tucker and Council (2014) showed that central banks are witnessing the digital transformation of central banking especially the digital transformation of money. They argued that, despite the digital transformation of central banking, central bank money will continue to be the final settlement asset and many financial intermediaries involved in payments services, clearing or liquidity-insurance should continue to have access to central bank money even though money becomes fully digital. Dow (2019) contributes to the debate about the digitalisation of central banking. Dow (2019) emphasized that the focus should not be on developing digital currencies, rather the focus should be on upgrading regulation to make it fit for the digital age and to address other digital innovations that generate credit and liquidity in the financial sector. Raskin and Yermack (2016) showed that the digital transformation of central banking is challenging classical monetary economics because emerging digital innovations, such as central bank digital currencies and blockchain technologies, are helping to narrow the relationship between citizens and the central bank, and may eliminate the need for the public to keep deposits in fractional reserve commercial banks, thereby, challenging classical banking and monetary economics.

Other studies analyse the role of artificial intelligence in finance. Milana and Ashta (2021) support the AI revolution in finance and showed that AI could offer better efficiency, generation of new data and risk management advantages in the financial sector. Bahrammirzaee (2010) showed that AI may be helpful in dealing with non-linear financial problems. They argued that traditional models demonstrate some difficultly in dealing with nonlinearities in financial markets, and that artificial intelligence techniques, particularly those that involve artificial neutral networks, expert systems and hybrid intelligence systems may be immensely helpful in addressing non-linear problems in financial markets. Königstorfer and Thalmann (2020) showed artificial intelligence has applications in banking especially in the areas of investment banking and in back-office banking services. They found that the use of artificial intelligence may reduce credit losses, increase payment efficiency, automate compliance-related work, and improve customer service. Veloso et al (2021) emphasise that artificial intelligence has great application in the financial services industry where financial institutions process huge cross-border payments daily, while stock markets and exchanges execute substantial amounts of trades and transactions.

Furthermore, Goodell et al (2021) conducted a literature survey and found that there are three common areas of research scholarship related to artificial intelligence in finance which are (a) portfolio and investor behaviour, (b) analysis of financial fraud and financial distress, and (c) sentiment inference and forecasting. Buchanan (2019) argued that artificial intelligence could disrupt the financial services industry. However, the author conducted a literature survey and notes that there is limited discussion about the econometric aspects of artificial intelligence applications in finance. Tadapaneni (2019) suggests some areas for considerations when using AI in finance. The considerations include the benefits to clients and firms, dealing with data privacy, data protection issues and the reduction in human labour which could create unemployment. Lin (2019) argued that despite the known applications of artificial intelligence in finance, the risks are still too great such as the risks related to cybersecurity and competition. Other studies such as Kahyaoglu (2021), Qian (2019), and Lopez-Corleone, Begum and Sixuan (2022) point to the use of artificial intelligence (AI) and machine learning to enhance the functionality, security, and efficiency of central bank products such as a central bank digital currency (e.g. the digital yuan, eNaira, DCash or the Sand Dollar).

While the literature has examined the digital transformations in central banking and the various applications and benefits of artificial intelligence in the financial sector, there is little or no discussion or research on the role, benefits and risks of artificial intelligence in central banking. This paper fills this gap in the literature by identifying the potential benefits and risks of artificial intelligence in central banking.

## 3. BENEFITS OF ARTIFICIAL INTELLIGENCE IN CENTRAL BANKING

The use of artificial intelligence in central banking offers many benefits. The benefits are identified below.

### 3.1. It Will Encourage Central Banks to Develop Information Technology (IT) and Data Science Capabilities

Deploying artificial intelligence systems in a central bank would give central banks an opportunity to develop information technology and data science capabilities. Many central banks lag behind private financial institutions in IT and data science capabilities. Therefore, deploying artificial intelligence systems in central banking will not only close the gap in IT and data science capabilities for central banks, but it will also enable central banks to enjoy the benefits that come with artificial intelligence and data science development.

### 3.2. AI Systems Can Assist in Detecting Financial Stability Risks

One of the objectives of a central bank is to maintain or preserve financial stability. Using artificial intelligence systems can assist a central bank in fulfilling this objective. Financial institutions, such as banks, often use artificial intelligence applications in ways that create value and create new risks or amplify existing financial and non-financial risks, and such risks could affect the soundness and safety of financial institutions. Financial institutions often submit financial returns to the central bank and to other regulators. A central bank can use AI systems to analyse the data in the financial returns submitted by commercial banks to the central bank. A central bank can use AI systems to detect quickly, within seconds, any abnormal change in the financial data submitted by financial institutions that may indicate a vulnerability or deteriorating condition of one or more financial institutions in the financial system. This would allow the central bank to make a timely assessment of the observed change and intervene in the financial system to mitigate risks before they become systemic in nature.

## 3.3. Searching the Internet for Granular Micro Economic/Non-Economic Data

Central banks can use AI tools to search the Internet and online media platforms (e.g., news media and social media) to obtain granular and micro data. There are lots of granular or micro economic and non-economic data about markets that ordinary people and businesses publish on the Internet (Shabsigh and Boukherouaa, 2023). These data, if utilised by central banks, could offer additional insights and improve central bank policy formulation. Many central banks rarely use such granular micro economic data either because they are unaware that such data exist on the Internet or because they are not confident in using unstructured third-party data for policy formulation. There is a need for central banks to use all data available, wherever it can be found, to improve policy decision making. Central banks may also use AI tools to obtain Internet information about what people think about central bank policies and their impact on households and businesses. This information can help central banks to improve policy formulation.

## 3.4. Using Synthetic Data on AI System Offers Benefits for Central Banks

Modern artificial intelligence systems can generate synthetic data that mimic real world data (Shabsigh and Boukherouaa, 2023). Many central banks will prefer to use both synthetic data and real-world data for AI algorithm training because they offer mutual benefits. However, some central banks may prefer to use synthetic data to train their enterprise AI algorithm because it would allow them to avoid using real-world data that contains personal and sensitive information, and it also allows them to bypass existing legal and regulatory bottlenecks associated with using real-world data on AI systems. The use of synthetic data has great appeal for central banks for three main reasons. One, it saves cost of finding real-world data. Two, it completely and perfectly diminishes all privacy risks because synthetic data do not contain personal or sensitive information. Three, it saves time that would be used to obtain real-world information from economic agents in the field or in markets. Central banks can also use synthetic data to emulate the behaviour patterns of economic agents and gain actionable insights for policy decision making. Despite the benefits of synthetic data, central banks should not be blinded to the risks of using synthetic data. It might be better and safer for central banks to use both synthetic and real-world data.

### 3.5. AI Systems Enable Task Automation for Central Banks

Artificial intelligence systems can automate several aspects of central bank operations. Central banks can use AI systems to automate repetitive tasks in central banking operations. This would allow central banks to reduce human errors, increase efficiency and save labour costs and time. Using artificial intelligence systems can also enable frictionless interaction between the internal operational systems in the central bank. It can also ease the interaction between central bank systems and the systems of financial institutions and enable frictionless and timely submission of regulatory and compliance reports to the central bank.

## 4. Risks of Artificial Intelligence in Central Banking

The use of artificial intelligence in central banking offers many benefits but it also poses some risks that should be minimised or avoided if possible. The risks include the following.

### 4.1. Data Privacy Risk

The use of artificial intelligence systems by central banks may violate privacy rules. This may occur by unintentionally unmasking private and confidential central bank data. The use of artificial intelligence systems by central banks may also lead to data leakages. There is also the risk that artificial intelligence systems can recall data about regulated entities and data about the central bank that were recorded in the training dataset after the data are used and deleted by the central bank. Therefore, central banks must be cautious about the potential for privacy violation when using artificial intelligence systems. If central banks must use artificial intelligence systems, they should upgrade artificial intelligence privacy rules and improve existing legal and regulatory frameworks to adhere to strong privacy standards. There is also the risk that the artificial intelligence systems used by central banks may intentionally or unintentionally collect and use personal information without obtaining explicit consent from the owners of such information (Shabsigh and Boukherouaa, 2023). While it is possible for central banks to develop an enterprise-level AI system that is relevant for central banking operations, such enterprise-level AI system may enhance data security for central banks, but residual privacy concerns may remain because low-level central bank employees may gain unauthorised access to central bank information which they do not need especially when the enterprise-level AI system remembers information or data that were deleted by top management.

## 4.2. Using Synthetic Data to Mimic Real-Word Data Could Lead to False Positives

There is the risk that deploying artificial intelligence systems might make central banks become lazy especially when central banks rely heavily on synthetic data. Instead of going out to the field to search for real-world data, central banks may prefer to utilize algorithm-created synthetic data that statistically mimic real-world data. Central banks may use algorithm-created synthetic data to train their artificial intelligence algorithms and the generated data may have poor quality and could give rise to many false positives in short-term or long-term forecasting of inflation and interest rates. The result generated by artificial intelligence systems using synthetic data, if implemented, could lead to wrong policy formulation, and may have disastrous effects on society (Shabsigh and Boukherouaa, 2023).

## 4.3. Elevated Risk of Embedded Bias

Embedded bias occurs when the data used by central banks to train the artificial intelligence system are discriminatory or unrepresentative or when the data reinforces existing prejudice and inequality in society. Such bias may also arise in the artificial intelligence system if the artificial intelligence algorithm is designed with human bias (Shabsigh and Boukherouaa, 2023). When this happens, it could lead to unfair central bank policy decisions. For example, a central bank may train the algorithm of its artificial intelligence system with data collected from economic agents who have personal bias and from a wide range of biased sources in urban areas to inform their monetary policy and financial stability decisions. Central banks may use this data and the artificial intelligence system to make policies that affect everyone in the country such as setting the policy interest rate. The AI-generated policy decision may be biased because the policy decisions generated by the AI system is a product of embedded bias, and the consequences are that it could lead to distrust of the central bank, and it could lead to economic hardship for people living in rural areas.

## 4.4. Difficulty in Explaining AI-Based Central Bank Policy Decisions

Central banks may find it difficult to explain AI-based policy decisions to members of the public, especially those decisions that were based on the solutions derived from artificial intelligence algorithms (Shabsigh and Boukherouaa, 2023). The ability to explain central bank policy decisions is at the core of sound central banking, but artificial intelligence systems could introduce complexity and complications in central bank's effort to explain the AI-based decisions because artificial intelligence solutions are derived from a set of interconnecting models whose assumptions and inputs may not be clearly known to a central bank. Therefore, many central banks may be reluctant to adopt artificial intelligence systems to support policy decision-making. Notwithstanding, central banks that are willing to develop an enterprise level artificial intelligence system must be prepared to deal with the complexity associated with explaining central bank policy decisions that are based on artificial intelligence systems.

### 4.5. Prone to Cybersecurity Risk

External hackers or malicious actors may use sophisticated hacking tools to gain access into the enterprise artificial intelligence systems used by central banks. Once, they gain entry into the artificial intelligence system, they may impersonate central banks through identity theft. Artificial intelligence systems are prone to data attacks at the data training stage as malicious actors may add destructive or disruptive elements to the training dataset to undermine the accuracy of artificial intelligence algorithms (see Shabsigh and Boukherouaa, 2023). Therefore, central banks may need to think deeply about the cybersecurity risks that may arise from adoption of artificial intelligence systems in central banking operations and decision making.

## 5. TECHNICAL DIFFICULTIES IN IMPLEMENTING AI IN CENTRAL BANKING

There are technical difficulties in implementing artificial intelligence in central banking. The first difficulty is the size of datasets for algorithm training. The datasets for algorithm training may be too small which could diminish AI model's predictive accuracy and mislead central banks into making wrong policy decisions, or the datasets may be too large and give out false positives which may also mislead central banks into making wrong policy decisions. Knowing the right size of datasets for algorithm training is difficult. Another technical difficulty relates to the quality of the data that is fed into the AI model used by central banks. Another difficulty is that central banks that use AI systems may face a situation where the AI infrastructure utilises significant computing resources for AI model training and deployment than is necessary. Lastly, central banks may find it difficult to deal with AI ethical and moral issues due to a host of factors such as the bias in algorithmic decision making caused by flawed training data prepared by human engineers. There is also the moral dimension which revolve around whether central banks are attempting to replace human workers with robots. And finally, there is concern about the inability of AI systems to explain the reasoning behind their decisions.

## 6. RESPONSIBLE AI: A CONSIDERATION FOR CENTRAL BANKS

An important consideration for central banks in the future will be how to design, develop and deploy artificial intelligence with good intentions and good ethics to support central bank policy decisions and improve the lives and welfare of everyone in a fair and meaningful way (Dignum, 2019), so that there will be greater trust in the central bank. A term used to describe this is 'responsible artificial intelligence' in central banking. Responsible artificial intelligence, if properly implemented, would reduce unintentional bias, increase transparency in artificial intelligence processes, protect data privacy, promote fairness, and create welfare benefits for those affected by central bank policy decisions. In the coming years, calls for the ethical and responsible use of artificial intelligence in central banking will increase, and central banks must be well-prepared for it. The major principles that will guide responsible artificial intelligence design and deployment will be fairness, privacy, security, and transparency (Dignum, 2019). But the major challenge that will arise for many central banks will be how to transition from 'principles' to 'practice' when deploying artificial intelligence systems. Central banks will also need to critically evaluate the different AI models used in central banking and how these models address security and data privacy concerns. AI models are programs or algorithms that rely on training data to recognize unique patterns and make predictions. As additional data points are added into an AI model, the more accurate the AI model will be in identifying unique patterns and in making forecast, and the greater the risk for data privacy and data security.

## 7. CONCLUSION

This paper assessed the benefits and risks of artificial intelligence in central banking. It showed that the benefits of artificial intelligence for central banks are that deploying artificial intelligence systems will encourage central banks to develop information technology (IT) and data science capabilities, it will assist central banks in detecting financial stability risks, it will aid the search for granular micro economic/non-economic data from the internet so that the data can support policy making, it enables the use of AI-generated synthetic data, and it enables task automation in central banking operations. However, the use of artificial intelligence in central banking poses some risks which include data privacy risk, the risk that using synthetic data could lead to false positives, high risk of embedded bias, difficulty in explaining AI-based central bank policy decisions, and cybersecurity risk. The implication is that the use of public or enterprise-level artificial intelligence systems have benefits for central banks, but they also pose some risks. Therefore, central banks should be cautious in deploying artificial intelligence systems. The risks they pose are significant, and if the risks materialise, they could tarnish the reputation of a central bank. Using artificial intelligence systems in central banking needs close monitoring by humans. The level of human monitoring should be proportionate with the risks that may arise from using artificial intelligence systems in central banking operations or decision making. Although robust regulatory frameworks to guide central banks in using artificial intelligence have not yet been developed, central banks should continue to monitor the evolving use of artificial intelligence in the financial sector and study the benefits, risks and applications of artificial intelligence in central banking so as to determine the best use case of artificial intelligence systems in central banking. While such monitoring may continue for a long time, many central banks will prefer to take a cautious approach to artificial intelligence due to the time and cost that would be involved in developing, training, and supervising artificial intelligence systems.

## REFERENCES

Bahrammirzaee, A. (2010). A comparative survey of artificial intelligence applications in finance: Artificial neural networks, expert system, and hybrid intelligent systems. *Neural Computing & Applications*, *19*(8), 1165–1195. doi:10.1007/s00521-010-0362-z

Blinder, A. S. (2010). How central should the central bank be? *Journal of Economic Literature*, *48*(1), 123–133. doi:10.1257/jel.48.1.123

Buchanan, B. (2019). Artificial intelligence in finance. A Report by the Alan Turing Institute.

Dignum, V. (2019). *Responsible artificial intelligence: how to develop and use AI in a responsible way* (Vol. 2156). Springer. doi:10.1007/978-3-030-30371-6

Dow, S. (2019). Monetary reform, central banks, and digital currencies. *International Journal of Political Economy*, *48*(2), 153–173. doi:10.1080/08911916.2019.1624317

Fernández, A. (2019). Artificial intelligence in financial services. *Banco de Espana Article*, *3*, 19.

Goodell, J. W., Kumar, S., Lim, W. M., & Pattnaik, D. (2021). Artificial intelligence and machine learning in finance: Identifying foundations, themes, and research clusters from bibliometric analysis. *Journal of Behavioral and Experimental Finance*, *32*, 100577. doi:10.1016/j.jbef.2021.100577

Goodhart, C. (1995). *The central bank and the financial system.* Springer. doi:10.1057/9780230379152

Goodhart, C. A. E. (2011). The changing role of central banks. *Financial History Review, 18*(2), 135–154. doi:10.1017/S0968565011000096

Hu, W., & Chen, Y. (2022, July). Application of Artificial Intelligence in Financial Risk Management. In *International Conference on Adaptive and Intelligent Systems* (pp. 180-188). Cham: Springer International Publishing. 10.1007/978-3-031-06794-5_15

Jackson, J. P., & Manning, M. J. (2007). Central bank intraday collateral policy and implications for tiering in RTGS payment systems. *The future of payment systems*, 138.

Johnson, K., Pasquale, F., & Chapman, J. (2019). Artificial intelligence, machine learning, and bias in finance: Toward responsible innovation. *Fordham Law Review, 88*, 499.

Kahyaoglu, H. (2021). The Impact of Artificial Intelligence on Central Banking and Monetary Policies. *The Impact of Artificial Intelligence on Governance, Economics and Finance, I*, 83–98.

Keister, T., & Sanches, D. (2023). Should central banks issue digital currency? *The Review of Economic Studies, b90*(1), 404-431.

Königstorfer, F., & Thalmann, S. (2020). Applications of Artificial Intelligence in commercial banks–A research agenda for behavioral finance. *Journal of Behavioral and Experimental Finance, 27*, 100352. doi:10.1016/j.jbef.2020.100352

Lin, T. C. (2019). Artificial intelligence, finance, and the law. *Fordham Law Review, 88*, 531.

Lopez-Corleone, M., Begum, S., & Sixuan Li, G. (2022). Artificial intelligence (AI) from a regulator's perspective: The future of AI in central banking and financial services. *Journal of AI. Robotics & Workplace Automation, 2*(1), 7–16.

Milana, C., & Ashta, A. (2021). Artificial intelligence techniques in finance and financial markets: A survey of the literature. *Strategic Change, 30*(3), 189–209. doi:10.1002/jsc.2403

Nabilou, H., & Prum, A. (2019). Central banks and regulation of cryptocurrencies. *Banking and Financial Law, 39*, 1003.

Neyapti, B. (2003). Budget deficits and inflation: The roles of central bank independence and financial market development. *Contemporary Economic Policy, 21*(4), 458–475. doi:10.1093/cep/byg025

Ozili, P. K. (2020). Does competence of central bank governors influence financial stability? *Future Business Journal*, *6*(1), 24. doi:10.1186/s43093-020-00031-y

Ozili, P. K. (2023a). *Big data and artificial intelligence for financial inclusion: benefits and issues*. Artificial Intelligence Fintech, and Financial Inclusion. doi:10.1201/9781003125204-1

Ozili, P. K. (2023b). Central bank digital currency research around the World: A review of literature. *Journal of Money Laundering Control*, *26*(2), 215–226. doi:10.1108/JMLC-11-2021-0126

Qian, Y. (2019). Central Bank Digital Currency: Optimization of the currency system and its issuance design. *China Economic Journal*, *12*(1), 1–15. doi:10.1080/17538963.2018.1560526

Raskin, M., & Yermack, D. (2016). *Digital currencies, decentralized ledgers, and the future of central banking (No. w22238)*. National Bureau of Economic Research. doi:10.3386/w22238

Shabsigh, G., & Boukherouaa, E. B. (2023). Generative Artificial Intelligence in Finance. *FinTech Notes*, *2023*(6).

Sinclair, P. J. (2000). *Central banks and financial stability*. Bank of England Quarterly Bulletin.

Swinburne, M. (1991). 25 Central Bank Independence and Central Bank Functions. In *The evolving role of central banks*. International Monetary Fund.

Tadapaneni, N. R. (2019). Artificial intelligence in finance and investments. *International Journal of Innovative Research in Science, Engineering and Technology*, *9*(5).

Tucker, P., & Council, S. R. (2014). The political economy of central banking in the digital age. *Bank of England Quarterly Bulletin*, Q1.

Veloso, M., Balch, T., Borrajo, D., Reddy, P., & Shah, S. (2021). Artificial intelligence research in finance: Discussion and examples. *Oxford Review of Economic Policy*, *37*(3), 564–584. doi:10.1093/oxrep/grab019

# Chapter 5
# Blockchain in Healthcare

**Fouad M. Ziade**
*Lebanese University, Lebanon*

**Malak Mohamad Daher**
https://orcid.org/0009-0002-9886-7763
*Jinan University, Lebanon*

**Mustapha F. Ziade**
*HHL Leipzig Graduate School of Management, Germany*

## ABSTRACT

*Blockchain technology has emerged as a solution to tackle challenges in the healthcare sector, such as fragmented data vulnerabilities in security and a lack of transparency. In this chapter, the authors provide an overview of blockchain and its potential benefits for the healthcare industry. These include collaboration, improved integrity and security of data, enhanced efficiency, empowerment of patients, and advancements in supply chain management. However, implementing blockchain faces obstacles like scalability issues, the absence of interoperability standards uncertainties regarding regulatory aspects, and usability concerns. To ensure the adoption of technology in healthcare, the authors propose a strategic roadmap for both short-term implementation at individual hospitals and long-term transformation of insurance and billing processes through smart contract automation. This requires integrating with existing IT systems training for staff members addressing ethical considerations effectively and customizing approaches based on regional requirements.*

DOI: 10.4018/979-8-3693-1046-5.ch005

## 1. INTRODUCTION TO BLOCKCHAIN TECHNOLOGY IN HEALTHCARE

In the field of healthcare there is a growing interest, in utilizing technology for purposes such as enhancing data management promoting interoperability ensuring security and increasing transparency in delivering care (Kuo et al., 2021). A blockchain is essentially a network that securely and permanently records transactions, among parties through a distributed ledger system (Agbo et al., 2019). The unique cryptographic validation and consensus mechanisms that form the foundation of architecture bring about benefits when applied to healthcare scenarios.

There are ways in which healthcare can benefit from technology. For example, using technology can help ensure the storage and sharing of electronic medical records (EMRs). It can also improve the process of insurance claim processing. Enable tracking of pharmaceuticals, in the supply chain. Additionally, blockchain systems can help manage telehealth data allowing patients to have control, over their health information while still maintaining privacy.

However, blockchain use in healthcare faces legislative, technical, and organizational obstacles. Concerns around data privacy and confidentiality, as well as scalability, usability, and a lack of standards, must be addressed (Dwivedi et al., 2019). Permissioned blockchains and decentralized IDs are two strategies that may help overcome restrictions. Overall, blockchain has the ability to significantly disrupt basic healthcare processes and improve service delivery throughout the patient journey.

This introduction discusses the benefits and drawbacks of blockchain technology in the healthcare industry. The parts that follow will provide an overview of blockchain basics, cover specific applications and use cases, go over implementation problems, and examine the technology's potential influence on healthcare.

## 2. THE CURRENT SITUATION OF BLOCKCHAIN ADOPTION AND DEVELOPMENT IN HEALTHCARE

Blockchain technology enables the establishment of a distributed, immutable, and secure transaction ledger. Blockchain has the potential to disrupt the healthcare sector by improving health data security, privacy, and interoperability, putting the patient at the center of the healthcare ecosystem, and enabling new forms of health information sharing. However, there are significant barriers to blockchain use in healthcare, including regulatory compliance, scalability, integration, and standardization. Based on a survey of recent literature and publications, this paper presents an overview of the current global position of blockchain usage and development in healthcare.

According to (Singh et al.), blockchain use in healthcare has been investigated from various angles, including electronic health records (EHR), healthcare management systems (HMS), decentralized applications (DApps), and consensus techniques. Data fragmentation, data security, data interoperability, data quality, and data ownership were recognized as existing difficulties in healthcare systems by the authors. They also conducted a comparative examination of existing blockchain-based healthcare apps and presented a solution taxonomy. According to the report, blockchain can deliver considerable benefits to healthcare systems in terms of data integrity, data provenance, data transparency, data sharing, and data governance.

Another study (Alshammari et al) looked at the current status of research in the field of blockchain application and integration in healthcare. The authors divided seven ACM Digital Library works into three categories: adoption, implementation, and integration. They discovered that while blockchain adoption has been extensively discussed in the literature, there is a need for additional research on blockchain implementation and integration for healthcare systems. They also identified unexplored study areas and possible future research fields.

Al-Mutairi's thesis evaluates the adoption of blockchain technology in EHR management in Kuwait. A survey among healthcare professionals and patients revealed low awareness of blockchain technology's benefits, but expressed positive attitudes towards its potential to improve EHR quality and security. The author suggests increased education and awareness campaigns to increase acceptance and knowledge of blockchain technology among stakeholders. While blockchain is still in its early stages, it has the potential to address challenges and opportunities in the healthcare sector.

These are some examples of how blockchain acceptance and development in healthcare are moving forward in various countries and areas. Blockchain technology is still in its early phases of research and implementation in healthcare, but it has showed promise in addressing some of the sector's core difficulties and opportunities. Blockchain may become a game changer for healthcare systems around the world as more study and innovation is performed in this subject.

## 3. BLOCKCHAIN TECHNOLOGY AND ITS POTENTIAL FOR HEALTHCARE INNOVATION:

Blockchain technology has the potential to revolutionize healthcare by addressing critical challenges such as data fragmentation, security vulnerabilities, and transparency gaps (Agbo et al., 2019). Healthcare systems today face major issues with fragmentation of patient data across various providers, care settings, and administrative silos (Dwivedi et al., 2019). This leads to incomplete health records, repetitive tests, medication errors, and a lack of interoperability. Blockchain's decentralized distributed ledger structure can integrate disjointed data sources into a unified system, ensuring a complete view of a patient's medical history for improved coordination of care (Kuo et al., 2021).

Additionally, blockchain's cryptographic foundations enhance security and prevent unauthorized tampering of medical records (Mettler, 2016). Consensus mechanisms verify transactions on the network while hashing and digital signatures protect data integrity. This addresses vulnerabilities in current systems that have led to ransomware attacks and data breaches impacting millions of patients worldwide (Lee & Lee, 2021).

Finally, the transparency inherent in blockchain's immutable ledger promotes accountability and trust (Almutairi et al., 2022). All parties can validate transactions, while smart contracts automate processes openly and impartially. This eliminates opacity and inspires confidence in data provenance. Overall, blockchain has transformative potential to enable decentralized collaboration, fortify security, and bridge transparency gaps in healthcare.

## 1. Decentralized Collaboration and Data Sharing

Blockchain's decentralized nature allows seamless and secure sharing of patient data among various healthcare stakeholders (Kuo et al., 2021; Dwivedi et al., 2019). The distributed ledger is maintained and updated through peer-to-peer collaboration, eliminating reliance on a central authority. This prevents siloed data storage as information can be transparently exchanged across providers, hospitals, labs, insurers, researchers, and other entities (Agbo et al., 2019).

For example, a blockchain-based linking system was developed to enable interconnected health information exchange networks across Austria, Germany, and Switzerland (Önder et al., 2020). This decentralized approach facilitated cross-border patient data sharing while maintaining security and privacy.

Another study found that a private blockchain solution improved transparency and trust in collaborative clinical trials through real-time sharing of time-stamped patient data across multiple sites (Benchoufi et al., 2022). The immutable nature of distributed ledgers establishes provenance and audit trails for healthcare transactions (Mettler, 2016).

Overall, blockchain's decentralized structure removes bottlenecks and data silos, enabling seamless, secure collaboration and information exchange among diverse healthcare stakeholders. This has been demonstrated through various implementations across providers, research, and insurance.

## 2. Enhanced Data Integrity and Security

Blockchain strengthens data integrity, provenance tracking, and accountability across interconnected healthcare systems through its inherent security mechanisms (Kaur et al., 2020; Lee & Lee, 2021). The distributed ledger structure establishes an immutable audit trail, ensuring no unauthorized changes or tampering of records as they are shared between entities (Dwivedi et al., 2019).

Cryptographic foundations like hashing and digital signatures enable proof of authenticity for medical data (Agbo et al., 2019). Transactions must be verified through consensus protocols like proof-of-work, which act as gatekeepers to prevent malicious actors (Mettler, 2016).

A systematic review found that blockchain-based systems significantly improved the security of electronic medical records by restricting access only to authorized users (Ghafoor et al., 2021). Another study demonstrated how blockchain preserved the integrity of archival medical images through fingerprinting and certificates (Kumar et al., 2021).

Overall, blockchain's cryptography, consensus rules, permanent ledgers, and other security mechanisms enhance integrity, provenance tracking, access control, and accountability of medical data as it is exchanged across diverse healthcare systems and users. This prevents unauthorized changes, enhancing security.

## 3. Pervasive Transformation and Efficiency

Blockchain technology has the potential to transform many aspects of healthcare and make processes more efficient. Specifically, blockchain could overhaul clinical trials, drug supply chains, insurance claims, and billing processes (Angraal, Krumholz, & Schulz, 2017). Clinical trials could benefit from blockchain through increased data integrity, real-time monitoring of adherence, and streamlined regulatory oversight (Benchoufi & Ravaud, 2017; Nugent, Upton, & Cimpoesu, 2016). Drug supply chains could use blockchain to prevent counterfeiting, enable end-to-end tracking, and automate transactions between parties (Mackey, Nayyar, & Hocquard, 2019). For insurance claims and billing, blockchain offers transparency, automation, and disintermediation to reduce friction and costs (Gordon & Catalini, 2018). In summary, blockchain may enable pervasive transformation across healthcare by enhancing security, streamlining processes, and removing inefficiencies.

### Automates Claim Processing, Reduces Administrative Costs, and Benefits Patients and Providers

Blockchain technology can automate and streamline the insurance claim processing workflow, reducing administrative costs and providing benefits for both patients and healthcare providers.

By using smart contracts on a blockchain network, claim submissions, approvals, payments, and record-keeping can happen automatically based on predefined rules and conditions. This eliminates many of the manual approval steps and paperwork that currently cause claim processing delays. Errors and improper claim rejections are also reduced through the transparent logic encoded in smart contracts.

For patients, automated claim processing means faster reimbursements and reduced hassles navigating paperwork and follow-ups. Providers benefit from faster payments and lower administrative overhead. Staff time is freed up to focus on patient care rather than managing claims. Inexpensive, efficient claim processing also helps lower operational costs for providers and removes waste from the system.

Blockchain-based claim automation provides significant cost and efficiency advantages over current manual processing methods. By automating workflows, improving transparency, and enabling real-time transactions, blockchain can accelerate claims payment, improve cash flow, reduce denied claims, and create savings that benefit both patients and healthcare providers. The end result is an improved system where administrative friction is reduced and value-based care delivery is enhanced.

## 4. PATIENT EMPOWERMENT AND PRIVACY

Patients gain control over their medical records and engage actively in their healthcare journey.

Blockchain technology enables greater patient empowerment and privacy over personal health information. By utilizing blockchain-based electronic medical records (EMRs), patients can take ownership of their own health data and control how it is shared (Ekblaw et al., 2016). This gives patients more autonomy in managing their care and selecting providers while maintaining data privacy (Azaria et al., 2016).

Specifically, blockchain-based EMR systems allow patients to provide fine-grained access permissions to their medical history (Peterson et al., 2016). Healthcare providers can be granted limited access to relevant information needed for treatment. Research studies can also request access with a patient's consent. At all times, patients retain control over their data and can monitor who is accessing it through the EMR's transparent ledger. This prevents information leaks or unauthorized sales of patient data.

Enhanced access and privacy empower patients to be more informed and engaged in treatment decisions (Husu et al., 2021). Patients can coordinate complex care needs, securely share information with new providers, and avoid redundancy in tests or procedures. Overall, blockchain EMRs support patient-centered care delivery through accurate medical histories, transparent records, and patient stewardship over personal health data.

## 5. SUPPLY CHAIN MANAGEMENT AND RESEARCH ENHANCEMENT

- Blockchain enables meticulous tracking and verification in the medical supply chain, enhancing transparency and efficiency.

The medical supply chain is complex, involving numerous stakeholders and transactions from raw material sourcing to the final delivery of medical devices and pharmaceuticals. Effective supply chain management is critical for healthcare organizations to deliver quality patient care. However, opacity in supply chains can lead to issues like counterfeit drugs, stock outs of critical supplies, and inflated costs. Blockchain technology presents an opportunity to transform medical supply chain operations by enabling greater transparency, traceability, and process efficiency. In this paper, we examine how blockchain can be leveraged to enhance supply chain management and research in the medical field. First, we provide background on blockchain technology and its core attributes of distributed ledgers, smart contracts, and cryptographic validation that allow robust tracking of transactions. We then outline key challenges in the medical supply chain like fragmentation, lack of coordination, and inadequate monitoring.

Next, we present examples of how blockchain has already been piloted to track pharmaceuticals, medical devices, and hospital supplies. Key benefits realized include better inventory management, prevention of counterfeits, and auditability across the supply network. We also discuss how blockchain can enable more advanced supply chain analytics through its data richness to derive insights. Finally, we examine emerging trends and future research directions needed to promote greater blockchain adoption. The immutability and transparency of blockchain make it highly promising for advancing medical supply chain management and addressing critical healthcare challenges. Realization of its full potential necessitates multi-stakeholder collaboration and thoughtful integration with legacy systems.

- Streamlines clinical trial management and sample tracking, accelerating research and drug development.

Blockchain technology has the potential to significantly enhance clinical trial management and medical research through its ability to seamlessly track samples and data. According to a study by Benchoufi and Ravaud (2017), blockchain establishes a permanent, shared record of trial transactions and events that can be securely accessed by multiple authorized parties. By maintaining a complete history of a sample from collection to analysis, blockchain can enable better monitoring and auditing throughout the clinical trial process. This level of transparency and immutability also facilitates compliance with regulatory requirements (Nugent et al., 2016). Additionally, blockchain streamlines data collection and exchange between research sites, sponsors, and regulators. A decentralized platform reduces bottlenecks that can delay trial progress and analysis. According to Cong and Wang (2019), these efficiencies enabled by blockchain can accelerate the overall medical research lifecycle, getting life-saving drugs and treatments to market faster. With its ability to enhance security, accountability, and integrity in clinical trials, blockchain holds much promise for advancing medical research.

## 6. EFFICIENT INSURANCE PROCESSING AND PATIENT-CENTRIC CARE

- Smart contracts driven by blockchain expedite insurance processes, reducing administrative expenses and clearance delays.

Administrative costs in healthcare are exorbitantly high, with estimates ranging from \$248 to \$265 billion lost annually due to billing, insurance-related, and operational inefficiencies (Shrank et al., 2019). The complexity of medical billing and insurance procedures is a major contributor. However, blockchain-based smart contracts promise to significantly optimize this process through automated adjudication and payment processing. As self-executing programs, smart contracts can be encoded with intricate clinical and insurance rules to validate claims and disperse appropriate funds between providers and payers (Kuo et al., 2017). This eliminates manual verification steps and speeds up payment settlement. One study found that using blockchain decreased transaction processing times from days to minutes (Roehrs et al., 2017). Faster claims processing means fewer administrative costs for providers. It also enables a better patient financial experience by reducing uncertainty and delays in insurance clearance and reimbursement. Blockchain's potential to add transparency and efficiency to insurance functions can translate to superior care delivery and economic value across healthcare.

- Empowers patients with access to medical records and treatment tracking for patient-centric healthcare decisions.

Patient empowerment is a crucial aspect of quality healthcare delivery. Blockchain technology can promote patient-centric care by providing secure, decentralized access to medical records. Through private keys, patients can control their health data and share it seamlessly with chosen providers and caregivers (Ekblaw et al., 2016). This prevents siloed record-keeping across organizations. Blockchain-enabled personal health records also allow patients to view test results, prescribed medications, and treatment plans to be better informed about their care (Azaria et al., 2016). Some systems even incorporate wearable devices to let patients monitor vital signs and disease markers. By having comprehensive access to their medical history, patients can collaborate more effectively with providers to make appropriate healthcare decisions. Blockchain returns control over health data to patients, enabling truly patient-centric medicine tailored to individual needs and priorities.

Blockchain's potential for healthcare innovation is boundless, offering transformative solutions that transcend existing limitations and revolutionize the way healthcare systems operate.

## 7. CHALLENGES AND LIMITATIONS OF BLOCKCHAIN ADOPTION

By enabling secure and transparent distributed ledgers, blockchain has emerged as a disruptive technology with the potential to alter industries such as finance, supply chain management, and healthcare. However, considerable hurdles and constraints to mainstream blockchain implementation remain.

Scalability, interoperability, regulation, and a lack of standards are among the obstacles that must be addressed before blockchain can reach its full potential.

The Bitcoin blockchain, for example, can only execute 3 to 7 transactions per second, significantly less than the thousands of transactions per second processed by major credit card networks (I. Lee and T. Lee, 2021). Furthermore, the lack of common standards makes interoperability across different blockchain platforms challenging (M. Mettler, 2016).

Uncertain legislation, a lack of user usability, and privacy and security issues are all problems (T.T.A. Dinh et al., 2018). While blockchain has great potential, resolving these restrictions is important for its widespread adoption across industry and government sectors.

## 8. THE FUTURE OF BLOCKCHAIN IN HEALTHCARE

The integration of blockchain into healthcare holds immense potential for both the short and long term. By following a strategic roadmap that encompasses individual adoption, hospital integration, insurance transformation, and billing revolution, the healthcare industry can harness blockchain's benefits to improve data management, transparency, and efficiency. This journey requires careful planning, technological expertise, employee training, and a deep understanding of regional considerations to ensure a successful and impactful implementation.

### Short-Term Implementation

Step 1 - Individual Technological Adoption: In the immediate future, individuals can start harnessing blockchain for their healthcare needs. Patients can use blockchain-powered apps to securely store and manage their medical records, enabling convenient access and sharing with healthcare providers. Additionally, wearable devices can leverage blockchain to ensure the integrity and privacy of personal health data, fostering trust and encouraging wider adoption.

Step 2 - Hospital Integration: Hospitals can take the lead in adopting blockchain technology to streamline their operations. Implementing blockchain for managing patient data can enhance data integrity, simplify data sharing between departments, and reduce data silos. Hospital staff would require training to understand blockchain's features, its security protocols, and its integration with existing systems.

### Long-Term Implementation

Step 3 - Insurance Industry Transformation: In the long term, the insurance sector can leverage blockchain to overhaul their operations. Blockchain can facilitate secure and transparent sharing of patient data between insurers and healthcare providers, leading to more accurate risk assessment and tailored insurance plans. Smart contracts can automate claims processing, reducing delays and administrative overhead.

Step 4 - Billing and Payments Revolution: Blockchain's impact on healthcare extends to billing and payments. Blockchain-based systems can simplify billing processes by ensuring transparency and reducing fraudulent claims. Automated smart contracts can streamline billing between healthcare providers and insurers, enhancing efficiency and reducing discrepancies.

## Key Considerations

Integration of IT Technology: The successful implementation of blockchain requires seamless integration with existing IT systems. Compatibility testing, data migration, and system updates must be meticulously managed to ensure a smooth transition without disrupting critical healthcare operations.

Employee Training: Comprehensive training programs are essential to equip healthcare professionals with the skills required to utilize blockchain effectively. Staff members need to understand blockchain's principles, security measures, and day-to-day operation to confidently incorporate it into their workflows.

Navigating Governmental, Ethical, and Legal Challenges: The adoption of blockchain in healthcare must navigate a complex landscape of regulations, ethical considerations, and legal requirements. Different regions might have varying data protection laws and healthcare standards, necessitating a thorough assessment of compliance before implementation.

Regional Variation: The application of blockchain in healthcare may need to be tailored to the specific needs and challenges of each region. Cultural norms, infrastructure availability, and economic factors can influence the adoption strategy, requiring a localized approach to implementation.

While blockchain use is still in its early stages, it has the potential to provide better patient-centered, secure, and integrated healthcare as digital transformation proceeds. Standards, scalability, and regulatory compliance are critical issues to handle. Overall, blockchain appears to be a vital technology that will shape the future of modernized healthcare.

## 9. CONCLUSION

In summary, blockchain technology has the enormous potential to revolutionize the healthcare industry by solving systemic issues including data fragmentation, security flaws, a lack of transparency, and ineffective processes. A more coordinated approach to care delivery is made possible by the decentralized, cryptographically secured structure of blockchain, which facilitates seamless and reliable data sharing across many healthcare stakeholders. Blockchain strengthens the security of medical records by strengthening the integrity, privacy, provenance tracking, and accountability of health data when it is transferred between entities. Within connected health networks, confidence and trust are increased because to the visible and unchangeable audit trails that come standard with blockchain ledgers.

Additionally, blockchain enables the automation and simplification of formerly time-consuming activities in areas like clinical trials, supply chain management, insurance claims, and billing. Costs are reduced, and essential healthcare operations are expedited. However, careful integration with existing systems, thorough testing, and employee training are necessary to fully reap the benefits of blockchain. Blockchain-related legal and regulatory ambiguities must also be aggressively resolved. Blockchain is a genuinely inventive technology that has the ability to put patients at the center of the healthcare ecosystem while addressing significant systemic issues, even though adoption is still in its early stages. Blockchain's potential to alter modern healthcare can be unlocked with a strategic roadmap, rigorous preparation, and execution.

## REFERENCES

Agbo, C. C., Mahmoud, Q. H., & Eklund, J. M. (2019). Blockchain technology in healthcare: A systematic review. *Health Care*, *7*(2), 56. PMID:30987333

Almutairi, A. F., Sarfraz, Z., & Basalamah, A. (2022). Blockchain in Healthcare: A Survey on Day-To-Day Applications and Challenges Ahead. *Applied Sciences (Basel, Switzerland)*, *12*(2), 679.

Angraal, S., Krumholz, H. M., & Schulz, W. L. (2017). Blockchain technology: Applications in health care. *Circulation: Cardiovascular Quality and Outcomes*, *10*(9), e003800. doi:10.1161/CIRCOUTCOMES.117.003800 PMID:28912202

Azaria, A., Ekblaw, A., Vieira, T., & Lippman, A. (2016). Medrec: Using blockchain for medical data access and permission management. *2016 2nd International Conference on Open and Big Data (OBD)*, 25-30.

Benchoufi, M., Porcher, R., & Ravaud, P. (2022). Blockchain protocols in clinical research: Transparency and traceability of consent through distributed ledgers. *F1000 Research*, 10.

Benchoufi, M., & Ravaud, P. (2017). Blockchain technology for improving clinical research quality. *Trials*, *18*(1), 1–5. doi:10.1186/s13063-017-2035-z PMID:28724395

Cong, L. W., & Wang, L. (2019). *Tokenomics and Blockchain-Enabled Transformation of the Healthcare Research Ecosystem.* Blockchain Research Institute. https://blockchainresearchinstitute.io/tokenomics-and-blockchain-enabled-transformation-of-the-healthcare-research-ecosystem/

Dwivedi, A. D., Srivastava, G., Dhar, S., & Singh, R. (2019). A decentralized privacy-preserving healthcare blockchain for IoT. *Sensors (Basel), 19*(2), 326. doi:10.3390/s19020326 PMID:30650612

Ekblaw, A., Azaria, A., Halamka, J. D., & Lippman, A. (2016). A case study for blockchain in healthcare: "MedRec" prototype for electronic health records and medical research data. *Proceedings of IEEE Open & Big Data Conference.*

Ekblaw, A., Azaria, A., Halamka, J. D., & Lippman, A. (2016). A Case Study for Blockchain in Healthcare: "MedRec" prototype for electronic health records and medical research data. *Proceedings of IEEE Open & Big Data Conference.* https://doi.org/10.13140/RG.2.2.30823.39849

Ghafoor, S., Hussain, O. K., Muhammad, Y., Al-Turjman, F., & Bakar, A. H. A. (2021). A framework for secure and decentralized sharing of electronic health records using blockchain technology. *Computer Communications, 174*, 64–72.

Gordon, W. J., & Catalini, C. (2018). Blockchain technology for healthcare: Facilitating the transition to patient-driven interoperability. *Computational and Structural Biotechnology Journal, 16*, 224–230. doi:10.1016/j.csbj.2018.06.003 PMID:30069284

Husu, H., Jussila, J., & Vuori, V. (2021). Blockchain in healthcare: A systematic literature review, synthesis, and future research agenda. *International Journal of Information Management, 57*, 102297.

Kaur, H., Alam, M. A., Javed, A., Anjum, A., & Alrasheedi, M. (2020). A blockchain-based communication infrastructure for future healthcare cybersecurity enhancement. *Electronics (Basel), 9*(12), 2133.

Kumar, A., Bandopadhyay, S., Das, P. K., Alazab, M., & Irish, Q. Y. (2021). Blockchain-Based Preservation of Archival Medical Images. *IEEE Journal of Biomedical and Health Informatics, 26*(2), 519–530.

Kuo, T. T., Kim, H. E., & Ohno-Machado, L. (2017). Blockchain distributed ledger technologies for biomedical and health care applications. *Journal of the American Medical Informatics Association : JAMIA, 24*(6), 1211–1220. doi:10.1093/jamia/ocx068 PMID:29016974

Kuo, T. T., Kim, H. E., & Ohno-Machado, L. (2021). Blockchain distributed ledger technologies for biomedical and health care applications. *Journal of the American Medical Informatics Association : JAMIA, 24*(6), 1211–1220. doi:10.1093/jamia/ocx068 PMID:29016974

Lee, I., & Lee, K. (2021). The Internet of Things (IoT) healthcare: Issues and challenges. *Cluster Computing*, *24*(1), 353–360.

Mackey, T. K., Nayyar, G., & Hocquard, J. (2019). Applying blockchain technology to improve healthcare supply chain management. In *Transforming healthcare with blockchain* (pp. 97–117). Apress.

Mettler, M. (2016). Blockchain technology in healthcare: The revolution starts here. In *2016 IEEE 18th International Conference on e-Health Networking, Applications and Services (Healthcom)* (pp. 1-3). IEEE.

Nugent, T., Upton, D., & Cimpoesu, M. (2016). Improving data transparency in clinical trials using blockchain smart contracts. *F1000 Research*, *5*, 5. doi:10.12688/f1000research.9756.1 PMID:28357041

Önder, I., Malinauskas, V., & Berniūnas, E. (2020). Blockchain-based decentralized management of cross-border healthcare data exchange: Methodology and framework. *BMC Medical Informatics and Decision Making*, *20*(1), 1–17. PMID:31906929

Peterson, K., Deeduvanu, R., Kanjamala, P., & Boles, K. (2016). A blockchain-based approach to health information exchange networks. *Proceedings of the NIST workshop blockchain healthcare*, 1-10.

Roehrs, A., da Costa, C. A., da Rosa Righi, R., da Silva, V. F., Goldim, J. R., & Schmidt, D. C. (2017). Analyzing the performance of a blockchain-based personal health record implementation. *JBI*, *78*, 169–178. doi:10.1016/j.jbi.2017.08.018

Shrank, W. H., Rogstad, T. L., & Parekh, N. (2019). Waste in the US Health Care System: Estimated Costs and Potential for Savings. *Journal of the American Medical Association*, *322*(15), 1501–1509. doi:10.1001/jama.2019.13978 PMID:31589283

Xia. (2017). *BBDS: Blockchain-Based Data Sharing for Electronic Medical Records*. Academic Press.

Zhang. (2018). *FHIRChain: Applying Blockchain to Securely and Scalably Share Clinical Data*. Academic Press.

# Chapter 6
# Blockchain Integration in Upstream Oil and Gas:
## Enhancing Performance Through Innovation

**Kaustubh Laturkar**
https://orcid.org/0000-0002-2643-3942
*Michigan State University, USA*

**Kasturi Laturkar**
https://orcid.org/0000-0002-4985-909X
*Validation Associates LLC, USA*

## ABSTRACT

*With its complex exploration and production processes, extensive information exchange and stringent safety standards, the upstream oil and gas industry is embracing cutting-edge technologies to maximize operational efficiency and improve data reliability. Blockchain technology has risen to prominence as an appealing solution offering decentralized, trustworthy, and immutable information management capabilities. An outline of the upstream oil and gas industry is provided to demonstrate its role and impact on societal development. The fundamental principles of blockchain are then discussed, emphasizing its potential to revolutionize data handling, transactions, and smart contracts. The chapter also provides examples of some of the current operational projects in the upstream oil and gas industry that are exploring its potential uses and the challenges associated with its implementation. Through the insights presented in this chapter, oil and gas companies and key stakeholders can utilize blockchain technology to boost business performance and enhance efficiency.*

DOI: 10.4018/979-8-3693-1046-5.ch006

## INTRODUCTION

In terms of its economic importance on a global scale, the oil and gas industry is one of the most significant segments of the energy industry (Stevens, 2018). Global energy demands will continue to rise as the world population and economy grow, and it must ensure that it can meet them. A key contribution to the oil and gas industry comes from the upstream sector which involves locating, exploring, extracting, and producing crude oil from wells or reservoirs. Around the world, this multibillion-dollar sector provides energy for households and businesses, and is a major source of employment and revenues (International Energy Agency (IEA), 2023). Upstream oil and gas companies are always looking for ways to improve productivity, reduce operational costs, improve efficiency and resolve environmental concerns. With its structured and quality-driven processes, this sector is increasingly embracing digital technology to gain insights into operations and optimize processes. Digitization enhances data protection, confidentiality, and streamlines information processing, helping them accomplish their goals more efficiently (Martinotti et al., 2014).

Blockchain technology is one such modern innovation that is helping the sector optimize reservoir resource utilization rates, improve output projections for thousands of drilling locations, and significantly enhance drilling operations' productivity and performance (Ahmad et al., 2022). In essence, blockchain is an immutable, distributed database that is designed to record and monitor information across a network of nodes in a transparent, reliable and tamper-resistant manner. A few additional benefits of incorporating this technology include the transformation of supply chains, development of energy markets, effective management of waste, and better worker safety (Q. Wang & Su, 2020). Each operation can be made more efficient by using blockchain technology. Its purpose is to store historical data, especially regarding energy efficiency and environmental performance (such as carbon footprint). The information is permanently and unalterably recorded in its transparent digital ledger, without intermediaries. It is possible to store and transfer sensitive financial information using this technology in a safe and secure manner. Due to the technology's ability to automate many processes and reduce the need for manual intervention, oil and gas companies can reduce their costs and increase the accuracy of their data. Moreover, it simplifies the process of collecting, verifying, and storing information.

The purpose of this article is to examine the benefits of blockchain technology and outline how it can be implemented in the upstream sector in order to support operational efficiency and achieve sustainable development targets. Moreover, this article explores a few examples of blockchain integration in the industry, as well as some of the possible challenges associated with its implementation.

## Overview of Upstream Oil and Gas Industry

In addition to providing a comprehensive overview of how the upstream oil and gas sector makes contributions to sustainable development, a structural analysis can also shed light on the obstacles it faces and the impact it has on society.

In the upstream oil and gas industry, which is the first stage in the energy production chain, there are a number of intricate processes used to extract valuable hydrocarbons. It is imperative that advanced technologies, multidisciplinary expertise, and strategic decision-making be used in exploration, drilling, and processing of minerals. Here is an outline of the key stages of the upstream sector, highlighting its technological solutions.

### 1. Geophysical Exploration of Subsurface Locations

In order to begin the exploration process, geologists. geophysicists, and other experts identify potential oil and gas deposits underground. Securing information about subsurface structures is carried out through seismic surveys, in which sound waves are generated and their reflections measured. As soon as promising areas are identified, exploration wells are drilled to confirm that hydrocarbons are present in the area (Jones, 2018). A high-risk, high-reward exploration process is immediately followed by an investment in the production infrastructure.

### 2. Drilling for the exploration of underground reserves

It is necessary to drill a well into the Earth's crust in order to be able to access the underground reservoirs of hydrocarbons buried beneath the surface. Depending on the depth of the reservoir, there are a wide variety of drilling techniques that can be used, depending on the location and depth of the reservoir. The most common methods of drilling include the use of rotary drills, directional drills, and cuttings on offshore platforms. By carrying the rock cuttings to the surface of the earth, drilling fluids, which are made of advanced materials and technologies, are responsible for cooling the equipment and carrying drilling bits to the surface of the earth. The production casing installed inside hydrocarbon-bearing rock formations prevents contamination and ensures the integrity of the well (Epelle & Gerogiorgis, 2020; Li et al., 2022).

### 3. Extraction and handling of hydrocarbons

Following the drilling of reservoirs, hydrocarbons are extracted from them during the production phase. A reservoir's natural pressure forces the oil and gas out from the depths to the surface. There is a possibility that when the reservoir pressure is declining, it might be necessary to employ a gas lift system or an electric submersible pump in order to enhance production. As soon as hydrocarbons are extracted from the ground, they are separated into crude oil and natural gas, as well as other substances. Surface facilities, such as wellheads, separators, and pipelines, are necessary to transport extracted resources to refineries for further processing (Li et al., 2022; Polyakov et al., 2019; Zhi & Caineng, 2019).

### 4. Refining and processing of raw materials

Refineries play a key role in turning crude oil into processed products by using chemical and physical methods, such as distillation, cracking, and catalytic reforming. Separation is accomplished based on the properties of crude oil's various components. This produces various hydrocarbon products such as gasoline, diesel, kerosene, natural gas, etc. It is necessary to remove or reduce certain impurities in petroleum products before they can be marketed. Water, metals and sulfur compounds like hydrogen sulfide and mercaptans are among the most common impurities (Tretjakov, 2013). Several techniques are available to remove impurities from hydrocarbons, including sweetening, mercaptan extraction, clay treatment, hydrogen treatment, and molecular sieving. Additives are added to purified products before distribution to change properties, characteristics, and/or performance (Tretjakov, 2013).

### 5. Addressing environmental and safety concerns

All of these processes need to be conducted with environmental and safety considerations in mind, which must be taken into account at every stage of the process. In order to protect human health, the environment, and ecosystems on a global scale, regulations and industry standards have been developed. There are various initiatives that are being undertaken to reduce the emission of greenhouse gases, prevent spills, restore habitats and minimize the impact of pollution. It has been observed that the industry is taking a number of measures to reduce its carbon footprint, including the use of energy-efficient practices, carbon capture and storage, and financially supporting the research on how renewable energy can be integrated into its various processes (Cordes et al., 2016; Waxman et al., 2020).

As a consequence of these factors, the upstream sector of the oil and gas industry has developed a culture of scientific knowledge, technological innovation, and environmental responsibility. Throughout the course of any project, from the initial seismic survey to the refinement of valuable resources, meticulous planning, rigorous execution, as well as continual adaptation to changing needs are all essential for its success. As the world strives to achieve a balance between energy needs and sustainability goals, it is beyond doubt that the upstream energy sector will play an increasingly important role in the global energy landscape as it strives to meet these demands.

## Value Proposition of Blockchain Technology

Blockchain technology has evolved rapidly and has become one of the most fascinating developments in the digital realm. In a network of nodes, it allows for the collection and analysis of information in an immutable, distributed manner. The chain of blocks in a blockchain are arranged systematically using a distributed governance algorithm (Laturkar & Laturkar, 2023a). The term "block" refers to a group of authorized transactions over a period of time. If the authorization requirements are met, a transaction request is considered authentic and valid. The chain of blocks in a blockchain are arranged systematically using a distributed governance algorithm. As new transaction blocks are added, they are linked to the blocks that have already been created, forming a blockchain (Laturkar & Laturkar, 2022). The entities in the network maintain a copy of the blockchain, which is a database containing all transactions. For instance, if two firms shared a blockchain containing relevant information about their joint supply network, each could be assured that the information was identical and hadn't been manipulated in any way. It will be possible for companies to audit the distribution chain without hesitation whenever necessary since there will be a permanent record of what has been accomplished. An overview of blockchain technology is presented in Figure 1 which elucidates the process of adding data blocks to the blockchain.

## Upstream Segment and Blockchain

The upstream oil and gas industry is a multifaceted ecosystem composed of a variety of entities, such as oil and gas exploration and production firms, equipment suppliers, service contractors, and government agencies (Doyle, 2019; Musienko, 2023; Startus-insights.com, n.d.). With the ever-growing demands for increased productivity, accountability, and reliability, a number of businesses have begun investigating how blockchain technology might be able to assist with these concerns. In terms of enhancing transparency, security, and efficiency, blockchain technology has the potential to significantly impact the upstream oil and gas industry in the near future, even though it is still in its infancy stage of implementation. Blockchain implementation examples in the several upstream oil and gas sectors are listed in this section. Figure 2 illustrates a summary of blockchain applications in several of these upstream oil and gas areas.

*Figure 1. Blockchain data blocks are added to the blockchain as the nodes verify a transaction based on network protocols*

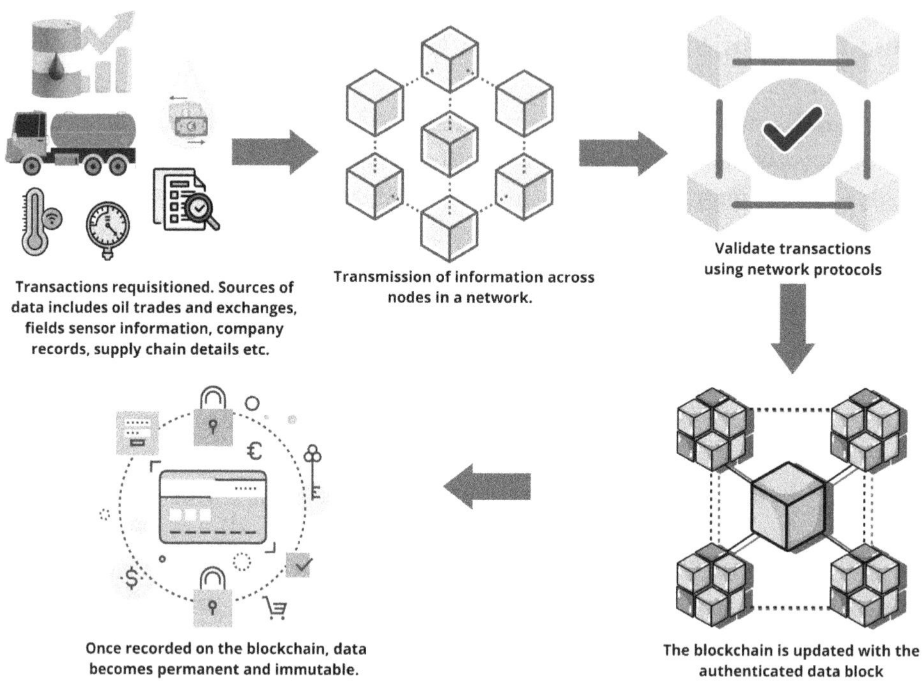


## 1. Inspecting pipelines and detecting spills

Petroleum-based oil and gas products can be transported over considerable distances with the help of the distribution system of oil and gas pipelines. Safety measures are taken to prevent spills or ruptures that can cause environmental disasters or human deaths. In mitigating undesirable events, pipeline tracking combined with timely alerts regarding tampering, interference, or a rupture of the pipeline can be crucial. Typically, pipelines are monitored by devices mounted on them. To aggregate and interpret measurements from sensors on the ground, centralized platforms are currently employed in monitoring and spill prevention systems (Lu et al., 2019). There is a risk that it would compromise the credibility, accessibility, and security of information necessary to identify, prevent, supervise, and predict pipeline ruptures. A blockchain-based solution can be used for monitoring pipeline ruptures and ensuring pipeline reliability. The application allows ensuring compliance with health and safety regulations in pipeline supervision, spill prevention, and maintenance. Various field-based smart monitoring equipment and drones can be utilized for validation to verify the integrity of information regarding the flow of fluid within pipelines. This will ensure that the measured data pertaining to oil and gas fuels and pipelines is highly credible, accurate, and reliable. By implementing smart contracts, pipeline operators can receive timely notifications of potential leaks, along with the coordinates and ID of the compromised pipeline segments for repairs. Pipeline operators can use blockchain technology to document systematically both the damage to pipelines and the maintenance performed on them. By using blockchains in these circumstances, information tampering can be minimized, producing robust and credible tools for pipeline condition assessment and integrity evaluation that can boost the efficiency of the oil and gas industry (Ahmad et al., 2022; Sircar et al., 2021).

## 2. Transportation

Transport vessels, freight trains, trucks, and pipelines deliver crude oil from drilling sites to refineries, where it is refined and shipped to industries or domestic consumers. Because of fragmented information, outdated recordkeeping methodologies, and overreliance on paper documentation, tracking the intricate infrastructure can be difficult and inaccuracies can develop (Mohammadpoor & Torabi, 2020). With Internet of Things (IoT) sensors, modern operations are able to track data related to temperature, pressure, humidity, volume, etc., thus minimizing product losses. The sensors can ensure that any unauthorized attempts to open oil and gas tanks are immediately detected. Furthermore, the tracking capabilities of these sensors enable precise geo-location of oil and gas tankers, shipment states, and transportation routes to be monitored, validated, and revised (Laturkar & Laturkar, 2023b; Wanasinghe, Gosine, et al., 2020). All the relevant data from the sensors is relayed to the blockchain network to secure quality and integrity and ensure compliance with all regulations. Blockchain systems have the benefit of being decentralized, which makes certain that records cannot be modified by unauthorized entities. Every update or modification to ownership of oil and gas-based products is automatically documented on the blockchain as they change hands and handling responsibilities. By using such records, oil and gas-based products can be authenticated and fraud related to them can be identified. Lastly, smart contracts automate the payment and collection processes between counterparties without the need for an intermediary once certain conditions are met (such as the quality and quantity of fuel). In most cases, these payments are instantaneous and reduce the risk of errors, lag times, and high costs (Ahmad et al., 2022).

## 3. Automation in Exploration and Production

With the advent of IoT-based monitoring devices, the crude oil industry is generating huge amounts of data related to the extraction and processing of oil and gas. For instance, data regarding rock formation characteristics, fluid concentrations, pressure, temperature, borehole conditions, steam infusion flowrates, drilling speeds, energy consumptions etc. are all recorded (Noshi et al., 2018; H. Wang et al., 2022; Zakir, 2022). In contrast to conventional networks, blockchain protects organizational information from manipulation, so that it cannot be altered or interfered with by adversarial entities or criminals. By doing so, oil and gas organizations can securely store all of their data, including confidential and sensitive material. This is done by issuing and recording the hash of the recorded information on a robust blockchain architecture. Modifications can be done in the global network at any time and at any node. The authenticity of the amendments to the global network can be independently verified and instantly reflected in the global chain (Rahardja et al., 2021). As a result, data is fingerprinted and made immutable, enhancing not just the security, but also the overall reliability of the global infrastructure to establish a robust autonomous system. By providing an integrated view of operational data that is accurate, up-to-date, and unified, organizations can share updated information regarding processes and deliverables in real-time, while mitigating potential obstacles encountered during exploration and production. In an implicit approach, the collected data can be loaded into AI-based models which can be used to detect patterns and help in training, revising, reinforcing, and consolidating the acquired knowledge for more efficient operations (Koroteev & Tekic, 2021). Blockchain can also be used for payment to vendors, contractors, and other affiliated businesses in a timely, transparent, and reliable manner.

## 4. Compliance Management

A regulation compliance program ensures that the business and operational activities of organizations in the oil and gas sector adhere to and comply with the laws and regulations in effect at a local, national, and international level. In order to ensure compliance with the set standards, it is the authorities' responsibility to provide appropriate guidelines, monitor the actions of the organization to ensure that they are being followed, and to give incentives or impose penalties for violations depending on the impact of the non-compliance (Saralaya et al., 2019). There is a lack of transparency, clarity, integrity, and confidentiality within the current record management systems that are being used to collect and manage the records that are required as part of compliance management. It can include a wide range of data such as wastewater utilization and disposal, chemical consumption, environmental emissions, payments to government entities, lease reports, drilling data, and so on (Ahmad et al., 2022). In addition to the privacy and logistics network tracking capabilities of blockchain, the integrity of information can be ensured by blockchain technology in order to protect people and the planet. It is possible for an oil and gas enterprise to document that safety protocols have been implemented. Auditors can confirm that said protocols have been validated, and anyone with permission on the open chain can verify that such actions have been carried out. In this way, it will be possible to eliminate any information manipulation, and, if an error does occur, it will be obvious where safety measures were not adequate in preventing that incident from taking place (Anjum et al., 2017). The diligent implementation of these guidelines safeguards the environment from harmful events, such as gas leaks and oil leaks.

## 5. Expedite Reconciliation

During a typical day, oil and gas companies carry out more than a million operations, including regular periods of buying and selling (X. Sun et al., 2023). There are several reasons why these operations cannot operate as efficiently and accurately as they could. These include poor operational procedures, individual negligence, outdated accounting methods, and other antiquated management practices (Lu et al., 2019). A blockchain-based ledger framework enables users to digitize key aspects of a crude oil exchange on a blockchain, which strengthens accountability, increases reliability, and maximizes the efficiency of an exchange. Another significant advantage of blockchain technology is the fact that it can be used to implement smart contracts (Laturkar & Laturkar, 2022). Smart contracts for performance monitoring may be created on the blockchain for oil and gas exploration and extraction, crude oil distribution, and oil and gas-based products marketing. These smart contracts verify that business transactions comply with specified standards. As a result of such contracts, specific actions are carried out automatically when predetermined criteria (such as grade and volume of oil) are met, resulting in automatic remittances and billings bypassing the requirement for an intermediary in the process (Alqahtani et al., 2020). In most cases, the transaction is immediate, so expenses, delay time, inaccuracies, and potential liability are minimized. Blockchain can be utilized by government agencies for monitoring, validating, and identifying a number of parameters pertaining to oil and gas shipments, such as the starting point, final destination, volume, composition, geographical location, and many other attributes (Ahmad et al., 2022; Aloqaily et al., 2020). Business records are also kept confidential, which enhances the credibility of oil and gas companies. By using smart contracts and distributed ledgers, blockchain allows contracts and agreements to be processed digitally instead of conventional methods, which are excessively time-consuming.

6. **Waste Management**

With the oil and gas industry producing different types of waste, including wastewater, chemicals found in drilling fluids and muds and hazardous emissions and gases, necessary measures must be taken in order to properly discard these wastes. In order to protect the environment, a portion of such waste products are recycled and the remainder is disposed of in landfills (Al-Hameedi et al., 2020). It is required by various laws and regulations to systematically treat oil and gas waste prior to disposal. Regulatory agencies employ methods to track and monitor waste. This ensures that waste collectors and recyclers adhere to ethical guidelines throughout the stages of sorting, categorization, transportation, processing, reprocessing, and disposal (United States Environmental Protection Agency, n.d.). At present, oil and gas waste handling technologies fail to provide sufficient confidence, reliability, and trustworthiness. Utilizing IoT sensors in conjunction with blockchain technology

*Figure 2. Summary of blockchain applications in several upstream oil and gas areas*

can streamline waste handling operations and minimize unauthorized dumping and transportation of waste by permanently storing records and transactions. It is possible to integrate IoT devices into oil and gas operations so that all waste generated is gathered, processed, and disposed of safely, with all relevant information captured on a distributed ledger and complying with environmental regulations (Hakak et al., 2020; Wanasinghe, Gosine, et al., 2020). With smart contracts, wait times can be substantially reduced, documents can be protected from tampering, and data integrity can be ensured. In transportation, processing, dumping, or recycling, the volume of waste lost can be determined by examining the details of the activities. Penalties can be imposed on responsible entities by imposing monetary fines. Blockchain protocols that are based on smart consensus can serve to enhance the credibility associated with oil and gas businesses and governing bodies through immutability, data traceability, and auditability capabilities (Ahmad et al., 2022; Baralla et al., 2023).

## Industry Projects

The upstream oil and gas industry is expected to undergo extensive transformations with the implementation of blockchain technology. By incorporating blockchain into various aspects of the industry's operations, transparency, efficiency, and security could be enhanced, processes would be streamlined, and costs could be reduced. Several business entities are currently assessing the capabilities of blockchain technology and exploring its potential use in the upstream oil and gas industry as highlighted in this section. Figure 3 illustrates a summary of some of these industrial entities which have undertaken Blockchain projects for the upstream oil and gas industry.

### 1. Blockchain for Energy

Blockchain for Energy (B4E) is a consortium that offers its member companies with revolutionary solutions and technologies for the energy industry. It is designed to enable organizations to accelerate their digital transformation to Web3 by being able to enable them with the capability of expediting their digitization transition. Among the current member organizations of the B4E are the American Petroleum Institute, Schlumberger, Chevron, Chesapeake Energy, ExxonMobil, ConocoPhillips, Devon Energy, Repsol, Pioneer Natural Resources and Katalyst Data Management (Businesswire, 2022). Recent developments in the consortium have culminated in the launch of their own network and platform, which marks the next step forward in their journey to Web3 which is a decentralized internet centered on blockchain technologies that is tailored to the needs of the industry and built specifically for it. Through the use of this framework, affiliated organizations are able to leverage their existing products and develop applications using Web3 building blocks, as well as design, test, and implement smart contracts in one place. The newly designed interface was recently used to launch the first commercially available product. It is a chemical delivery process that incorporates IIOT and Blockchain technology under the B4E Commodity Transport Program (Businesswire, 2023). B4E members will have first access to the program, with other energy companies to follow shortly after.

## 2. VAKT

With the VAKT blockchain platform, which was launched in 2018 by a group of global energy giants, commodity traders and financial institutions, all stakeholders in the oil and gas industry chain can connect digitally from the moment they initiate an exchange to its completion, while maintaining a transparent, immutable record of the transaction. These partnerships have enabled Shell, Equinor, Gunvor, Mercuria and BP to operate independently as VAKT's early adopters, integrating in tandem with their in-house solutions. ABN Amro, ING, Koch Supply & Trading, and Societe Generale are among VAKT's additional financial investors (Vakt.com, 2018). The first physical oil trade transactions utilizing VAKT technology were carried out in late 2022. The first firms to participate in this initiative were Gunvor Group and TotalEnergies Trading SA (TOTSA) (Vakt.com, 2022). Because physical oil trades are complex, the transaction process has traditionally been time-consuming and complicated. Creating standardized agreements straight from an energy trading risk management platform can be an arduous process for both the initiating and receiving parties. By introducing a fully digitized workflow, VAKT clients can confirm and verify transactions securely and effectively, which allows them to respond more rapidly to unforeseen circumstances. VAKT authentication process is automated, so the verification workflow is activated as soon as both entities register the transaction. This ensures that discrepancies between purchasers and suppliers can be identified and resolved at initialization, rather than later, thereby avoiding expensive delays.

## 3. Vertrax IBM

A blockchain solution built on Hyperledger fabric and powered by IBM Blockchain technology on Amazon AWS, the Vertrax Blockchain offers total asset traceability, provides insight into data flow throughout the oil and gas supply chain, and substantially reduces supply chain expenses (Vertrax, n.d.). In this innovative blockchain application, user information is integrated into a centralized, encrypted, access-controlled platform, utilizing predictive algorithms, which monitors inventory levels, transactions, and reconciliations. By integrating all IoT systems and transportation networks, this solution provides real-time tracking of products as they move through the supply chain while maintaining data security. This allows companies to share value through collaboration while protecting their most sensitive data assets. Monitoring and tracking large liquid orders can be optimized by analyzing production and demand relationships to ensure timely and accurate product delivery to retail establishments. As a result, costs are reduced, efficiency is increased, and supply chains are made more reliable and transparent. Furthermore, it can help ensure that the highest quality products are delivered to consumers. As a result of the smart contracts deployed on Blockchain, it's possible for organizations to make near real-time payments or apply for credit quickly, which can greatly improve their cash flow, which is one of the most important aspects of any business (Mullineaux, 2019). In addition to automating processes, smart contracts can also reduce human error risks by eliminating manual labor. The process can also minimize the need for intermediaries, resulting in further cuts in expenses.

4. **GumboNet**

To manage smart contracts in the energy industry, Data Gumbo developed the GumboNet and GumboNet ESG software platforms by integrating distributed ledger technology with the Industrial Internet of Things (IIoT). It provides enhanced functionality for monitoring environmental, social and governance approaches for tracking sustainable progress through its automated smart contract management system (Mittal & Kudapa, 2023). As a result of the large number of contractors and vendors in the oil and gas industry, supply chain management issues always arise, resulting in a delay in invoice processing, auditing, and disagreements, resulting in substantial financial losses. Through blockchain technology, workflows become straightforward, efficient, trustworthy, and reliable. By utilizing the smart contract management system, records are maintained, invoices are processed, reconciled, and settled without human intervention, and disagreements are reduced with higher accuracy (Datagumbo.com, n.d.). Smart contracts consist of clauses and performance metrics organizations use to gauge progress. These may include on-time delivery of goods, contractual obligations etc. Depending on the system, data may include business operations reports, daily updates, or technical information. By employing this smart contract management system, raw information is gathered and standardized to be easily accessible and secure. A single block or ledger record is generated by the process, and every entity involved in the operation has a node and a copy of the blockchain that can be used for verification and approval. Upon the confirmation and endorsement of the outcome by all stakeholders, the payment is automatically processed. The blockchain will archive all the original information, computations, and outcomes of the project. This will help the organization conduct future evaluations of its work and ensure compliance.

*Figure 3. Blockchain projects undertaken by several industrial entities for the upstream oil and gas industry*

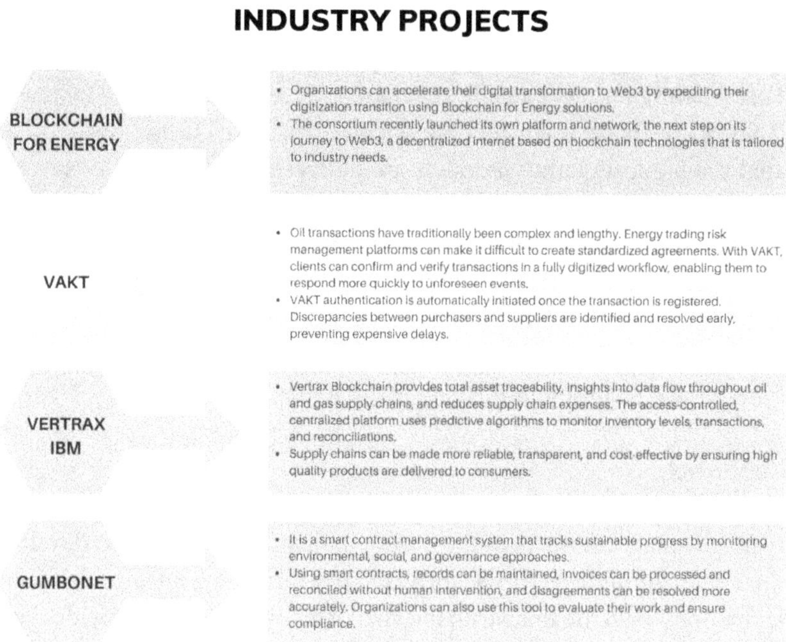


## Implementation Challenges

It is possible to secure records and exchanges related to oil and gas exploration, extraction, transportation, and a variety of industrial activities using blockchain technology, which employs robust consensus protocols and immutable cryptographic information encryption techniques. There are however a number of vulnerabilities that exist as a result of the inadequacies of protocol specifications and security measures incorporated into this technology. Listed below are a few of the challenges associated with the implementation of this technology in the upstream oil and gas industry.

### 1. Security and Privacy

The number of potential security breaches and failure scenarios for blockchain implementation is insufficient for a risk assessment, and since the technology is in its infancy, there is the possibility of an unforeseen safety hazard. This means evaluating the process and mitigating any potential risks that may arise will require some resources and attention. There are several difficulties associated with blockchain implementation, including interface problems, misuse of open and confidential access keys, and the lack of protocols and government oversight. Majority hacks are possible when more than 50% of distributed ledger nodes are controlled (Upadhyay, 2020). If this happens, the entire process of adding blocks to the network can be compromised, resulting in invalid blocks being created. Malicious actors can manipulate the record of several operations by splitting and presenting a different or fabricated version of the transaction by possessing an equivalent amount of computational capacity as all existing nodes. If transactions can be linked to IP addresses, personal information can be revealed and identities and keys can be lost or stolen. It is possible for external entities to track users' personal information, transactions, and records, which can then be exploited and compromised (Monrat et al., 2019). These situations raise privacy concerns. To prevent this kind of data leakage, it is imperative that key protection and architecture access are thoroughly scrutinized during the implementation of any blockchain service.

2. **Scalability**

Various sources, such as seismic surveys, drilling operations, and production activities, generate vast amounts of data for the upstream oil and gas industry. Each transaction in the blockchain's distributed ledger must be recorded and verified by multiple nodes. With a growing data volume, the blockchain network's performance and speed can be negatively affected. In particular, blockchain networks using proof-of-work consensus algorithms might have transaction throughput limitations. These networks only process a limited number of transactions per second, which delays transactions and increases costs (Monrat et al., 2019). Oil and gas upstream operations can experience significant congestion when dealing with massive numbers of real-time transactions. Moreover, blockchain networks are decentralized, so consensus and transaction validation requires participation by multiple nodes. As the number of nodes in the network increases, there is a possibility that scalability issues can arise. Depending on the time required by all nodes to come to a consensus, there may be a slowdown in transaction speeds and congestion on the network (Chen et al., 2020). In order to overcome these scalability issues, blockchain networks need to be optimized in order to ensure that transactions are as fast and secure as possible. It is necessary to develop new technologies and protocols that can be used to support high-speed and large-scale transactions in order to achieve this goal.

### 3. Interoperability

The upstream oil and gas sector involves a variety of stakeholders including exploration and production businesses, service operators, regulators, and financial institutions. There are various data infrastructures, proprietary formats, information repositories, and protocol specifications maintained by each of these entities, which makes it inconvenient for information to be seamlessly transmitted, resulting in fragmented ecosystems. As a result of the disparate nature of these platforms, interoperability becomes a significant issue when implementing blockchain technology (Ahmad et al., 2022; Upadhyay, 2020). Across the industry, there are no standardized data specifications and protocols, which is a major obstacle to interoperability. Information flow is hindered and blockchain technology's possible applications are limited because of incompatible data structures. The oil and gas industry relies substantially on legacy systems developed and operated over a long period of time. In order to facilitate interoperability between existing legacy applications and the innovative blockchain architecture in a reliable manner, it is imperative that strategies be identified to bridge the disconnect in an innovative manner (Zehir et al., 2022). This necessitates an extensive understanding of already established systems and comprehensive knowledge of blockchain based architectures.

### 4. Regulations

There are many regulatory and administrative complications associated with the upstream oil and gas industry due to its multifaceted nature. A number of confidential data types are handled in the industry, including privileged exploration and production records, commercial proprietary information, and personally identifiable information. The inherent accessibility and immutability of blockchain technology raises privacy and security concerns. The implementation of blockchain solutions should be carefully considered in light of regulatory compliance mandates, such as information protection guidelines and industry-specific regulations (Brilliantova & Thurner, 2019; Hassani et al., 2020). Furthermore, each nation or geographic area may have its own regulatory framework and compliance requirements. The process of implementing blockchain across geographical boundaries can be complicated and time-consuming due to the need to deal with multiple legal and regulatory structures. Regulatory guidelines may require the modification of existing compliance processes, and any changes to compliance processes need to be understood and accepted by organizations. Last but not least, organizations need to ensure that blockchain transactions can be audited and traced, which can be a challenging task, especially considering the technology's decentralized nature (Chang et al., 2020).

## 5. Integrating Data From Different Sources

In the upstream oil and gas industry, a great deal of data is generated from various sources, such as drilling equipment, sensors, IoT devices, geological surveys, reservoir simulations, and production facilities. There is a lot of information included in this data, such as well performance, production levels, maintenance records, safety reports, and much more (Behounek et al., 2017; E. Allison & B. Mandler, 2018). It is quite challenging to integrate this data into a blockchain network because of the variety of data formats and standards involved. With the help of blockchain technology, critical data can be stored in blocks and a distributed and immutable ledger can be created. Whenever a block is added to the chain, it is the record of a transaction or data point, and once it is added to the chain, it cannot be changed or removed, which ensures that the data is as accurate as possible. As part of the blockchain network, not all the data should be visible to all the participants. To ensure that only authorized parties have access to specific information, access control and permissions should be implemented in the system. Sensitive information such as that related to exploration, reserves, and proprietary technologies should be protected in this manner. It may be necessary, in some cases, to integrate data from off-chain sources using something called a data oracle. A data oracle can be a trusted source of off-chain data that can be used to trigger smart contracts or update blockchain records in real time. If these oracles are present, then the blockchain can accurately represent data from the physical world (Acharya et al., 2019; Maleh et al., 2023). Blockchain networks should also be able to integrate and process real-time data, so they can respond instantly to events or conditions that are critical.

## 6. Training and Education

It may be difficult for many industry professionals to implement and manage blockchain solutions effectively because blockchain is a relatively new technology. This gap must be bridged through training and education programs. Companies should also consider investing in research and development efforts to ensure that they are staying up to date with the latest developments in the blockchain space (Mohammed et al., 2020; Vermeulen et al., 2018). Additionally, working with experienced experts in the field can help organizations better understand the potential of blockchain solutions. In order to assist employees and management in navigating resistance to adopting new technologies, employees and management must be equipped with change management skills. To demonstrate the benefits of blockchain technology and how it can be used to improve processes and outcomes in the oil and gas industry, examples of successful blockchain implementations as well as case studies of blockchain implementations in other industries must be shared. In order to be able to integrate blockchain with existing systems, technical training will need to be provided to IT and development teams. The training should cover such topics as blockchain architecture, APIs, and how to integrate data effectively with the blockchain. When a blockchain solution depends on a particular vendor or platform, it is important to make sure that the appropriate personnel have received training from the vendor or third-party experts as part of the solution. Finally, companies should create a comprehensive strategy to incorporate blockchain technology into their operations and ensure the success of their initiatives (Ajao et al., 2019; Hassani et al., 2020).

## 7. Confidentiality and Consent

Partnering with regulators and sharing sensitive data is often a part of upstream operations. It can be a complex legal and technical challenge to implement blockchain solutions while respecting data privacy laws. Companies must ensure they have the necessary processes and systems in place to protect customer data and ensure compliance with relevant regulations. Additionally, companies should ensure that their blockchain solutions are designed to securely store and process customer data. Companies should also consider implementing a data governance framework to ensure that customer data is handled responsibly. There must be clear mechanisms in place for obtaining explicit consent from individuals or organizations before their data can be stored on a blockchain, and this consent must be obtained beforehand. Consent should be given in an informed, revocable, and well documented manner (Rantos et al., 2019; Varma Kakarlapudi et al., 2021). The process of automating consent can be achieved using smart contracts. Smart contracts, for example, can be used to trigger consent requests when new data is added to the blockchain. To allow data sharing and transactions on the blockchain without leaking any of the actual data content, it is necessary to explore zero-knowledge proofs or secure multi-party computation, to allow privacy-preserving techniques to be implemented. It is imperative that robust identity management systems be implemented in order to verify the identity of participants on the blockchain. In this way, sensitive data can be accessed only by authorized individuals and organizations. Individuals should be able to gain more control over the use of their personal information by using decentralized identity solutions and self-sovereign identity principles. Finally, companies should regularly review their blockchain solutions to ensure that customer data remains secure and private (Ahmad et al., 2022).

## 8. Issues Related to the Environment

A blockchain network typically uses a lot of computational power, which raises environmental concerns, especially when it comes to an industry that is increasingly concerned with sustainability and reducing its carbon footprint. This has led to the development of energy-efficient blockchains such as proof-of-stake and proof-of-authority (Asif & Hassan, 2023; Schletz et al., 2020). These protocols use a fraction of the energy of traditional proof-of-work systems, making them a more sustainable alternative. Additionally, these protocols are also more secure, as they require fewer resources to verify transactions. This makes them an attractive option for organizations looking to reduce their environmental impact while still maintaining a high level of security. There is a tendency for blockchain networks to rely on data centers to run their nodes, and these data centers consume a considerable amount of energy. The amount of energy consumed can have a significant impact on the carbon footprint. It is important to invest in energy-efficient data center infrastructure, such as cooling systems and server optimization, in order to reduce energy consumption in the data centers (Hintemann & Hinterholzer, 2019; Luntovskyy & Hara, 2021). It would be beneficial to locate data centers in areas that are abundant in renewable energy sources. Investments should be made in carbon offsetting initiatives to neutralize the carbon emissions caused by blockchain operations. A few examples of these efforts can be planting trees, undertaking renewable energy projects, and other actions that contribute positively towards the environment.

To summarize, adopting blockchain in the upstream oil and gas sector requires detailed planning, consideration of industry-specific challenges, and an understanding of technical, regulatory, and organizational hurdles. Managing these challenges effectively will require collaboration between industry stakeholders and technology experts. A successful implementation also requires a clear strategy, thoughtful implementation, and continued investment to ensure long-term success.

## FUTURE OF BLOCKCHAIN IN UPSTREAM OIL AND GAS

There are both opportunities and challenges associated with the future of blockchain in the upstream oil and gas industry. Despite the fact that the adoption of blockchain technology has been relatively slow in this industry due to its complexity and conservative nature, there are several trends and developments that suggest blockchain will continue to play a substantial role in shaping the future of the industry.

### 1. Enhanced Data Management

As a result of blockchain technology, there will be an increase in the use of secure, transparent, and safe data management in the future. In the era of IoT devices and sensors, blockchain technology can help secure the integrity and authenticity of data generated by them, making it vital for decision-making, compliance, and audit purposes. Blockchain is also a powerful tool for data security and privacy, as it allows data to be encrypted and stored in a decentralized network (Das et al., 2021). This reduces the risk of data theft and misuse, making it more secure and reliable. Blockchain technology makes it possible to share data efficiently and securely between various parties involved in the oil and gas value chain, such as exploration companies, drilling contractors, service providers, and regulatory agencies. Data sharing agreements can be automated with the use of smart contracts, making information readily available to authorized parties while maintaining the confidentiality and ownership of the data. In the area of analytics and machine learning, blockchain technology offers a comprehensive and secure data source. With the help of data analytics, it is possible to extract valuable insights from the vast amounts of data generated during upstream operations, which can lead to better reservoir management, maintenance predictions, and cost optimization (Deepa et al., 2022).

## 2. The Optimization of the Oil and Gas Supply Chain

Oil and gas supply chains can be made more transparent and efficient with the use of blockchain technology. In the future, companies will increasingly use blockchain technology in order to track the movement of assets, equipment, and materials in the supply chain, reducing fraud, errors, and delays in the process. Additionally, blockchain technology can be used to automate processes, such as payments and contract management, reducing costs and streamlining operations (Aslam et al., 2022; Laturkar & Laturkar, 2022). Blockchain technology can also be used to monitor environmental impact and sustainability of oil and gas supply chains. This data can be used to make informed decisions and to assess the performance of companies. Due to its tamper-proof nature and the ability to execute smart contracts, blockchain has the potential to reduce the incidence of fraud and errors in the supply chain significantly. With smart contracts, it is possible to automate and enforce agreements, ensuring that the transactions and delivery of goods are carried out in accordance with predefined conditions. There is a reduction in disputes and discrepancies in invoicing, payments, and order fulfillment, as well as the elimination of intermediaries and manual reconciliation processes, which greatly reduces the probability of human error (Omar et al., 2020). Supplier onboarding and verification can be streamlined with blockchain technology. To ensure that all suppliers comply with industry standards and regulations, companies can quickly identify and mitigate supplier-related risks by recording all supplier credentials, certifications, and performance history on the blockchain.

## 3. Smart Contracts

It is expected that smart contracts will become more prevalent in upstream operations in the coming years. In addition to being self-executing, these contracts can also automate complex processes, such as royalty payments, joint venture agreements, and compliance checks, reducing the need for intermediaries and streamlining operations as a result. This will enable companies to more efficiently manage their contracts and reduce the risk of errors. Smart contracts will also help to reduce costs associated with manual processes, as the need for human input will be minimized (Sarrakh et al., 2019). Smart contracts will also allow companies to track and monitor the performance of their agreements in real-time, allowing them to spot any issues quickly and take corrective action. This will help to ensure that parties are held accountable for their actions. With smart contracts, drilling contracts can be automated to ensure that payment is triggered automatically based on meeting predefined conditions such as the performance of the wells, drilling milestones, or production volumes, ensuring that settlements are made on time. All aspects of asset lifecycle management, from procurement, to decommissioning, will be covered in contracts. It will be possible to automate asset management procedures, such as asset records, maintenance schedules, and retirement processes, using smart contracts. Inventory management can be automated, with orders being automatically generated if the inventory level reaches predefined thresholds, thus reducing storage costs and maximizing the use of resources (Ahmad et al., 2022; Lu et al., 2019).

## 4. Achieving Regulatory Compliance

Using blockchain technology, companies will be able to provide an immutable and auditable record that will enable them to comply with industry specific regulations and reporting requirements with ease. A blockchain could also be utilized by regulators as a means of monitoring compliance in real-time, on a primary basis. This would provide greater visibility and accountability, as well as reduce the risk of fraud and human error (Ahamed N et al., 2023; Ahmad et al., 2022). Additionally, blockchain technology can be used to automate the process of collecting and analyzing data, making it easier for businesses to stay compliant with regulations. It also helps to reduce operational costs and increase efficiency. Companies can also use blockchain technology to track and trace products, ensuring they are compliant with quality standards and regulations. This can help to protect consumer health and safety, as well as protect the environment. A more comprehensive set of regulatory requirements will be imposed on ESG reporting in the coming years. There is a need for companies to disclose data on emissions, social responsibility initiatives, and governance practices in order to meet the demands of investors and regulatory bodies. It is anticipated that the use of digital twin technology, which creates virtual replicas of physical assets, will become more prevalent for the purpose of risk assessment and incident response planning in the near future. In conjunction with advanced analytics, artificial intelligence, and machine learning, blockchain will enable compliance risk monitoring and regulatory change prediction for all these virtual assets, enabling a real-time change management for physical assets (Lu et al., 2019; Wanasinghe, Wroblewski, et al., 2020).

## 5. Technology Integration

It is expected that blockchain technology will be integrated with other emerging technologies such as artificial intelligence, machine learning, and edge computing in order to provide actionable insights derived from the data collected in the field. It is expected that these technologies will work in concert to maximize the efficiency of exploration, drilling, and production. Blockchain will be used to store and process data, while AI, machine learning, and edge computing will provide the ability to analyze and interpret the data (Elijah et al., 2021). This will enable companies to make better informed decisions about their operations and gain a competitive advantage. Additionally, these technologies will enable companies to significantly reduce costs, improve safety, and increase sustainability. It is anticipated that the adoption of IoT sensors will continue to spread widely, allowing for the collection of real-time data and constant monitoring of equipment, processes, and operations. Drilling rigs, pipelines, and reservoirs will be equipped with these sensors in order to improve the operational efficiency and the safety of drilling operations. In order to monitor, inspect, and maintain remote assets, pipelines, and offshore platforms, drones and UAVs will play a very important role in the future. Besides assisting with regular operations and maintenance, they will also monitor the upstream environment and respond to emergencies (Al-Rbeawi, 2023). With the help of telepresence and augmented reality technologies, experts will be able to provide remote assistance to aid with complex tasks, maintenance, and troubleshooting.

## 6. Changing Energy Landscape

As the oil and gas industry evolves, it is becoming more diverse in its energy mix. In addition to supporting the integration of renewable energy sources into existing infrastructure, blockchain can facilitate the tracking and trading of renewable energy certificates. Blockchain can also be used to reduce fraud and ensure the authenticity of renewable energy certificates. Additionally, blockchain coupled with IoT sensors can be used to track carbon emissions and incentivize companies to reduce their emissions. Blockchain can also be used to facilitate the exchange of energy between renewable and traditional energy sources, allowing for a more balanced energy mix. This can help to reduce energy consumption from traditional sources and create a more sustainable energy system (Saraji & Chen, 2023). Blockchain can also be used to provide greater transparency in the energy market, making it easier for consumers to make informed decisions. Oil and gas companies in the upstream sector can invest in Carbon Capture and Storage technologies as a way to capture and store carbon emissions from their operations, thus reducing their environmental impact. By combining improved seismic imaging techniques with artificial intelligence and machine learning, companies will be able to detect more efficient and sustainable reserves through improved exploration efforts. A combination of automation, robotics, and remote monitoring will reduce the need for on-site personnel, making operations safer and more cost-effective as well. It is expected that upstream companies will invest in resilience strategies in order to adapt to the changing climate conditions and to mitigate the impacts of extreme weather events on their operations (Desai et al., 2021; Vera, 2020).

## 7. Expansion on a Global Scale

Blockchain technology can play a significant role in verifying the authenticity of data and transactions across borders as the industry expands into new regions and markets, thereby reducing the risks associated with international operations. It can also help to reduce fraud, improve data security, and streamline processes (Lakhanpal & Samuel, 2018; J. Sun et al., 2021). Additionally, it can improve customer engagement and provide better customer service. It can be implemented to create more efficient supply chains, reduce transaction costs, and improve regulatory compliance. Blockchain technology can also be utilized to automate manual processes, reduce costs, and increase transparency. In the coming years, emerging markets with significant oil and gas reserves will increasingly adopt blockchain technology to enhance transparency and attract investments as blockchain technology becomes more accessible. As a result, the oil and gas industry will be able to provide investors and stakeholders with detailed assessment of the sustainability practices of oil and gas companies around the world that are using environmental, social, and governance (ESG) metrics in a standardized and transparent way. This data can also be used to identify opportunities for improvement and help companies make better decisions about their operations. Blockchain technology can also assist organizations measure their carbon footprint more accurately (Elijah et al., 2021; Lu et al., 2019; Sarrakh et al., 2019).

## 8. Ecosystem of Innovation

A number of startups and technology innovators are looking into blockchain as a means of addressing challenges that are specific to the upstream sector (Businesswire, 2023; Datagumbo.com, n.d.; Vakt.com, 2018; Vertrax, n.d.). Blockchain solutions tailored to the needs of specific industries will be developed as a result of this innovation ecosystem. This will provide new opportunities for oil and gas companies to improve their operations. It will also bring efficiency and cost savings to the entire industry. This might lead to increased competition in the industry, which will ultimately benefit consumers and stimulate economic growth. As a result, there will be increased innovation in the oil and gas industry, as well as improved security, transparency and accountability. As blockchain technology integrates with the Internet of Things (IoT) and sensor technologies, drilling equipment, pipelines, and offshore platforms will be able to securely transmit real-time data to the blockchain for analysis and for making timely decisions based on the data. In order to derive insights from blockchain data, advanced analytics will be used in combination with artificial intelligence (AI) in order to improve predictive maintenance, reservoir management, and operational efficiency. AI can be used to automate processes and provide insights into complex data, while advanced analytics can help to identify patterns and trends. This combination of AI and advanced analytics will help organizations to optimize their operations and gain a competitive edge (Ahmad et al., 2022; Elijah et al., 2021).

It should be noted that blockchain adoption in the upstream oil and gas industry has been gradual, but it is poised for growth and transformation in the future. It is anticipated that blockchain will play an increasingly important role in modernizing and optimizing operations in this critical sector as organizations begin to recognize the benefits of enhanced data management, transparency, and automation. To realize the full potential of blockchain technology in the industry, however, the integration, security, and regulatory compliance challenges will need to be addressed.

# CONCLUSION

The use of blockchain technology has the potential to solve many challenges in the upstream oil and gas sector. As a result of the implementation of blockchain technology, transaction expenses are expected to decrease, standardization can be improved, better transparency can be achieved, supply chain management can be enhanced, contracts can be better managed, processes can be streamlined, security and trust can be enhanced, etc. It can assist businesses in reducing their carbon footprint by improving their operations. While blockchain technology is still in its infancy, oil and gas companies are keenly interested in adopting it as a game-changing technology despite the difficulties in its adoption.

Companies should consider partnering with innovative blockchain technology enterprises to ensure successful implementation. Additionally, they should consider setting up a research and development teams to keep exploring the potential of blockchain technology. They should be open to adopting new versions of blockchain technologies as they come out, as this can help them stay ahead of the competition. They should also be proactive in creating partnerships with other companies and stakeholders to ensure successful adoption. Their focus should be on providing training and education to their employees to ensure that they are up-to-date with the latest information on blockchain technologies. Finally, they should consider investing in blockchain technology to ensure long-term success. Collaboration, innovation, and a commitment to addressing these challenges are essential to the successful adoption of blockchain technology in the upstream oil and gas industry.

In the coming years, blockchain technology will continue to mature and gain experience, transforming the way upstream operations are conducted, resulting in more efficient and transparent processes that benefit both companies and the overall energy ecosystem. The industry is highly regulated and complex, so achieving its full potential will require ongoing effort and investment. As governments and industry work together, they'll be able to develop and execute policies and regulations that shape blockchain technology's future in the upstream oil and gas sector. This will ensure that the industry can capitalize on the potential of the technology to transform the industry. In addition, it will ensure that the technology is used responsibly and ethically for the best interests of all stakeholders.

## REFERENCES

Acharya, V., Yerrapati, A. E., & Prakash, N. (2019). *Oracle Blockchain Quick Start Guide: A practical approach to implementing blockchain in your enterprise*. Packt Publishing Ltd.

Ahamed, N. N., Ayesha, A., & Karthikeyan, P. (2023). Industry 4.0: Features Adopting Digital Technologies in the Oil and Gas Industry. In Sustainable Digital Technologies: Trends, Impacts, and Assessments (pp. 69–89). CRC Press. doi:10.1201/9781003348313-4

Ahmad, R. W., Salah, K., Jayaraman, R., Yaqoob, I., & Omar, M. (2022). Blockchain in oil and gas industry: Applications, challenges, and future trends. *Technology in Society*, *68*, 101941. Advance online publication. doi:10.1016/j.techsoc.2022.101941

Ajao, L. A., Agajo, J., Adedokun, E. A., & Karngong, L. (2019). Crypto Hash Algorithm-Based Blockchain Technology for Managing Decentralized Ledger Database in Oil and Gas Industry. *J — Multidisciplinary Scientific Journal, 2*(3), 300–325. doi:10.3390/j2030021

Al-Hameedi, A. T. T., Alkinani, H. H., Albazzaz, H. W., Dunn-Norman, S., & Alkhamis, M. M. (2020). Insights into the applications of waste materials in the oil and gas industry: state of the art review, availability, cost analysis, and classification. In Journal of Petroleum Exploration and Production Technology (Vol. 10, Issue 5, pp. 2137–2151). Springer. doi:10.1007/s13202-020-00865-w

Al-Rbeawi, S. (2023). A Review of Modern Approaches of Digitalization in Oil and Gas Industry. *Upstream Oil and Gas Technology, 11*, 100098. Advance online publication. doi:10.1016/j.upstre.2023.100098

Allison, E., & Mandler, B. (2018). *Subsurface Data in the Oil and Gas Industry Probing beneath the Earth's surface for exploration and hazard mitigation*. www.americangeosciences

Aloqaily, M., Boukerche, A., Bouachir, O., Khalid, F., & Jangsher, S. (2020). An energy trade framework using smart contracts: Overview and challenges. *IEEE Network, 34*(4), 119–125. doi:10.1109/MNET.011.1900573

Alqahtani, S., He, X., Gamble, R., & Papa, M. (2020). Formal Verification of Functional Requirements for Smart Contract Compositions in Supply Chain Management Systems. *Hawaii International Conference on System Sciences*. https://aisel.aisnet.org/cgi/viewcontent.cgi?article=1658&context=hicss-53

Anjum, A., Sporny, M., & Sill, A. (2017). Blockchain Standards for Compliance and Trust. *IEEE Cloud Computing, 4*(4), 84–90. https://doi.org/https://doi.org/10.1109/MCC.2017.3791019

Asif, R., & Hassan, S. R. (2023). Shaping the future of Ethereum: Exploring energy consumption in Proof-of-Work and Proof-of-Stake consensus. *Frontiers in Blockchain, 6*, 1151724. Advance online publication. doi:10.3389/fbloc.2023.1151724

Aslam, J., Saleem, A., Khan, N. T., & Kim, Y. B. (2022). Blockchain Technology for Oil and Gas: Implications and Adoption Framework Using Agile and Lean Supply Chains. *Processes (Basel, Switzerland), 10*(12), 2687. Advance online publication. doi:10.3390/pr10122687

Baralla, G., Pinna, A., Tonelli, R., & Marchesi, M. (2023). Waste management: A comprehensive state of the art about the rise of blockchain technology. In *Computers in Industry* (Vol. 145). Elsevier B.V. doi:10.1016/j.compind.2022.103812

Behounek, M., Hofer, E., Thetford, T., White, M., Yang, L., & Taccolini, M. (2017). Taking a Different Approach to Drilling Data Aggregation to Improve Drilling Performance. *SPE/IADC Drilling Conference and Exhibition*, 14–16.

Brilliantova, V., & Thurner, T. W. (2019). Blockchain and the future of energy. *Technology in Society*, *57*, 38–45. doi:10.1016/j.techsoc.2018.11.001

Businesswire. (2022, October 13). *The Energy Industry Pivots Toward New Levels of Efficiency With a Proven Smart Contracts Solution*. Businesswire.Com.

Businesswire. (2023, February 7). *Blockchain for Energy Launches an Inclusive Platform to Access and Build Smart Contract Solutions*. Businesswire.Com.

Chang, Y., Iakovou, E., & Shi, W. (2020). Blockchain in global supply chains and cross border trade: A critical synthesis of the state-of-the-art, challenges and opportunities. *International Journal of Production Research*, *58*(7), 2082–2099. doi:10.1080/00207543.2019.1651946

Chen, Y. J., Wang, L. C., & Wang, S. (2020). Stochastic Blockchain for IoT Data Integrity. *IEEE Transactions on Network Science and Engineering*, *7*(1), 373–384. doi:10.1109/TNSE.2018.2887236

Cordes, E. E., Jones, D. O. B., Schlacher, T. A., Amon, D. J., Bernardino, A. F., Brooke, S., Carney, R., DeLeo, D. M., Dunlop, K. M., Escobar-Briones, E. G., Gates, A. R., Génio, L., Gobin, J., Henry, L. A., Herrera, S., Hoyt, S., Joye, M., Kark, S., Mestre, N. C., . . . Witte, U. (2016). Environmental impacts of the deep-water oil and gas industry: A review to guide management strategies. In Frontiers in Environmental Science (Vol. 4, Issue SEP). Frontiers Media S.A. doi:10.3389/fenvs.2016.00058

Das, M., Tao, X., & Cheng, J. C. P. (2021). BIM security: A critical review and recommendations using encryption strategy and blockchain. *Automation in Construction*, *126*, 103682. Advance online publication. doi:10.1016/j.autcon.2021.103682

Datagumbo.com. (n.d.). *GumboNet™ blockchain powers the world's largest B2B ecosystem*. Retrieved June 11, 2023, from https://www.datagumbo.com/platform#enterprise-blockchain

Deepa, N., Pham, Q. V., Nguyen, D. C., Bhattacharya, S., Prabadevi, B., Gadekallu, T. R., Maddikunta, P. K. R., Fang, F., & Pathirana, P. N. (2022). A survey on blockchain for big data: Approaches, opportunities, and future directions. In *Future Generation Computer Systems* (Vol. 131, pp. 209–226). Elsevier B.V. doi:10.1016/j.future.2022.01.017

Desai, J. N., Pandian, S., & Vij, R. K. (2021). Big data analytics in upstream oil and gas industries for sustainable exploration and development: A review. In *Environmental Technology and Innovation* (Vol. 21). Elsevier B.V. doi:10.1016/j.eti.2020.101186

Doyle, H. M. (2019, August 7). *Government agency seeks blockchain solution to strengthen oil trading*. https://www.reutersevents.com/downstream/supply-chain-logistics/government-agency-seeks-blockchain-solution-strengthen-oil-trading#:~:text=The%20U.S.%20Government%20would%20like%20to%20use%20the,companies%20interested%20in%20testing%20this%20project%20this%20year

Elijah, O., Ling, P. A., Rahim, S. K. A., Geok, T. K., Arsad, A., Kadir, E. A., Abdurrahman, M., Junin, R., Agi, A., & Abdulfatah, M. Y. (2021). A Survey on Industry 4.0 for the Oil and Gas Industry: Upstream Sector. *IEEE Access : Practical Innovations, Open Solutions*, *9*, 144438–144468. doi:10.1109/ACCESS.2021.3121302

Epelle, E. I., & Gerogiorgis, D. I. (2020). A review of technological advances and open challenges for oil and gas drilling systems engineering. *AIChE Journal. American Institute of Chemical Engineers*, *66*(4), e16842. Advance online publication. doi:10.1002/aic.16842

Hakak, S., Khan, W. Z., Gilkar, G. A., Haider, N., Imran, M., & Alkatheiri, M. S. (2020). Industrial Wastewater Management using Blockchain Technology: Architecture, Requirements, and Future Directions. *IEEE Internet of Things Magazine*, *3*(2), 38–43. doi:10.1109/IOTM.0001.1900092

Hassani, M., Bazaeeand, G., & Shahmansouri, A. (2020). Identifying Blockchain Technology Maturity's Levels in the Oil and Gas Industry. *Petroleum Business Review*, *4*(3), 43–61. https://doi.org/https://doi.org/10.22050/pbr.2020.256181.1138

Hintemann, R., & Hinterholzer, S. (2019). Energy consumption of data centers worldwide. *Business, Computer Science (ICT4S)*. https://www.researchgate.net/publication/341427004

International Energy Agency (IEA). (2023). *World Energy Investment 2023*. https://iea.blob.core.windows.net/assets/8834d3af-af60-4df0-9643-72e2684f7221/WorldEnergyInvestment2023.pdf

Jones, C. M. (2018). The oil and gas industry must break the paradigm of the current exploration model. In Journal of Petroleum Exploration and Production Technology (Vol. 8, Issue 1, pp. 131–142). Springer Verlag. doi:10.1007/s13202-017-0395-2

Koroteev, D., & Tekic, Z. (2021). Artificial intelligence in oil and gas upstream: Trends, challenges, and scenarios for the future. *Energy and AI*, *3*, 100041. Advance online publication. doi:10.1016/j.egyai.2020.100041

Lakhanpal, V., & Samuel, R. (2018). Implementing Blockchain Technology in Oil and Gas Industry: A Review. *SPE Annual Technical Conference and Exhibition*, 24–26. https://doi.org/https://doi.org/10.2118/191750-MS

Laturkar, K., & Laturkar, K. (2022, April). Blockchain and the downstream segment: Increasing efficiency through technology. *Hydrocarbon Processing*, 75–78. https://www.hydrocarbonprocessing.com/magazine/2022/april-2022/digital-technology/blockchain-and-the-downstream-segment-increasing-efficiency-through-technology

Laturkar, K., & Laturkar, K. (2023a). A Blockchain-Based Approach to Revolutionizing Healthcare. In Revolutionizing Digital Healthcare Through Blockchain Technology Applications (pp. 44–73). doi:10.4018/978-1-6684-6509-7.ch003

Laturkar, K., & Laturkar, K. (2023b). Internet of Things: Architectures, Applications, and Challenges. In T. Murugan & N. E. (Eds.), Handbook of Research on Data Science and Cybersecurity Innovations in Industry 4.0 Technologies (pp. 456–475). IGI Global. doi:10.4018/978-1-6684-8145-5.ch023

Li, Z., Xie, R., Wu, Y., & Yuan, J. (2022). Progress and prospect of CNOOC's oil and gas well drilling and completion technologies. *Natural Gas Industry B*, *9*(2), 209–217. doi:10.1016/j.ngib.2021.08.020

Lu, H., Guo, L., Azimi, M., & Huang, K. (2019). Oil and Gas 4.0 era: A systematic review and outlook. In Computers in Industry (Vol. 111, pp. 68–90). Elsevier B.V. doi:10.1016/j.compind.2019.06.007

Luntovskyy, A., & Hara, T. (2021). Green IT: Energy Efficient Constructions and Applications for Data Centers and Clusters. In M. Choraś, R. S. Choraś, M. Kurzyński, P. Trajdos, J. Pejaś, & T. Hyla (Eds.), *Proceedings of the Conference (CORES, IP&C, ACS)*. https://www.springer.com/series/15179

Maleh, Y., Alazab, M., & Mounir, S. (Eds.). (2023). *Computational Intelligence for Cybersecurity Management and Applications*. CRC Press. doi:10.1201/9781003319917

Martinotti, S., Nolten, J., & Steinsbø, J. A. (2014). *Digitizing oil and gas production*. https://www.mckinsey.com/~/media/McKinsey/Industries/Oil%20and%20Gas/Our%20Insights/Digitizing%20oil%20and%20gas%20production/Digitizing%20oil%20and%20gas%20production.pdf

Mittal, A., & Kudapa, V. K. (2023). A Short Review on the Application of Blockchain Technology in Petroleum Industry. *AIP Conference Proceedings*, *2558*, 020014. Advance online publication. doi:10.1063/5.0120673

Mohammadpoor, M., & Torabi, F. (2020). Big Data analytics in oil and gas industry: An emerging trend. In Petroleum (Vol. 6, Issue 4, pp. 321–328). KeAi Communications Co. doi:10.1016/j.petlm.2018.11.001

Mohammed, A., Potdar, V., & Yang, L. (2020). Key Factors Affecting Blockchain Adoption in Organizations. In Y. Tian, T. Ma, & M. K. Khan (Eds.), Big Data and Security (pp. 455–467). Springer Singapore. doi:10.1007/978-981-15-7530-3_35

Monrat, A. A., Schelén, O., & Andersson, K. (2019). A survey of blockchain from the perspectives of applications, challenges, and opportunities. In *IEEE Access* (Vol. 7, p. 117134–117151). Institute of Electrical and Electronics Engineers Inc. doi:10.1109/ACCESS.2019.2936094

Mullineaux, V. (2019, December 5). *Collaboration: Key to the First Multicloud Blockchain Deployment.* https://insights.vertrax.com/blog/collaboration-key-to-first-multicloud-blockchain-deployment

Musienko, Y. (2023, February 13). *How to use Blockchain in oil and gas industry?* https://merehead.com/blog/use-blockchain-oil-gas-industry/#:~:text=In%20 2018%2C%20BP%2C%20Shell%2C%20Repsol%2C%20Gazprom%20and%20 other,projects%20to%20solve%20logistics%2C%20trade%20and%20financial%20 problems

Noshi, C. I., Assem, A. I., & Schubert, J. J. (2018). The Role of Big Data Analytics in Exploration and Production: A Review of Benefits and Applications Data Analytics and Artificial Intelligence. *SPE International Heavy Oil Conference and Exhibition*. 10.2118/193776-MS

Omar, I. A., Jayaraman, R., Salah, K., Debe, M., & Omar, M. (2020). Enhancing vendor managed inventory supply chain operations using blockchain smart contracts. *IEEE Access : Practical Innovations, Open Solutions*, *8*, 182704–182719. doi:10.1109/ACCESS.2020.3028031

Polyakov, V. N., Chizhov, A. P., Kotenev, Y. A., & Mukhametshin, V. S. (2019). Results of system drilling techniques and completion of oil and gas wells. *IOP Conference Series. Earth and Environmental Science*, *378*(1), 012119. Advance online publication. doi:10.1088/1755-1315/378/1/012119

Rahardja, U., Hidayanto, A. N., Lutfiani, N., Febiani, D. A., & Aini, Q. (2021). Immutability of Distributed Hash Model on Blockchain Node Storage. *Scientific Journal of Informatics*, *8*(1), 137–143. doi:10.15294/sji.v8i1.29444

Rantos, K., Drosatos, G., Kritsas, A., Ilioudis, C., Papanikolaou, A., & Filippidis, A. P. (2019). A Blockchain-Based Platform for Consent Management of Personal Data Processing in the IoT Ecosystem. *Security and Communication Networks*, *2019*, 1–15. Advance online publication. doi:10.1155/2019/1431578

Saraji, S., & Chen, S. (2023). *Sustainable Oil and Gas Using Blockchain* (Vol. 98). Springer Nature. doi:10.1007/978-3-031-30697-6

Saralaya, S., Saralaya, V., & D'Souza, R. (2019). Compliance Management in Business Processes. In *Digital Business: Business Algorithms, Cloud Computing and Data Engineering*. Springer International Publishing AG. https://doi.org/https://doi.org/10.1007/978-3-319-93940-7

Sarrakh, R., Renukappa, S., Suresh, S., & Al Nabt, S. (2019). Smart Solutions in the Oil and Gas Industry: A Review. *Journal of Clean Energy Technologies*, *7*(5), 72–76. doi:10.18178/JOCET.2019.7.5.512

Schletz, M., Cardoso, A., Dias, G. P., & Salomo, S. (2020). How can Blockchain technology accelerate energy efficiency interventions? A use case comparison. *Energies*, *13*(22), 5869. Advance online publication. doi:10.3390/en13225869

Sircar, A., Yadav, K., Rayavarapu, K., Bist, N., & Oza, H. (2021). Application of machine learning and artificial intelligence in oil and gas industry. In Petroleum Research (Vol. 6, Issue 4, pp. 379–391). KeAi Publishing Communications Ltd. doi:10.1016/j.ptlrs.2021.05.009

Startus-insights.com. (n.d.). *Discover 5 Top Blockchain Startups impacting the Oil & Gas Sector*. Retrieved June 11, 2023, from https://www.startus-insights.com/innovators-guide/discover-5-top-blockchain-startups-impacting-the-oil-gas-sector/

Stevens, P. (2018). The Role of Oil and Gas in the Economic Development of the Global Economy. In T. Addison & A. Roe (Eds.), Extractive Industries: The Management of Resources as a Driver of Sustainable Development (pp. 71–90). Oxford University Press. doi:10.1093/oso/9780198817369.003.0004

Sun, J., Zhao, G., & Wang, R. (2021). Application of Blockchain Technology in Oil and Gas Industry. *ACM International Conference Proceeding Series*, 9–13. 10.1145/3460537.3460538

Sun, X., Wei, Y., Jin, Y., Song, W., & Li, X. (2023). The evolution of structural resilience of global oil and gas resources trade network. *Global Networks*, *23*(2), 391–411. doi:10.1111/glob.12399

Tretjakov, A. E. (2013). *Benefits of additives using in oil-refining industry*. Academic Press.

United States Environmental Protection Agency. (n.d.). *Compliance Monitoring Programs*. Epa.Gov. Retrieved June 19, 2023, from https://www.epa.gov/compliance/compliance-monitoring-programs

Upadhyay, N. (2020). Demystifying blockchain: A critical analysis of challenges, applications and opportunities. *International Journal of Information Management*, *54*, 102120. Advance online publication. doi:10.1016/j.ijinfomgt.2020.102120

Vakt.com. (2018, November 18). *November 2018: VAKT Goes Live with World First Enterprise-grade Blockchain Platform*. Vakt.Com.

Vakt.com. (2022, September 7). *World first as physical oil trade confirmations are digitised using VAKT*. Vakt.Com.

Varma Kakarlapudi, P., Mahmoud, Q. H., & Systematic, Q. A. (2021). A Systematic Review of Blockchain for Consent Management. *Health Care*. Advance online publication. doi:10.3390/healthcare PMID:33535465

Vera, F. (2020). Unlocking Oilfield Development using Blockchain. *SPE Latin American and Caribbean Petroleum Engineering Conference, Virtual*. https://doi.org/https://doi.org/10.2118/199170-MS

Vermeulen, E., Fenwick, M., & Kaal, W. (2018). Why Blockchain will Disrupt Corporate Organizations: What can be Learned from the "Digital Transformation.". *The Journal of the British Blockchain Association*, *1*(2), 1–10. doi:10.31585/jbba-1-2-(9)2018

Vertrax. (n.d.). *About Vertrax Blockchain*. Retrieved June 11, 2023, from https://vertrax.com/blockchain/

Wanasinghe, T. R., Gosine, R. G., James, L. A., Mann, G. K. I., De Silva, O., & Warrian, P. J. (2020). The Internet of Things in the Oil and Gas Industry: A Systematic Review. *IEEE Internet of Things Journal*, *7*(9), 8654–8673. doi:10.1109/JIOT.2020.2995617

Wanasinghe, T. R., Wroblewski, L., Petersen, B. K., Gosine, R. G., James, L. A., De Silva, O., Mann, G. K. I., & Warrian, P. J. (2020). Digital Twin for the Oil and Gas Industry: Overview, Research Trends, Opportunities, and Challenges. In IEEE Access (Vol. 8, pp. 104175–104197). Institute of Electrical and Electronics Engineers Inc. doi:10.1109/ACCESS.2020.2998723

Wang, H., Huang, H., Bi, W., Ji, G., Zhou, B., & Zhuo, L. (2022). Deep and ultra-deep oil and gas well drilling technologies: Progress and prospect. *Natural Gas Industry B*, *9*(2), 141–157. doi:10.1016/j.ngib.2021.08.019

Wang, Q., & Su, M. (2020). Integrating blockchain technology into the energy sector - From theory of blockchain to research and application of energy blockchain. In *Computer Science Review* (Vol. 37). Elsevier Ireland Ltd. doi:10.1016/j.cosrev.2020.100275

Waxman, A. R., Khomaini, A., Leibowicz, B. D., & Olmstead, S. M. (2020). Emissions in the stream: Estimating the greenhouse gas impacts of an oil and gas boom. *Environmental Research Letters*, *15*(1), 014004. Advance online publication. doi:10.1088/1748-9326/ab5e6f

Zakir, R. V. (2022). Thermal methods for oil and gas recovery. *Galaxy International Interdisciplinary Research Journal, 10*(5). https://giirj.com/index.php/giirj/article/view/3295/3202

Zehir, C., Zehir, M., Borodin, A., Mamedov, Z. F., & Qurbanov, S. (2022). Tailored Blockchain Applications for the Natural Gas Industry: The Case Study of SOCAR. *Energies*, *15*(16), 6010. Advance online publication. doi:10.3390/en15166010

Zhi, Y., & Caineng, Z. (2019). "Exploring petroleum inside source kitchen": Connotation and prospects of source rock oil and gas. *Petroleum Exploration and Development*, *46*(1), 181–193. doi:10.1016/S1876-3804(19)30018-7

# Chapter 7
# Blockchain Technology Through Bitcoin and Ethereum:
## A Comprehensive Review of Their Interdependent Relationship

**Najib Saab**
*Lebanese International University, Lebanon*

**Mahmoud El Samad**
https://orcid.org/0000-0002-6396-1509
*Lebanese International University, Lebanon*

## ABSTRACT

*With a focus on the two most important cryptocurrencies, Bitcoin and Ethereum, this chapter explains the significance of blockchain in today's environment and analyzes its implementation in both networks as well as investigates how they work, describing their transactions, unique characteristics, benefits, and necessities, noting how Ethereum addressed some of Bitcoin's shortcomings with the introduction of smart contracts. They both depended on the proof of work (PoW) consensus mechanism at first, which Ethereum has moved to proof of stake (PoS) in its new upgrade as Ethereum 2.0. They examine the benefits and differences of these consensus protocols and other ones that deserve consideration and shed light on how they both have dealt with their challenges and drawbacks. Moreover, they analyze the prospects and likely improvements in blockchain technology, as they hope to illustrate the potential of blockchain along with Bitcoin and Ethereum to spark future innovation and address contemporary difficulties through their capabilities and network applications.*

DOI: 10.4018/979-8-3693-1046-5.ch007

## I. INTRODUCTION

Nowadays, blockchain is among the fastest-growing technologies, with its roots tracing back to the groundbreaking work of Satoshi Nakamoto, who introduced the concept of blockchain in 2008 and developed it in 2009 (Nakamoto, 2008). It is essentially a decentralized, distributed public ledger of records in which every network participant can access and examine the same information without obtaining control over it. The records are stored in a linear, chronological manner, with each block having a hash of the previous block, forming a chain of connected blocks. This chain of blocks provides a secure and tamper-proof database, ensuring data integrity and immutability (Andreev et al., 2018). Moreover, it facilitates peer-to-peer transactions by using a consensus validation procedure via a network of computers (Michael et al., 2018). Multiple nodes compete to validate the most recent block entries in order to obtain a reward for maintaining the blockchain. All validated transactions are saved in a chain of blocks that grows as new blocks are added to it. Because the block validation mechanism is immutable, all transactions, old and new, are kept indefinitely and cannot be removed. Further, Anyone on the network can access the ledger via a dedicated website, providing all participants with an up-to-date record of the most recent transactions or changes. Decentralization, persistency, anonymity, and auditability are key characteristics of blockchain technology, which operates in a decentralized environment by combining essential technologies such as cryptographic hash, digital signature (based on asymmetric cryptography), and distributed consensus mechanism, allowing transactions to take place in a decentralized manner. This builds confidence, which, as we'll see, accelerates transactions and provides cost-saving efficiency in a variety of transactional interactions (Bambara & Allen, 2018).

Blockchain technology is primarily intended to decentralize data control and administration, and as opposed to traditional centralized systems, blockchain runs on a peer-to-peer network, eliminating the need for middlemen and building trust through consensus procedures (Aste et al., 2017). This decentralization improves security and gives people direct authority over their digital assets and information (Zheng et al., 2018). Another essential feature of blockchain is its immutability. Once a transaction has been recorded on the blockchain, it is nearly hard to change or erase it. This property is attained by cryptographic procedures, which ensure that historical data remains intact and tamper-proof. This capability is vital in businesses such as supply chain management, where data integrity is crucial (Casino et al., 2018). Furthermore, blockchain's design incorporates anonymity, which gives users a sense of privacy and pseudonymity. While blockchain transactions are public and transparent, they are also pseudonymous, with cryptographic addresses rather than personal information being used to identify them. This delicate balance between transparency and privacy has serious implications for security and confidentiality. Also, the characteristic of auditability is an essential key of blockchain's architecture. Every transaction on the blockchain is accessible to all network participants, increasing accountability and providing transparency that traditional systems cannot match. This ease of access extends to auditors and regulators, who can easily analyze transaction histories, assuring regulatory compliance, and lowering the risk of fraud (Kouhizadeh & Sarkis, 2018).

Blockchain technology can be used in a variety of financial services, including digital assets, remittances, and online payments, due to its capacity to facilitate transactions without the involvement of banks or middlemen (Peters et al., 2015; Foroglou and Tsilidou, 2015). Furthermore, blockchain technology is regarded as one of the most promising for the next generation of Internet interaction systems, such as smart contracts (Kosba et al., 2016), public services (Akins et al., 2013), the Internet of Things (IoT) (Zhang and Wen, 2015), reputation systems (Sharples and Domingue, 2015), and security services (Noyes, 2016a) (Zheng et al., 2018).

Moving on, Bitcoin, the world's first cryptocurrency, is frequently regarded as the forerunner of this blockchain revolution. In 2009, it was launched by the pseudonymous Satoshi Nakamoto (2008), introducing a digital currency that defies geographical borders and central authorities. Its decentralized nature, powered by a process known as "mining", has turned it into a global phenomenon, attracting both enthusiastic supporters and harsh critics. Bitcoin's rise from obscurity to widespread acceptance has been defined by huge price swings, regulatory difficulties, and ongoing arguments about its position in the global financial ecosystem (Aste et al., 2017). Ethereum, on the other hand, is a big advancement in the blockchain field. It was created by Vitalik Buterin and published in 2015, pioneered the notion of "smart contracts", which are self-executing agreements that can automate a wide range of jobs and transactions (Buterin, 2013). This advancement broadened the utility of blockchain technology beyond simple currency transfers, paving the way for decentralized applications (DApps) and the larger world of decentralized finance (DeFi). Ethereum's programmable and adaptable blockchain has fostered an ecosystem of innovation, resulting in the creation of hundreds of tokens and initiatives (Buterin, 2013; Community, n.d.).

The objective of this review paper is to emphasize the critical necessity of blockchain technology and provide a comprehensive view of its landscape and implications in today's interconnected, digitized world. To do so, we will shed light extensively on the use of blockchain in two of the most well-known cryptocurrencies, Bitcoin and Ethereum, delving into how each of them operates and what distinguishes one from the other. Besides the questioning on what about the new upgrade of Ethereum (known as Ethereum 2.0) and its transition to the Proof of Stake (PoS) consensus protocol, and whether there is a prospect for alternative consensus mechanisms, that have attempted to fix many of the problems with the existing ones? We will also cover the limitations and downsides of both Bitcoin and Ethereum networks, as well as the potential for future improvements in the blockchain arena.

Following that, we will go first into the blockchain architecture, defining its structure, cryptographic function, and taxonomy. Later on, we will delve into Bitcoin and Ethereum consecutively, which have used blockchain technology to completely transform the financial environment, describing their transactions, consensus, unique characteristics, benefits, and necessities, noting how Ethereum addressed some of Bitcoin's shortcomings with the introduction of smart contracts and increased flexibility. Both Bitcoin and Ethereum depended on the Proof of Work (PoW) consensus mechanism at first, which brought them together in blockchain development. Moreover, we will look at and examine the benefits and differences of other consensus protocols, such as Proof of Activity (PoA), Practical Byzantine Fault Tolerance (PBFT), Delegated Proof of Stake (DPoS), and Proof of Stake (PoS) which Ethereum has moved to, in its new upgrade as Ethereum 2.0. On the other hand, even as blockchain technology gains traction, it is not without its own set of challenges and drawbacks, such as scalability issues, energy consumption concerns, decentralization quandaries, oracle problems, and vulnerability to cyber and network-based attacks. We will shed light on how Bitcoin and Ethereum have dealt with and handled these difficulties. Looking ahead, we will open new scopes, investigating the integration of blockchain with new technologies such as big data analytics, artificial intelligence (AI), machine learning, and the internet of things (IoT), which these synergies hold enormous promise for opening up new paths for research, development, and transformational applications.

The paper structure is as follows: Section II talks about the Blockchain Paradigm, while Section III delves into Bitcoin currency, in addition to the Ethereum network in Section IV, and Consensus Protocols in Section V. Addressing the Challenges and Drawbacks of Bitcoin and Ethereum are in Section VI, followed by Future Scope in Section VII, and finally Conclusion and Summary in Section VIII.

## II. BLOCKCHAIN PARADIGM

Understanding blockchain technology may seem complex, but breaking it down into its components can make it more accessible. Blockchain, at its heart, is a network of interconnected blocks that records transactions like a standard public ledger. Along with notions like immutable ledgers, it also makes use of well-known cryptographic methods and practices from computer science, including hash functions, digital signatures, and asymmetric-key cryptography. We'll go into more detail on each of these topics in this part.

In Section 2.1, we introduce the block structure, followed by the cryptographic hash functions in Section 2.2, then the digital signature in Section 2.3 in addition to the cryptographic nonce in Section 2.4, while Section 2.5 presents the blockchain taxonomy.

## 2.1 Block Structure

The genesis block is the first block in a blockchain and does not have a parent block. As shown in Figure 1, a block consists of two major components: the block header and the block body. The block header contains block-specific metadata, whereas the block body comprises a list of approved and legitimate transactions submitted to the blockchain network. Each transaction's legality and authenticity are ensured by ensuring that it is properly formed and that the suppliers of digital assets indicated in the transaction's "input" values have all cryptographically signed the transaction. This verification ensures that digital asset providers had access to the private key required to sign over the available digital assets. When a block is published, the authenticity and validity of all transactions contained in the block are validated by other full nodes on the network. Other nodes will not accept the block if it contains incorrect transactions.

A blockchain's block header typically contains numerous pieces of critical metadata. These are some examples (Zheng et al., 2018):

- Block version: It defines which set of validation rules should be utilized for the block.
- Parent block hash: A 256-bit hash value indicating the previous block in the chain. The blockchain establishes a tamper-evident record of all transactions by connecting each block to its parent.
- Merkle tree root hash: The hash value of all transactions in the block is stored in this field. The Merkle tree enables the network to efficiently validate the inclusion of a transaction in a block without having to process the full block.
- Timestamp: This is the current time in seconds since January 1st, 1970.
- nBits: This is a concise representation of the current hashing target. It contributes to the network's ability to maintain a steady rate of block production.
- Nonce: This is a 4-byte field that is used to change the hash value of the block header. With each hash computation, miners increase the nonce value in order to discover a block header that fulfills the current hashing objective.

*Figure 1. Block structure*

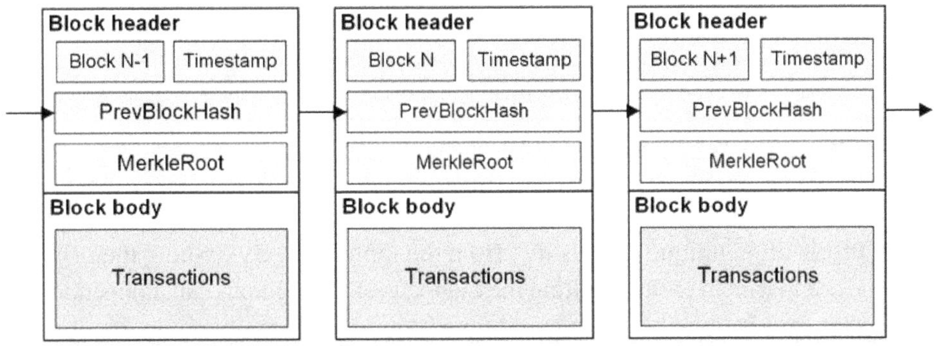


The block body comprises a list of transactions that have been validated and authenticated and have been sent to the network. The structure of the block body varies depending on the blockchain implementation, however, it typically includes:

- Transaction counter: This value indicates the total number of transactions in the block.
- Transactions: This is a list of transactions that have been validated and authenticated and have been submitted to the network. Each transaction normally comprises the sender, receiver, money, and any additional data required to complete the transaction.

The maximum number of transactions that a block can contain is determined by several parameters, including block size and transaction size. To prevent the blockchain from getting too huge and unmanageable, blocks are often designed to be limited in size. The maximum block and transaction sizes may differ based on blockchain technology.

Chaining blocks together is done by inserting the hash digest of the preceding block's header in each new block, resulting in the formation of a blockchain. If any previously published block is changed, it will have a unique hash, causing all subsequent blocks to have unique hashes as well, because they also contain the prior block's hash. This method makes it simple to detect and reject any modified blocks (Yaga et al., 2019). The block structure of a generic chain is depicted in Figure 1.

## 2.2 Cryptographic Hash Functions

Cryptographic hash functions are essential in many processes in blockchain technology. Applying a cryptographic hash function to data produces a message

*Table 1. Samples of input text corresponding to SHA-256 digest value*

| *Input Text* | ***SHA-256 Digest Value*** |
|---|---|
| ***A*** | 0x559aead0 8264d57 95d390 9718cdd0 5abd495 72e84fe55 590eef31a88 a08fdffd |
| ***B*** | 0xdf7e7 0e502154 4f483 4bbee6 4a9e3789fe bc4be81470 df629c ad6ddb033 20a5c |
| ***AB*** | 0x38164f bd17603 d73f696 b8b4d726 64d735 bb6a7c885 77687 fd2ae33fd6 964153 |

digest that is often unique and distinct from the input data. By hashing the original data and comparing it to the resulting message digest, individuals can independently verify that data has not been tampered with. Any modifications to the input data, no matter how modest, will result in a dramatically different message digest output.

The Secure Hash Algorithm (SHA) with an output size of 256 bits is a cryptographic hash function that is widely utilized in blockchain applications. Many computers support this algorithm in hardware, making it quick to compute. SHA-256 produces 32 bytes, which is equivalent to 256 bits. As seen in Table 1, this output is often written as a 64-character hexadecimal string.

It should be **noted** that even changing a single character in the input text would result in an entirely different SHA-256 digest value.

Cryptographic hash functions are utilized for a variety of applications, including unique identifier generation, address generation, block data security, and block header security. A publishing node hashes the block contents to generate a digest, which is then stored in the block header for security. If the network uses the proof of work consensus process, as we will see later, the publishing node must hash the block header with multiple nonce values until the puzzle requirements are met. The hash digest of the current block header is integrated into the header of the subsequent block, protecting the contents of the current block. As a result, when the block header digest is included in the subsequent block, the block data is also protected.

## 2.3 Digital Signature

Asymmetric-key cryptography, commonly known as public key cryptography, is used in blockchain technology. This cryptographic method uses two mathematically linked keys: a public key and a private key. The public key is freely shared among blockchain network participants, whereas the owner keeps the private key secret. Asymmetric-key cryptography enables secure transaction signatures, encryption, and verification in the blockchain. The private key is used to ensure the validity and integrity of transactions. On the other hand, the public key is used to authenticate signatures and encrypt data that can only be decrypted with the associated private key. Figure 2 depicts an example of a digital signature in a blockchain system.

*Figure 2. Digital signature in blockchain*

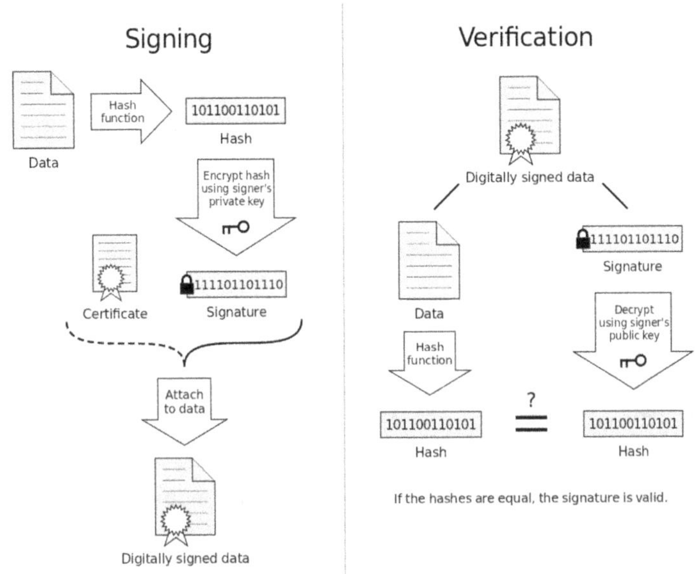


Referring to Figure 2, the procedure of a digital signature requires two separate phases: the signing phase and the verification phase. Assume a user wants to sign a transaction. First, he or she creates a hash value from the transaction data. He/she then encrypts this hash value using his/her private key and delivers it, together with the original data, to the destination. The receiver validates the transaction in the verification phase by comparing the decrypted hash (using the sender's public key) with the hash value derived from the received data, using the same hash function as the sender; if the hashes are equal, the signature is valid and the data was not tampered with. This comparison confirms the transaction's integrity and legitimacy.

Established digital signature methods, such as the Elliptic Curve Digital Signature Algorithm (ECDSA) (Johnson et al., 2001), are routinely used in blockchain systems. These algorithms provide strong security features to ensure the integrity and confidentiality of blockchain network transactions (Zheng et al., 2018).

## 2.4 Cryptographic Nonce

A cryptographic nonce is a one-time use random or pseudo-random number in a cryptographic communication or procedure. A nonce can be used in conjunction with data, such as a message or key, to generate a unique hash digest for each nonce value, ensuring that each communication or protocol is unique and cannot be tampered with or replayed.

Assume a sender wishes to convey a message to a recipient using a cryptographic hash function. To confirm the message's integrity (data transmitted = data received), the sender can append a cryptographic nonce to it before hashing it. The nonce value is picked at random and is only used once. The resulting hash digest will be specific to the message and nonce combination, preventing an attacker from tampering with the message or replaying an old message.

```
Digest = hash (data + nonce) (Yaga et al., 2019)
```

Overall, encrypting data using a cryptographic nonce is a critical approach for maintaining the security and validity of cryptographic communications and protocols.

## 2.5 Taxonomy of Blockchain Systems

Blockchain systems are classified into multiple kinds depending on various parameters. Commonly used classifications:

1. Accessible blockchains include public, private, and consortium blockchains. Table 2 provides a comparison between them.
2. Proof of Work, Proof of Stake, Delegated Proof of Stake, and other mechanisms based on consensus.
3. Blockchain based on purpose: currency-based, asset-based, and application-based.
4. Platform-based: Bitcoin, Ethereum, Hyperledger, Corda, and others.
5. Blockchain architecture: monolithic, modular, and hybrid.
6. Blockchain network topology: centralized, decentralized, and distributed

It should be **noted** that these categories are not necessarily mutually exclusive, and a given blockchain system may fall into more than one.

# III. BITCOIN

## A. Bitcoin Overview

Bitcoin is a game-changing digital currency and a revolutionary technological invention that has captivated the attention of individuals, businesses, and financial institutions worldwide. It has radically changed how we think about money, finance, and the concept of trust in the digital era since its creation in 2009 by someone called Satoshi Nakamoto. His seminal work offers a groundbreaking answer to digital

*Table 2. Comparison between public, private, and consortium blockchain*

| | *Public* | *Private* | *Consortium* |
|---|---|---|---|
| ***Access*** | Open to all | Restricted | Restricted |
| ***Consensus Process*** | Permissionless | Permissioned | Permissioned |
| ***Consensus Mechanism*** | PoW, PoS, DPoS | PBFT, RAFT | PBFT |
| ***Transparency*** | Fully transparent | Depends on design | Depends on design |
| ***Privacy*** | Pseudonymous | Depends on design | Depends on design |
| ***Transaction Speed*** | Slow | Fast | Fast |
| ***Scalability*** | Limited | Good | Good |
| ***Immutability*** | Almost Impossible to tamper | Could be tampered | Could be tampered |
| ***Efficiency*** | Low | High | High |
| ***Governance*** | Decentralized | Centralized | Decentralized |
| ***Examples*** | Bitcoin, Ethereum, EOS | IBM Hyperledger Fabric | R3 Consortium |

currency issues, particularly the issue of double spending (Nakamoto, 2008). While Nakamoto's exact identity is unknown, it is known that he actively contributed to the Bitcoin project until 2010, when he handed over development to the community (Tschorsch & Scheuermann, 2016). In Nakamoto's proposal, a peer-to-peer (P2P) distributed timestamp server that serves as a generator of computational evidence for maintaining the chronological order of transactions was introduced (Nakamoto, 2008). He characterized an electronic coin as a chain of digital signatures, which we discussed in section 2.3, with each transaction consisting of a digitally signed hash of the previous transaction and the subsequent owner's public key. As shown in Figure 3, the private key is used to sign the transaction, while the public key is utilized for transaction verification.

Bitcoin's price has fluctuated significantly over the years, garnering both fervent advocates and critics. Its value has fluctuated dramatically, but its fundamental technology and ideals have gained traction. Beyond its usage as a digital currency, Bitcoin has paved the way for the creation of a thriving ecosystem of cryptocurrencies, blockchain apps, and cutting-edge financial services. It is critical to understand that blockchain and bitcoin are not synonymous, as bitcoin is only one successful application of blockchain technology (Monrat et al., 2019).

Later in this part, we'll delve into the Bitcoin transactions in Section B, followed by Proof of Work (PoW) in Section C, in addition to the advantages of Bitcoin and other cryptocurrencies in Section D.

*Figure 3. The structure of transaction in a Bitcoin blockchain*

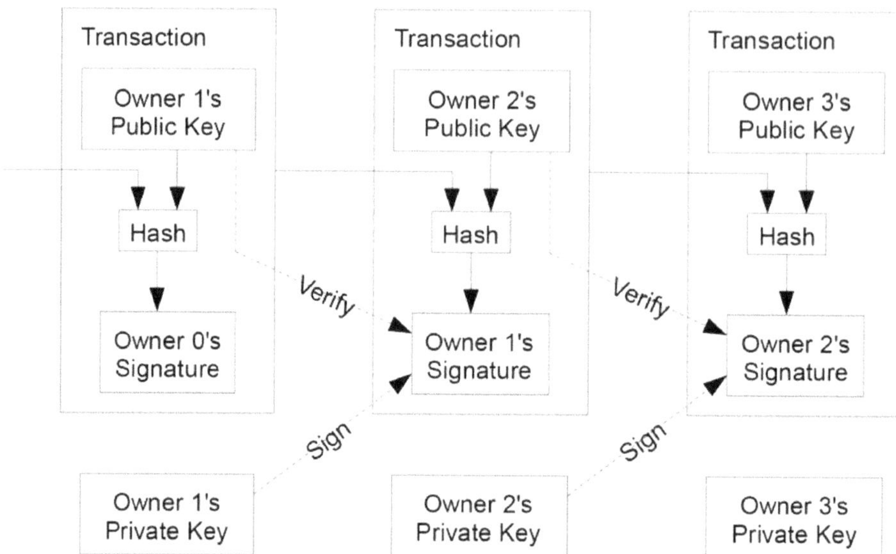


## B. Bitcoin Transactions

Each transaction's signature is a 256-bit value, making it extremely difficult to forge or fake the signature in order to conduct a fraudulent transaction. The number of possible guesses is 2256, which is an astronomically high number that is almost impossible to compute (Monrat et al., 2019). This level of security ensures that transactions' legitimacy and integrity are preserved inside the blockchain network. In addition to validating the sender's signature, the verifier must determine whether the sender has sufficient cash to transfer to the receiver. Examining the ledger, which contains information about all previous successful transactions, is part of the verification process. The verifier can confirm if the sender has the necessary cash to complete the transaction by referring to the ledger.

The Bitcoin ledger functions as a state transition system, with a state representing the ownership status of all bitcoins in existence and a state transition function that is executed via transactions. The state transition function accepts the current state as input and outputs a new state. This process modifies the states of the sender and recipient engaged in the transaction, assuming the sender has enough bitcoins to complete the transaction. Otherwise, an error occurs, indicating that the balance is insufficient (Vujicic et al., 2018). The Bitcoin ledger protects the integrity and consistency of Bitcoin ownership records using this state transition system. Each transaction causes a state change, indicating that ownership has been transferred from the sender to the recipient. The ledger's decentralized nature, maintained by a network of nodes, ensures transparency and immutability of state changes, prohibiting fraudulent or unauthorized changes to ownership data.

## C. Proof of Work (PoW)

Bitcoin is, at its heart, an electronic currency created using distributed systems. Unlike traditional currencies, the issuance of Bitcoin is governed by a consensus competition between dispersed network nodes utilizing proof-of-work (PoW) mining. Proof-of-work is a proof-based consensus algorithm. Its basic premise is to detect and select a node capable of adding a new block to the existing blockchain by demonstrating sufficient proof of computational effort (Monrat et al., 2019). A user can publish the next block under the proof of work (PoW) model by solving a computationally demanding puzzle faster than other users. This puzzle's answer serves as "proof" that the user has worked. The puzzle is purposefully meant to be tough to solve, but it is simple to check whether a given solution is correct. This allows other full nodes to swiftly verify the proposed next block, and any block that does not match the puzzle's requirements is rejected (Yaga et al., 2019).

To prevent or lessen the danger of a user attempting to manipulate the network and perform double-spending attacks by issuing multiple transactions of the same coin to different users, the Bitcoin network requires each validating node to produce proof of work. Furthermore, a user might create several instances to prove their initial intent and carry out a Sybil attack. To avoid this, nodes must execute computationally intensive tasks to verify their legitimacy as network members. The system will stay stable as long as the cumulative processing capacity of the honest nodes exceeds that of the attacker, and all genuine transactions will be confirmed (Vujicic et al., 2018). Miners are the nodes responsible for computing hashes and solving the computationally hard puzzle to validate transactions, and mining is the proof-of-work technique they use. Because the authentication computation takes time, Nakamoto devised an incentive mechanism in 2008, such as granting a small fraction of Bitcoins to the miner (Andreev et al., 2018; Nakamoto, 2008; Zheng et al., 2018).

Miners include their personal Coinbase transaction along with the transaction data they want to authenticate and confirm while mining a block. A Coinbase transaction, which is generated solely by miners, is a different type of Bitcoin transaction. It only has outputs, and for each newly mined block on the network, a new Coinbase transaction is made. It mostly performs two functions:

- Block Reward: Indicates where the reward of this block is allocated, that allowing the miner to claim them.

- Transaction Fees: Provides a space for miners to collect fees from the transactions included in the block.

The miner who finds the correct nonce first by solving the computational puzzle in the PoW process wins the competition and earns the right to build the next block. The winner is then rewarded with a fixed amount of newly minted bitcoin, takes transactions from the memory pool, and arranges them in decreasing order of their related transaction fees into a new block. This new block is then broadcasted to the whole blockchain network, and other nodes accept it only if the transactions contained inside it are genuine and have not already been received. The other nodes then append this new block to the main chain, and the consensus process begins once more with the fight for the right to bundle new transactions into the next block (Yuan & Wang, 2018).

Bitcoin employs the proof of work approach, which modifies the puzzle difficulty every 2016 blocks, to maintain a block publication pace of roughly ten minutes. The modification is achieved by raising or lowering the number of leading zeros necessary, which affects the puzzle's complexity level. As the difficulty level increases, the puzzle becomes more difficult to solve because there are fewer alternative answers. Reducing the difficulty level, on the other hand, makes the puzzle easier to complete because there are more alternative solutions. This modification is required to preserve the computational difficulty of the puzzle as well as the Bitcoin network's primary security mechanism. The puzzle difficulty generally grows with the number of publishing nodes and available processing power. Changes are made to the difficulty goal of blockchain networks that use the proof of work consensus process to prevent any single entity from monopolizing block generation, while this increases the number of resources necessary to solve the cryptographic puzzles. Because of the considerable resource consumption associated with various proof-of-work blockchain networks, there is a trend to include publishing nodes in places where there is an abundance of inexpensive electricity. The computing effort needed to answer a challenge has no effect on the chance of solving current or future puzzles, which is an important component of the proof of work concept. As a result, when a user receives a legitimate block from another user, they are driven to stop their current work and instead begin building off the freshly received block, knowing that other publishing nodes will do the same (Yaga et al., 2019).

Consider a puzzle in which a machine must find a hash value that matches certain target parameters, known as the difficulty level. The SHA-256 algorithm, a popular cryptographic hash function, is used in this puzzle.

```
SHA256("proofwork" + Nonce) = Hash Digest starting with "0000"
```

The SHA-256 algorithm accepts an input and returns a fixed-size output, which is commonly represented as a hexadecimal value (Gilbert & Handschuh, 2003). The difficulty level of the problem is determined by the precise criteria that the hash value must meet. For example, the target criterion could demand a particular number of leading zeros in the hash value (Target criteria in this this example is Hash Digest starting with 0000).

To solve the problem, the computer produces alternative input values known as nonces and uses the SHA-256 algorithm to determine the matching hash values. The resulting hash values are then compared to the target criteria. This process is repeated until the computer finds a hash value that meets the difficulty level. The puzzle's difficulty level can be changed to influence the computational work necessary to solve it. The number of attempts required to find a correct hash value rises as the difficulty level increases, making the challenge more complex.

This example shows how blockchain technology uses cryptographic puzzles and the SHA-256 algorithm to ensure the integrity and immutability of transaction records in a blockchain network (Yaga et al., 2019).

```
SHA256("proofwork")= 0x427bd8e09 730e47123 7a6941d 033ad
4b36885c71 a19823f bf2e6330 4d767c f9f (not solved)
SHA256("proofwork1")= 0x12ed50d 97b7 22f4c58df ba106e42
fb3654b7 7676ebdd 14a8b11 0c18bf1f 0765d (not solved)...
SHA256("proofwork076576")= 0x0000b3 5c03625 8c424fa 17bae75
b9773dd 0d50d7e450b ed4cf101b85b 3b5c4a 33190 (solved)
```

Not Solved: Hash Digest still not contains the four necessary leading zeros, which means the nonce value is still incompatible, that's why not solved yet.

Solved: The winner miner has found the correct nonce value of the block, which leads to a hash digest that starts with four leading zeros, which means that the specific block is signed.

The transactions within a block in the Bitcoin network are arranged and hashed using a data structure known as a Merkle tree. Merkle trees are binary trees in which the leaf nodes represent individual transactions and the root is a hash value computed from the hashes of the tree's child nodes. Figure 4 depicts a Merkle tree with hashed transactions. This hierarchical structure makes it possible to efficiently verify the integrity and consistency of transactions within a block. Using a Merkle tree, any irregularity or tampering in the transactions will be noticed somewhere along the tree, assuring the blockchain's long-term viability. Furthermore, the Merkle tree enables efficient storage on network nodes. Once the transactions have been included in a block and the block has been confirmed, the network discards all intermediate hashes in the tree, leaving only the root hash in the block header.

*Figure 4. Merkle tree of transaction hashes*

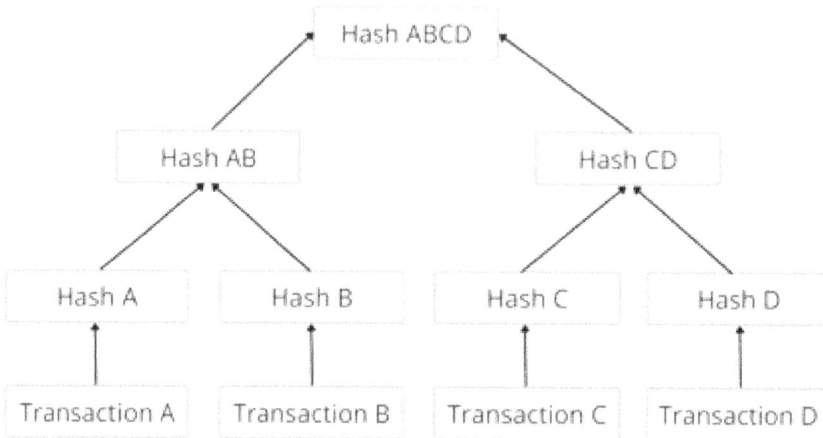


This pruning procedure contributes to the reduction of storage capacity required to store the blockchain on network nodes (Vujicic et al., 2018).

To further improve resource utilization, Bitcoin introduces Simplified Payment Verification (SPV). With SPV, network nodes are not needed to keep a complete record of all transactions. Instead, they just need to keep copies of the block headers from the longest chain (Nakamoto, 2008). This enables lightweight nodes to participate in the network and validate transactions without the requirement for large storage resources.

## D. Bitcoin and Cryptocurrencies Advantages

Experts believe that the Blockchain technology can be used to address problems in a variety of different sectors. Bitcoin has been one of the most successful applications of blockchain technology to date. According to the most current data posted on the monitoring website Blockchain.info, around 400,000 transactions totaling $120 million were registered in the Bitcoin blockchain ledger on a daily basis. Furthermore, almost 800,000 blocks have been manufactured thus far. According to Coinmarketcap.com, there are about 22,932 different types of cryptocurrencies traded in blockchain-powered markets, with a total market capitalization of $1.1 trillion. Bitcoin maintains its market dominance, accounting for about 50% of the total market cap, while ETH (Ethereum) and USDT (Tether) are second and third, respectively. Bitcoin's decentralized structure has permitted the establishment of a worldwide economy with the worth of a mid-sized developed country, all based on trust and consensus via algorithms. In other words, Bitcoin has demonstrated that decentralized digital money can operate globally without the use of traditional intermediaries. Experts believe that by 2027, blockchain technology will have stored nearly 10% of the world's GDP (Yuan & Wang, 2018).

Thus, Bitcoin and other cryptocurrencies like Ethereum, Ripple, and Litecoin have various advantages over traditional electronic cash systems, such as:

- Decentralization: Cryptocurrencies are decentralized, which means they are not governed by a centralized authority or government. Transactions are recorded on the blockchain, a public ledger that is maintained by a network of participants (known as "nodes"). Because of the system's decentralized structure, it is difficult for any single entity to manipulate it.
- Security: The blockchain is protected by cryptographic methods, making it nearly impossible to edit or tamper with transaction records. Furthermore, before being added to the blockchain, transactions are validated by a network of participants to ensure that they are legitimate.
- Limited Supply: Bitcoin has a finite quantity, with a total of 21 million bitcoins available for creation. Because of its scarcity, it has increased in value and popularity.
- Anonymity: Because Bitcoin transactions are pseudonymous, users can stay anonymous while transacting. This feature has made it popular among privacy-conscious consumers.
- Global Acceptance: Bitcoin and other cryptocurrencies may be used globally without the need for currency translation, making international transactions more efficient and cost-effective.
- Lower Transaction Fees: Credit cards and bank transfers are two examples of traditional electronic cash systems that incur hefty transaction fees. Bitcoin, on the other hand, offer reduced transaction fees, making them more appealing for minor transactions.
- Programmability: Cryptocurrencies are programmable, which means they can be used to perform smart contracts, which we shall discuss in more detail later.

These attributes have all led to the growing popularity and adoption of cryptocurrencies in general and Bitcoin in particular in today's society.

# IV. ETHEREUM

## A. Ethereum Overview

The concept of Ethereum was created and presented in Vitalik Buterin's whitepaper, "Ethereum White Paper: A Next-Generation Smart Contract & Decentralized Application Platform." The article, which was published in late 2013, introduced the concept of a decentralized platform that is more than just a cryptocurrency like Bitcoin (Buterin, 2013). Ethereum is a blockchain platform that allows not just digital money transactions but also a Turing-complete programming language. This enables developers to immediately install smart contracts and decentralized apps (DApps) into the Ethereum network, and we'll delve into each one intensely later in this section. Because of the platform's versatility and programmability, it may be used to develop a variety of apps and organizations that are decentralized, permissionless, and censorship-resistant (Buterin, 2013).

Smart contracts in Ethereum are often written in the programming language Solidity, which we'll go over later in this section. One of Ethereum's primary benefits is its Turing completeness, which attracted to many developers because of the flexibility it provides in constructing complicated and powerful smart contracts. However, Ethereum's capacity to store and save state is much more critical. A stateful system in computing is one that can detect and retain changes to information across time. This means that Ethereum's blockchain can update and record changes made by smart contracts while maintaining the system's present state. This consistency is essential for assuring the correct and consistent execution of smart contracts and DApps on the Ethereum platform (Community, n.d.).

Later in this segment, we'll look at how Bitcoin's shortcomings were overcome in Section B, while Section C covers Ethereum Accounts, and Section D discusses the Ethereum Transaction Essentials. Section E delves into Ethereum Messages, followed by Smart Contracts in Section F, and finally, Section G explores Decentralized Apps (DApps) on the Ethereum blockchain.

## B. Overcome Bitcoin's Shortcomings

Let's consider a computer without a hard drive. Its capability would be severely limited, similar to that of a calculator, with the contents of its memory being fleeting and impermanent. A blockchain's ability to construct interactions between users in the future and under certain conditions is a huge improvement. It enables programmers to incorporate control flow and conditional logic into cryptocurrency transaction programming (Dannen, 2017). This is the most major difference between Ethereum and Bitcoin, however, as you shall see, it is far from the only one. Vitalik highlighted numerous limitations in Bitcoin's programming language that Ethereum attempted to remedy in the whitepaper (Buterin, 2013):

- Bitcoin's scripting language is purposefully constrained in order to ensure security and prevent potential flaws. This, however, limits the kind of apps that may be built on top of the Bitcoin network. Ethereum's goal was to provide a more expressive and Turing-complete programming language, implying that any computable function may be implemented on the Ethereum platform.
- Lack of Native Support for Smart Contracts: While Bitcoin supports simple programming, it does not support more complicated smart contracts. The major goal of Ethereum was to provide a specialized platform for building and executing smart contracts, which are self-executing agreements with the terms directly put into code.
- Centralized Development: During Bitcoin's early days, the majority of its development was focused on the core protocol. Ethereum, on the other hand, aimed to establish a decentralized ecosystem in which developers could independently construct applications and deploy smart contracts on the Ethereum blockchain.
- Deterministic Gas Model: To manage resource allocation and prioritize transactions, Ethereum adopted a deterministic gas model. Bitcoin, on the other hand, uses a more traditional fee-based method for transaction prioritizing.
- Faster Block Times: Ethereum sought to achieve faster block times than Bitcoin, aiming for 15-second block intervals as opposed to Bitcoin's 10-minute blocks. This shorter block time allowed for speedier transaction confirmations and improved responsiveness for decentralized applications.

Ultimately, Ethereum's design solved these flaws to provide a more versatile and developer-friendly platform that enables the development of a wide range of decentralized applications beyond simple cryptocurrency transactions. As time passed, Ethereum evolved into one of the main blockchain platforms for developing decentralized apps and executing smart contracts.

## C. Ethereum Accounts

The state of Ethereum is organized around things called "accounts". A 20-byte address uniquely identifies each account, and state transitions include direct transfers of value and information between these accounts (Jani, 2017). Ethereum supports two sorts of accounts: externally owned accounts (EOAs) managed by private keys and contract accounts governed by their contract code (Community, n.d.). These

*Table 3. Comparison between EOAs and contract accounts*

| | *Externally Owned Accounts (EOAs)* | *Contract Accounts* |
|---|---|---|
| ***Purpose*** | Used to hold and transfer Ether (crypto) | Used to represent deployed smart contracts |
| ***Control*** | External users' private keys | The smart contract code that has been deployed |
| ***Cost*** | Nothing | Because you're using network storage, there is cost |
| ***Transactions*** | Can initiate transactions (e.g., value transfers) | Can receive transactions (smart contract calls) |
| ***Balance*** | Holds Ether (ETH) balance | Can hold and manage Ether sent to it |
| ***Nonce*** | Has a nonce for transaction ordering | Does not have a nonce |
| ***State*** | Does not have an internal state or storage | Has internal state and storage for contract variables |
| ***Usage*** | Used by individual users and external entities | Used for implementing decentralized applications |

accounts are critical in facilitating Ethereum blockchain state transitions. Refer to Table 3 to see the primary differences between the two.

A Ethereum account is comprised of four fields (Ethereum accounts, n.d.):

1. Nonce: A nonce is a sequential number that is intended to prevent replay attacks and ensure that each transaction from an account is distinct. The nonce is incremented each time an account sends a transaction.
2. Balance: The account's balance shows how much Ether or cryptocurrency it has. This balance indicates the amount of Ether held by EOAs. It represents the amount of Ether held by the contract in contract accounts.
3. Code Hash: The Code Hash in Ethereum refers to the code of the account on the Ethereum Virtual Machine (EVM). When a message call is received by a contract account, these code fragments are programmable and capable of performing numerous tasks. Unlike other account values, it is immutable and cannot be changed once the contract is launched. For future retrieval, all code fragments are securely saved in the state database under their individual hashes. Externally owned accounts in the Ethereum ecosystem are governed by private keys, the Code Hash field includes the hash of an empty string. Moreover, it ensures the integrity and security of smart contract execution, making it a critical component.
4. Storage Root: In Ethereum, the Storage Root is a 256-bit hash that represents the root node of a Merkle Patricia tree (trie), which acts as a mapping structure to encapsulate an account's store contents. The Keccak-256 cryptographic

hash function is used to efficiently organize the data as a mapping between 256-bit integer keys and their matching RLP-encoded 256-bit integer values. The Storage Root variable, which is initially empty by default, dynamically updates as the connected smart contract interacts with and adjusts its internal state variables. This technique maintains the confidentiality and integrity of smart contract data, enabling transparency and auditability in the decentralized environment of the Ethereum network.

## D. Transaction Essentials

A transaction is a fundamental action that enables users to communicate with the Ethereum network. It denotes the process of sending or performing a certain network operation, such as transferring Ether (Ethereum's native coin) from one account to another or invoking a smart contract. Transactions that change the state of the Ethereum Virtual Machine (EVM) must be broadcast to the whole network in Ethereum (Wood, 2018). Any node in the network can request that a transaction be conducted on the EVM. Once the request is made, a validator inside the network will execute the transaction and then notify all other nodes in the network of the resulting state change. This ensures that all nodes have a consistent and up-to-date view of the blockchain's status when the transaction is completed (Community, n.d.).

### Transaction Types

There are three types of transactions on the Ethereum blockchain (What are Ethereum Transactions?, 2023):

1. Regular Transactions: These are transactions in which Ether (ETH) is transferred from one account to another. In a standard transaction, the sender enters a recipient address and the quantity of Ether they want to transfer into the "to" box. These transactions may contain data if necessary, but their primary goal is to transfer Ether between accounts.
2. Contract Deployment Transactions: A particular sort of transaction is utilized when installing a new smart contract on the Ethereum network. The "to" column is left empty or set to zero in this scenario, while the "data" field includes the bytecode representing the produced smart contract code. This transaction starts the process of constructing the smart contract on the blockchain, and once it is mined into a block successfully, a new contract address is produced.
3. Smart Contract Execution: When a smart contract is implemented, it becomes an entity with a unique address on the Ethereum network. Users must submit transactions with the contract's address defined in the "to" field to interact

with it and execute its operations. The "data" element holds the function call's encoded input data, including any parameters. Smart contract transactions can do more than just transfer Ether; they can also initiate sophisticated computations, update the contract's state, or interact with other contracts in the Ethereum ecosystem.

Regular transactions and contract deployment transactions, respectively, are used to update the account status by updating balances and generating new contracts. The execution of a contract, on the other hand, involves the execution of code within the smart contract, which can result in changes in the contract's internal state and interactions with other contracts (Community, n.d.).

## Gas and Gas Cost

Gas is a measuring unit used in the Ethereum blockchain to determine the computational effort required to execute network operations. It represents the cost of processing transactions and smart contracts on the Ethereum network. Every activity in a transaction, whether it's a simple value transfer or a sophisticated smart contract function call, requires a certain quantity of gas.

The "gas cost" or "gas fee" for each operation in the Ethereum Virtual Machine (EVM) is a specified quantity of gas. The cost of gas is dictated by the operation's complexity and resource requirements. Simple processes use less gas, while more sophisticated or computationally intensive operations use more gas. When a user starts a transaction, they must select a gas limit, which is the most quantity of gas they are prepared to pay for the transaction to be completed. The gas limit is a safety feature that prevents infinite loops or too expensive computations from draining all of the user's funds. If the transaction consumes more gas than the given gas limit, the transaction is automatically reverted, and the transaction's state changes are undone (Transactions, n.d.).

For instance, when checking a user's balance on the Ethereum blockchain, it costs 400 Gas, whereas making a transaction costs 21,000 units of Gas. It's important to note that the gas cost for various operations remains constant, as opposed to the gas price, which fluctuates over time. The concept of GWEI (Giga Wei) is presented to address the issue of this fluctuating:

- One Ether (ETH) = 1,000,000,000,000,000,000 Wei (one quintillion Wei).
- 1 Giga Wei = 0.000000001 Ether.

Users can set gas prices at a more manageable and user-friendly level by utilizing GWEI, a considerably lower denomination. So Let us take an example to an Ethereum transaction to make things more understandable, Suppose that Alice wants to send money to Bob, but first she needs to consider a few things:

1. The transaction costs 21,000 units of Gas.
2. The price of Ethereum fluctuates constantly. Currently, the Ethereum rate is almost $1,850 per 1 Ether (ETH/USD, n.d.).
3. The gas price, which can change depending on how quickly she wants the transaction to be completed. Higher gas prices result in speedier transaction processing. The Ethereum Average Gas Price, according to recent statistics, is nearly 25 GWEI (ETH/USD, n.d.).

Now, let's calculate the total cost of the transaction:

- Gas Price: 25 GWEI = 0.000000025 Ether
- Cost of Transaction = Gas Price * Gas Units = 0.000000025 Ether * 21,000 Gas Units = 0.000525 Ether
- Cost of Transaction in Dollar = 0.000525 Ether * $1,850 = $0.97125

Be aware that when the network is busy and experiencing congestion, the cost of gas may go up, resulting in higher transaction fees than usual.

## Transaction Architecture

An Ethereum transaction must include the following elements (Transactions, n.d.):

- Sender Address: This is the account that initiates the transaction, also known as the "from" address. It must be a genuine Ethereum address with enough coins to cover the transaction cost and any additional fees.
- Recipient Address: This is the Ethereum address of the account or smart contract that will receive the transaction or be the target of the contract execution. It is also known as the "to" address.
- Transaction Signing: A transaction must be signed by the sender's private key before it can be sent to the Ethereum network. This signature serves as cryptographic proof that the transaction originated from the account linked with that private key, ensuring the transaction's security and authenticity.
- The quantity of Ether (ETH) transmitted from the sender to the receiver is indicated by the Ether Value. This amount may be zero for contract interactions if the transaction is used merely to trigger a function on the contract without transferring Ether.

- Transaction Data: This field is normally empty for regular value transfers. When engaging with a smart contract, however, this field includes the input data required to perform a specific function within the contract.
- A nonce is a one-time identifier that is used to prevent duplicate transactions from being conducted. Each transaction from an account must have a unique nonce and must be performed in the correct order.
- The gas limit is a notion used by Ethereum to measure the computing power required to perform a transaction or smart contract. The gas limit specifies the maximum quantity of gas that the transaction may utilize.
- The gas price tells how much Ether the sender is willing to pay per unit of gas. It calculates the transaction charge by multiplying the gas price by the amount of gas utilized.

A transaction is broadcast to the Ethereum network when it is initiated by a user. Network validators collect and validate transactions before grouping them into blocks, such as a valid signature, a correct nonce, a sufficient balance in the sender's account to cover the transfer and the transaction charge, and adherence to gas restrictions and prices (Wood, 2018). To be included in a block, the sender must pay the transaction fee, which is determined as the gas price multiplied by the amount of gas utilized. When a transaction is included in a block and uploaded to the blockchain, it is deemed final and irrevocable. If the transaction involves a money transfer, the recipient's account balance is updated. If the transaction interacts with a smart contract, the contract's code is performed, and the contract state may be changed based on the logic of the function (Community, n.d.).

## Transaction Lifecycle

Following the submission of a transaction, a sequence of cryptographic and network procedures occur (Community, n.d.):

1. Transaction Hash Generation: A unique transaction hash is generated when a user initiates a transaction on a blockchain network. This hash acts as a digital fingerprint for that transaction, allowing it to be identified and tracked.
2. Broadcast and Transaction Pool: The transaction is broadcast to the network and added to a pool of pending transactions known as the "mempool" or "transaction pool." All pending transactions are stored here until they are picked up by validators and included in a new block.
3. Validator Selection and Block Inclusion: Validators are in charge of choosing transactions from the pool and incorporating them into a new block. When a

validator forges a block successfully, it includes a set of transactions, including yours, in that block.

4. Verification and Justification: Once your transaction has been placed in a block, the network begins to validate it. The block is distributed across the network, and other nodes (computers) authenticate that the transactions within it follow the blockchain protocol's rules. As more blocks are added on top of the block containing your transaction, the likelihood that your transaction is valid increases. This is commonly referred to as the block being "justified."
5. Finalization: As more blocks are added to the blockchain, the block containing your transaction gets more "finalized." The network has reached a high level of consensus that the transactions included within the block are genuine and irreversible. The deeper your transaction is buried behind successive blocks, the more difficult and expensive it is to change it.

It's worth **noting** that Ethereum first used the Proof of Work (PoW) consensus protocol, which required miners to solve complex mathematical puzzles. However, Ethereum 2.0, also known as Eth2 or Serenity, is a significant upgrade to the Ethereum blockchain that is migrating from the Proof of Work (PoW) consensus method to the Proof of Stake (PoS) consensus mechanism. In this upgraded method, PoS relies on the stake concept, miners are replaced with validators, and instead of mining blocks it will be forging when creating a new block. The upcoming section will thoroughly investigate the PoS concept, its functions, and its advantages over PoW.

The launch of Ethereum 2.0 was planned to occur in three phases (Gu, 2023):

- On December 1$^{st}$ 2020, Phase 0 known as "Beacon Chain" was completed, introducing the Proof of Stake to the Ethereum network.
- Phase 1 titled "The Merge", involved merging phase 0 (Eth2) with the original Proof of Work (Eth1) to create a unified network that uses the same ETH coin. This phase was successfully completed on September 15$^{th}$ 2022.
- Phase 2 known as "Sharding", is expected to be released in 2024. Its purpose is to horizontally split the database to distribute the load evenly on the Ethereum network.

## E. Ethereum Messages

Messages in Ethereum refers to the interactions and communications that occur between accounts, specifically when a smart contract is activated or a transaction is sent. These messages are a critical component of how the Ethereum blockchain functions and allows decentralized applications (DApps) to work (Jani, 2017).

A message is made up of numerous components that specify its aim and how it should be carried out, let us talk about them:

1. Sender and Recipient Addresses: These addresses identify the sender and the account or contract to whom the message will be delivered. These addresses are 20-byte identifiers that can be associated with either an externally owned account (EOA) or a contract account.
2. Ether Value: If the message involves the transfer of Ether, the sender can specify how much Ether (in Wei) should be delivered with the message. This number represents the monetary transaction related to the message.
3. Input Data: The encoded function call and its arguments are contained in the input data for contract interactions. This data directs the contract on how to perform the function and gives any relevant parameters. It is based on the function signature and arguments encoded in accordance with the ABI (Application Binary Interface) specification.
4. Gas Limit: The gas limit specifies how much gas the sender is willing to provide for message execution. It prevents infinite loops and resource-intensive procedures.

Depending on the situation, sending a message might result in a variety of activities. If the recipient is an externally owned account (EOA), the message may include an Ether transfer. If the recipient is a contract account, the message may cause the contract to execute a certain function. The sender's gas pays for the computational labor required to process the message, and transaction fees paid in Ether compensate validators for putting the transaction in a block (Jani, 2017).

## F. Smart Contracts

### Background and Definition

Nick Szabo created the term "Smart Contract" in 1994. Smart contracts, according to Szabo, are self-executing contracts in which the provisions of the agreement are immediately integrated into the code and enforced automatically by a computer network. The primary goals of smart contract design include satisfying basic contractual constraints such as payment terms, liens, and confidentiality and minimizing purposeful and accidental exceptions. Smart contracts attempt to decrease the reliance on trusted third middlemen, such as banks or attorneys, for executing and enforcing contractual agreements by utilizing cryptography and decentralized networks (Szabo, 1994). It's worth noting that, while Szabo pioneered the notion of smart contracts in the 1990s, it was the advancement of blockchain technology, most notably the establishment of Ethereum in 2013, that provided the required infrastructure for smart contracts to be widely implemented. Ethereum-based blockchain technologies enable the implementation of sophisticated and programmable agreements, ushering in a new era of decentralized apps and automated transactions.

Smart contracts make use of and expand on blockchain technology. They are made up of code and data, also known as functions and states, and are distributed on the blockchain network through cryptographically signed transactions. Nodes in the blockchain network carry out the execution of a smart contract. It is critical that all participating nodes have identical results when the smart contract is executed, and that these results are then posted on the blockchain. Users can build transactions that interact with smart contract public functions. These transactions contain information that is sent to the smart contract, which subsequently performs the relevant procedure to provide a certain service or function. Since the code is on the blockchain, it is also tamper-evident and resistant, and can thus be utilized as a trustworthy third party. This means that once a smart contract has been launched and validated on the blockchain, its code cannot be changed or tampered with without being detected. This attribute adds a layer of trust and security to contract execution, removing the requirement for a typical trusted third party. Smart contracts are adaptable and can accomplish activities other than financial operations. They can execute calculations, store information, reveal properties that reflect the contract's publicly exposed status, and even send funds to other accounts if programmed to do so. It is crucial to note, that not every blockchain network supports smart contracts, as others may have distinct purposes or limits that make smart contract execution difficult or impracticable (Introduction to smart contracts, n.d.).

Let's look at an example to better understand how smart contracts function. If you wish to sell your home or rent out your apartment, you can simply deploy a smart contract in an existing blockchain network. Property information can be kept on the blockchain, and anyone with access to that network can view it but not change it. You can locate a buyer for your house this way without the assistance of a third party (Mohanta et al., 2018).

## Advantages

Blockchain-based smart contracts could provide a number of advantages for a wide range of potential applications (Introduction to smart contracts, n.d.):

- Precision: Smart contracts work using predetermined and immutable code. The contract's terms and conditions are clearly written, leaving no possibility for misunderstanding or human error. This accuracy fosters trust and lowers the chance of contract disputes caused by unclear or conflicting contract wording.

- Reduced execution risk: Smart contracts reduce execution risks by exploiting the tamper-evident and tamper-resistant features of blockchain technology. The automated and transparent execution of preset contract conditions means that all parties involved can have confidence in the conclusion, eliminating the need for intermediaries to check or enforce the agreement.
- Quickness and real-time updates: Smart contracts on a blockchain can speed up transaction processing and updating times. Once the contract conditions are met, the execution is automatic and immediate, removing the need for manual processing or the need to wait for intermediaries to validate and execute the transaction. This allows for real-time updates and faster process completion.
- Fewer intermediaries: Traditional methods may involve many intermediaries, such as brokers, agents, or legal counsel, which can add complexities, delays, and expenses. Smart contracts simplify the process by automating contract execution and eliminating the need for middlemen. This has the potential to result in more direct and efficient interactions between parties.
- Reduce Cost: Smart contracts can dramatically cut costs by eliminating intermediaries and automating operations. Transactions become more cost-effective by removing the need for third-party services and avoiding manual intervention. These cost savings can assist a variety of businesses, including finance, supply chain management, and real estate.
- Innovative business or operational models: Smart contracts allow for the development of novel business models and operational frameworks. Blockchain-based smart contracts enable new types of cooperation, peer-to-peer interactions, and decentralized apps by automating processes and enabling decentralized, trustless transactions.

It's crucial to note that Smart contracts must be deterministic, which means they must always create the same output given the same set of inputs. This deterministic behavior is required to maintain consistency and predictability in smart contract execution across all nodes on the blockchain network. The term "Oracle" in the context of smart contracts refers to a method or service that delivers external data to the smart contract. Smart contracts are often incapable of directly accessing or retrieving data from sources outside the blockchain network. If a smart contract requires external data, such as real-world occurrences, market prices, or weather conditions, the contract relies on Oracles to retrieve and supply such data. Oracles serve as interfaces between the blockchain and external data sources. They obtain the necessary data from off-chain sources and pass it on to the smart contract as input parameters. The smart contract can then process the inputs and carry out its logic. By allowing smart contracts to connect with real-world data, oracles play a critical role in expanding their functionality and use cases. While Oracles make it easier to use external data in smart contracts, they also present a potential point of trust and vulnerability. Because the smart contract is dependent on the quality and dependability of the data provided by Oracle, the Oracle service's integrity and security become critical. Maintaining the overall trust and reliability of the smart contract system requires ensuring Oracle's trustworthiness (Yaga et al., 2019).

## How It Works

When publishing new blocks, several blockchain implementations, particularly in permissionless networks like Ethereum execute the smart contract code simultaneously. The following are the main points (Introduction to smart contracts, n.d.):

- Simultaneous Execution: In some blockchain systems, when new blocks are published, publishing nodes run the smart contract code at the same time. This distributed execution ensures node consensus and agreement on the state changes caused by smart contract execution.
- Validation Nodes: In some blockchain systems, nodes do not run smart contract code but rather validate the results produced by the executing nodes. This separation of execution and validation can aid in network scalability and efficiency.
- Cost of Execution: In permissionless blockchain networks such as Ethereum, the user initiating a transaction to a smart contract bears the cost of code execution. This cost, known as "gas," is a measure of the computing effort required to run the code. The higher the gas cost, the more complex the code and the longer it takes to perform.
- Execution Time and Gas Limits: The amount of execution time and gas that can be utilized by a single call to a smart contract is limited. This limit is in place to avoid infinite loops or actions that consume an excessive amount of resources from interrupting the network. If the execution time or gas limit is exceeded, the transaction is discarded, and the user is still responsible for the associated charges.
- Rewards and Denial of Service Prevention: The mechanism of charging users for the cost of code execution not only incentivizes publishing nodes to execute smart contract code but also acts as a deterrent against malicious users deploying contracts capable of performing denial-of-service attacks. It inhibits resource-intensive or potentially hazardous code from being

distributed and performed on the network by setting cost limitations and demanding users pay for execution.

These methods contribute to the stability, security, and efficient operation of the blockchain network by ensuring that the computational burden is correctly distributed and harmful activities are mitigated.

The performance of smart contracts is developing as an important topic of study. The use of smart contract-based applications is projected to increase dramatically as interest in blockchain technology grows in both the public and private sectors. As a result, investigating and improving the performance of smart contracts is becoming increasingly crucial.

## G. Decentralized Apps (DApps)

### Definition and Characteristics

A decentralized application (DApp) is a program that is created on a decentralized network and includes both a smart contract and a front-end user interface. Smart contracts as we discussed above, in the context of Ethereum are accessible and transparent, similar to open APIs. This means that your DApp can use a smart contract written by someone else. DApps differ from standard programs in that their backend code, rather than being confined to a single machine, operates on a blockchain or a peer-to-peer (P2P) network of computers. This decentralized architecture does away with the necessity for centralized authority and offers DApps autonomy. They, like traditional apps, can be created with frontend code and user interfaces in any programming language. This frontend layer allows users to interact with the DApp and make calls to its backend, allowing for a more seamless user experience while taking advantage of the benefits of decentralized technology (Glomann et al., 2020; Metcalfe, 2020).

The characteristics of decentralized apps (DApps) highlight their distinct features within the Ethereum ecosystem:

- Decentralized: DApps are decentralized because they run on Ethereum, a public, open, and decentralized platform over which no single entity has control. Transparency, immutability, and inclusivity are all ensured by the distributed structure of the system.
- Deterministic: DApps behave consistently regardless of the execution environment. Their functions produce the same outputs independent of location, improving predictability and reliability.

- Turing Complete: DApps may perform a wide range of operations, assuming they have access to the relevant resources. This "Turing completeness" enables the integration of complicated and diversified features.
- Isolated: DApps operate in a safe, segregated environment known as the Ethereum Virtual Machine (EVM). This separation ensures that any flaws or bugs within a smart contract do not jeopardize the entire stability and operation of the blockchain network.

These characteristics highlight DApps' unique and robust nature, allowing them to run autonomously, securely, and reliably on the Ethereum blockchain.

## Centralized vs. Decentralized App

Before we proceed to explore the benefits of DApps, let's briefly compare a centralized with a decentralized app, in addition to a real-world example.

A single entity owns and controls the software in a centralized application. The software for this application is hosted on servers owned and managed by the owner. You interact with the app as a user by downloading it, and your interactions consist of sending and receiving data to and from the company's server. A decentralized application (DApp), on the other hand, operates within a blockchain or a network of networked computers. Transactions take place directly between users in this model, with no need for a central authority. Users of DApps often pay the developer with cryptocurrency to gain access to and use the program's source code. This source code, known as a smart contract, allows users to conduct transactions while retaining their anonymity because no personal information is necessary to execute these transactions. Because DApps are decentralized, they promote greater autonomy and peer-to-peer interactions (Frankenfield, 2023).

A traditional web application, such as Facebook or Netflix, runs on a computer system owned and controlled by a firm with control over the service's activities. Regardless of the number of users, the corporation retains control of the app's backend operations. DApps, on the contrary hand, can run on either a peer-to-peer (P2P) or a blockchain network. Applications such as BitTorrent, Tor, and Popcorn Time, for example, operate within a P2P network, allowing multiple individuals to access, exchange, or contribute to the content. As previously stated, DApps operate within a public, open-source, decentralized ecosystem that is immune to manipulation or control by any single party. Consider the following scenario, a developer creates a DApp similar to Facebook; This DApp is hosted on a blockchain, and any user can contribute to the feed, even the DApp creators are unable to remove a post once it has been made, resulting in an immutable and censorship-resistant ecosystem (Frankenfield, 2023).

## Benefits

Decentralized applications have a number of compelling advantages that distinguish them from typical centralized applications. These advantages include higher openness, improved security, less reliance on intermediaries, and user empowerment through greater control over their data and interactions. DApps use blockchain technology to build a new paradigm of trustless and self-sufficient platforms, stimulating innovation and transforming industries across the digital landscape. Let us delve in more details about these benefits (Frankenfield, 2023; Introduction to dapps, n.d.):

- Enhanced Privacy: Unlike traditional apps, users can utilize the features of DApps without revealing any personal information. Smart contracts are crucial in DApps because they allow transactions to take place directly between anonymous individuals without the need for a central authority. Decentralization and anonymity improve user privacy and security, making DApps desirable to users that value data security.
- Resistance Against Censorship: Because of its fundamental principles, a decentralized social media platform is naturally resistant to censorship. Messages and information are recorded on a blockchain in such a network, ensuring that no single member, even the site's administrators or designers, has the right to arbitrarily delete or prohibit messages.
- Continuous Availability: Once a smart contract is implemented on the blockchain, the entire network stays operational at all times, ensuring that users engaging with the contract receive uninterrupted service. This resilience effectively thwarts bad actors' attempts to disrupt specific DApps via denial-of-service attacks.
- Uncompromised Data Integrity: Due to advanced encryption technologies, the information saved on the blockchain is unchangeable and incorruptible. This cryptographic basis assures that once data is made public, it remains unchanged and untouchable by bad individuals.
- Verifiable and Trustworthy Execution: Because smart contracts are transparent and analyzable, they enable predictable and dependable execution without relying on a centralized authority. This divergence from traditional approaches removes the need to invest trust in centralized institutions, reducing possible risks.

## V. CONSENSUS PROTOCOLS

To begin, consensus requires the use of protocols, which govern how nodes in a network establish agreement on the ledger they have and the order in which transactions are recorded on a freshly created block. It can be difficult to complete this process without the assistance of consensus algorithms, as these methods fulfill two critical requirements: safety (ensuring that a confirmed block committed to the blockchain cannot be altered) and liveness. In other words, if an honest person attempts to submit a block that has been verifiably demonstrated to be genuine, they will eventually be approved. As a result, a strong decentralized blockchain relies largely on a reliable consensus algorithm to govern the network, allowing nodes to achieve an agreement and maintain an updated blockchain. Furthermore, by thoroughly researching the consensuses used by the blockchain platforms with the biggest market capitalization, this section intends to provide a comprehensive picture of how consensus is attained in blockchains (Merrad et al., 2022).

In this part, we'll delve into the Proof of Stake (PoS) consensus protocol which has been implemented and worked out recently in the new version of Ethereum (Eth2), and also we'll describe the most well-known consensus mechanisms nowadays, such as Delegated Proof of Stake (DPoS), Proof of Activity (PoA), and the Practical Byzantine Fault Tolerance (PBFT), while Proof-of-Work (PoW) consensus protocol has been discussed in detail in section 3.3.

The Proof of Stake (PoS) is based on the concept of stake and differs from Proof of Work (PoW) by replacing miners with validators that are chosen based on their network stake. Delegated Proof of Stake (DPoS) overcomes a significant difficulty of PoS like the requirement for a large number of participants to validate blocks. DPoS addresses this issue by employing a fewer number of validators than standard PoS. Proof of Activity (PoA) is a hybrid consensus system that combines aspects of PoW and PoS. It strives to remove existing constraints and provide a unique method to consensus by merging their key ideas. On the other hand, Practical Byzantine Fault Tolerance (PBFT), distinguishes itself from the aforementioned algorithms by introducing an enhanced consensus protocol based on a voting-based method.

### A. Proof of Stake (PoS)

Proof-of-stake was a notion that was proposed in the Bitcoin community as early as 2011. This consensus was established in an effort to provide a superior alternative to the previously employed Proof-of-Work (PoW) technique, which was ineffective and inadequately shielded from the delegate's unprofessional behavior due to the cryptocurrency's dependence on energy consumption, operating such networks incurs enormous overhead costs that are passed on to users in the form of inflation and transaction fees, in addition that PoS systems may offer faster transaction confirmation times (Saad & Radzi, 2020). Proof-of-stake can be a more energy-efficient alternative to proof-of-work (PoW), since the miner doesn't have to use a lot of computer power to solve the mathematical puzzle using this consensus approach. Instead, participation in the block-building process depends on holding a large enough interest in the system. The stake or wealth of the participating node completely determines the likelihood of being given the chance to validate a block (Monrat et al., 2019).

The proof-of-stake (PoS) paradigm is based on the idea that users who have a larger investment stake in the system are more likely to support its success and less likely to sabotage it. Stake is the amount of cryptocurrency that a user contributes to the blockchain network, it serves as collateral and indicates their dedication to network security and integrity. This can be accomplished in a variety of ways, including locking it with a certain transaction type, sending it to a specified address, or storing it in specialist wallet software. When a cryptocurrency is staked, it often becomes unspendable. The amount of stake a person has in a proof-of-stake blockchain network impacts their likelihood of publishing new blocks (Yaga et al., 2019). Depending on how PoS is implemented, the particular process of selecting validators and creating blocks may differ. However, the following are the general operating principles of PoS:

- Validator Selection: Validators are chosen to build new blocks and validate transactions depending on the amount of cryptocurrency they own and stake in the network. Validators with higher stakes have a better probability of being selected.
- Block Creation: Selected validators generate new blocks containing a collection of transactions. The validator must include a "proof" in the block proving ownership of the stake.
- Block Validation: Other validators in the network validate the newly produced block and associated transactions. They validate the creator's proof and ensure that the transactions adhere to the network's rules and consensus requirements.
- Block Addition: A block is added to the blockchain when it has been validated by a sufficient number of validators. As an incentive for participating in the consensus process, validators are rewarded with transaction fees or newly minted bitcoin.
- Security and Consensus: Security and Consensus: The security of a PoS network is dependent on validators having an economic incentive to operate honestly. If a validator acts maliciously or attempts to attack the network,

they risk losing the cryptocurrency they have staked. This economic penalty serves as a deterrent to fraudulent behavior.

This consensus process, however, has certain disadvantages. Because validators are chosen based on their stakes, nodes with larger wealth may be given more chances to validate blocks, potentially leading to an uneven distribution or centralization within the network. PoS is also more prone to malicious attacks than PoW because the mining cost and effort required are far lower. Another issue that has lately been uncovered is the "Nothing-at-stake" problem. This problem occurs as a result of the lack of reliance on physical reality to provide a coordinating point for consensus (Monrat et al., 2019).

To address these issues, contemporary PoS systems, such as Ethereum's Casper, are actively including penalties for malicious behavior by validators (Buterin & Griffith, 2017). Several alternatives have evolved that combine the stake size with other parameters to decide the validator who will be able to construct the next block. For example, King et al. launched Peercoin, which uses an age-based stake selection, giving older and larger groups of currencies higher priority for block mining (King & Nadal, 2012). Vasin et al. introduced Blackcoin, a cryptocurrency that uses randomness to choose the next block generator based on the lowest hash value in combination with stake amount (Vasin, 2014). Furthermore, several consensus algorithms combine concepts from PoS and PoW, frequently with additional characteristics. Bentov et al., for example, suggested Proof-of-Activity (PoA), which we'll also delve into it after a few, it combines aspects of PoW, and PoS to ensure validators are picked in a pseudorandom but uniform manner (Bentov, Lee, Mizrahi, & Rosenfeld, 2014).

## B. Delegated Proof of Stake (DPoS)

Delegated proof-of-stake (DPoS) is an optional consensus technique that allows network nodes with a stake to delegate transaction validation to another node via voting. Proof-of-stake (PoS) is a direct democratic method, whereas DPoS is a representative democratic method. Stakeholders choose witnesses, who are in charge of generating and certifying blocks. This group of chosen nodes proposes blocks and verifies data states. They vote for blocks on behalf of their stakeholders and validate the legitimacy of prior blocks in turn. Many systems incorporate a replacement pool with standby validators to address node outages.

In comparison to PoS, DPoS requires a smaller number of participants for block validation, resulting in faster block production and transaction confirmations, as well as lower latency, which is highly appealing on IoT networks. Furthermore, network characteristics such as block size and intervals can be changed to improve efficiency. The fundamental disadvantage of this consensus method is its tendency to centralize.

Participants with a large stake in the outcome can manipulate voting to become validators and influence others. Stakeholders, on the other hand, have the option to vote out dishonest witnesses who engage in malevolent behavior. Bitshare is an example of a platform that used the DPoS consensus process (Monrat et al., 2019).

## C. Proof of Activity (PoA)

As previously stated, both PoS and PoW algorithms have restrictions. While the PoW algorithm improves chain dependability and robustness by making block mining difficult, it suffers from drawbacks like as excessive power consumption and high processing requirements. These issues raise worries about monopolization and the environment. The PoS algorithm, on the other hand, provides a greener alternative with lower energy consumption and the potential to prevent network monopolies. However, the simplicity with which blocks can be added in PoS enhances the likelihood of the "nothing at stake" dilemma, which leads to double spending of coins. As a result, it may be claimed that a hybrid of PoW and PoS algorithms could provide an optimal approach for obtaining consensus in blockchain, which we called in nowadays: The proof of activity (PoA) (Merrad et al., 2022).

The Proof of Activity (PoA) protocol is adapted from the Bitcoin consensus protocol and adds extra network node verifications. In PoA, these nodes are required to do more complex validations than Bitcoin network nodes. Our contention is that this increased burden has certain benefits (Bentov, Lee, Mizrahi, & Rosenfeld, 2014). The PoA system is an attempt to combine the best features of both the PoW and PoS systems. The mining process in PoA begins similarly to that of PoW, with numerous miners competing with greater processing power to discover a new block. When a new block is discovered or mined, the system switches to PoS, and the newly discovered block contains only a header and the miner's reward address. A new group of validators is picked at random from the blockchain network using the information provided in the block header. These selected validators are in charge of validating or signing the new block. The number of coins possessed by each validator influences the selection process, with those with more coins having a better chance of being picked as signers. Once all of the chosen validators have signed the newly discovered block, it is considered complete and is identified and uploaded to the blockchain network. On this block, transactions begin to be logged. If some of the designated signers are unable to finish the signing process, the operation proceeds to the next successful block, with a new set of validators chosen at random based on their coin stake. This process is repeated until a winning block achieves the required number of signers, at which point it is considered a complete block. The mining fees or rewards are distributed among the miner and the numerous validators who contributed by signing off on the block in their respective roles.

Because of its combination of PoW and PoS, the PoA system has been chastised for just utilizing one of the two methods. It is claimed that there is still a significant need for processing power during the PoW phase, which can result in excessive energy consumption. Furthermore, the amount of coins held influences the selection process for signers in the PoS phase, potentially favoring those with more coins and letting them accrue bigger virtual currency incentives. These issues of controversy and criticism have been aimed at the PoA system.

## D. Practical Byzantine Fault Tolerance (PBFT)

To achieve this type of voting-based consensus, advanced consensus protocols, particularly Byzantine fault-tolerant protocols (BFT), are used. These protocols allow for the achievement of consensus in a distributed network even in the presence of hostile or technically faulty nodes. A BFT protocol, which is a replication technique designed to withstand Byzantine faults, is an example of Practical Byzantine fault tolerance (PBFT) (Merrad et al., 2022).

As a high-performance consensus algorithm, PBFT considers the presence of dishonest or malfunctioning nodes and relies on a network of trusted nodes. The nodes in PBFT are grouped sequentially, with one node serving as the leader and the rest nodes functioning as backups. When the leader node receives a request, it notifies the backup nodes and begins processing it. The results are communicated to the request originator via the leader node, who then awaits confirmation from additional nodes. The majority votes are used to make decisions, and each node communicates with other nodes to verify the origin and integrity of the signed message. Each round of the consensus process establishes a new block and selects a leader node based on predefined rules. The leader node is in charge of ordering transactions within the block. The PBFT consensus algorithm, released in 2015, was chosen for its capacity to handle up to one-third of malicious Byzantine replicas. The Hyperledger Fabric consensus process is separated into three stages: pre-prepared, prepared, and commit. During each phase, a node advances to the next step if it receives votes from more than two-thirds of the nodes. This indicates that PBFT requires every node in the network to be known. Similarly, Mazieres's Stellar Consensus Protocol (SCP), proposed in 2015, is a Byzantine agreement protocol. SCP, unlike PBFT, does not use a hashing technique. SCP allows individuals to choose which group of other participants to trust. Antshares (now known as NEO) announced their delegated Byzantine Fault Tolerance (dBFT) consensus mechanism, which was inspired by PBFT. Instead of involving all nodes in the network, dBFT selects a selection of professional nodes to record transactions (Zheng et al., 2018).

Numerous research papers have attempted to compare between Proof of Work (PoW), Proof of Stake (PoS), Delegated Proof of Stake (DPoS), Proof of Activity

(PoA), and Practical Byzantine Fault Tolerance (PBFT) that have been influencing the blockchain technology landscape. These assessments frequently emphasize the critical differences between all these various consensus algorithms. While the breadth and focus of these comparisons vary, they all emphasize the trade-offs between characteristics like energy consumption, transaction speed, security measures, decentralization levels, and scalability. It is critical to understand that the suitability of each consensus algorithm is largely dependent on the specific use case, network goals, and technological constraints. Researchers are constantly improving our grasp of the subtleties of these algorithms and their real-world ramifications, allowing for more informed decisions about blockchain implementations.

## VI. CHALLENGES AND DRAWBACKS

Bitcoin and Ethereum are cryptocurrency pioneers, leading the push toward a decentralized financial future. Both platforms have achieved extraordinary success, transforming our perceptions of traditional banking and currency systems. However, as with any game-changing innovation, they are not without their challenges and drawbacks. As these digital currencies acquire traction, it is critical to investigate and address the inherent complexity and constraints that may undermine their long-term viability and scalability. In this investigation, we will look into the fundamental issues that Bitcoin and Ethereum confront, providing light on areas of concern that require careful consideration in the continuous development of these disruptive technologies.

In section A, we shall address the challenges of scalability and energy usage, Section B will investigate the concerns of decentralization in both Bitcoin and Ethereum. In addition, section C will explore the Oracle problem, followed by section D's considerations for user experience. Finally, section E will cover cyber and network-based attacks in Bitcoin and Ethereum.

### A. Scalability and Energy Consumption

Both Bitcoin and Ethereum encountered significant scalability and energy consumptions issues early in their development because of their reliance on the Proof of Work (PoW) consensus method, which the new version of Ethereum (Eth2) did not rely on it anymore. Let's talk about these problems with both networks, and how each one dealt with them.

The first blockchain-based cryptocurrency, Bitcoin, was intended to be a decentralized and secure digital currency. However, The blockchain gets heavier as more transactions are made. This necessitates the storage of every transaction for validation, adding to the blockchain's overall weight. With the original block size restriction of 1MB and the delay between generating new blocks, the Bitcoin network unfortunately has a restricted processing capability. It cannot handle the real-time processing of millions of transactions because it can only process roughly 7 transactions per second. Due to the restricted block capacity, miners may prioritize transactions with greater fees, which may result in delays for smaller transactions. While raising the block size helps alleviate scalability issues, it may potentially cause blockchain branches and delay propagation speed. This makes scaling a difficult problem to address (Poon & Dryja, 2016).

Ethereum, on the other hand, sought to complement Bitcoin's capabilities by creating a framework for executing smart contracts and decentralized applications (DApps). However, due to its PoW consensus process and the greater scope of its use cases, it ran into similar scaling challenges. The inclusion of smart contracts increased transaction complexity, necessitating more computer resources for execution, resulting in higher block sizes and slower transaction processing times. Furthermore, the increase in DApp usage resulted in increased network activity, where popular DApps and token sales (ICOs) could cause network congestion, increasing transaction costs and delaying confirmation times (Vukolic, 2015).

As previously stated, Both Bitcoin and Ethereum rely on PoW, which no longer exists in Ethereum 2.0, but using this consensus requires miners to perform complex mathematical computations to validate transactions and add new blocks to the blockchain. This process is competitive and energy-intensive, as miners race to solve these computational puzzles in order to earn rewards (O'Dwyer & Malone, 2014). The energy consumption concern has raised environmental issues and led to debates about the sustainability of PoW-based blockchain networks. The carbon footprint associated with mining activities has drawn criticism, especially given the growing awareness of climate change and the need to transition towards more eco-friendly technologies.

In response to these issues, both networks proposed a variety of remedies, which resulted in the deployment of multiple soft and hard forks within the Bitcoin network. Soft forks involve changes that preserve backward compatibility, allowing existing software to validate freshly created blocks as valid. Hard forks, on the other hand, entail software changes that incorporate new network rules, rendering outdated software incompatible with detecting new blocks (Castor, 2017). Bitcoin implemented the Segregated Witness (SegWit) protocol upgrade to address its scaling issues. It was added to the Bitcoin protocol as a backward-compatible enhancement. This means that SegWit enabled nodes that had upgraded to the new rules to continue communicating and interacting with nodes that had not upgraded, preserving the network's overall integrity. The primary goal of SegWit was to address the issue of transaction malleability and enhance the capacity of Bitcoin's blocks by decoupling transaction signature data (witness data) from transaction data, allowing more transactions to fit inside the same block size limit (Cointelegraph, n.d.). This upgrade was built in such a way that it did not require all nodes to upgrade at the same time, resulting in a soft fork.

Furthermore, Ethereum 2.0 represents a concerted effort to improve both scalability and energy consumption by shifting from Proof of Work (PoW) to Proof of Stake (PoS) consensus. PoS replaces the resource-intensive mining method, lowering energy usage and environmental effect. Also, Ethereum 2.0 features shard chains, a sharding technique that divides the blockchain into smaller components known as shards. This enables the network to handle numerous transactions and smart contracts at the same time, significantly expanding the Ethereum ecosystem's overall transaction capacity.

It should also be mentioned that prior to the advent of Ethereum 2.0 (Eth2), both Ethereum and Bitcoin researched solutions for their scalability and energy consumption issues. Notably, both networks had an interest in the concept of Layer 2 scaling. This included looking into Layer 2 options such as Bitcoin's Lightning Network and Ethereum's rollup solutions (Poon & Dryja, 2016). These ideas sought to solve scalability difficulties by allowing a large volume of transactions to be performed off-chain. Following that, these off-chain transactions would be settled on the principal blockchain on a regular basis, improving overall network scalability, significantly lowering the burden on the PoW consensus, and consequently lowering energy consumption.

## B. Decentralization

Decentralization is a significant issue in both the Bitcoin and Ethereum 2.0 networks, though in different ways. The mining process, in which players compete to solve intricate mathematical problems in order to validate transactions and create new blocks, jeopardizes the network's decentralized nature in the case of Bitcoin. While protecting the network, the proof-of-work (PoW) consensus method introduces the risk of centralization, as concentrating mining power in a few entities could undermine the network's intended decentralized structure (Yaga et al., 2019).

Ethereum 2.0, the upgraded version of the Ethereum blockchain, tackles the decentralization challenge by switching from a proof-of-work (PoW) consensus process to a proof-of-stake (PoS) consensus mechanism. The change is intended to improve scalability, environmental sustainability, and participation. However, decentralization remains a primary priority in Ethereum 2.0. The Proof-of-Stake (PoS) system is based on validators who are chosen to create new blocks depending on the amount of cryptocurrency they "stake" as collateral. However, the danger arises when a tiny group amasses an excessive amount of staking power, thus leading to the concentration of governance and decision-making. This occurrence, known colloquially as the "51% attack," emphasizes the importance of maintaining a large and diverse number of validators to ensure the network's stability and adherence to decentralized ideals.

A 51% attack on a permissionless blockchain network, such as Bitcoin and Ethereum, occurs when an attacker controls more than 51% of the network's computational power or mining resources (Majority Attack, n.d.). The attacker can establish an alternate chain of blocks by controlling the bulk of the network's mining power, effectively exceeding the block generation rate of the network's honest players. This allows the attacker to generate a longer blockchain, which becomes the legal chain according to the consensus rules of most blockchain systems. A 51% attack against a big and well-established blockchain network, like the above networks, is regarded as extremely costly and resource-intensive. It often necessitates massive amounts of computer power, rendering it impracticable for most individual attackers. Such an attack would be better carried out by state-level actors or entities with significant resources (Greenspan, 2017).

Finally, the permissionless blockchain's security and integrity are dependent on its decentralized structure and vast distribution of mining power among network participants. The 51% attack emphasizes the significance of having a varied and decentralized network to protect against malevolent actors aiming to undermine the blockchain's trust and immutability.

## C. Oracle Problem

In the blockchain context, the term "Oracle problem" refers to the security, authenticity, and trust conflict that develops between third-party oracles and the trustless execution of smart contracts. The topic of the Oracle problem has been discussed and recognized by several members of the blockchain community. The name derives from a Reddit post by user Dalovindj (Dalovindj, n.d.), who highlighted the difficulty of confirming the reliability of external data without jeopardizing the trustless nature of blockchain consensus methods. This understanding of the Oracle problem predates the release of the Ethereum platform, which popularized the use of smart contracts (Caldarelli, 2020).

In both the Bitcoin and Ethereum ecosystems, the problem of oracles is a major challenge, although it has a different degree of importance. The Oracle problem is smaller in the case of Bitcoin, which serves primarily as a peer-to-peer Internet currency but focuses on value transfer and storage. However, situations may arise where external data needs to be integrated into Bitcoin-based applications, such as smart contracts, which may lead to Oracle problems. Secure and reliable obtaining of real-world data, which is integrated into the Bitcoin blockchain in such a way as to ensure that it remains true and trustworthy are key challenges (Buck, 2017).

On the other hand, the Oracle problem is increasingly visible in Ethereum, a platform built to handle more complicated decentralized apps and smart contracts. External data is frequently required for smart contracts on Ethereum to execute predetermined actions, such as initiating payments depending on real-world events such as market prices. The Oracle problem occurs when this external data is vulnerable to manipulation or inaccuracy, possibly jeopardizing the security and dependability of smart contract outcomes. Decentralized finance (DeFi) applications built on Ethereum, for example, rely significantly on oracles to offer reliable price feeds for a variety of assets, emphasizing the need of addressing the oracle problem (Oracles, ).

Moreover, the Oracle problem continues to be much the same as Ethereum 2.0 is moving towards a new consensus mechanism. The need for reliable data is not altered when it comes to efficient contract execution, despite the improvement in scalability. The Oracle problem has not been entirely addressed with the enhanced efficiency of Ethereum 2.0. In order to provide trusted information for their functionality, DeFi applications in Ethereum 2.0 continue to rely heavily on Oracle solutions, and this indicates that there is a renewed need for strong mechanisms from Oracle.

So Eventually, when blockchain networks interact with the actual world, validating the authenticity and correctness of the input data is difficult. Data can come from a variety of sources, including human input and sensor information from the actual world. However, it can be difficult to determine whether the input data truly replicates real-world events. Inaccurate data may be produced by malfunctioning sensors, and humans may supply incorrect information, either purposefully or accidentally. It is crucial to stress that these challenges are not exclusive to blockchain networks, but are common in all digital systems (Buck, 2017). However, dealing with data misrepresentation from external sources becomes especially difficult for blockchain networks, which frequently operate in a pseudonymous way in which real-world identities are not directly linked to blockchain addresses (Yaga et al., 2019).

Maintaining the confidence and reliability of blockchain networks requires ensuring the integrity of external data. To address the Oracle problem, various approaches are being investigated, including trusted oracles, decentralized oracle networks, data verification procedures, and reputation systems. These solutions seek to reduce the dangers associated with data misrepresentation while also improving the security and quality of information obtained from external sources. As a result of overcoming the Oracle issue, blockchain networks can improve their ability to connect with the real world in a trusted and dependable manner, broadening their uses beyond exclusively digital systems.

## D. User Experience

Navigating the realm of blockchain technology, particularly the Bitcoin and Ethereum networks, is an intriguing yet complex journey. However, obstacles await newcomers behind the promise of decentralized creativity. This introduction digs into a critical aspect of this journey: the User Experience. Individuals that enter these networks face complications such as wallet maintenance, transaction fees, and comprehending the mechanics of blockchain transactions. These difficulties, visible in both Bitcoin and Ethereum, highlight the need for user-centric solutions that demystify the complexities of these networks, allowing novices to easily embrace the benefits of decentralized systems.

On the Bitcoin network, managing the user experience can be difficult, especially for newbies. The concept of wallets and private keys might be intimidating, as users must safely manage these cryptographic keys in order to access and control their assets. The obligation of safeguarding private keys might cause concern about potential loss or theft. Additionally, knowing transaction fees and optimizing them for speedy confirmations might be difficult. During times of network congestion, new users may not completely understand the complexities of transaction fee dynamics. The confirmation time variability adds to the uncertainty. Furthermore, understanding the technological complexities of how transactions are executed on the blockchain might be difficult. The requirement to wait for confirmations to secure transaction finality, as well as the various layers of the Bitcoin network (e.g., Lightning Network for speedier transactions), add layers of complexity that may discourage beginners from completely embracing the technology (Krombholz et al., 2017).

On the contrary, with its emphasis on smart contracts and decentralized applications (DApps), Ethereum creates its own set of user experience issues. Understanding gas fees, which users pay to conduct transactions and engage with smart contracts, is essential for navigating Ethereum. Gas fee volatility, which is caused by network demand and congestion, can result in unpredictable costs for consumers. Furthermore, during moments of strong DApp activity, Ethereum's network congestion can result in delayed transactions and higher fees. Interacting with DApps and smart contracts entails a number of processes, including transaction approval and confirmation on the blockchain, which might be confusing for newbies. Another degree of complexity is added by wallet compatibility and security precautions (Glomann et al., 2020). Furthermore, the transition to Ethereum 2.0's proof-of-stake mechanism brings both opportunities and problems for users, as they must comprehend how the change affects their involvement and possible rewards as validators.

As a whole, the complexity of wallet maintenance, comprehending transaction fees, and managing the technical nuances of blockchain transactions characterize the user experience challenges on both the Bitcoin and Ethereum networks. These barriers can be especially daunting for newcomers, potentially impeding widespread adoption. To improve the user experience and make blockchain technology more accessible to a wider audience, efforts must be made to simplify user interfaces, provide educational resources, and build intuitive tools for wallet management and transaction optimization.

## E. Cyber and Network-Based Attacks

While blockchain technology provides intrinsic security through tamper-evident and tamper-resistant design, it is critical to understand that some attack routes and vulnerabilities may still exist in blockchain networks such as Bitcoin and Ethereum, and their applications. Let's us talk about some of them (Yaga et al., 2019):

- Unconfirmed Transactions: As previously have discussed, the PoW consensus mechanism was adopted by both the Bitcoin and Ethereum networks, which leads to unconfirmed transactions that are vulnerable to attacks because they were not included in a published block. A transaction is vulnerable to double-spending attacks or manipulation until it is validated and uploaded to the blockchain by the miners. Ethereum 2.0's innovative consensus method, Proof of Stake (PoS) considerably reduces the inherent vulnerability to double-spending attacks. Validators are assigned to forge new blocks based on the amount of cryptocurrency they "stake" as collateral in this system. As a result of this configuration, validators are financially driven to work with integrity, as any malicious activities will imperil their staked funds, preventing malicious activity.
- Time-Related Attacks: Manipulating timestamps or altering a member of an ordering service's clock can affect the order or validity of transactions. This could be used to exploit weaknesses or acquire a competitive advantage in the network. It is not entirely eliminated in Ethereum 2.0, because it can still influence the order of transactions in any blockchain network that uses timestamps.
- Denial of Service Attacks: Denial of service (DoS) attacks can target Bitcoin and Ethereum networks, and the apps developed on top of them. These attacks are designed to disrupt or disable network operations, making it difficult for legitimate users to complete transactions or access network resources (Valdeolmillos et al., 2020). Furthermore, DoS attacks in Eth2 can target the network's availability rather than its consensus mechanism. However, shard chains and increased scalability may make it more difficult for attackers to take down the entire network.

- Network Scanning and Exploitation: Malicious actors may conduct network scanning and reconnaissance in order to uncover weaknesses in a blockchain network like Bitcoin and Ethereum. Once detected, vulnerabilities can be exploited, potentially resulting in unauthorized access, control, or disruption of the network or its applications. While Eth2 improves network design, the underlying network security principles and the possibility for vulnerabilities remain.
- Smart Contract Vulnerabilities: As with any software, newly generated smart contracts may involve coding errors, vulnerabilities, or deployment flaws. Attackers can take advantage of these flaws to undermine the smart contract's functioning, security, or funds. While Bitcoin does have some basic scripting capabilities, they are not as complicated as Ethereum's smart contract features, and because Ethereum 2.0 retains the ability to execute smart contracts, the possibility of smart contract vulnerabilities remains.

To prevent these threats, it is critical to use security best practices such as thorough code reviews, vulnerability assessments, penetration testing, and regular security upgrades. Furthermore, continuing research, community participation, and audits can help uncover and address possible vulnerabilities or weaknesses in both Bitcoin and Ethereum networks and their associated applications.

## VII. FUTURE SCOPE

We divert our attention away from the current environment of blockchain technology and its tremendous impact on financial institutions and toward the intriguing horizons that lay ahead. The intricate interplay between blockchain networks, illustrated by Bitcoin and Ethereum, has ushered in a new era of decentralized innovation and digital trust, as outlined in the preceding sections. However, this is only the beginning of what promises to be a revolutionary journey as we investigate potential options for further expansion and advancement. In this section, we will look at the novel technologies, that have the potential to synergize with blockchain, hence creating new opportunities, and concentrating on their delicate relationship with the Bitcoin and Ethereum networks. Our goal is to identify significant areas that require additional research, development, and refinement.

This section will provide an overview of the potential applications of blockchain technology, with a focus on Big Data Analytics in Section A, Artificial Intelligence (AI) in Section B, Section C about Machine Learning, in addition to the Internet of Things (IoT) in Section D.

## A. Big Data Analytics

The integration of Bitcoin and Ethereum networks with advanced big-data analytics has immense promise in the ever-changing landscape of blockchain technology and digital currency. As these networks grow, they produce an incredible amount of transactional and operational data. Big data analytics applied to these blockchain ecosystems has the potential to transform different areas of their functionality. Insights can be gained by employing sophisticated data processing techniques, predictive modeling, and artificial intelligence, which not only improve network security and performance but also provide vital market knowledge (Muheidat et al., 2021).

Incorporation of big data analytics with the Bitcoin and Ethereum networks could allow for real-time monitoring of transactions and addresses, allowing for the early detection of anomalies or questionable activity. This proactive security technique could increase the trustworthiness of these networks and encourage greater use. Furthermore, big data analytics could aid in refining consensus processes and protocol upgrades, resulting in greater scalability and transaction speed, both of which are essential aspects in solving the issues of mainstream adoption (Muheidat et al., 2021). From a market standpoint, combining on-chain and off-chain data might provide a full view of user behavior, investment trends, and sentiment analysis. This useful information would benefit investors, regulators, and businesses alike, encouraging a more informed and stable environment for cryptocurrency-related activity.

## B. Artificial Intelligence (AI)

As the Bitcoin and Ethereum networks intersect with the world of artificial intelligence (AI), an exciting vision of possibilities arises in the quickly evolving terrain of blockchain technology and digital currency. These mentioned networks, which are growing into vast stores of diverse and granular data, are on the verge of a revolutionary era in which the incorporation of AI has far-reaching implications beyond technical enhancement.

The combination of AI and blockchain expands its effect into areas such as governance, sustainability, and socioeconomic empowerment. AI-driven consensus algorithms may pave the way for more inclusive decision-making processes inside these networks. These algorithms, by dynamically assessing patterns and actions, could promote consensus among participants with previously impossible efficiency and fairness. This not only strengthens the decentralization spirit of blockchain but also allows varied stakeholders to play a more active part in defining the network's destiny. Furthermore, their combination has the potential to stimulate sustainable practices. These networks could optimize energy usage patterns and resource distribution using advanced predictive analytics. This has the potential to reduce the environmental impact of cryptocurrency mining and transactions, coinciding with worldwide initiatives to create a greener, more environmentally responsible digital landscape. The socioeconomic repercussions are also significant. By assessing creditworthiness based on a broader range of characteristics, AI-powered analytics could usher in a new era of financial inclusion, expanding banking services to underrepresented communities. Smart contracts might initiate micro-loans or insurance payouts on their own, bridging access gaps to financial services. Moreover, AI-augmented networks have the potential to transform supply chain transparency, ensuring ethical sourcing and decreasing fraud in complicated global trade networks (C, 2023).

## C. Machine Learning

The combination of blockchain technology, as illustrated by the Bitcoin and Ethereum networks, with the power of machine learning holds huge potential in the future years. As time goes on, it is expected that these two breakthrough technologies will work together to provide creative solutions to the current restrictions and challenges that both systems confront.

Machine learning algorithms are capable of analyzing historical transaction data, identifying patterns, and accurately forecasting network congestion. These models can proactively alter transaction processing settings to enhance efficiency and alleviate congestion by projecting periods of increased activity. This predictive feature not only improves the user experience challenge by providing speedier transaction confirmations, but it also reduces the likelihood of network slowdowns during peak usage periods. Further, the incorporation of machine learning has the potential to alter the way transaction fees are decided. Moreover, These algorithms can also dynamically change charge suggestions by taking into account real-time parameters such as network demand, transaction urgency, and current congestion levels. This provides consumers with insights into ideal charge amounts that balance timely confirmations with cost-effectiveness. The consequences of these developments go far beyond the immediate benefits to users. From microtransactions to large-scale financial operations, a more efficient and dependable network can encourage broader adoption and use cases. As a result, the mainstream adoption of cryptocurrencies as viable methods of trade accelerates (Data, 2022).

## D. Internet of Things (IoT)

A compelling merger is on the horizon in the fast-growing domain of digital currencies and blockchain technology, as the Bitcoin and Ethereum networks embrace the transformational potential of the Internet of Things (IoT). The convergence of these technologies represents a watershed moment in the growth of the digital landscape as well as the way we interact with the world around us. The integration of IoT devices provides an unprecedented opportunity to extend their capabilities beyond traditional transactions, imagining a future in which connection and blockchain combine in remarkable ways.

Consider a world in which commonplace objects equipped with IoT sensors and gadgets connect effortlessly with blockchain networks. This confluence has the potential to create a world of smart contracts that are executed autonomously by interconnected devices, enabling new levels of efficiency and automation. Smart appliances, automobiles, and even wearables have the potential to begin and settle transactions, altering ideas such as ownership, sharing, and commerce. The synergy of IoT and blockchain goes beyond transactions since it has the potential to improve supply chain transparency. IoT devices might track and record each step of a product's journey, creating immutable records on the blockchain. This guarantees that consumers receive unbiased information about the origin, journey, and authenticity of a product, boosting trust and ethical consumption. Furthermore, IoT could spur data-driven innovation in the Bitcoin and Ethereum space. Data from IoT devices in real-time could provide insights into industry trends, customer behavior, and environmental implications. When paired with blockchain's security and immutability, this data has the potential to reshape how cryptocurrencies are valued, handled, and used (Sharma & Nanda, 2023).

## VIII. CONCLUSION AND SUMMARY

In conclusion, this comprehensive review has shed light on the remarkable world of blockchain technology, with a specific focus on two of its most notable applications: Bitcoin and Ethereum. Several major discoveries emerged during our investigation, providing vital insights into the distinct characteristics and potential of different blockchain ecosystems. Our journey began with an introduction to blockchain technology, highlighting its critical role in constructing a decentralized architecture within a peer-to-peer network. This design distinguished itself by ensuring dependable interactions among network nodes without the need for central authorities, and the integrity of data transmitted between nodes.

On the other hand, We delved into the currency dynamics of Bitcoin with an overview introduction, followed by the Proof of Work (PoW) consensus method. We demystified the duties of miners and the complexities of the mining process using an understandable example, illuminating the benefits of cryptocurrencies in today's quickly changing financial scene. Moving on, we looked into the Ethereum network, outlining its history and emphasizing its advances in addressing some of Bitcoin's shortcomings. We went over the fundamentals of Ethereum transactions, like the significance of gas and gas costs with a detailed instance, the transaction account, architecture, lifecycle, and messages. We looked also at the highly anticipated Ethereum 2.0 (Eth2), which includes three separate phases, each one having a specific task to implement in this upgrade. Moreover, We proceeded with an in-depth look into smart contracts, including their definition, benefits, and operational processes. Our investigation resulted in a look at decentralized applications (dApps), comparing them to their centralized equivalents and emphasizing the numerous advantages of dApps in fostering trust and transparency. Our examination also included consensus protocols such as Proof of Stake (PoS), Delegated Proof of Stake (DPoS), Proof of Activity (PoA), and Practical Byzantine Fault Tolerance (PBFT), each of which offering unique solutions and innovations in the blockchain space. Furthermore, we went into crucial concerns like as scalability, energy consumption, decentralization, oracle problem, user experience, and the ever-present threat of cyber and network-based attacks to address the challenges and drawbacks encountered by both Bitcoin and Ethereum. We explored how each of them tackled these issues and provided possible solutions. Looking ahead, the potential for the Bitcoin and Ethereum networks appears limitless. The integration of big data analytics, artificial intelligence (AI), machine learning, and the internet of things (IoT) holds enormous promise for these blockchain ecosystems, opening up new paths for research, development, and transformational applications.

In closing, this review served as a comprehensive guide through the complex landscapes of blockchain, Bitcoin, and Ethereum, providing insight into their distinct capabilities, problems, and limitless promise for altering the future of finance, technology, and beyond.

## REFERENCES

Andreev, R.A., Andreeva, P.A., Krotov, L.N., & Krotova, E.L. (2018). Review of Blockchain Technology: Types of Blockchain and Their Application. *Intellekt. Sist. Proizv, 16*(1), 11-14.

Aste, T., Tasca, P., & Di Matteo, T. (2017). Blockchain technologies: The foreseeable impact on society and industry. *Computer, 50*(9), 18–28. doi:10.1109/MC.2017.3571064

Bambara, J. J., & Allen, P. R. (2018). *Blockchain. A practical guide to developing business, law and technology solutions*. McGraw-Hill Professional.

Bentov, I., Lee, C., Mizrahi, A., & Rosenfeld, M. (2014). Proof of activity: Extending bitcoin's proof of work via proof of stake. IACR Cryptology ePrint Archive, 452. doi:10.1145/2695533.2695545

Bentov, I., Lee, C., Mizrahi, A., & Rosenfeld, M. (2014). Proof of activity: Extending bitcoin's proof of work via proof of stake [extended abstract]. *Performance Evaluation Review*, *42*(3), 34–37. doi:10.1145/2695533.2695545

Buck, J. (2017). *Blockchain Oracles, Explained*. Cointelegraph. https://cointelegraph.com/explained/blockchain-oracles-explained

Buterin, V. (2013). *Ethereum white paper: a next generation smart contract & decentralized application platform*. http://www.theblockchain.com/docs/Ethereum_white_papera_next_generation_smart_contract_and_decentralized_application_platf orm-vitalik-buterin.pdf

Buterin, V., & Griffith, V. (2017). Casper the friendly finality gadget. *arXiv preprint arXiv:1710.09437*.

C. (2023, May 3). *Use Cases of AI in Blockchain. Chainlink Blog*. https://blog.chain.link/blockchain-ai-use-cases

Caldarelli, G. (2020). Understanding the blockchain oracle problem: A call for action. *Information (Basel)*, *11*(11), 509. doi:10.3390/info11110509

Casino, F., Dasaklis, T. K., & Patsakis, C. (2018). A systematic literature review of blockchain-based applications: Current status, classification and open issues. *Telematics and Informatics*.

Castor, A. (2017). *A short guide to Bitcoin forks*. https://www.coindesk.com/short-guide-bitcoin-forks-explained/

Cointelegraph. (n.d.). *SegWit explained*. Available at: https://cointelegraph.com/explained/segwit-explained

Community, E. (n.d.). *A next-generation smart contract and decentralized application platform*. White Paper. Available at: https://github.com/ethereum/wiki/wiki/White-Paper

Dalovindj, U. (n.d.). *The Oracle Problem*. Available online: https://www.reddit.com/r/Bitcoin/comments/2p78kd/ the_oracle_problem/

Dannen, C. (2017). *Introducing Ethereum and solidity* (Vol. 1). Apress. doi:10.1007/978-1-4842-2535-6

Data, L. Y. (2022, July 7). *Blockchain and AI: The Best of Both Worlds. Label Your Data.* https://labelyourdata.com/articles/blockchain-and-machine-learning

Ethereum accounts. (n.d.). https://ethereum.org/en/developers/docs/accounts/

ETH/USD: Convert Ethereum to US Dollar. (n.d.). https://www.coinbase.com/converter/eth/usd

Frankenfield, J. (2023, April 16). *Decentralized Applications (dApps): Definition, Uses, Pros and Cons.* Investopedia. https://www.investopedia.com/terms/d/decentralized-applications-dapps.asp

Gilbert, H., & Handschuh, H. 2003, August. Security analysis of SHA-256 and sisters. In *International workshop on selected areas in cryptography* (pp. 175-193). Springer Berlin Heidelberg.

Glomann, L., Schmid, M., & Kitajewa, N. 2020. Improving the blockchain user experience-an approach to address blockchain mass adoption issues from a human-centred perspective. In *Advances in Artificial Intelligence, Software and Systems Engineering: Proceedings of the AHFE 2019 International Conference on Human Factors in Artificial Intelligence and Social Computing, July 24-28, 2019, Washington DC, USA 10* (pp. 608-616). Springer International Publishing. 10.1007/978-3-030-20454-9_60

Greenspan, G. (2017). *The Blockchain Immutability Myth.* CoinDesk. https://www.coindesk.com/blockchain-immutability-myth/

Gu, M. (2023, April 14). *Ethereum 2.0: Here's what you NEED to know.* Boxmining. https://boxmining.com/ethereum-2/

Introduction to dapps. (n.d.). https://ethereum.org/en/developers/docs/dapps/

Introduction to smart contracts. (n.d.). https://ethereum.org/en/developers/docs/smart-contracts/

Jani, S. (2017). An overview of ethereum & its comparison with bitcoin. *International Journal of Scientific and Engineering Research, 10*(8), 1–6.

King, S., & Nadal, S. (2012). *Ppcoin: Peer-to-peer cryptocurrency with proof-of-stake.* https://peercoin.net/assets/paper/peercoin-paper. pdf

Kouhizadeh, M., & Sarkis, J. (2018). Blockchain practices, potentials, and perspectives in greening supply chains. *Sustainability (Basel), 10*(10), 3652. doi:10.3390/su10103652

Krombholz, K., Judmayer, A., Gusenbauer, M., & Weippl, E. (2017). The other side of the coin: User experiences with bitcoin security and privacy. In *Financial Cryptography and Data Security: 20th International Conference, FC 2016,* Christ Church, Barbados, February 22–26, 2016, *Revised Selected Papers 20* (pp. 555-580). Springer Berlin Heidelberg.

Lee, J. Y. (2019). A decentralized token economy: How blockchain and cryptocurrency can revolutionize business. *Business Horizons*, *62*(6), 773–784. doi:10.1016/j.bushor.2019.08.003

Majority Attack. (n.d.). In *Bitcoin Wiki.* https://en.bitcoin.it/wiki/Majority_attack

Merrad, Y., Habaebi, M., Islam, M., Gunawan, T., Elsheikh, E., Suliman, F. E., & Merad, M. (2022). Blockchain: Consensus Algorithm Key Performance Indicators, Trade-Offs, Current Trends, Common Drawbacks, and Novel Solution Proposals. *Mathematics*, *10*(15), 2754. Advance online publication. doi:10.3390/math10152754

Metcalfe, W. (2020). Ethereum, smart contracts, DApps. *Blockchain and Crypt Currency, 77.*

Michael, J., Cohn, A. L. A. N., & Butcher, J. R. (2018). Blockchain technology. *The Journal*, *1*(7), 1–11.

Mohanta, B. K., Panda, S. S., & Jena, D. (2018, July). An overview of smart contract and use cases in blockchain technology. In *2018 9th international conference on computing, communication and networking technologies (ICCCNT)* (pp. 1-4). IEEE. 10.1109/ICCCNT.2018.8494045

Monrat, A. A., Schelen, O., & Andersson, K. (2019). Survey of Blockchain from the Perspectives of Applications, Challenges and Opportunities. *IEEE Access : Practical Innovations, Open Solutions*, *7*, 1–1. doi:10.1109/ACCESS.2019.2936094

Muheidat, F., Patel, D., Tammisetty, S., Tawalbeh, L. A., & Tawalbeh, M. (2021). Emerging Concepts Using Blockchain and Big Data. *Procedia Computer Science*, *198*, 15–22. doi:10.1016/j.procs.2021.12.206

Nakamoto, S. (2008). *Bitcoin: A peer-to-peer electronic cash system*. Available at: https://bitcoin.org/bitcoin.pdf

O'Dwyer & Malone. (2014). *Bitcoin mining and its energy footprint*. Academic Press.

Oracles. (n.d.). https://ethereum.org/en/developers/docs/oracles/

Poon, J., & Dryja, T. (2016). *The bitcoin lightning network: scalable off-chain instant payments*. Available at: https://lightning.network/lightning-network-paper.pdf

Saad, S. M. S., & Radzi, R. Z. R. M. (2020). Comparative review of the blockchain consensus algorithm between proof of stake (pos) and delegated proof of stake (dpos). *International Journal of Innovative Computing*, *10*(2).

Sharma, M., & Nanda, A. (2023). The Future of Blockchain Technology in Internet of Things: Opportunities and Challenges. *International Journal of Next-Generation Computing.*, *14*, 206–217. doi:10.47164/ijngc.v14i3.1299

Szabo, N. (1994). *Smart Contracts*. https://www.fon.hum.uva.nl/ rob/Courses/ InformationInSpeech/ CDROM/Literature/ LOTwinterschool2006/ szabo.best.vwh.net/smart.contracts.html

The Bitcoin Forum Index. (2021). Available online: https://forum.bitcoin.com/technical-support/unconfirmed-bitcoin-transaction-for-more-than-5-days-t57444.html

Transactions. (n.d.). https://ethereum.org/en/developers/docs/transactions/

Tschorsch, F., & Scheuermann, B. (2016, March). Bitcoin and beyond: A technical survey on decentralized digital currencies. *IEEE Communications Surveys and Tutorials*, *18*(3), 2084–2123. doi:10.1109/COMST.2016.2535718

Valdeolmillos, D., Mezquita, Y., González-Briones, A., Prieto, J., & Corchado, J. M. (2020). Blockchain technology: a review of the current challenges of cryptocurrency. In *Blockchain and Applications: International Congress* (pp. 153-160). Springer Interna 10.1007/978-3-030-23813-1_19

Vasin, P. (2014). *Blackcoins proof-of-stake protocol v2*. https://blackcoin. co/ blackcoin-pos-protocol-v2-whitepaper. pdf

Vujicic, D., Jagodic, D., & Randic, S. (2018). Blockchain technology, bitcoin, and Ethereum: A brief overview. *2018 17th International Symposium INFOTEH-JAHORINA (INFOTEH).*

Vukolic, M. (2015). The quest for scalable blockchain fabric: Proof-of-work vs. bft replication. In *International workshop on open problems in network security*. Springer.

What are Ethereum Transactions? (2023, August 18). https://www.quicknode.com/guides/ethereum-development/transactions/what-are-ethereum-transactions

Wood, G. (2018). *Ethereum: a secure decentralised generalised transaction ledger, Byzantium version*. Available at: https://ethereum.github.io/yellowpaper/paper.pdf

Yaga, D., Mell, P., Roby, N., & Scarfone, K. (2019). *Blockchain technology overview. arXiv preprint arXiv:1906.11078.*

Yuan, Y., & Wang, F.-Y. (2018). Blockchain and Cryptocurrencies: Model, Techniques, and Applications. *IEEE Transactions on Systems, Man, and Cybernetics. Systems*, *48*(9), 1421–1428. doi:10.1109/TSMC.2018.2854904

Zheng, Z., Xie, S., Dai, H. N., Chen, X., & Wang, H. (2018). Blockchain challenges and opportunities: A survey. *International Journal of Web and Grid Services*, *14*(4), 352–375. doi:10.1504/IJWGS.2018.095647

# Chapter 8
# Blockchain-Based Smart Contracts:
## Technical and Usage Aspects

**Gulbir Singh**
*MMICT & BM, India*

## ABSTRACT

*Blockchains are decentralized, distributed, and immutable ledgers that can execute contracts on the blockchain, called smart contracts. Blockchain-based smart contracts have different challenges, opportunities, and applications in various fields like cryptocurrency systems, real estate, agriculture, logistics, and fire industry. The codes that can be executed and which operate on top of a blockchain to facilitate, implement, and enforce agreements between numerous parties in the absence of a trusted third party are called smart contracts. This chapter uses a taxonomy to classify different processes, such as comparing and contrasting the strengths and weaknesses of various methods and identifying research gaps and unanswered questions. The chapter also outlines some promising research guidelines for blockchain-based smart contracts and discusses the benefits and challenges. Researchers and practitioners in the field of blockchain-based smart contracts may find this chapter useful because it offers an overview of current and emerging developments in the field.*

## INTRODUCTION

The purpose of this study is to give a complete assessment of the existing literature on blockchain-based smart contracts from both a technical and an application standpoint. We make use of a taxonomy to classify the papers in accordance with

DOI: 10.4018/979-8-3693-1046-5.ch008

several criteria, such as blockchain platforms, smart contract languages, security issues, scalability solutions, privacy upgrades, and programmability factors, amongst others (Bogner et al., 2016; Khan et al., 2021; Petersen et al., 2008; Taherdoost, 2021). We evaluate and contrast the positives and negatives of a variety of approaches, as well as uncover research gaps and outstanding issues. We also examine the possible benefits and obstacles of pursuing these interesting future research avenues for blockchain-based smart contracts and offer some future research directions for blockchain-based smart contracts.

A blockchain is a distributed, decentralized, and unchangeable ledger that is built of a chain of record collection that is linked cryptographically. Blockchains are used in cryptocurrencies like bitcoin and ethereum. Transactions and events are terms that are used to refer to the individual records themselves, while blocks are terms that are used to refer to groups of data. Each individual who is a part of the blockchain network has a copy of the distributed ledger stored in the account that they use to access the network. These transactions are added to the distributed ledger only after passing through a process of verification and agreement with the other parties involved in the blockchain. Blockchain technology is distinguished by a number of basic qualities, the most important of which are immutability, decentralization, and a cryptographic link.

**Immutability:** The fact that the records of transactions in the ledger, which continue to be spread across the nodes, are permanent and cannot be modified is what is meant by the term "immutability." The immutability of the data stored on a blockchain is a property that distinguishes it from centralized database systems and raises to a higher level the level of data integrity that may be maintained on a ledger.

As long as the cryptographic links are in place, it will be difficult to manipulate the records via computational means.

**Decentralization:** As a result of blockchain's decentralization, the network's participants are given equal authority over the distributed ledger. In contrast to centralized systems that are managed by a reliable third party, the blockchain has a feature that ensures redundancy, and this sets it apart from other types of systems. Through decentralization, the service availability can be guaranteed, the risk of failure can be reduced, and ultimately, the trust in the service may be improved (Buterin, 2014; Nakamoto, 2009; Wang, 2018).

**Cryptographic Link:** The block is what establishes the chain of integrity throughout the remainder of the blockchain. It is a link between each record ordered in chronological order. A blockchain is a decentralized database that logs transactions. During the validation of each record's digital signature, hashing techniques and asymmetric key cryptography are employed. This ensures the record's authenticity and prevents manipulation. Any modification to a block or transaction record constitutes a violation of integrity (Wright & Filippi, 2015), resulting in the invalidation of both the record and the block.

In addition, cryptocurrencies enable seamless peer-to-peer payments and disseminate the financial context while emphasizing that they are the first public blockchain generation. Moreover, cryptocurrencies enable payments to be made between parties who are not acquainted with one another. Cryptocurrencies are a type of digital currency that can only be used on the blockchain, which is an online-only distributed ledger. Bitcoin (Alharby & Moorsel, 2017) is the world's first significant cryptocurrency that facilitates peer-to-peer financial transactions without the need for trusted third parties such as international payment channels. Previously, these types of transactions were only possible through international payment channels. Prior to this juncture, this type of transaction could only be completed using foreign payment methods.

A third party is not required for the operation of the system, and the verification of transactions that are committed to the network is taken care of by specialized nodes known as miners who employ cryptographic techniques.

In centralized systems, the use of a trustworthy third party, like a bank, is required so that participants who do not trust one another can connect with one another and send and receive financial transactions with one another. When you rely on a trustworthy third party, on the other hand, you run the risk of encountering issues with both your privacy and your data's security (Udokwu, 2018), in addition to experiencing higher transactional expenses. Blockchain technology was created with the intention of resolving this issue by allowing parties who do not trust one another to reach an accord over their transactions and communications without a trusted third party. The blockchain can be viewed as a decentralized database that documents and maintains the history of all blockchain network transactions (el al Aggarwal, 2019; Seijas et al., 2016). This is one approach to conceptualize the blockchain. Bitcoin, the first decentralized digital money, was constructed on top of a technological advancement known as the blockchain, which acted as the underlying infrastructure for the currency. In addition to its use in the financial sector, the blockchain technology has progressed to the point that it can now support a wide range of decentralized applications. A number of these applications depend on the deployment and execution of smart contracts on the blockchain in order to function properly.

A smart contract (Bterin, 2018) is a computer program that encodes the agreement between parties that do not trust one another and that is carried out in accordance with certain pre-defined circumstances. This agreement is carried out in accordance with some pre-defined conditions. As a component of a blockchain transaction, smart contracts are gaining in popularity, and one or more blockchain systems may be used to construct or carry out a smart contract (Alharby & Moorsel, 2017). A smart

*Figure 1. Different smart contract platforms*

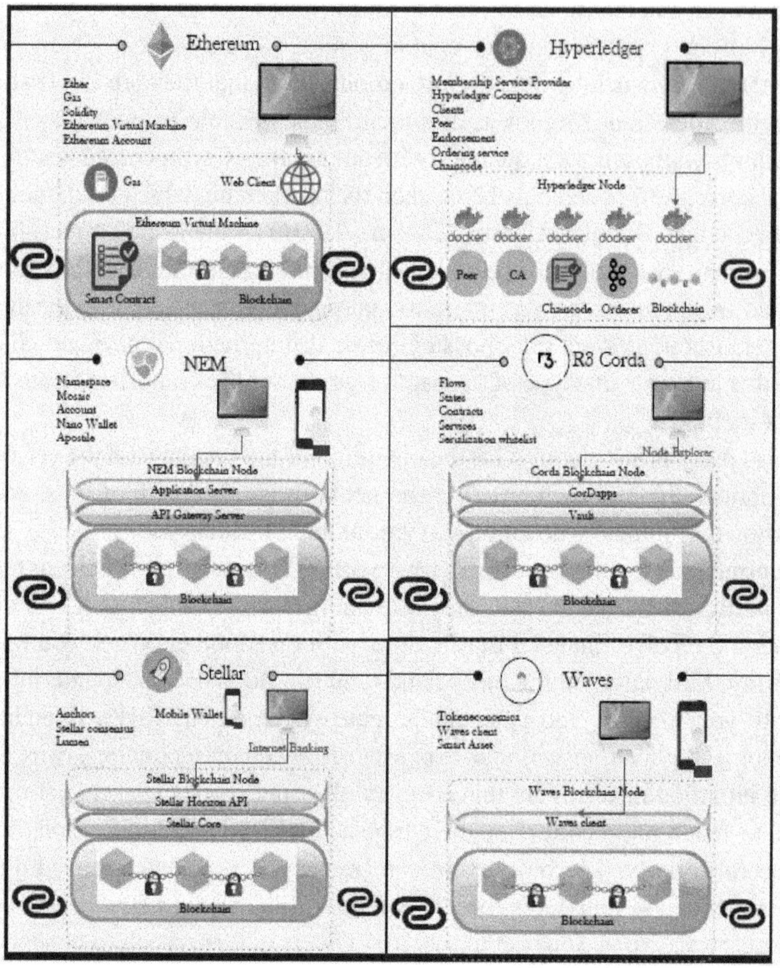


contract may also be referred to as an intelligent contract. Miners are a special category of participant in the blockchain network that are responsible for the deployment of new contracts as well as the execution of contracts that already exist in the system. Miners are paid for their efforts based on the amount of computational work that is required to fulfill the contracts. This determines how much compensation miners earn. Currently, Ethereum and Hyperledger Fabric are the two platforms that have the largest market share when it comes to providing support for the deployment and execution of smart contracts.

The usage of smart contracts enables the regulations of the company to be rewritten as computer programs. As a result of the diverse requirements imposed by various industries, a number of distinct platforms for smart contracts have recently come into existence (Polyzos & Fotiou, 2022).

Every single one of the several platforms for smart contracts comes with its own one-of-a-kind collection of features that are geared specifically for the use case in question. To give just one illustration, the primary concentration of effort that has been put into the development of Ethereum (Wust & Gervais, 2018) has been on applications that require tokenization. Almost every platform includes the fundamental components of a smart contract system, including immutable computer code, a decentralized ledger, and a consensus layer. These components are necessary for the system to implement smart contracts. The consensus layer is one of these constituents (Crawford, 2017; Guo, 2018). Fig. 1 depicts the most prominent smart contract systems that are presently available.

In order to achieve its objectives, this study will first identify and categorize all previous research conducted on the topic of smart contract technology, and then have other academicians evaluate the relevant prior research. It is essential to note that we do not endeavor to cover all of the most recent breakthroughs in technical, financial, or political matters that have been disseminated via other channels, primarily the Internet (Hans et al., 2017). This is something we believe should be clarified. The longitudinal (year after year) characteristics of academic contributions to smart contracts are of particular interest to us because they will allow us to not only document and evaluate the growth in research outputs, but also compare the emphasis placed on various issues across the board. In addition, the purpose of this study is to identify open issues in smart contracts that, once resolved, will necessitate further research. We came to the conclusion that the most efficient approach to proceed would be to use the method of systematic mapping study described in (Bogner et al., 2016; Petersen et al., 2008) to construct a classification map and search for relevant papers in the most important scientific databases. We reached this conclusion after determining that this method would be the most effective means of achieving our goal. The generated map can be used to obtain a deeper understanding of both the issues of interest and the gaps that must be filled in terms of future work (Bartoletti & Pompianu, 2017; Peters & Panayi, 2016).

This study makes a contribution to the existing body of research by offering a comprehensive, up-to-date, and methodical review of blockchain-based smart contracts. This overview includes both theoretical and practical elements. Additionally, it provides some observations and suggestions for future work that can assist in advancing the research and development of smart contracts that are based on blockchain technology.

The remaining parts of this essay are structured as follows: In section 2, we cover some of the fundamentals of blockchain technology and smart contracts. The methods that we used to conduct our literature review is discussed in Section

3. In Section 4, we will discuss the findings that emerged from our analysis of the relevant literature in light of our taxonomy. In the fifth section, we address potential future research directions for smart contracts that use blockchain technology. The final section of the paper is section 6.

## BACKGROUND

We will provide some background knowledge on blockchain technology and smart contracts in the next section. We discuss the fundamental ideas, characteristics, and issues associated with these technologies, as well as how they are related to one another.

### Blockchain Technology

The unchangeable, decentralized, and distributed ledger that blockchain technology use to record transactions that take place between several parties in a peer-to-peer network is known as the blockchain. A blockchain is a distributed ledger that is made up of a chain of blocks that are connected by cryptographic hashes (Bartoletti & Pompianu, 2017; Sengupta et al., 2020). A consensus process used by the nodes in the network verifies the validity of a set of transactions that are contained within each block. The consensus mechanism ensures that all nodes agree on the validity and sequence of transactions, preventing double spending as well as malicious attacks. It also ensures that all nodes agree on the validity and order of transactions. It is impossible to modify or delete a block once it has been added to the blockchain since doing so would break the chain of hashes, which renders the blockchain both tamper-proof and transparent (Sankar et al., 2017; Singh et al., 2020).

Blockchain technology has several features that make it suitable for various applications, such as:

- **Decentralization:** The blockchain network is not governed or controlled by a centralized authority or an intermediary because there isn't one. Each node in the network is capable of independently verifying transactions and taking part in the network. This lowers the likelihood of there being a single point of failure, as well as the chances of censorship and corruption (Chen, 2017; Clack et al., 2016).
- **Immutability:** Transactions that are recorded on a blockchain cannot be undone and are therefore permanent. Because of this, the data that is recorded on the blockchain is guaranteed to be accurate and trustworthy, and it also provides auditability and accountability (Sousa et al., 2018; Xu, 2017).

- **Cryptographic link:** Cryptographic methods, like as digital signatures and encryption, are utilized to ensure the safety of all transactions carried out on the blockchain. This not only protects the transactions from illegal access and modification, but it also guarantees the transactions' legitimacy and confidentiality (Marino & Juels, 2016).
- **Smart contracts:** It is possible to pre-program transactions on the blockchain so that they carry out automatically when certain circumstances are satisfied. These exchanges are what are known as "smart contracts," and they are computer protocols that facilitate, verify, and enforce agreements between many parties.

However, blockchain technology also faces some challenges that limit its scalability, efficiency, and usability, such as:

- **High resource consumption:** The majority of blockchains use a consensus mechanism, which requires a large amount of both processing power and energy. This is done to validate transactions and assure the continuous safety of the blockchain network. As a consequence of this, the operation and upkeep of a blockchain network incurs enormous expenses and has an adverse impact on the natural environment (Norta, 2016).
- **Low throughput:** The amount of transactions that may be handled in a single second by a blockchain network is constrained by the block size as well as the block time. This leads in low throughput and excessive latency of transactions, which affects the performance and user experience of blockchain apps.
- **Privacy issues:** All nodes in the network are able to view all transactions that take place on the blockchain publicly. Concerns about users' ability to maintain the confidentiality of their identities and data are prompted by this development. In addition, certain transactions might include private or confidential information that shouldn't be seen by the public on the blockchain.
- **Interoperability issues:** Architectures, protocols, standards, and language implementations might vary widely amongst different blockchains. Because of this, it is difficult for them to communicate and share data with other internal systems as well as with systems that are external to their organization. This makes it more difficult to integrate blockchain apps in a variety of contexts and ensure that they are compatible with one another.

## Smart Contracts

- Smart contracts are executable codes that operate atop a blockchain to facilitate, implement, and enforce agreements between multiple parties in the absence of a trusted third party. Other programming languages, such as Solidity for Ethereum, Java for Hyperledger Fabric, and JavaScript for NXT, can also be used to construct smart contracts. The ability of smart contracts to communicate with one another and with other data sources, commonly referred to as oracles, enables the execution of complex logic and actions. The use of smart contracts rather than regular contracts has a number of benefits, including the following:
- **Automation:** Smart contracts can execute automatically when predefined conditions are met. This reduces the need for manual intervention and human errors (Moyano & Ross, 2017).
- **Efficiency:** Smart contracts can process transactions faster and cheaper than traditional contracts. This saves time and money for the parties involved.
- **Security:** Smart contracts are secured by cryptography and the immutability of the blockchain. This prevents fraud, manipulation, and breach of contract.
- **Transparency:** Smart contracts are visible and verifiable by all parties on the blockchain. This ensures trust and accountability among the parties.

However, smart contracts also have some limitations and challenges that need to be addressed, such as:

- **Design flaws:** Smart contracts are prone to bugs, errors, or vulnerabilities in their code or logic. These flaws can lead to unexpected outcomes or malicious attacks that can compromise the functionality or security of smart contracts (Hu, 2018).
- **Legal issues:** In the majority of nations, smart contracts are not recognized by the law and are not enforceable. The use of smart contracts is not governed by any specific legal framework or law. In addition, there is no process for the resolution of disputes or any other kind of remedy for smart contract disagreements (Macrinici et al., 2018).
- **Usability issues:** In order to design, deploy, and use smart contracts, one must first acquire the necessary technical skills and knowledge. For the creation of smart contracts and their subsequent interactions, there is a dearth of user-friendly tools and interfaces. In addition, there is a lack of standardization as well as interoperability between the various platforms for smart contracts (Feng et al., 2019; Luu, 2017).

*Table 1. Summarizes the main application contexts and related works*

| Platforms | Major Application Contexts | Related Works |
|---|---|---|
| Ethereum | • Financial<br>• Asset trading | • DAI (Bauer et al., 2018; Sengupta et al., 2020)<br>• Cryptokitties (Manzoor, 2018) |
| Corda | • Insurance | • Energy Block Exchange (Guo & Liang, 2016)<br>• MonetaGo (Peters & Panayi, 2016) |
| Hyperledger Fabric | • Supply chain Management<br>• Stock trading<br>• Trade finance | • Everledger diamond blockchain (Rosner & Kang, 2015)<br>• IBM Food Trust (Hopwood et al., 2016) |
| Stellar | • Remittance | • StellarX (Rathore et al., 2022)<br>• Tempo (Alphand, 2023)<br>• TillBilly (Nagothu, 2023) |

# METHODOLOGY

In this section, we describe the methodology of our literature review. We explain how we searched, selected, categorized, and analyzed the relevant papers on blockchain-based smart contracts.

## Search Strategy

To conduct a comprehensive and systematic literature search, we followed the PRISMA guidelines. We used the following keywords and their combinations to search for papers on blockchain-based smart contracts: blockchain, smart contract, distributed ledger, decentralized application, DApp, Ethereum, Hyperledger Fabric, NXT, Solidity, security, scalability, privacy, programmability. We searched the following databases: Google Scholar, Scopus, Web of Science, IEEE Xplore, and ACM Digital Library. We also searched the references of the retrieved papers to identify any additional relevant papers.

We applied the following inclusion and exclusion criteria to filter the papers:

- **Inclusion criteria:** The paper must be written in English; it must be published in a journal or conference that is subject to peer review; the study's primary focus must be on blockchain-based smart contracts, either from a technical or an application standpoint; and the paper's publication date must fall between 2015 and 2023.

- **Exclusion criteria:** The paper is not written in English; the article is not published in a journal or conference that is subject to peer review; the paper does not focus on blockchain-based smart contracts or only briefly mentions them; the paper was published before 2015 or after April 2023; and the paper was published before or after those dates.

In April of 2023, we carried out the search of the relevant literature and came up with a total of 3356 papers. Following the application of the criteria for inclusion and exclusion, we settled on 539 papers for further investigation.

## Categorization and Analysis

A taxonomy that we built ourselves based on the previous research was utilized by us in order to classify and evaluate the papers that were chosen. The taxonomy is comprised of six different dimensions: a blockchain platform, a smart contract language, a security issue, a solution to scalability, an enhancement to privacy, and an aspect of programmability. Each dimension is broken down into multiple subcategories that each indicate a particular strategy or method that was utilized by the papers. As an illustration, some of the platforms that fall under the umbrella of blockchain technology are Ethereum, Hyperledger Fabric, NXT, and others. Vulnerabilities can be broken down into its component parts, such as code vulnerability, transaction vulnerability, network vulnerability, and others (He, 2017; Zheng et al., 2018).

We classified each publication by assigning it to one or more subcategories for each dimension according to the primary contribution or focus that it presented in the paper. In addition, we retrieved some descriptive information from each of the papers, such as the title, authors, year of publication, kind of publication (journal or conference), type of research (empirical or theoretical), type of technique (qualitative or quantitative), and the primary findings or implications.

In order to provide a concise summary of the distribution and frequency of the papers across a variety of dimensions and subcategories, we made use of descriptive statistics. In addition, we utilized thematic analysis in order to recognize the predominant patterns and ideas that surfaced across the papers. We analyzed the various approaches and methods described in the papers and compared and contrasted their positive and negative characteristics. In addition to this, we uncovered the study voids and unanswered questions that must be answered by subsequent investigations.

# RESULTS

In this section, we will describe the findings of our literature review in accordance with the taxonomy that we developed. We describe the distribution of the papers throughout the various dimensions and subcategories, as well as the frequency of their appearance. In addition, we analyze the papers to determine the most prominent recurring themes and trends.

## Distribution and Frequency of Papers

The breakdown of the papers into their respective publication years is presented in Fig.2. Since 2015, we can see that the number of papers on blockchain-based smart contracts has dramatically increased, hitting a peak in 2022 with 158 publications. This indicates that the number of papers is expected to continue to climb. This suggests that both researchers and practitioners are becoming increasingly interested in and attentive to this topic.

The breakdown of the papers into their respective types of publishing is presented in Fig. 3. We can observe that the majority of the papers were presented at conferences (82%) rather than being published in journals (18%). This shows that blockchain-based smart contracts are still a developing and active study subject that

*Figure 2. Distribution of papers by year of publication*

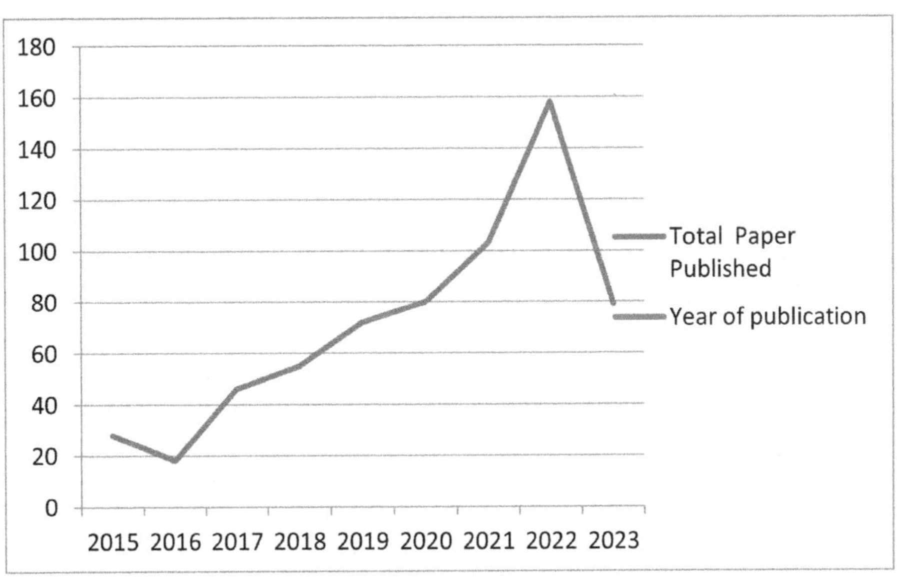

*Figure 3. Distribution of papers by type of publication*

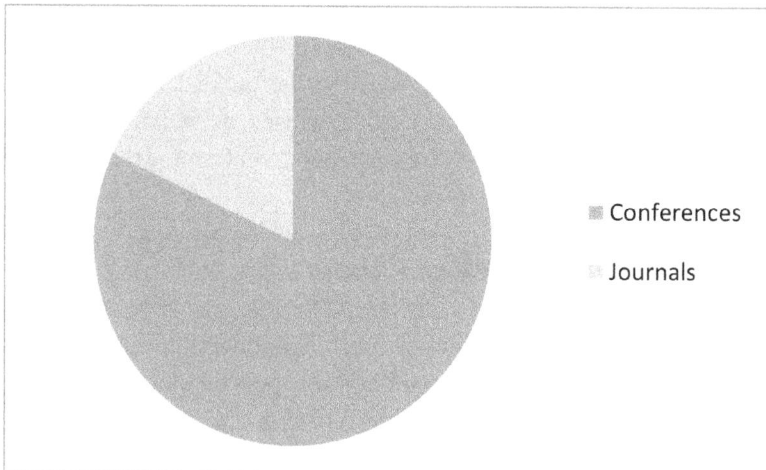


needs additional investigations that are more rigorous and mature before they can be published in journals.

Figure 4 illustrates the breakdown of the publications into the several categories of research. It is clear that the majority of the publications (71%) were empirical, whilst only 29% of the studies were theoretical. This indicates that research on smart contracts that are based on blockchains is mostly conducted from a more applied viewpoint, employing experiments, case studies, surveys, or simulations to evaluate the performance, usability, or application of blockchain-based smart contracts.

The breakdown of the publications into their respective methods is presented in Figure 5. It is clear that the majority of the publications (63%) focused on quantitative research, while just 37% of the papers explored qualitative topics. This suggests that the quality, efficacy, or efficiency of blockchain-based smart contracts is evaluated primarily through the use of numerical data, such as metrics, measurements, or statistics.

The distribution and frequency of the papers can be seen in Table 2, which is broken down by dimension and subcategory. We can observe that the majority of the papers (67%) utilized Ethereum as their blockchain platform of choice, followed by Hyperledger Fabric (16%), NXT (7%) and others (10%). The majority of the research articles (58%) made use of the smart contract programming language Solidity. This was followed by Java (15%), JavaScript (8%) and other languages (19%). The most common type of security issue that was discussed in the papers was code vulnerability, which accounted for 42% of the total, followed by transaction vulnerability (24%), network vulnerability (18%), and other types of vulnerability (16%). Sharding was the scalability approach that was proposed in the studies the most frequently (35%)

*Figure 4. Distribution of papers by type of research*

*Figure 5. Distribution of papers by type of approach*

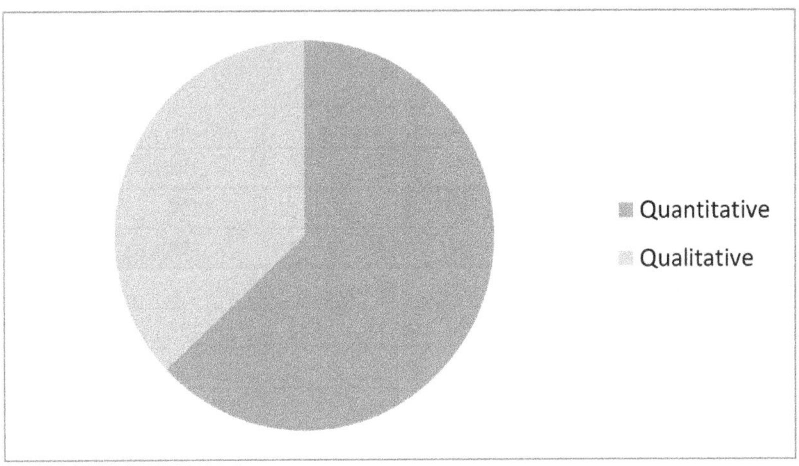


followed by off-chain computation (25%), sidechains (20%), and other scalability solutions (20%). The technique of enhancing privacy with zero-knowledge proof was utilized by the majority of the papers (40%), followed by encryption (30%), ring signature (15%), and other privacy enhancement methods (15%). The majority of the publications (45%) focused on formal verification as the primary method for evaluating programmability, followed by testing (25%), debugging (15%), and other methods (15%).

*Table 2. Distribution and frequency of papers by dimension and subcategory*

| Dimension | Subcategory | Frequency | Percentage |
|---|---|---|---|
| Blockchain platform | Ethereum | 82 | 67% |
| Hyperledger Fabric | 20 | 16% | |
| NXT | 9 | 7% | |
| Others | 12 | 10% | |
| Smart contract language | Solidity | 71 | 58% |
| Java | 18 | 15% | |
| JavaScript | 10 | 8% | |
| Others | 23 | 19% | |
| Security issue | Code vulnerability | 52 | 42% |
| Transaction vulnerability | 30 | 24% | |
| Network vulnerability | 22 | 18% | |
| Others | 19 | 16% | |
| Scalability solution | Sharding | 43 | 35% |
| Off-chain computation | 31 | 25% | |
| Sidechains | 25 | 20% | |
| Others | 24 | 20% | |
| Privacy enhancement | Zero-knowledge proof | 49 | 40% |
| Encryption | 37 | 30% | |
| Ring signature | 18 | 15% | |
| Others | 18 | 15% | |
| Programmability aspect | Formal verification | 55 | 45% |
| Testing | 31 | 25% | |
| Debugging | 18 | 15% | |
| Others | 19 | 15% | |

## Themes and Patterns

Based on our thematic analysis of the papers, we identified four main themes and patterns that emerged from our literature review:

- **Theme A:** Smart contracts built on blockchain technology make it possible to create new applications and business models in a variety of industries, including cryptocurrency systems, supply chain management, agribusiness, real estate, and energy trading, amongst others. These applications make use of the capabilities and advantages offered by smart contracts, such as automation, efficiency, safety, and transparency. On the other hand, they are also subject to a number of difficulties and constraints, including regulatory uncertainty, user uptake, interoperability, and so on.

- **Theme B:** Blockchain-based smart contracts require high-quality code to ensure their correct functionality and security. However, writing smart contract code is not easy due to its complexity, novelty, and irreversibility. Therefore, many papers propose methods and tools to improve the quality of smart contract code, such as formal verification, testing, debugging, etc.
- **Theme C:** Blockchain-based smart contracts suffer from scalability issues due to their high resource consumption and low throughput. Therefore, many papers propose solutions to enhance the scalability of smart contracts, such as sharding, off-chain computation, sidechains, etc. These solutions aim to reduce the load on the main blockchain or increase its capacity without compromising its security or decentralization.
- **Theme D:** Blockchain-based smart contracts raise privacy concerns due to their public visibility and traceability. Therefore, many papers propose techniques to enhance the privacy of smart contracts, such as zero-knowledge proof, encryption, ring signature, etc. These techniques aim to protect the identity or data of smart contract users or transactions without affecting their functionality or verifiability.

## FUTURE RESEARCH DIRECTIONS

Following the completion of our literature study, we will now present several possible future research areas for smart contracts that are based on blockchain technology. We examine the possible benefits as well as the obstacles that may arise from following these areas, and we offer some suggestions or guidelines for future work.

### Cross-Chain Smart Contracts

Cross-chain smart contracts are smart contracts that can interact with different blockchains or other external systems. This is one of the future research directions that will be pursued in order to enable cross-chain smart contracts. The interoperability and usefulness of blockchain-based systems, such as decentralized exchanges, cross-border payments, supply chain management, and other similar applications, can be improved with the help of cross-chain smart contracts. However, cross-chain smart contracts also present some technical and security challenges, such as how to ensure the consistency and atomicity of transactions across different blockchains, how to verify the validity and authenticity of data from external sources, how to prevent malicious attacks or frauds, and so on. These are just some of the challenges. As a result, future effort ought to concentrate on building innovative protocols, structures, and standards with the purpose of making it easier to design, deploy, and carry out execution of cross-chain smart contracts.

## Machine Learning-Based Smart Contracts

Integration of machine learning methods with smart contracts, which are smart contracts that can learn from data and adapt to changing environments, is another potential study direction. Smart contracts are smart contracts that can learn from data. Applications built on blockchain technology, such as prediction markets, insurance policies, recommendation systems, and so on, can have their intelligence and efficiency improved by the use of smart contracts that are powered by machine learning. Nevertheless, machine learning-based smart contracts face a number of challenges and limitations. These include the following: how to ensure the privacy and security of data used for training and inference; how to deal with uncertainty and noise in data and models; how to balance the trade-off between complexity and performance of models; how to handle ethical and legal issues related to the outcomes of machine learning; and so on. As a result, work that will be done in the future should concentrate on establishing unique methodologies, tools, and frameworks that will enable the construction, deployment, and assessment of smart contracts that are based on machine learning.

## Human-Centric Smart Contracts

The adoption of a human-centric approach to smart contracts, which are smart contracts that take into consideration the requirements, preferences, and actions of human users, is the third future research direction that will be pursued. The usability and general acceptability of blockchain-based applications, such as e-commerce platforms, social networking platforms, gaming platforms, and so on, can be improved with the help of human-centric smart contracts. However, human-centric smart contracts also raise a few challenges and questions, such as how to design user-friendly interfaces and interactions for smart contracts, how to incorporate human factors and emotions into the logic of smart contracts, how to align the outcomes of smart contracts with human values and norms, and how to resolve conflicts and disputes that arise from the execution of smart contracts, among other things. In light of this, work that will be done in the future should concentrate on establishing unique concepts, models, and approaches to support the design, implementation, and evaluation of human-centric smart contracts.

## CONCLUSION

In this chapter, we have provided a comprehensive evaluation of the literature on blockchain-based smart contracts, both from a technical and an application standpoint. We have provided a taxonomy of the currently available blockchain-based smart contract solutions, categorized the included research papers, and discussed the various blockchain-based smart contract-based studies. In addition, we have identified and analyzed the major themes and patterns that emerged from our review of the pertinent literature. On the basis of our findings, we have suggested some potentially fruitful future research avenues for blockchain-based smart contracts and analyzed their potential benefits as well as potential drawbacks.

According to the findings of our study, blockchain-based smart contracts are an emerging and rapidly developing research topic that may be used to a variety of contexts and present a range of opportunities as well as difficulties. Nevertheless, blockchain-based smart contracts confront a number of challenges, both technological and usage-related, that need to be addressed by researchers and practitioners in the field. As a result, we have high hopes that our study will be able to operate as a helpful reference and guide for subsequent research on smart contracts based on blockchain technology.

## REFERENCES

AlharbyM.MoorselA. V. (2017). *Blockchain-based smart contracts: A systematic mapping study*. doi:10.5121/csit.2017.71011

Alphand, O. (2023). *IoTChain: A Blockchain Security Architecture for the Internet of Things. In 2018 IEEE Wireless Communications and Networking Conference (WCNC)*. IEEE.

Atzei, N. (2018). SoK: Unraveling Bitcoin Smart Contracts. In L. Bauer & R. Küsters (Eds.), Lecture Notes in Computer Science: Vol. 10804. *Principles of Security and Trust. POST 2018*. Springer.

Bartoletti, M., & Pompianu, L. (2017). An empirical analysis of smart contracts: platforms, applications, and design patterns. In *International conference on financial cryptography and data security*. Springer. 10.1007/978-3-319-70278-0_31

Bogner, A., Chanson, M., & Meeuw, A. (2016). A Decentralised Sharing App Running a Smart Contract on the Ethereum Blockchain. In *Proceedings of the 6th International Conference on the Internet of Things*. ACM. 10.1145/2991561.2998465

Bterin, V. (2018). *A next-generation smart contract and de-centralized application platform*. Available online at: https://github.com/ethereum/wiki/wiki/White-Paper/

Buterin, V. (2014). *A Next-generation Smart Contract and Decentralized Application Platform*. White paper 3: 37.

Chen, L. (2017). Decentralized Execution of Smart Contracts: Agent Model Perspective and its Implications. In *International Conference on Financial Cryptography and Data Security*. Springer. 10.1007/978-3-319-70278-0_29

Clack, C. D., Bakshi, V. A., & Braine, L. (2016). Smart Contract Templates: Essential Requirements and Design Options. *arXiv preprint arXiv:1612.04496*

Crawford, M. (2017). The Insurance Implications of Blockchain. *Risk Management*, *64*, 24.

el al Aggarwal, S. (2019). Blockchain for Smart Communities: Applications, Challenges and Opportunities. *Journal of Network and Computer Applications*, *144*, 13–48. doi:10.1016/j.jnca.2019.06.018

Feng, Q., He, D., Zeadally, S., Khan, M. K., & Kumar, N. (2019). A Survey on Privacy Protection in Blockchain System. *Journal of Network and Computer Applications*, *126*, 45–58. doi:10.1016/j.jnca.2018.10.020

Guo, Y. (2018). WISChain: An Online Insurance System based on Blockchain and DengLu1 for Web Identity Security. *2018 1st IEEE International Conference on Hot Information-Centric Networking (HotICN)*, 242–243.

Guo, Y., & Liang, C. (2016). Blockchain application and outlook in the banking industry. *Financial Innovation*, *2*(1), 24. doi:10.1186/s40854-016-0034-9

Hans, R., Zuber, H., Rizk, A., & Steinmetz, R. (2017). Blockchain and Smart Contracts: Disruptive Technologies for the Insurance Market. *2017 Americas Conference on Information Systems*, 1-10.

He, P. (2017). Survey on Blockchain Technology and its Application Prospect. *Computer Science*, *44*, 1–7.

Hopwood, D., Bowe, S., Hornby, T., & Wilcox, N. (2016). *Zcash Protocol Specification*, Tech. rep. 2016–1.10. Zerocoin Electric Coin Company.

Hum Y. (2018). *A Delay-Tolerant Payment Scheme Based on the Ethereum Blockchain*. CoRR abs/1801.10295

Khan, S. N., Loukil, F., Ghedira-Guegan, C., Benkhelifa, E., & Bani-Hani, A. (2021). Blockchain smart contracts: Applications, challenges, and future trends. *Peer-to-Peer Networking and Applications*, *14*(5), 2901–2925. doi:10.1007/s12083-021-01127-0 PMID:33897937

Luu, L. (2017). Practical Decentralized Pooled Mining. *26th fUSENIXg Security Symposium (fUSENIXg Security 17),* 1409–1426.

Macrinici, D., Cartofeanu, C., & Gao, S. (2018). Smart Contract Applications within Blockchain Technology: A Systematic Mapping Study. *Telematics and Informatics*, *35*(8), 2337–2354. doi:10.1016/j.tele.2018.10.004

Manzoor, Y. (2018). A Delay-Tolerant Payment Scheme on the Ethereum Blockchain. *2018 IEEE 19th International Symposium on A World of Wireless, Mobile and Multimedia Networks (WoWMoM),* 14–16.

Marino, B., & Juels, A. (2016). Setting Standards for Altering and Undoing Smart Contracts. *International Symposium on Rules and Rule Markup Languages for the Semantic Web*, 151–166. 10.1007/978-3-319-42019-6_10

Moyano, J. P., & Ross, O. (2017). KYC Optimization Using Distributed Ledger Technology. *Business & Information Systems Engineering*, *59*(6), 411–423. doi:10.1007/s12599-017-0504-2

Nagothu, D. (2023). A Microservice-enabled Architecture for Smart Surveillance using Blockchain Technology. *2018 IEEE International Smart Cities Conference (ISC2),* 1–4.

Nakamoto, S. (2009). *Bitcoin: A Peer-to-peer Electronic Cash System.* http://www:bitcoin:org/bitcoin:pdf

Norta, A. (2016). Designing a Smart-contract Application Layer for Transacting Decentralized Autonomous Organizations. *International Conference on Advances in Computing and Data Sciences*, 595–604.

Peters, G. W., & Panayi, E. (2016). *Understanding modern banking ledgers through blockchain technologies: Future of transaction processing and smart contracts on the internet of money. In Banking beyond banks and money.* Springer.

Petersen, K., Feldt, R., Mujtaba, S., & Mattsson, M. (2008). Systematic mapping studies in software engineering. *EASE*, *8*, 68–77.

Polyzos, G. C., & Fotiou, N. (2022). Blockchain-Assisted Information Distribution for the Internet of Things. *2017 IEEE International Conference on Information Reuse and Integration (IRI),* 75–78.

Rathore, S., Kwon, B. W., & Park, J. H. (2022). Blockseciotnet: Blockchain-based decentralized security architecture for iot network. *Journal of Network and Computer Applications*, *143*, 167–177. doi:10.1016/j.jnca.2019.06.019

Rosner, M. T., & Kang, A. (2015). Understanding and Regulating Twenty-first Century Payment Systems: The Ripple Case Study. *Michigan Law Review*, *114*, 649.

Sankar, L. S., Sindhu, M., & Sethumadhavan, M. (2017) Survey of Consensus Protocols on Blockchain Applications. *2017 4th International Conference on Advanced Computing and Communication Systems (ICACCS),* 1–5.

Seijas, Thompson, & McAdams. (2016). Scripting smart contracts for distributed ledger technology. *IACR Cryptology ePrint*, 1156.

Sengupta, J., Ruj, S., & Bit, S. D. (2020). A Comprehensive Survey on Attacks, Security Issues and Blockchain Solutions for IoT and IIoT. *Journal of Network and Computer Applications*, *149*, 102481. doi:10.1016/j.jnca.2019.102481

Singh, A., Click, K., Parizi, R. M., Zhang, Q., Dehghantanha, A., & Choo, K.-K. R. (2020). Sidechain Technologies in Blockchain Networks: An Examination and State-of-the-art Review. *Journal of Network and Computer Applications*, *149*, 102471. doi:10.1016/j.jnca.2019.102471

Sousa, J., Bessani, A., & Vukolic, M. (2018). A Byzantine Fault-tolerant Ordering Service for the Hyperledger Fabric Blockchain Platform. *2018 48th annual IEEE/IFIP international conference on dependable systems and networks (DSN),* 51–58.

Taherdoost, H. (2021). Smart Contracts in Blockchain Technology: A Critical Review. *Information (Basel)*, *14*(2), 117. doi:10.3390/info14020117

Udokwu, C. (2018). *An Exploration of Blockchain Enabled Smart-contracts Application in the Enterprise.* Technical Report 2.2:36464.97287

Wang, S. (2018). An Overview of Smart Contract: Architecture, Applications, and Future Trends. *2018 IEEE Intelligent Vehicles Symposium (IV),* 108–113. 10.1109/IVS.2018.8500488

WrightA.FilippiP. D. (2015). Decentralized Blockchain Technology and the Rise of Lex Cryptographia. doi:10.2139/ssrn.2580664

Wust, K., & Gervais, A. (2018). Do You Need a Blockchain? *2018 Crypto Valley Conference on Blockchain Technology (CVCBT),* 45–54. 10.1109/CVCBT.2018.00011

Xu, X. (2017). A taxonomy of Blockchain-based Systems for Architecture Design. *2017 IEEE International Conference on Software Architecture (ICSA),* 243–252. 10.1109/ICSA.2017.33

Zheng, Z., Xie, S., Dai, H. N., Chen, X., & Wang, H. (2018). Blockchain Challenges and Opportunities: A Survey. *International Journal of Web and Grid Services, 14*(4), 352–375. doi:10.1504/IJWGS.2018.095647

# Chapter 9
# Cotton Health-Guard: AI-Enhanced Crop Health Assessment Through Image Classification

**Manohar Kapse**
https://orcid.org/0000-0002-1258-8599
*Symbiosis Centre for Management and Human Resource Development, Symbiosis International University, India*

**Vinod Sharma**
https://orcid.org/0000-0002-0815-8502
*Symbiosis Centre for Management and Human Resource Development, Symbiosis International University, India*

**Jeanne Poulose**
*School of Business and Management, Christ University, India*

**N. Elangovan**
https://orcid.org/0000-0002-4551-6081
*Christ University, India*

**Yogesh Mahajan**
*Symbiosis Centre for Management and Human Resource Development, Symbiosis International University, India*

## ABSTRACT

*Crop loss due to illness is the main issue that farmers deal with. The second issue is the delay in identifying which disorders to treat. Thus, the purpose of this study is to use the image classification technique to determine if the crop is healthy or sick. R software was used to implement picture categorization and machine learning techniques. The diseased leaf has been identified by the process of picture*

DOI: 10.4018/979-8-3693-1046-5.ch009

*classification. In order to accomplish this, images of both healthy and diseased cotton crops were gathered from the fields. According to the study, the support vector machine algorithm is more accurate than other machine learning algorithms, which makes it suitable for real-time disease diagnosis and categorization.*

## 1. INTRODUCTION

In recent times because of the decrease in the cost of hardware and the availability of high-processing computers, there has been tremendous growth in AI, Machine Learning, and Deep Learning techniques. AI and ML have been extensively used by corporations, industries, and even small firms to solve their problems and make decisions. There has been extensive use of AI and ML nowadays in agriculture as well (Sood et al., 2021). There has been extensive digitalization in India in every field after the COVID-19 pandemic. Agriculture is also not intact with it, the process of agricultural digitization can be grouped into two general fields, the biological and the mechanical (ETC Group, 2016). The initial use of technology was done by using GPS (Larsen et al., 1994), AI, ML, and IOT to manage and identification of farm animals, management of sheep and pigs in big farms done successfully (Fogarty et al., 2018; Halachmi et al., 2019). In India also use of technology is done for weather forecasting, identification of the best crop for a particular region, managing agricultural equipment, and so on. However, the cost of technology is a little bit higher for small farmers in India due to which they are not very popular and used by them. After COVID-19 people have found technology to be very user-friendly due to the excessive availability of smartphones and the Internet. If the technology is based on smartphones and the internet it will be accepted by the farmers in India.

## 2. PURPOSE OF THE STUDY

India is an agriculture-based economy, though the service sector is also contributing to thc growth of thc cconomy. In India, the major employment is provided by agriculture, nearly one-third of the population is employed in agriculture ("FAO in India," n.d). The contribution of the agriculture sector to the GDP is nearly 20% of the economy. Cotton (Gossypium hirsutum L.), popularly known as "white gold", is a natural fiber crop that is grown in India (Nikam et al., 2017).

As per (Cotton Manufacturing Companies, Cotton Manufacturers and Exporters in India, 2022; Cotton update, 2022) the production of cotton in India is 352.48 lakh bales for the year 2021 and estimated to be 340.62 lakh bales for the year 2022. As per the ICAC report, 37% of the world's cotton cultivation area is in India, making it the highest cotton-producing country (Cotton Corporation India Ltd, 2022). However, one of the problems the farmers are facing is the damage caused to the plants by insect pests, notably those caused by Helicoverpa armigera, commonly referred to as American Bollworm (Yadav & Goel, 2019). Nearly 40% of the pesticides used in India are only for the cotton crop (Mollaee et al., 2019; Training Manual on "Cultivation of Long Staple Cotton (ELS)," 2007). The basic purpose of this study is to create a model that can be used to identify the cotton crop's infection based on the image of the leaf. Using the image, we will be classifying whether the crop is infected or not. Using a drone and mobile camera, an image will be captured and fed into the model, which will inform the farmers how much is the infection in the plant and on the farm, based on it we can also suggest the pesticides required.

## 2.1. Cotton Production in India

In this paper, we are working on a problem faced by Indian farmers who are involved in cotton production in India. In India, cotton is one of the major cash crops grown(NFSM: National Food Security Mission, n.d.). It plays a dominant role in the industrial and agricultural economy of the country. Cotton is the basic raw material for the cotton textile industry. Cotton in India provides direct livelihood to nearly 6 million farmers and about 40 -50 million people are employed in the cotton trade and its processing directly and indirectly. Cotton is a kharif crop and is generally cultivated in early April-May in northern India and is delayed as we proceed down south. The major states where cotton is grown are Punjab, Haryana, Rajasthan, Uttar Pradesh, Madhya Pradesh, Gujarat, Maharashtra, and parts of Andhra Pradesh & Karnataka. Tarun Satsangi, AGM-Research, Origo e-Mandi, estimates cotton production for 2022-23 to increase by 8.5 percent percent to 34.2 million bales (ETMarkets, 2022).

As per the report published in the Economics Times, "Government agency Cotton Corporation of India (CCI), which carries out cotton procurement operations when prices fall below the minimum support price (MSP), has pegged India's 2022-23 cotton production higher by 15% to 360 lakh bales of 170 kilograms each. Prices of Indian cotton had increased from Rs 60,000 per candy (of 356 kilograms) in January 2022 to Rs 1,10,000 per candy by May 2022. Due to this, the area under cotton sowing has increased by 7% to 8%" (Bhosale Jayashree, 2022).

## 3. REVIEW OF LITERATURE

Before applying any classification algorithms, the image is processed so that machine learning algorithms can be applied (Russ, 1990). Image classification plays a major role in the detection of objects and analysis of images. There are a lot of techniques available for image classification now. Lots of studies have been conducted on satellite image classification techniques. However, deciding the best technique of all available techniques is not easy because of the dependency of accuracy on several factors (Kalra et al., 2013).

This research focuses on finding various algorithms to improve the efficiency of image classification. The image is soothingly done on noisy images. The noise represents the unexpected change in the pixel measures which are occurred during the image acquisition, the transformation of images, and the communication methodology. Image sharpening is the process of increasing the contrast along the edges where different colours coincide. This image sharpening process is used to increase the component of high frequency in the image. Findings showed that hard and soft classification models could get better results (Hu et al., 2014). The shadow effect of images is treated as noise and the removal of shadow noise is very much essential. The removal means nothing but the improvement in brightness or restoration of luminance of shadowed parts in the image. Results show that under contingency conditions by using the Shapley value approach, massive saving is done. (Khare et al., 2015). Many researchers used logistic regression for the classification of images using logistic regression. To estimate gender through morphometric landmark indices in facial image logistics regression (Verma et al., 2021), similarly, classification of edible bird's nest was also done using logistic regression. The validation result demonstrates that the model exhibits a high level of diagnostic accuracy in categorizing the EBN type, based on the mineral ratio (Ang et al., 2022).

To classify hyperspectral images different ML algorithms were used by researchers. The researchers also used Deep Neural Network (DNN), Gaussian Mixture Model (GMM), K Nearest Neighbour (KNN), and K Means (KM) classifiers. The results demonstrate that the SVM had superior performance compared to the other classification techniques (Okwuashi & Ndehedehe, 2020), for breast image classification also support vector machine, and KNN was used by researchers such as (Ding et al., 2015; Lo & Wang, 2012) in their research work. For brain tumor detection, using images and SVM were used. The comparative results indicate that while the difference between the performance metrics is minimal, SVM demonstrates higher precision and lower error rates (Chandra et al., n.d.). Even researchers have used decision trees for image classification (Fakhari & Moghadam, 2013; Jajodia et al., 2020; Yang et al., 2003). To estimate deforestation naïve, the Bayes classifier was also used by researchers (Ramesh Kumar & Vijaya, 2022; Zhang et al., 2015). Author Knecht et al. gave an open-source platform, Image Harvest high-throughput plant image processing, and analysis, and has been widely for image classification, they used Python libraries for developing the platform (Knecht et al., 2016). Recently many researchers have been working on using images for classification.

Images of scan sonar, multibeam, remotely operated vehicles using SVM, and speeded-up Robust Features were also used. The performance assessment of both the training and testing datasets yielded superior results (Raj & Murugan, 2019). Even in medical fields images are analyzed using ML techniques (Perez-Careta et al., 2022), for mammograms and during the coronavirus pandemic for various purposes (Bhattacharya et al., 2021; Lehman et al., 2015).

Though there is a lot of work done in image classification for classification and prediction using various tools, techniques, and algorithms in various domains, still very little work is done in the agriculture domain that also for classification (El Amraoui et al., 2022; Nesteruk et al., 2021). In this research paper, we are working on classification in the agricultural domain with a single crop for the detection of pests using leaf images.

## 4. RESEARCH METHODOLOGY

The objective of the study is to find a machine-learning algorithm that can detect infected and healthy plants. For the study, we are considering the cotton plant leaves to detect the infection of pests in the crop. The study focuses on the identification of infection of pests in a crop, which is a major cause of loss to farmers in India. If the infection is detected at an early stage, it can help in decreasing the loss that will be caused by the pest in the plant. The early detection of infection will help in early treatment and less use of pesticides, which in turn help in saving the environment.

### 4.1. Research Design

For the study CRISP-DM methodology which stands for the cross-industry standard process for data mining is applied, which is widely used in the industry for data mining (Chapman et al., 2000; Martínez-Plumed et al., 2021).

#### 4.1.1. Business Understanding

Business understanding is more of what to accomplish from a business perspective. The ultimate aim of this stage is to find out the important factors that might affect the outcome (Schröer et al., 2021). The primary objective is to detect the infected and healthy leaves, which in turn will be used to identify the level of infection in the cotton plant and the farm.

*Figure 1. Infected leaves and healthy leaves (as per data collected by the researcher)*

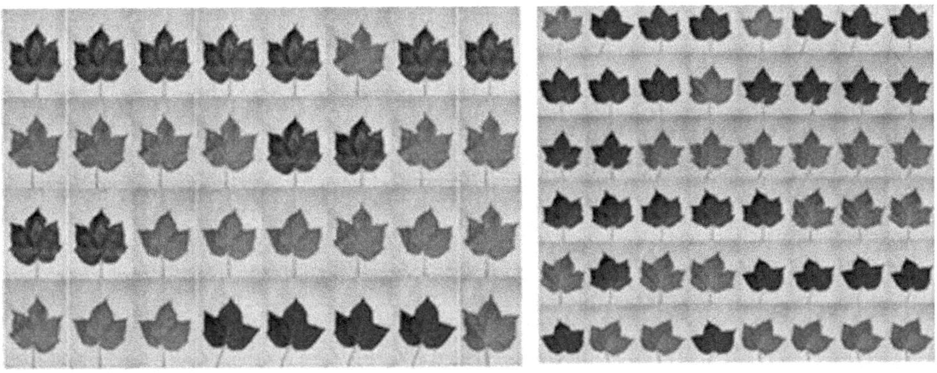

### 4.1.2. Data Collection

For the study, we are considering images of cotton plant leaves as the study's data. We collected fresh leaves from the farm that were infected by the pests and also from those plants that were healthy and not infected by pests. The images are taken with a white background. The images are then divided into two groups, group 1 as infected and Group 2 as healthy. The study is conducted during August and September 2022, since the cotton crop is being shown during this period in India. For the study, we collected 16 infected leaves and 48 healthy leaves. Due to the limitation of computation resources, a small sample size was considered for the study.

### 4.1.3. Data Analysis Tools

Now for image analysis lot of software and data analysis tools are used such as R, Python, Azure, and so on. For the present study, we are using R programming software for data analysis. The packages which are used for the analysis are imager, dplyr (Wickham et al., 2018), caret (Kuhn, 2021), tidyr (Wickham & Girlich, n.d.), and so on. We will be using logistic regression, k-nearest neighbor, support vector machine, and neural network algorithms for the classification of the infected and healthy leaves in this study.

### 4.1.4. Describe Data

Examining the properties of the dataset of the paper is a data description, which includes the format, quantity, identities, etc. The dataset gathered for the paper consists of images of cotton leaves. The sample images for both infected and healthy leaves are collected and given in Figure 1.

## 4.2. Data Preparation

The third phase of CRISP-DM methodology is where the dataset is finalized with all of the preprocessing steps which include the sub-stages as shown below:

### 4.2.1. Data Selection

The images of leaves are taken and created in two folders in the local system where one folder has infected images, and the other folder has healthy ones.

### 4.2.2. Converting Images to the Data Point

The images need to be converted to pixel data for applying the ML algorithms, where the pixel is the smallest unit of a digital image or graphic that can be displayed and represented on a digital display device (Hayes, 1999). The images are also labeled as infected and healthy. For converting the images to data points that are pixels, we first converted them to grey images. The colored image has been converted to a grey image using the code grey scale from the imager package. Since all the images are of different sizes, they all are resized to 100*100 pixels using the code resize from the imager package. The images are converted to 100*100 pixels, here the gray image pixel value is what color it has, the pixel value is 0 for black and as it becomes brighter the magnitude increases to 1. These numbers are converted to numbers from 0 to 1 for all the images. A database is created with a variable id which is the pixel number, group1 which is infected and healthy, which is the image file name, and v is the value of the pixel which ranges from 0 to 1. Now we have a data set with the dependent variable as group 1 which has two categories infected and healthy image. The independent variable will be the 100*100-pixel points, which are converted to 10,000 variables. The data set created is used for modeling. The models that are applied are binary logistic regression, K-nearest neighbor, and Support vector machine.

## 4.3. Modeling

There are hundreds of models which are available in machine learning for classification. The common model which is used for classification is binary logistic regression, K-nearest neighbour, and Support vector machine. Logistic Regression is a classification modeling technique used when the dependent variable is categorical and the independent variable is either categorical or a scale or a combination of both (Cramer, 2002; O'Fallon et al., 1983). The dependent variable in this paper is the Target variable group1. Logistic regression has various types out of which we used "Binomial Logistic Regression" because the output variable has two possible outcomes. One of the very popular models popularly known as KNN is used for classification in Machine Learning. It can be used for both regression and also for classification (Cover & Hart, 1967). It is widely used by researchers in their studies for classification as well as regression. Support Vector Machine (Maldonado & Weber, 2009; Qu et al., 2010; Sun et al., 2014) is a supervised machine learning algorithm that can be used for both classification or regression challenges and is widely used for classification. In the SVM algorithm, we plot each data item as a point in n-dimensional space (where n is the number of features you have) with the value of each feature being the value of a particular coordinate. Then, we perform classification by finding the hyper-plane that differentiates the two classes very well. From the r software using the caret package the accuracy of the model was calculated using linear, polynomial, and sigmoid kernel.

Naïve Bayes is a classification technique based on Bayes' Theorem with an assumption of independence among predictors. In simple terms, a Naive Bayes classifier assumes that the presence of a particular feature in a class is unrelated to the presence of any other feature. The naive Bayes model is easy to build and particularly useful for very large data sets. Along with simplicity, Naive Bayes is known to outperform even highly sophisticated classification methods. A decision tree is a graphical representation of a decision-making process that uses a tree-like model of decisions and their possible consequences, including chance event outcomes, resource costs, and utility (Breiman et al., 1984; Quinlan, 1986).

After the application of algorithms, it is found that most of the algorithms have high accuracy of classification. The algorithms which were used are binary logistic regression, k-nearest neighbor, support vector machine, decision tree, and naïve Bayes classification algorithms. Table 1 gives a comparative accuracy table for all the algorithms applied.

From the accuracy table, it is clear that the support vector machine is one of the best classifiers for classifying images of infected and healthy leaves. The accuracy of the SVM- linear kernel was 0.9882, followed by SVM- Polynomial Kernel with 0.9765, logistics with 0.9529, and decision tree with 0.9529. The lowest accuracy was received from k-nearest with 0.9294 and the naïve Bayes classifier with 0.9176. From the analysis, it is also found that most of the sensitivity and specificity were also high, which makes the classifier appropriate for classification.

*Table 1. Comparative accuracy of algorithms*

| | Logistics Regression | K-Nearest Neighbor | SVM-Linear Kernel | SVM-Polynomial Kernel | SVM-Sigmoid Kernel | Naïve Bayes | Decision Tree |
|---|---|---|---|---|---|---|---|
| Accuracy | 0.9529 | 0.9294 | 0.9882 | 0.9765 | 0.9412 | 0.9176 | 0.9529 |
| 95% Confidence Interval | (0.8839, 0.987) | (0.8827, 0.9737) | (0.9362, 0.9997) | (0.9176, 0.9971) | (0.8680, 0.9806) | (0.8377, 0.9662) | (0.8839, 0.9870) |
| No Information Rate | 0.5765 | 0.5765 | 0.5765 | 0.5765 | 0.5765 | 0.5765 | 0.5765 |
| P-Value | 0.000 | 0.000 | 0.000 | 0.000 | 0.000 | 0.000 | 0.000 |
| Kappa | 0.9043 | 0.8586 | 0.976 | 0.9522 | 0.88 | 0.8307 | 0.905 |
| McNamar's Test P-Value | 0.6171 | 0.04123 | 1 | 0.4795 | 1 | 1 | 0.1336 |
| Sensitivity | 0.9722 | 1 | 1 | 1 | 0.9444 | 0.8889 | 1 |
| Specificity | 0.9388 | 0.8776 | 0.9796 | 0.9592 | 0.9388 | 0.9388 | 0.9184 |
| Positive Predicted Value | 0.9211 | 0.8571 | 0.973 | 0.9474 | 0.9189 | 0.9143 | 0.9 |
| Negative Predicted Value | 0.9787 | 1 | 1 | 1 | 0.9583 | 0.92 | 1 |
| Prevalence | 0.4235 | 0.4235 | 0.4235 | 0.4235 | 0.4235 | 0.4235 | 0.4235 |
| Detection Rate | 0.4118 | 0.4235 | 0.4235 | 0.4235 | 0.4 | 0.3765 | 0.4235 |
| Detection Prevalence | 0.4471 | 0.4941 | 0.4353 | 0.4471 | 0.4353 | 0.4118 | 0.4706 |
| Balanced Accuracy | 0.9555 | 0.9388 | 0.9898 | 0.9796 | 0.9416 | 0.9138 | 0.9592 |

## 5. FINDINGS

After the application of algorithms, it is found that most of the algorithms have high accuracy of classification. The algorithms which were used are binary logistic regression, k-nearest neighbour, support vector machine, decision tree, and naïve Bayes classification algorithms. This is in line with the past literature (See (Chandra et al., n.d.) Table 1 gives a comparative accuracy table for all the algorithms applied.

From the accuracy table, it is clear that the support vector machine is one of the best classifiers for classifying images of infected and healthy leaves. The high accuracy obtained with the SVM validates its efficacy as a state-of-the-art algorithm for hyperspectral image classification (Okwuashi & Ndehedehe, 2020). The accuracy of the SVM- linear kernel was 0.9882, followed by SVM- Polynomial Kernel with 0.9765, logistics with 0.9529, and decision tree with 0.9529. The lowest accuracy was received from k-nearest with 0.9294 and the naïve Bayes classifier with 0.9176 (Ramesh Kumar & Vijaya, 2022). From the analysis, it is also found that most of the sensitivity and specificity were also high, which makes the classifier appropriate for classification.

From the classification algorithms, it is clear that a Support vector machine can be applied for the classification of infected and healthy leaves of cotton crops (Jenifa et al., 2019). Farmers can send the images of the leaves randomly collected from their farms through their mobile by emailing it, WhatsApp, or any other source. From where it will be saved on a system and then the algorithms will be applied which will give the number of leaves infected and healthy based on this result, we will be able to tell the extent of infection in the farm and also the amount of pesticide required.

## 6. CONCLUSION

We can use machine learning algorithms for image classification, which has been used earlier by many researchers in their work to detect objects, images, and many other things. Using various machine learning algorithms such as logistic regression, support vector machine, naïve Bayes, and decision tree we can classify images into infected or not infected (Okwuashi & Ndehedehe, 2020). The suggested program utilizes automated snapshots of the crops at each step, analyzing them early to identify any defects, hence preventing any financial and product losses for the farmer (Patil & Szambre, 2014). A system can be created where the farmers can send the images via any media using their smartphone to the concerned person who will apply the algorithms and will give the result to the farmers, even an app or a webpage can be developed where the farmers will upload the image of the leaves and will get the results instantly. Using the output of this research we can help the farmers to identify the pests' infection in the cotton plant by the image of the leaves (Usha Kumari et al., 2019). The images can be taken from the farm directly using a smartphone or drones for a larger farm and based on the image analysis we can detect the extent of infection caused to the crop. We can even calculate the number of pesticides required on the farm per acre.

### 6.1. Suggestions for Areas of Improvement and Future Research

This study is on classification based on image, nowadays there has been tremendous growth in the technology. Every now a day new and advanced algorithms are coming up. Even there are new and free resources that can be easily integrated with mobile and apps can also be developed, though some cost is also required for the same. This study is limited to a few of the classification algorithms only because of the limitation of training the algorithms using GPUs. More training can be done using Google Colab or Microsoft-azure or using paid services for using high computing facilities. More classification algorithms such as neural networks can also be used for classification in the future.

Since there are lots of varieties of cotton, grown across India with different climatic and soil conditions, which causes different types of pest infection in the plant. There is an infection in the plant at every stage of the plant growth, starting from the seed growth till it gives the fruits. Some infections are caused by the seeds, stems, leaves, and later on the fruits. In this study, we are limiting pest infection in the leaves only.

## 7. Limitations of the Study

Since there are lots of varieties of cotton, grown across India with different climatic and soil conditions, which causes different types of pest infection in the plant. There is an infection in the plant at every stage of the plant growth, starting from the seed growth till it gives the fruits. Some infections are caused by the seeds, stems, leaves, and later on the fruits. In this study, we are limiting pest infection to the leaves only.

## REFERENCES

Ang, K.-M., Seow, E.-K., Fam, P.-S., & Cheng, L.-H. (2022). Classification of edible bird's nest samples using a logistic regression model through the mineral ratio approach. *Food Control*, *137*, 108921. doi:10.1016/j.foodcont.2022.108921

Bhattacharya, S., Maddikunta, P. K. R., Pham, Q.-V., Gadekallu, T. R., Krishnan, S. S. R., Chowdhary, C. L., Alazab, M., & Piran, M. (2021). Deep learning and medical image processing for coronavirus (COVID-19) pandemic: A survey. *Sustainable Cities and Society*, *65*, 102589. Advance online publication. doi:10.1016/j.scs.2020.102589 PMID:33169099

Bhosale Jayashree. (2022, September 19). *Cotton production: India's cotton production to increase by 15% in 2022-23 - The Economic Times*. https://economictimes.indiatimes.com/news/economy/agriculture/indias-cotton-production-to-increase-by-15-in-2022-23/articleshow/94288018.cms

Breiman, L., Friedman, J., Stone, C. J., & Olshen, R. A. (1984). *Classification and Regression Trees*. CRC Press.

Chandra, S., Bhat, R., Singh, H., & Chauhan, D. S. (n.d.). Detection of brain tumors from MRI using gaussian RBF kernel-based support vector machine. *IJACT*, *1*(1), 46–51.

Chapman, P., Clinton, J., Kerber, R., Khabaza, T., Reinartz, T., Shearer, C., & Wirth, R. (2000). *CRISP-DM 1.0 step-by-step data mining guide*. Academic Press.

Cotton Corporation India Ltd. (2022). *National Cotton Scenario*. https://cotcorp.org.in/national_cotton.aspx

*Cotton Manufacturing Companies, Cotton Manufacturers and Exporters in India*. (2022). India Brand Equity Foundation. https://www.ibef.org/exports/cotton-industry-india

*Cotton update*. (2022). International Cotton Advisory Committee; International cotton advisory committee. https://icac.org/Content/PublicationsPdfFiles/35f65863_c1fa_48c6_8570_cb3ca9225152/CU_2022_05_19.pdf.pdf

Cover, T., & Hart, P. (1967). Nearest neighbor pattern classification. *IEEE Transactions on Information Theory*, *13*(1), 21–27. doi:10.1109/TIT.1967.1053964

CramerJ. S. (2002). *The Origins of Logistic Regression*. doi:10.2139/ssrn.360300

Ding, J., Cheng, H. D., Xian, M., Zhang, Y., & Xu, F. (2015). Local-weighted Citation-kNN algorithm for breast ultrasound image classification. *Optik (Stuttgart)*, *126*(24), 5188–5193. doi:10.1016/j.ijleo.2015.09.231

El Amraoui, K., Ezzaki, A., Masmoudi, L., Hadri, M., El Belrhiti, H., El Ansari, M., & Amari, A. (2022). Machine learning algorithm for Avocado image segmentation based on quantum enhancement and Random Forest. In B. Benhala, K. Mansouri, A. Raihani, & M. Qbadou (Eds.), *2022 2nd international conference on innovative research in applied science, engineering and technology (iraset'2022)* (pp. 149–155). 10.1109/IRASET52964.2022.9738360

ETMarkets. (2022, September 24). *Kharif production: Origo Commodities' estimate suggests a drop in kharif production - The Economic Times*. https://economictimes.indiatimes.com/markets/commodities/news/origo-commodities-estimate-suggests-a-drop-in-kharif-production/articleshow/94413715.cms

Fakhari, A., & Moghadam, A. M. E. (2013). Combination of classification and regression in decision tree for multi-labeling image annotation and retrieval. *Applied Soft Computing*, *13*(2), 1292–1302. doi:10.1016/j.asoc.2012.10.019

FAO in India. (n.d.). *India at a Glance | FAO in India | Food and Agriculture Organization of the United Nations*. Food and Agriculture Organization of the United Nations.

Fogarty, E. S., Swain, D. L., Cronin, G., & Trotter, M. (2018). Autonomous on-animal sensors in sheep research: A systematic review. *Computers and Electronics in Agriculture*, *150*, 245–256. doi:10.1016/j.compag.2018.04.017

Group, E. T. C. (2016). *Software vs. hardware vs. nowhere*. ETCGroup.org. https://www.etcgroup.org/sites/www.etcgroup.org/files/files/software_vs._hardware_vs._nowhere_-_briefing_dec_2016.pdf

Halachmi, I., Guarino, M., Bewley, J., & Pastell, M. (2019). Smart animal agriculture: Application of real-time sensors to improve animal well-being and production. *Annual Review of Animal Biosciences*, *7*(1), 403–425. doi:10.1146/annurev-animal-020518-114851 PMID:30485756

Hayes, B. (1999). Computing Science Seeing Between the Pixels. *American Scientist*, *87*(3), 202–207. doi:10.1511/1999.24.202

Hu, T., Wu, W., & Liu, L. (2014). Combination of hard and soft classification method based on adaptive threshold. *2014 IEEE Geoscience and Remote Sensing Symposium*, 4180–4183. 10.1109/IGARSS.2014.6947409

Jajodia, A., Amrith, B., Madhukar, A., Chaturvedi, A., Mehta, A., Kapur, R., Dewan, A., Agarwal, M., Mahwar, V., Yadav, V., Pasricha, S., & Koyyala, V. P. B. (2020). 286P Improved diagnostic accuracy on MR imaging in post-surgical recurrent head and neck SCC lesions using decision tree classification system. *Annals of Oncology : Official Journal of the European Society for Medical Oncology*, *31*, S1353. doi:10.1016/j.annonc.2020.10.280

Jenifa, A., Ramalakshmi, R., & Ramachandran, V. (2019, April 1). Classification of Cotton Leaf Disease Using Multi-Support Vector Machine. *IEEE International Conference on Intelligent Techniques in Control, Optimization and Signal Processing, INCOS 2019*. 10.1109/INCOS45849.2019.8951356

Kalra, K., Kumar Goswami, A., & Gupta, R. (2013). A Comparative Study of Supervised Image Classification Algorithms for Satellite Images. *International Journal of Electronics*, *1*(10), 2320–2084.

Khare, S., Khan, B., & Agnihotri, G. (2015). A Shapley value approach for transmission usage cost allocation under contingent restructured market. *2015 1st International Conference on Futuristic Trends in Computational Analysis and Knowledge Management, ABLAZE 2015*, 170–173. 10.1109/ABLAZE.2015.7154987

Knecht, A. C., Campbell, M. T., Caprez, A., Swanson, D. R., & Walia, H. (2016). Image Harvest: An open-source platform for high-throughput plant image processing and analysis. *Journal of Experimental Botany*, *67*(11), 3587–3599. doi:10.1093/jxb/erw176 PMID:27141917

Kuhn, M. (2021). *CARET: Classification and Regression Training*. https://cran.r-project.org/package=caret

Larsen, W., Nielsen, G., & Tyler, D. (1994). Precision navigation with GPS. *Computers and Electronics in Agriculture*, *11*(1), 85–95. doi:10.1016/0168-1699(94)90054-X

Lehman, C. D., Wellman, R. D., Buist, D. S. M., Kerlikowske, K., Tosteson, A. N. A., Miglioretti, D. L., & Surveillance, B. C. (2015). Diagnostic Accuracy of Digital Screening Mammography with and Without Computer-Aided Detection. *JAMA Internal Medicine*, *175*(11), 1828–1837. doi:10.1001/jamainternmed.2015.5231 PMID:26414882

Leisch, D. M. (2021). *e1071: Misc Functions of the Department of Statistics, Probability Theory Group (Formerly: E1071)*. TU Wien.

Lo, C.-S., & Wang, C.-M. (2012). Support vector machine for breast MR image classification. *Computers & Mathematics with Applications (Oxford, England)*, *64*(5), 1153–1162. doi:10.1016/j.camwa.2012.03.033

Maldonado, S., & Weber, R. (2009). A Wrapper Method for Feature Selection Using Support Vector Machines. *Information Sciences*, *179*(13), 2208–2217. doi:10.1016/j.ins.2009.02.014

Martínez-Plumed, F., Contreras-Ochando, L., Ferri, C., Hernández-Orallo, J., Kull, M., Lachiche, N., Ramírez-Quintana, M. J., & Flach, P. (2021). CRISP-DM Twenty Years Later: From Data Mining Processes to Data Science Trajectories. *IEEE Transactions on Knowledge and Data Engineering*, *33*(8), 3048–3061. doi:10.1109/TKDE.2019.2962680

Mollaee, M., Mobli, A., Mutti, N. K., Manalil, S., & Chauhan, B. S. (2019). Challenges and Opportunities in Cotton Production. In *Cotton Production* (pp. 371–390). John Wiley & Sons, Ltd. doi:10.1002/9781119385523.ch18

Nesteruk, S., Shadrin, D., Pukalchik, M., Somov, A., Zeidler, C., Zabel, P., & Schubert, D. (2021). Image Compression and Plants Classification Using Machine Learning in Controlled-Environment Agriculture: Antarctic Station Use Case. *IEEE Sensors Journal*, *21*(16), 17564–17572. doi:10.1109/JSEN.2021.3050084

NFSM: National Food Security Mission. (n.d.). *Brief Note on Cotton*. Retrieved September 28, 2022, from https://www.nfsm.gov.in/

Nikam, T. A., Latpate, C. B., Ramesh, K. B., & Thakare, V. S. (2017). Efficacy of conventional and newer insecticides against leafhopper, Amarasca biguttula biguttula (Ishada) in Bt cotton under high density planting system. *Bull Environ Pharmacol Life Sci*, *6*(2), 274–281.

O'Fallon, J. R., Cormack, R. M., & Bithell, J. F. (1983). Obituaries. *Biometrics*, *39*(4), 1107–1111.

Okwuashi, O., & Ndehedehe, C. E. (2020). Deep support vector machine for hyperspectral image classification. *Pattern Recognition*, *103*, 107298. doi:10.1016/j.patcog.2020.107298

Patil, S. P., & SZambre, R. (2014). Classification of Cotton Leaf Spot Disease Using Support Vector Machine. In *Journal of Engineering Research and Applications* (Vol. 4, Issue 5). www.ijera.com

Perez-Careta, E., Guzman-Sepulveda, J.-R., Lozano-Garcia, J.-M., Torres-Cisneros, M., & Guzman-Cabrera, R. (2022). Classification of medical images using machine learning. *Dyna (Bilbao)*, *97*(1), 35–38. doi:10.6036/10117

Qu, Z., Feng, H., Zeng, Z., Zhuge, J., & Jin, S. (2010). A SVM-based pipeline leakage detection and pre-warning system. *Measurement*, *43*(4), 513–519. doi:10.1016/j.measurement.2009.12.022

Quinlan, J. R. (1986). Induction of Decision Trees. *Machine Learning*, *1*(1), 81–106. doi:10.1007/BF00116251

Raj, M. V., & Murugan, S. S. (2019). Underwater Image Classification using Machine Learning Technique. In P. R. S. Pillai, M. H. Supriya, & A. A. Balakrishnan (Eds.), *Proceedings of the 2019 international symposium on ocean technology (sympol 2019)* (pp. 166–173). IEEE. doi:10.1109/SYMPOL48207.2019.9005299

Ramesh Kumar, P., & Vijaya, A. (2022). Naïve Bayes machine learning model for image classification to assess the level of deformation of thin components. *Materials Today: Proceedings*. https://doi.org/https://doi.org/10.1016/j.matpr.2022.08.489

Russ, J. C. (1990). Image Processing. In Computer-Assisted Microscopy: The Measurement and Analysis of Images (pp. 33–69). Springer US. doi:10.1007/978-1-4613-0563-7_3

Schröer, C., Kruse, F., & Gómez, J. M. (2021). A Systematic Literature Review on Applying CRISP-DM Process Model. *Procedia Computer Science, 181*, 526–534. doi:10.1016/j.procs.2021.01.199

Sood, A., Sharma, R. K., & Bhardwaj, A. K. (2021). Artificial intelligence research in agriculture: a review. *Online Information Review*. doi:10.1108/OIR-10-2020-0448

Sun, J., Xiao, Q., Wen, J., & Wang, F. (2014). Natural gas pipeline small leakage feature extraction and recognition based on LMD envelope spectrum entropy and SVM. *Measurement, 55*, 434–443. doi:10.1016/j.measurement.2014.05.012

*Training Manual on "Cultivation of Long Staple Cotton (ELS)."* (2007). Central Institute for Cotton Research, Regional Station, Coimbatore.

Usha Kumari, C., Arun Vignesh, N., Panigrahy, A. K., Ramya, L., & Padma, T. (2019). Fungal disease in cotton leaf detection and classification using neural networks and support vector machine. *International Journal of Innovative Technology and Exploring Engineering*, *8*(10), 3664–3667. doi:10.35940/ijitee.J9648.0881019

Verma, R., Bhardwaj, N., Singh, P. D., Bhavsar, A., & Sharma, V. (2021). Estimation of sex through morphometric landmark indices in facial images with strength of evidence in logistic regression analysis. *Forensic Science International. Reports, 4*, 100226. doi:10.1016/j.fsir.2021.100226

Wickham, H., François, R., Henry, L., & Müller, K. (2018). *DPLYR: A Grammar of Data Manipulation.* Academic Press.

Wickham, H., & Girlich, M. (n.d.). *TIDYR: Tidy Messy Data. R package version 1.2.0.* Academic Press.

Yadav, R. D., & Goel, R. (2019). Problems of Cotton Farmers in Haryana. *Int. J. Curr. Microbiol. App. Sci* (Vol. 8, Issue 03, pp. 2139–2142). https://doi.org/https://doi.org/10.1016/S0308-521X(02)00051-3

Zhang, X., Hao, S., Xu, C., Qian, X., Wang, M., & Jiang, J. (2015). Image classification based on low-rank matrix recovery and Naive Bayes collaborative representation. *Neurocomputing, 169*, 110–118. doi:10.1016/j.neucom.2015.01.085

# Chapter 10
# The Role of Social Media Presence, Technology, and Personalization in Increasing Sales and Achieving Sustainable Business Growth


**Lilian Shmait**
*University of Balamand, Lebanon*

**Christine Ghassan Haidar**
*University of Balamand, Lebanon*

**Lea Hamati**
*University of Balamand, Lebanon*

**Sana Nasr**
*University of Balamand, Lebanon*

**Barbara Remlaoui**
*University of Balamand, Lebanon*

**Rita Nasr**
*University of Balamand, Lebanon*

**Nour Khalil**
*University of Balamand, Lebanon*

**Sam El Nemar**
*University of Balamand, Lebanon*



## ABSTRACT

*While most businesses are now aware of the importance of focusing their marketing efforts on online advertising, many still struggle to effectively target their audience and convert online users to loyal customers. Nowadays, one of the main challenges faced by businesses is achieving sustainable growth and making profit in the long run while meeting the constantly changing demands of customers. Taking into consideration the psychology of consumer behaviour, the marketing strategies implemented, and the external factors that influence individuals, a comprehensive understanding of all those factors combined is necessary to plan and execute well-defined strategies for marketing professionals to follow. For that reason, a conceptual framework was*


DOI: 10.4018/979-8-3693-1046-5.ch010

*designed to display all elements that contribute to increasing sales and achieving sustainable business growth by utilizing social media and technology strategically. Those factors were grouped into four main themes that cover effective marketing strategies, good customer relationships, personalization, and data collection.*

## GENERAL OVERVIEW

With 4-5 billion people viewing others' content on their phones most of the day, we can expect to see the extent to which their behaviour, thoughts and actions are influenced by social media. Online reviews and ratings, brand products and services, e-commerce stores and others are all accessible to the public. When it comes to regular users, a new opportunity of connecting with others and exchanging information on any topic has been created. Businesses, on the other hand, benefit from collecting data and analysing algorithms to improve their presence, selling their products, and engaging more efficiently with their customers and building long-lasting relationships. Many themes such as customer satisfaction, value creation, customer relationships, brand awareness and acquiring new customers are taking a new shape in the presence of social media (Dwivedi et al., 2021). So, measuring those criteria is important to get a clearer understanding on how social media functions and ways to benefit from it. For instance, measuring the growth of followers on the long term, the increase in brand mentions within a specific timeframe, and the change in engagement rate on different content types are some of many metrics used by marketing professionals (Infante & Mardikaningsih, 2022). With so much information available on it, social media has become a very "useful" tool for both parties involved in the buying and selling of products, which has made it a key factor that determines businesses' overall performance (Chatterjee et al., 2021).

Ideally, from a business perspective, businesses plan to leverage data collected from social media to understand and accordingly modify the purchase behaviour of consumers – now and in the future. Keeping in mind that a main driving force that shapes a consumer's opinion is the external environment: including social pressures and technological advancements, businesses aim to be one of the influencing factors triggering favourable behaviour from customers. As Mark Twain says: "The average man is not interested in contriving an opinion of his own, by study and reflection, but is only anxious to find out what his neighbour's opinion is and slavishly adopt it." For that purpose and to achieve sustainable growth, businesses must take advantage of various media channels to build their brands, improve consumer knowledge about their products, improve their practices, and invest in media literacy programs to encourage informed purchases (Chatterjee et al., 2021; Cai, 2020). Not only that, they should also do this continuously, in a studied and well-planned manner to ensure consistency, efficiency, and long-term viability. By collecting current data on demographics, search history, and brand interests/dislikes on a large audience, they can expect patterns of purchase in the future and plan on how to influence accordingly.

Based on the theory of Elaboration Likelihood Model (ELM), the more relevant a message is to a potential customer receiving it, the more likely they are to exert thoughtful effort in considering it. Therefore, it is important that businesses use the data available to meet those expectations by tailoring advertisements to fit their personal preferences. By doing so, they create a sense of familiarity and relevance with the customer which can possibly lead to a stronger bond that lasts longer. In media analytics terms, the more personalized the messages are, the higher the click-through rates, profile visits, followers, and online total purchases. Considering numbers were not promising from the start, having a marketing strategy that is customer-centric in place will still hold more value as it guides professionals and helps them point out necessary modifications (Constantinescu et al., 2019). Regularly reflecting on social media processes is very important on the long-term to guarantee satisfied customers, profit generation, and business continuity in the market. With no doubt, this is made easier with the advent of technological advancements, the ease of access to resources and skilled personnel, and the sharing of knowledge. However, companies' understanding of the importance of social media is still missing the know-how to effectively leveraging it to achieve sustainable business models (Constantinescu et al., 2019).

## PURPOSE

Seeing the increased dependency on digital presence, this study explores how businesses currently utilize social media and how they can leverage technology to choose business models and plan their marketing strategies to promote a sustainable brand and achieve sales on the long-term. It highlights the emergence of new tools and software that support businesses in analysing current customer behaviour and making informed decisions on future outreach strategies. It also explores must-have elements that impact consumers' buying behaviour now and in the future: knowledge on available products, personalization, customer relationships, and effective marketing strategies. Acknowledging that some businesses might find it challenging to implement sustainable practices, this article explains how a sustainable approach to marketing operations specifically optimizes social media performance, positively impacts business profit, and promises long-term business growth.

## IMPORTANCE

Since social media influences the decision-making process of consumers nowadays, it is crucial that businesses understand how consumers interact with this technology to set a strategy that places them under the "positive decision outcome". Integrating social media and all its competitive features in marketing practices will restructure the shopping experience for both business and consumers. However, it is insufficient to implement a practice without building an all-inclusive marketing strategy with a clear vision on the audience it will target, how it will target different customer segments, and what metrics will be used to measure success (increased market share, higher sales, business profit, etc). The strategy building process should be aligned with the business's goals and objectives. The more they complement each other, the more likely the business is to achieve those goals. Additionally, orienting objectives towards a sustainable approach is even more rewarding because it sheds the light on the responsible practices a business applies while seeking profit. This approach is more likely to resonate with customers as it has higher chances to represent their values and promises them a safer option to consider when purchasing. Sharing this brand message fosters long-term loyalty with any potentially interested individual as it differentiates it from other competing business. By attracting a wider customer base who value sustainably, businesses increase their chances of succeeding in meeting their financial and sustainable marketing objectives. Therefore, this article will highlight the practices required to guide businesses through the process of creating sustainable value to achieve long-term business growth.

## CONTRIBUTION

First and foremost, the content of this article helps businesses understand how crucial it is to streamline marketing practices and plan ahead before executing to ensure effective outcomes. It brings forward multiple recommendations that can be adopted while creating a marketing strategy for the purpose of reaching a larger audience that is more likely to convert. The approach suggested in this article also aims to shed the light on the difference it makes when considering sustainability in creating a positive brand image, attracting new customers, and maintaining long-lasting relationships. Also, it encourages businesses to use this approach while engaging with their audience by integrating it as a focal point in their business goals and marketing strategy. The article includes best practices and emerging trends on effective social media features that can be used to complement a sustainable marketing strategy that aligns with both consumers' needs and business goals. This will help raise awareness on the importance of setting smart prospective strategies and prove to what extent their implementation influences sales and growth rates of businesses.

## LITERATURE REVIEW

### Introduction

The impact of social media on consumers' behavior and the effectiveness of personalization as a marketing strategy have witnessed high interest in recent years. Personalizing product advertisements and client outreach has led to great improvements in business performance; for instance, increase in consumers' happiness and loyalty and higher possibility of purchase, due to the generation of more accurate customer data (Gupta & Joshi, 2022; Alzoubi et al., 2022; Leung et al., 2022). Many tools ranging from artificial intelligence and machine learning to social media platforms have been involved in collecting and processing market information, from gathering clients' needs, creating specific marketing plans that feed into these needs, to collecting data reports that are later analyzed and shared with many companies (N. Sadeq et al., 2023; Li & Huang, 2017). AI helps recognize patterns using modern statistical methods and chunks of data, suggesting more accurate customer approaches that are more likely to generate desired outcomes (El Samad et al., 2023). The good thing is, the introduction of a personalized customer-based approach taps into the personal and specific tastes of the target audience. This led to companies making more customer happy, achieving higher sales, and consequently making more profit.

Studying consumers and how they make decisions is a crucial step to target more clients and widen a firm's customer base. Even in the presence of technology, it is still necessary to brainstorm what would encourage the audience to connect with a particular brand and prefer it over any other. There are various personal elements that impact a person's purchase choice, e.g their mental and emotional state (Islam et al., 2023). Also, external factors play a crucial role, the social influence and accessibility to information from different sources (Weismueller et al., 2020). The ability to influence is no longer restricted to friends and family but has expanded to include online reviews and recommendations. As for information accessibility, the more data available about a product, the more likely a consumer will approach it positively (Hoegl & Cordery, 2015). In the case of businesses, it is quite similar. Social media has affected attitudes and intentions of consumers towards advertisements and product purchase. A company's presence online plays a huge role on the clients' purchase decisions. How a company presents itself, its brand and products, how it interacts with people, what values it has, etc. are all factors that either encourage or discourage an online user to approach it. Now, a "participatory culture" is created, stressing on the ability users have to share information and opinions on a variety of offerings trusted as real and honest information provided by company representatives (Ashman et al., 2015). This only proves how impactful social media is and to what extent it can shape a business' image or reputation on the long-term.

Building brand recognition and leaving a positive impression are some of the strategies in which a brand can utilize social media to achieve higher revenues. Social media presence now allows audience outreach on a larger scale by creating engaging content and providing incentives such as coupons and promotions (Aji et al., 2020). By showing the authenticity of the brand – sharing user-generated information, such as customer reviews and images, and collaborating with influential figures, they build a relationship of trust with their customers (Bolton et al., 2013). Another customer-centric technique would be improving online customer service by answering questions, sharing comments, and addressing problems spot on (Gummerus et al., 2012). Chatbots, a form of limited memory AI system, are a widespread automated customer service application integrating technology e.

Personalization has a major impact on consumer behavior, showing increased customer happiness, purchase intent, and perceived value (Li et al., 2019). The data collected from all content online has been a growing area of significance in marketing as it is the base to improving advertising efficacy, targeting particular groups, and meeting customers' interests (Tran et al., 2021). It has multiple moderating characteristics such as the nature of the product being promoted, the level of participation and complexity of the product, the customer knowledge, culture, and experience, as well as the channel through which personalization is being delivered (Li et al., 2019; Verhoef et al., 2019). By applying those characteristics effectively when planning ad networks, the performance and effectiveness of advertising is boosted even more, especially when the right audience is targeted. This personalized approach encourages customers to pay for premium offers and services (Kim & Ko, 2012). According to the theory of mind, AI technologies that possess the ability to understand human behavior, can predict future behaviors and influence decisions. This means that they are aware of the needs of customers, can identify their emotion, and predict their preferences and interests (El Samad et al., 2023). However, it has some drawbacks, including the reluctance of customers towards sharing personal information (Chua et al., 2019). In other cases, firms might over-personalize their messages, losing their uniqueness and brand value/purpose (Homburg et al., 2017).

Influencer marketing has become a remarkable digital marketing strategy. Having accumulated millions of followers due to a certain online persona and performance, some people deem to be better influencers and hence better marketeers when it comes to promoting a product or a service (Vdovichena et al., 2021). Celebrities, for example, directly influence consumers' purchasing intentions by spreading word of mouth.

With the use of interactive advertisements such as filters or even eye-catching or positive-shock elements (discounts, limited offers, etc.), users have more enjoyable experiences (Flavian et al., 2022). Given that the brand content is shared by users more frequently than the brand's publications, brands should include information regarding product capabilities and attributes that highlight the exceptional qualities of the product in the brand content strategies.

## Sustainable Practices and Sustainable Growth

Almost all businesses have access to social media nowadays. With no doubt, this competitive market poses a big challenge on SMEs and their survival, compared to bigger firms with higher capacity to use high-end technology (Lin et al., 2020). What triggers the shift from "using digital technology" to "maximizing market outcomes" is providing value through sustainable business models that encourage innovation (Yang et al., 2017). For firms to start building this framework, the first step is to identify "uncaptured value" and search for opportunities to meet sustainable goals leading to the innovation of their business model (Yang et al., 2017). What a business provides is what a customer receives, and the cycle goes on. As customers interact with the business, more information is collected on their needs and preferences. Consequently, this data is used by businesses to provide value proposition that puts customers as a focal point around which they operate (Freudenreich et al., 2020). These days, AI algorithms are being used in big data analytics in addition to data-mining methods, making accurate forecasts and coming up with wise decisions (Samad et al., 2022).

In addition to being a game changer in optimizing internal processes, the use of technology, if effectively highlighted in marketing strategies, can guarantee sustainable growth in the market. This is because the end-user is aware of the user-centric practices that the company is applying as it provides its product/service (Kapitan et al., 2019; Lin et al., 2020). Therefore, to be on top of all changes happening in the market, businesses should approach decision making from consumers' perspective, taking into consideration: trust, safety, and good quality (Lin et al., 2020). Particularly in the marketing scope, the use of digital technology has been proved to be essential for business growth and strategy implementation (Manninen & Huiskonen, 2022; Lin et al., 2020). With access to digital platforms, marketing professionals can interact with their target audience, explore chances of cutting-edge approaches, experiment on a wider scale in the market, and learn from customer feedback through multiple channels (Russo et al., 2022). Codifying internal processes makes available huge data sets that can be reported and analyzed to forecast customer needs and preferences and make important decisions related to business development (Sivarajah et al., 2020). As a result, strategies related to internal operations and marketing can be customized and enhanced to add value to customers and predict their future behavior (Sivarajah et al., 2020). With the use of AI technologies, algorithms can analyze customer feedback, determine strength and weakness, and help companies tailor their brand messages according to their customer preferences (N. Sadeq et al., 2023).

Online presence on multiple platforms not only facilitates data collection, but also supports businesses in enhancing relationships with current customers, builds a bigger network, and most importantly helps generate a brand image that aligns with business goals and vision. With that being said, organizations have higher chances and more opportunities to reach out to a large audience and display their product/service, which provides the following benefits: generate revenue, reduce costs (operational and marketing), and access a bigger data pool (Russo et al., 2022). It is a fast and more direct communication channel that allows both the company and its potential customers to share their sustainable objectives creating a form of commitment from the business to continue serving its audience. By doing that, companies build a long-term value providing brand which creates competitive advantage (Russo et al., 2022).

Applying those practices efficiently can also be measured financially. As a business builds its model to meet sustainable objectives, it differentiates itself and its product/service for consumers which makes it more competitive. Users who prefer sustainable products are more likely to value innovation and socially responsible behavior (Hull, 2022). Prioritizing customers value and considering monetary goals as a secondary outcome, promises more economic benefits (Freudenreich et al., 2020). Interestingly, this concept goes both ways because the need to generate profit will encourage businesses to satisfy stakeholders. It is not a choice of either surviving or applying a sustainable business model; on the contrary, it is a collective power to remain competitive and aim for profitability (Hull, 2022).

To achieve that, having a resilient system in place is necessary to maintain high performance that continuously satisfied the end-user (Winnard et al., 2014). Managers must keep an eye on industry needs and grasp its nature to explore the best practices needed to achieve market growth and profitability at a particular time (Hull, 2022). The ability to shift strategies, adjust boundaries, and optimize functions is crucial to meet customer expectations and business goals (Winnard et al., 2014). In other words, managers should have the ability to see things from a bird's eye view, utilizing their leadership skills to study all factors, including ethical and social terms in their strategies as long as they're dealing with their stakeholders. Moreover, they should anticipate any potential external factors that could play as opportunities or threats to the implementation of their strategies and act accordingly to remain competitive on the long-run (Manninen & Huiskonen, 2022).

## Conducting Market Research and Data Collection

Businesses can learn a lot about the requirements, desires, and behaviors of their customers by studying their target audience through market research (Craig & Doughlas, 2001). The process entails data gathering and analysis on a certain market, including details about consumers, rivals, and market trends (Luchs et al., 2015). By compiling accurate and reliable data, businesses can make informed decisions about product/service development, pricing, promotion, and plan more sustainable marketing strategies (Constantinescu et al., 2019; Mooi & Sarstedt, 2011; Wilson & Abel, 2001).

The importance of market research and data collection in business decision-making has been thoroughly examined in a number of academic articles, textbooks, and industry studies (Popovik et al., 2012). By utilizing a wide collection of information, businesses can meet the unique requirements and preferences of their clients which increases levels of satisfaction and loyalty; thus, higher earnings and business success. However, the process of data collection can be challenging: biased information and sample size, and data quality issues (Wang & Strong, 2015). Data quality is another issue that corporate entrepreneurs may encounter. Given the nature of big data, it is essential to regulate the quality of generated data, as it may contain a number of errors, such as inaccurate, disorganized, and incomplete data (Samad et al., 2022). A key component of corporate entrepreneurship is creative decision-making, which includes converting data and information into actionable knowledge so that judgments are based on precise and relevant facts (Samad et al., 2022). The main challenge with big data isn't merely storing and integrating the data; rather, analyzing the data to get valuable insights at the right time and target the correct audience (Samad et al., 2022). To get beyond these obstacles, there are a variety of methods that can be utilized, depending on the study goals and intended audience, including surveys, interviews, focus groups, and observation (Bryman & Bell, 2019).

Market research not only gives businesses useful information about consumer behavior and tastes, but it also equips companies with the knowledge they need to stay competitive in a market that is continuously changing. Businesses can find new possibilities to make more informed strategic decisions which provides them a competitive edge and helps achieve sustainable development by closely observing market developments and their rivals (Kotler & Keller, 2022). One practical approach could be the implementation of AI as a rational non-biased tool to support in accurate decision making (N. Sadeq et al., 2023). In order to improve the added value of the new technology in workplaces, specialists in information technology, or IT, have recently been trying to merge AI with big data, more specifically, big data processing, data analysis, and cleaning (Samad et al., 2022). To sum up, gathering information and performing market research are essential steps for firms to take in order to understand their target market, consumer behavior, preferences, and trends. It helps make decisions on what channels are most effective, what strategies generated the most engagement, what customer segment resonated more with brand messages, etc. Accordingly, this knowledge can help businesses build more individualized customer experiences, boost client retention rates, and ultimately raise their success and revenues. To better implement AI and reap its benefits, business entrepreneurs should allocate resources towards training existing staff members and employing new data scientists (Samad et al., 2022).

## Customer Analysis

In today's fiercely competitive business world, firms must prioritize comprehending their target customer - the particular client group that a business seeks to serve or draw in with its products or services. Conducting target market research has many advantages in this regard, one of which is helping businesses develop more successful marketing strategies. They can create marketing messages that resonate with customers more successfully by understanding the needs and preferences of their target audience. As a result, there may be an uptick in sales, customer involvement, and brand recognition (Kotler & Keller, 2022). An added benefit is increased customers satisfaction and loyalty, for businesses have the data needed to provide their customers with a more customized experience by tailoring goods and services to meet their needs. As a result, repeated purchase is promoted and positive word of mouth is achieved (Anshari et al., 2019). With that being said, businesses can boost their bottom line, making more money from increased sales (Kotler & Keller, 2022).

Target market research has a lot of advantages, but it can also present some difficulties for firms. It might be difficult to ensure the quality of the data: sample size, availability of needed data, date, and much more. However, there are many advantages to conducting target market research that far outweigh any potential disadvantages.

## Competitor Analysis

Competitor analysis is a crucial step in developing a business strategy that can assist organizations in understanding their competitive landscape and creating winning business plans. The accuracy of competition analysis, however, depends on a number of variables, including the data's quality, the research techniques employed, and the company's capacity to put its created strategies into action (Slater,1994; Adom et al., 2016). Two basic methods of competitor analysis are the direct and indirect methods. Direct competitor analysis, focusing on companies that directly compete with the organization in the same market, studies leading rivals in the industry (Chen, 1996). On the other hand, indirect competitor analysis is more focused on those in other markets (Brock, 1984). Several sources, including public records, websites, trade shows, and industry reports, are available for the data (Kahaner, 1997).

For direct analysis, there are multiple tools used. SWOT analysis is one of the best since it helps determine businesses' competitive position and plan ahead to lead the market (Gurl, 2017). Another technique, Benchmarking, measures company performance against rivals, highlighting opportunities for improvement and optimization (He et al., 2015). For indirect analysis, Porter's Five Forces is one of the best techniques used because it studies industry level competitive forces that help businesses spot market trends and opportunities, and accordingly create winning plans to beat out the competition (Grundy, 2006).

The practice of competitor analysis, which involves finding and assessing the advantages and disadvantages of rivals in the market, is crucial to company strategy. The quality of the data, the research techniques employed, and the company's capacity to implement the created plans are just a few of the variables that affect how effective the analysis will be. Therefore, businesses must make investments in data collection and analysis tools and methods and make sure that they choose the best analysis techniques based on their unique requirements and objectives.

## Market Analysis

The two primary methods for looking for market opportunities are either product-oriented or market-oriented. Product-oriented strategies focus on creating new goods and services first, then identifying markets for them (Slater & Narver, 1999). On the contrary, market-oriented approaches identify customer needs and market trends, then develop products or services that address these needs. The product-oriented strategy is based on the importance of innovation: cutting-edge offerings may open up new markets and spur development (Herppich et al., 2018). Businesses must spend money on R&D in order to stay abreast of market developments in this process (Selden & MacMillan, 2006). Diversification is a different strategy employed in product-oriented approaches. Creating new goods or services that are distinct from those already available is a component of diversification. By reducing their reliance on current markets, this process aids businesses in expanding into new ones (Hako, 1972).

The market-oriented strategy follows the rationale that customer wants should drive product development and organizations should adapt accordingly to remain competitive (Grönroos,1989). Market research is one of the best tools for market-oriented strategies. By doing so, businesses can uncover market trends and produce goods and services that address client preferences. Another is Customer relationship management (CRM), which facilitates the process of understanding customers and their taste through establishing strong relationships (Kotorov, 2003). However, the efficiency of the market opportunity search depends on a number of variables, including the accuracy of the data, the techniques used for analysis, and the organization's capacity to put its developed strategies into practice (Fosfuri & Tribó, 2008).

## Effective Marketing Strategies

### Current Marketing Trends of Advertisement on Social Media

With the advent of new platforms and the growth of established ones, businesses must remain current on the newest trends in social media advertising in order to gain an edge over their competitors, increase brand awareness, improve customer engagement and loyalty, and ultimately achieve their business goals and objectives (Dutta, 2018; Kumar, 2018; Pires & Stanton, 2018). Nowadays, consumers are exposed to immersive and interactive experiences online through augmented reality, which could assist in boosting brand engagement and loyalty. Although it is still in its early stages, it is very important for online businesses to include the right elements to create enjoyable experiences, positive digital interactions, and easy access to new material (Flavian et al., 2022). In addition, advertising on social media is increasingly more targeted and personalized now. Due to the abundance of data on social media users, advertisers are now able to target their adverts to particular demographic groups or people based on their interests and activities. The growing significance of data-driven marketing and the need to improve the efficacy of advertising efforts have been the driving forces behind this development. With perceived personalization, brand objectives like brand self-expression, consumer-brand engagement, and brand relationship show positive results (Tran et al., 2021).

With the vast collection of items available for selection, it can be argued that eye-catching elements positively correlate with purchase intention and have a significant impact on it. It may be attributed to the notion that any inclusion or reduction of characteristics distinguishes an item from the competition in the current digital era. If particular data have an advantageous shock value, consumers might be pushed to bypass multiple phases of the decision-making procedure and create a purchasing desire soon. Some examples include restricted supply statements, price cuts, and other similar occurrences. Most of the time, people are cautious about where they allocate their cash, and this is particularly true when it is something they see on social media (Kamath et al., 2021). For that reason, building an emotional attraction with the customer can build a favorable relationship with them and significantly influence their purchase intention. Also, commercials with emotionally appealing material may promote word-of-mouth (Swani et al., 2013). However, it is important to note that following trends without a defined plan can be detrimental to the business and can have unfavorable effects (Pires & Stanton, 2018). For that reason, monitoring and modifying marketing tactics is crucial to creating better customer experiences and establish closer relationships (Dutta, 2018). Also, AI technologies can help in assessing the most effective pricing strategies for different customers based on company databases such as cookies, visit frequency, searches, and other information (N. Sadeq et al., 2023).

## Influencer Marketing

Social media advertising is expanding to keep up with changing customer tastes and advances in technology, influencer marketing being one major introduction. This method has gained popularity as an effective marketing strategy for brands to promote their products and services online in recent years (Khamis et al., 2017). Because online users preferred specific social media identities (SMI) and their content over everybody else, influencers gained countless followers and now played a significant role in shaping opinions of customers, especially after evaluating TikTok videos, the world's most popular online gadget for brief clips (Kurdi et al., 2022). This emerging form of advertising is a social networking promotion whereby retail companies collaborate with a SMI to create branded material that includes product recommendations or raises awareness on brand products (Lou & Yuan, 2019).

A lot of companies feel that this latest form of promotion will end up resulting in increased profits; therefore, it has grown into a vital part of their digital marketing strategies with the intent to influence consumers' intentions and attitudes. For instance, Amazon leverages marketing power to market its brand by recruiting prominent bloggers to produce videos about the firm (Vdovichena et al., 2021). Celebrity presence in ads, for the most part, enhanced consumer consciousness of firms' marketing efforts and the products and services that they provide, resulting in higher revenue and sales (Nelson & Deborah, 2017). Retailing marketers have found themselves attracted to the current condition of SMIs and are measuring the success of implementing this marketing strategy. Research by Khamis et al., (2017) suggests that engagement rates (such as likes, comments, and shares) are a particularly important metric to measure the success of influencer marketing campaigns. In accordance with a market survey (Linqia, 2019), 86% of brand advertisers employed influencer marketing in their advertising campaigns in 2017 and 92% of them considered it effective. Rather than employing it as a one-time, tactical effort, 42% of marketers indicated they want to utilize influencer marketing on a continuous basis. Therefore, the strategy of engaging the audience in a collaborative conversation by enlisting well-known influencers or product consumers is found to be effective.

## Email Marketing

To successfully connect with their target audience, businesses can implement email marketing, a crucial part of digital marketing that involves sending promotional emails or newsletters to a specific group of email subscribers, to fulfill their marketing objectives (Chaffey & Smith, 2022). Email marketing is a successful marketing strategy because it connects businesses with customers in an instantaneous, practical, highly targeted, and quantifiable method that easy to use and measure (Jenkins, 2008). Building and keeping up a high-quality email list with subscribers who have agreed to get emails from the company is essential for the effectiveness of email marketing efforts (Chaffey et al., 2019). By sending interesting and pertinent emails to current or potential customers, businesses can proactively involve consumers in the communication process, and make emails relevant enough attract new clients and keep hold of current ones (Hartemo, 2016).

Additionally, segmenting email lists based on customer behavior and preferences can help deliver more targeted and relevant content that will more likely resonate with the recipient. In terms of measuring the effectiveness of email campaigns, tracking metrics like open rates, click-through rates, and conversion rates is crucial (Chaffey et al., 2019). When compared to other marketing channels, email marketing can produce a higher return on investment (ROI), which is one of its main advantages (Chaffey & Smith, 2022). It is important to note that emails with personalized content did even better in terms of performance and sales. The likelihood that the email recipient would open the email improved by 20% when the receiver's name was added to its subject line. This resulted in a 31% increase in sales leads and a 17% decrease in the number of people who unsubscribed from the marketing email campaign (Sahni et al., 2018).

## Sharing Effective Content on Social Media Platforms

Sharing quality information is a powerful marketing tactic that helps firms position themselves as industry thought leaders and develop trust and credibility with their audience (Chung & Koo, 2016; Safko, 2015). Safko (2015) defines valuable content as material that is informative, relevant, and beneficial to the intended audience. By adapting this method, businesses have the potential to increase their visibility and website traffic because their audience is more likely to connect to their content and share it with their own networks. It helps build stronger relationships and fosters a sense of reciprocity and trust with their audience, leading to improved loyalty and repeated purchase (Chung & Koo, 2016; Safko, 2015). Additionally, rankings and their website's search engine optimization SEOs (Chung & Koo, 2016) making it more visible to search engines like Google (Safko, 2015). On the contrary, sharing unnecessary or harmful material can be detrimental and can harm a company's reputation (Safko, 2015).

### Providing Purchase Incentive

One of the key benefits of offering client purchase incentives is that it can boost sales volume and income by attracting new customers while retaining existing ones (Kotler & Armstrong, 2021). Discounts and promotions, for example, might entice people to buy by lowering the price or providing additional benefits. By doing that, businesses are boosting customer satisfaction and enhancing their perception of the brand (Panda, 2017). Customers may feel more valued and appreciated by a company when they receive offers or discounts. With that being said, a satisfied customer becomes more loyal and is more likely to recommend the brand to others through positive word-of-mouth.

With no doubt, this method has some drawbacks, one of which are diminished business profit margins (Panda, 2017). Discounting too frequently or without proper planning may result in reduced profit margins for the company and it may not be effective for all customer segments, as some may be uninterested in the rewards (Kotler & Armstrong, 2021). Despite these potential limitations, a variety of purchase incentive tactics can be implemented to increase consumer purchases and loyalty. Loyalty programs, for example, can be adapted by giving prizes for recurrent purchases (Panda, 2017), promotions can be strategically targeted to certain client categories to boost purchases during sluggish times (Batra & Kazmi, 2018), coupons can be provided to clients who purchase a particular number of items online (Kumar, 2016), and many more, all promoting consumer loyalty and sales (Kotler & Armstrong, 2021). However, it is important to ensure that the incentive programs represent the business's sustainable mindset, align with their goals and objectives, and provide a unique experience for different customer segments (Khan & Iqbal, 2015; Constantinescu et al., 2019).

## Maintaining and Securing Good Customer Relationships

### Effective Communication and Frequent Follow-Up With Online Customers

Maintaining and developing positive customer relationships is crucial for any business to live in the market and grow. Making available multiple options for easy and professional communication with online clients is one of the factors that help connect the business with their clients. This results in sustainable social performance (Edwin Cheng et al., 2021), for the business is offering multiple channels, including chat, social media platforms, phone, and email to provide fast, helpful, and informative responses to client's questions and concerns. With the advancements in technology, some businesses are adapting AI chatbots to reply to simple client concerns 24/7. For instance, nearly 1 out of 4 customer service organizations employ AI-driven chatbots to serve their customers (Gartner, 2019). Also, many AI systems are now able to identify textual and/or auditory patterns and translate them from one language to another. This application on instant messaging apps allows marketers to communicate in their preferred language and guarantees that the message is well understood by the customer through translated text or audio messages (El Samad et al., 2023). Artificial intelligence can also help in presenting previous customer data to make recommendations on innovative approaches to communicate with their customers and maintain long-lasting relationships (N. Sadeq et al., 2023). As it is important to initiate communication, it is also crucial to follow up with online customers frequently in case of any suggestion, feedback, or to make sure the clients' needs are being addressed. This method increases customer satisfaction and loyalty, and drives them to purchase from the brand. Moreover, personalizing advertisements and client outreach based on the data collected from follow-ups, leads to increased consumer's happiness and loyalty, and consequently improves business performance in terms of sales and profit (Gupta & Joshi, 2022; Alzoubi et al., 2022).

## Transparent Feedback Shared Online

Online platforms, including internet search engines, e-commerce sites, and social media networks frequently share asymmetric information. As a result, a very critical threat on consumer trust in the brand and brand reliability. In this context, an experiment conducted to test the impact of increased transparency in search result presentation, identity of sellers, and user reviews and ratings, proved an increased probability of product selection (Veltri et al., 2020). When customers make purchase decisions, they tend to rely on store websites or on opinions of other peoples' experiences online, especially when it involves time and money (Ramanathan et al., 2017; Cambria et al., 2013; Ind, 1997). The presence of negative reviews discourages future customers and impacts how any potential interested individual feels towards the store (Ramanathan et al., 2017). For this reason, it is of utmost importance to analyze customer feedback, make smart improvements accordingly (Liu, 2012; Kazmaier & van Vuuren, 2020), and communicate them online to show potential customers the accountability of the brand and willingness to improve.

## Personalization

### Personalizing Product Advertisements and Customer Outreach

In order to improve client engagement and boost sales, personalization of product marketing and customer outreach has grown in popularity in recent years. Customizing marketing initiatives to the unique demands and tastes of individual clients is one of the main advantages of personalized product promotions and customer outreach (Gupta & Joshi, 2022). Offering a more relevant and tailored experience, personalized marketing activities can increase consumer happiness and loyalty (Alzoubi et al., 2022). Additionally, as customers are more likely to interact with marketing communications that are pertinent to their needs and interests, personalized marketing activities can also boost the possibility that customers will make a purchase (Leung et al., 2022).

The utilization of consumer data to guide marketing initiatives is a crucial component of individualized product promotions and customer engagement (Bag et al., 2021). It was discovered that by recognizing consumer wants and preferences, customer data may be leveraged to generate effective marketing strategies. Also, by identifying customers who are likely to leave and focusing targeted marketing efforts on them, customer data can be utilized to increase customer retention (Boshoff & Gray, 2004). The use of digital technology, for instance AI, is an efficient tool to customize product marketing and client outreach (Nugroho, 2023; Li & Huang, 2017). Social media sites have also developed into a crucial tool for tailored product promotions and customer outreach.

### The Effect of Personalization on Consumer Behavior

It is true that consumers are influenced by one another when making purchase decisions. However, does this have to indicate that they have similar interests? Not necessarily. Personalizing messages better encourages purchases among users within the same market segment (Bonabeau, E., 2004). According to the theory of Elaboration Likelihood Model (ELM), the more relevant a message is to a potential customer receiving it, the more likely they are to exert thoughtful effort in considering it. Those who felt deeply connected to the brand message will more probably engage in high purchase behavior. On the other hand, sending out random automated messages can be a major reason why potential customers are more skeptical about advertisements. Even if it led to a purchase once, it is not enough to consider this customer loyal to that brand, for this particular purchase might be influenced. Personalization efficiency varies depending on the channel. Personalized recommendations, for example, are more successful in email marketing than in internet marketing. Similarly, individualized recommendations on social media outperform those on websites (Hajli et al., 2019). The channel used to execute personalization is determined by the features of the product, the target audience, and the marketing objectives. Customized suggestions, including tailored emailed marketing messages, boost client happiness, which in turn boosts customer loyalty and retention (Li et al., 2019; De Bellis et al., 2019). Increased purchase intention is another beneficial effect of personalization on customer behavior. Customized marketing messages have been shown to be more successful in capturing consumers' attention and enticing them to make a purchase. Also customized suggestions raise purchase intention and boost the perceived value of items, which might impact their willingness to pay a premium for products and services (Lee et al., 2017; Kim & Ko, 2012; Verhoef et al., 2019). With that being said, simplifying personalized messages is essential and it should be considered to enhance its effectiveness (N. Sadeq et al., 2023).

Yet, personalization has a detrimental impact on customer behavior. Privacy issues are one of them. Customization is based on the acquisition and use of customer data, which might cause consumers to be concerned about their privacy. To overcome this issue, businesses must be honest about their data gathering and usage procedures, as well as give customers with data control. Another disadvantage of personalisation is the possibility of over-personalization. can elicit negative feelings from clients, such as uneasiness and a sensation of being exploited (Homburg et al., 2017). Companies must establish a balance between personalisation and maintaining customers' sovereignty to prevent over-personalization.

## Conceptual Framework

The conceptual framework attached below aims to display the factors that businesses can take into consideration when planning their online marketing strategy and campaigns. With the main purpose to achieve higher sales and sustainable business growth, it is important to categorize key elements that need attention neatly and explore each individually. To reach this goal, the below conceptual framework suggests businesses capture online customers by implementing four themes: Effective Marketing Strategies, Market Research and Data Collection, Good Customer Relationships, and Personalization.

By executing effective marketing strategies, businesses are utilizing multiple tools that encourage customer acquisition and retention. One of the main pillars of a successful marketing campaigns is sharing value-content that engages the audience and educates them on products/services they are interested in. By sharing this information, customers build an impression on the brand and make well-informed decisions with regards to the business's value. The format through which information is shared is also crucial because different customer segments are triggered by different stimuli. Some are encouraged to purchase or try only by being provided an incentive (promotion, discount, package offer, etc.), others are more interested in businesses that follow trends and provide easy and trusted access to trending products/services. Some trending marketing strategies now are email and influencer marketing. Both play a significant role in promoting sustainable business growth. With email marketing, businesses can reach out to different target segments, personalize their emails according to their preferences, level of familiarity with the products, and likelihood to continue purchasing from the business. The ability to automate the application of this strategy also helps focus on more creative aspects of this to guarantee higher conversion rates. In terms of influencer marketing, businesses can explore collaborations with influencer who have strong online presence from different market niches as long as they responsibly represent the brand. This helps increase the reach of the brand in a very short amount of time, especially when all the other marketing strategy elements are applied too.

Conducting market research is one of the most important steps to achieving business growth since it provides businesses with the data needed to plan a sustainable marketing strategy. For instance, marketing professionals must have an idea about their potential customers. Some important details they could study are their needs, preferences, and behaviors. This information differs across age groups, gender, location, personality traits, etc, so those factors must be taken into consideration. Also, after customers try the product/service, additional data can be collected like their feedback on customer service, product quality, and general review. In some cases, data collected can be internal and not from the customer themselves, such as how frequently do they buy, the value of their purchases, etc. All those elements create a clearer understanding on customers and can be used to apply new or modify existing marketing strategies to fit all customers. On the other hand, exploring competitors in the market is also fundamental for businesses to keep track of the competitive landscape and assess existing strategies to audit their own. By doing so, businesses can reflect on current applied processes and find better ways to differentiate their offerings from others. They can find gaps that they can fill by optimizing their internal operations and developing new approaches to perform better on the short and long run. While doing that, businesses can analyze the market they are part of: growth rate, trends, market segments, and make strategic decisions regarding their marketing plans. An in-depth analysis of the market helps identify opportunities for growth and expansion within and across markets. This enhances the performance of a business, increases its sales, and consequently supports its growth.

Building good customer relationships is one of the key determinants to achieving higher sales. By fostering good connections, customers are more likely to repeat purchases and recommend the brand to others. Some important factors that facilitate those relationships are: providing transparent feedback, following up with customer frequently, communicating effectively with buyers, and personalizing messages. As businesses seek feedback from their customers, they gain valuable insight on products they offer and their overall brand experience. This allows them to collect big data on market needs and preferences and makes it easier to spot necessary improvements that should be made to enhance product quality. It also helps businesses anticipate future requirements and tailor their marketing efforts based on market needs. This positively reflects on the brand image customers build in their minds as they feel. Constantly reaching out to customers is also a good technique to maintain and nurture client relationships through sending check-in emails, post-purchase surveys, etc.. Taking this approach helps businesses prove their commitment towards satisfying customers and encourages marketing professionals to experiment with introducing new products or services that can further drive sales and sustainable business growth. A vital component in fostering this strong relationship would be effective and clear communication with the customer base. Marketers can tailor their content plans and product descriptions when they understand their target audiences' preferences. They can explore more sustainable initiatives that align with their offerings and their customers' values, allowing them to build trust and differentiate themselves in the market.

Last but not least, personalization is one of the themes that could help optimize marketing research and client relationships in case its implementation was well-planned. As more customer data is collected and analyzed, more insight is generated on customer preferences and purchase behaviors. Personalizing connections with potential buyers is more likely to convert them to loyal customers. Applying a marketing approach that prioritizes customers' preferences allows businesses to offer product suggestions and recommendations that resonate with different customer segments. This customization creates a unique customer experience that delivers value to customers, promotes satisfaction, and encourages sharing positive word-of-mouth, all of which contributes to sustainable business growth. On the other hand, customers become more actively engaged in product offerings and are more likely to make purchases frequently from this brand. As a result, a more loyal customer base is established, recommending the business to other potential buyers. In business terms, this is translated in increased sales, bigger market share, and higher profitability.

This inter-connection of elements is reflected in the below framework.

## CONCLUSION

To wrap up, using social media to target customers nowadays through personalized and tailored marketing campaigns is a big wave to surf. However, it is achievable once a clear business goal and vision is set to direct operations and marketing

*Figure 1. Conceptual framework presenting marketing elements that contribute to achieving higher sales and sustainable business growth online*

strategies accordingly. Initially, digital platforms were a trend that the minority of companies hopped on, but now a necessity if they plan to remain competitive in the market. Many tools are being created to help marketers reach out to potential customers through social media platforms effectively; however, there is always room for more innovation and improvement. In that sense, having a detailed marketing strategy that outlines targets, objectives, and goals helps marketing professionals focus their efforts on building long lasting connections with end-users who are the source of all collected data. Upon collecting and analyzing customer data and insights, businesses can test out multiple approaches and collect feedback on each approach to learn more and expand their database. The process of studying consumers' buying behavior involves a lot of factors, both internal and external. Every individual has a set of preferences, interests, and character traits that guide their behavior. As they experience life, those details are modified and they become unrepresentative of those people. With that being said, constant data collection and analytics must be performed to understand what exactly do customers need and want at the moment. Moving on to the external environment, multiple elements influence purchase decisions: economic state, cultural reality, social pressures, demographic area, etc. The aforementioned points shape and shift purchases choices consumers make whether they are representative or not of their own preferences. By using social media, individuals (influencers or regular users) and businesses are able to guide other people's behaviors and thoughts. Businesses improve their marketing strategies by using different platforms that help them connect with their customers, collect data, and track their satisfaction. As a result, they can brainstorm products, services, or advertising campaigns that can present company value, share brand awareness, even if non-existent. On the other hand, businesses can use this to encourage well-educated consumers to make informed purchase decisions by searching more about the product. A lot of information is present on any possible product in the market instantaneously, including online reviews. This means companies can use reviews to improve their online reputation and word-of-mouth, but also consumers can assess product quality and criticize online marketing campaigns objectively relying on many references.

As important as it is to maintain effective marketing practices and be active online, the role of the management in this scope cannot be neglected. Resilient systems that are built to satisfy customers constantly are necessary for achieving sustained development and profitability. When engaging stakeholders, managers should be aware of the needs of the industry, adjust their strategies as necessary, and take moral and ethical considerations into account. They should also plan ahead for outside influences on their competitiveness-preserving measures. Managers may optimize operations, make wise judgments, and align with business goals and stakeholder interests by using their leadership abilities and strategic foresight.

In this study, the connection between each of the elements mentioned is explored in depth. All factors essential to promoting long-term business growth have been thoroughly researched and identified by a thorough literature review. It is crucial to keep in mind that those components contribute proportionally to overall corporate profit and it can differ across industries and companies, necessitating a tailored approach to their implementation. Also, what may have been successful in the past may not always produce the same results in the future as firms develop and the external environment changes. Therefore, in order for businesses to remain competitive in a dynamic market on the long term, they must constantly evaluate the relevance and effectiveness of each component of their growth strategy. Given the unpredictability and constant change of the business environment, it is imperative to place a high priority on flexibility and adaptation in the strategy for corporate success. Upcoming technological improvements will be introduced, especially in the world of social media, consequently offering unique factors that will have an impact on business success.

For that reason, this study's conceptual framework provides an extensive understanding of the interrelated components that lead to sustainable and well-founded corporate growth. Although the in-depth analysis of the literature served as the foundation for the framework, opportunities for improvement and adaptation can take place upon actual implementation and empirical testing of the conceptual framework in practical setting. It is important to mention that this is one of the limitations of this study: the conceptual framework presented has not been empirically tested; therefore, the applicability and effectiveness in real-world settings hasn't been evaluated and was only guided by a thorough examination of the literature in the field. This drawback emphasizes the need for additional study to empirically evaluate and improve the conceptual framework in relevant settings. It can be studied by interested researchers or business experts by deploying it within marketing firms and corporations. Through this process, it might be possible to spot areas where the framework could benefit from additions, deletions, or modifications in order to better suit the particular needs and constraints of various businesses and industries. Such a strategy would offer insightful information about the framework's effectiveness and its usefulness in realistic situations. Eventually, findings will lead to a clearer understanding of the variables and help formulate more efficient strategies for businesses' sustainable growth.

## REFERENCES

Adiyono, N. G., Rahmat, T. Y., & Anindita, R. (2021). Digital Marketing Strategies to Increase Online Business Sales through Social Media. *Journal of Humanities, Social Science Public Administration and Management*, *1*(2), 31–37.

Adom, A. Y., Nyarko, I. K., & Som, G. N. K. (2016). Competitor analysis in strategic management: Is it a worthwhile managerial practice in contemporary times. *Journal of Resources Development and Management*, *24*(1), 116–127.

Agnihotri, Kothandaraman, Kashyap, & Singh. (2012). Bringing "Social" Into Sales: The Impact of Salespeople's Social Media Use on Service Behaviors and Value Creation. *The Journal of Personal Selling and Sales Management*, *32*, 333-348. https://www.researchgate.net/publication/260178184_Bringing_Social_Into_Sales_The_Impact_of_Salespeople'S_Social_Media_Use_on_Service_Behaviors_and_Value_Creation

Aji, P., Nadhila, V., & Sanny, L. (2020). Effect of social media marketing on Instagram towards purchase intention: Evidence from Indonesia's ready-to-drink tea industry. *International Journal of Data and Network Science*, *4*(2), 91–104. doi:10.5267/j.ijdns.2020.3.002

Anshari, M., Almunawar, M. N., Lim, S. A., & Al-Mudimigh, A. (2019). Customer relationship management and Big Data enabled: Personalization & Customization Of Services. *Applied Computing and Informatics*, *15*(2), 94–101. doi:10.1016/j.aci.2018.05.004

Ashley, C., & Tuten, T. (2015). Creative strategies in social media marketing: An exploratory study of branded social content and consumer engagement. *Psychology and Marketing*, *32*(1), 15–27. doi:10.1002/mar.20761

Aula, P. (2010). Social media, reputation risk and ambient publicity management. *Strategy and Leadership*, *38*(6), 43–49. doi:10.1108/10878571011088069

Ba, S., Jin, Y., Li, X., & Lu, X. (2020). One size fits all? The differential impact of online reviews and coupons. *Production and Operations Management*, *29*(10), 2403–2424. doi:10.1111/poms.13233

Batra, S., & Kazmi, S. H. H. (2018). Sales incentives and employee performance: A review of the literature. *Journal of Management Development*, *37*(3), 219–231. doi:10.1108/JMD-08-2016-0159

Behera, R. K., Gunasekaran, A., Gupta, S., Kamboj, S., & Bala, P. K. (2020). Personalized digital marketing recommender engine. *Journal of Retailing and Consumer Services*, *53*, 101799. doi:10.1016/j.jretconser.2019.03.026

Bolton, R. N., Parasuraman, A., Hoefnagels, A., Migchels, N., Kabadayi, S., Gruber, T., & Solnet, D. (2013). Understanding Generation Y and their use of social media: A review and research agenda. *Journal of Service Management*, *24*(3), 245–267. doi:10.1108/09564231311326987

Bonabeau, E. (2004). The Perils of the Imitation Age. *Harvard Business Review*, *82*(6), 45–54. PMID:15202286

Bowen, M. D., Lai-Bennejean, C. J., Haas, A., & Rangarajan, D. (2021). Social media in B2B sales: Why and when does salesperson social media usage affect salesperson performance? *Industrial Marketing Management*, *96*, 166–182. doi:10.1016/j.indmarman.2021.05.007

Brock, J. J. (1984). Competitor analysis: Some practical approaches. *Industrial Marketing Management*, *13*(4), 225–231. doi:10.1016/0019-8501(84)90017-8

Bryman, A., & Bell, E. (2019). *Business research methods*. Oxford University Press.

Cai, G. (2020). Impact of media use on consumer product knowledge. *Social Behavior and Personality*, *48*(2), 11–24. Advance online publication. doi:10.2224/sbp.8558

Cambria, E., Schuller, B., Xia, Y., & Havasi, C. (2013). New avenues in opinion mining and sentiment analysis. *IEEE Intelligent Systems*, *28*(2), 15–21. doi:10.1109/MIS.2013.30

Chaffey, D., & Ellis-Chadwick, F. (2019). *Digital marketing*. Pearson UK.

Chaffey, D., & Smith, P. R. (2022). *Digital marketing excellence: planning, optimizing and integrating online marketing*. Taylor & Francis. doi:10.4324/9781003009498

Chaker, N. N., Nowlin, E. L., Pivonka, M. T., Itani, O. S., & Agnihotri, R. (2022). Inside sales social media use and its strategic implications for salesperson-customer digital engagement and performance. *Industrial Marketing Management, 100*, 127–144. doi:10.1016/j.indmarman.2021.10.006

Chatterjee, S., Chaudhuri, R., Sakka, G., Grandhi, B., Galati, A., Siachou, E., & Vrontis, D. (2021). Adoption of social media marketing for sustainable business growth of SMEs in emerging economies: The moderating role of leadership support. *Sustainability (Basel)*, *13*(21), 12134. doi:10.3390/su132112134

Chen, M. J. (1996). Competitor analysis and interfirm rivalry: Toward a theoretical integration. *Academy of Management Review*, *21*(1), 100–134. doi:10.2307/258631

Chen, Y., Fay, S., & Wang, Q. (2011). The role of marketing in social media: How online consumer reviews evolve. *Journal of Interactive Marketing, 25*(2), 85-94. doi:10.1016/j.intmar.2011.01.003

Cheung, C. M. K., Xiao, B. S., & Liu, I. L. B. (2014). Do actions speak louder than voices? The signaling role of social information cues in influencing consumer purchase decisions. *Decision Support Systems*, *65*, 50–58. doi:10.1016/j.dss.2014.05.002

Choi, S. M., & Rifon, N. J. (2012). It is a match: The impact of congruence between celebrity image and consumer ideal self on endorsement effectiveness. *Psychology and Marketing*, *29*(9), 639–650. doi:10.1002/mar.20550

Chua, A. Y. K., Banerjee, S., & Kim, Y. (2019). Understanding consumers' responses to personalized advertising: A privacy calculus perspective. *Journal of Interactive Marketing*, *46*, 86–98.

Chung, Y. J., & Koo, C. (2016). The effects of social media marketing on brand loyalty: A case study of online fashion brand. *Journal of Global Fashion Marketing*, *7*(3), 204–213. doi:10.1080/20932685.2016.1193386

Constantinescu, M., Orindaru, A., Pachitanu, A., Rosca, L., Caescu, S.-C., & Orzan, M. C. (2019). Attitude evaluation on using the neuromarketing approach in social media: Matching company's purposes and consumer's benefits for sustainable business growth. *Sustainability (Basel)*, *11*(24), 7094. doi:10.3390/su11247094

Cozzolino, A., Corbo, L., & Aversa, P. (2021). Digital platform-based ecosystems: The evolution of collaboration and competition between incumbent producers and entrant platforms. *Journal of Business Research, 126*, 385–400. doi:10.1016/j.jbusres.2020.12.058

Dash, R., McMurtrey, M., Rebman, C., & Kar, U. K. (2019). Application of artificial intelligence in automation of supply chain management. *Journal of Strategic Innovation and Sustainability, 14*(3), 43–53.

De Bellis, E., Lassar, W. M., & Carr, C. T. (2019). The impact of personalization on email marketing metrics: Evidence from a field experiment. *Journal of Business Research, 98*, 214–223.

de Vries, L., Gensler, S., & Leeflang, P. S. H. (2012). Popularity of brand posts on brand fan pages: An investigation of the effects of social media marketing. *Journal of Interactive Marketing, 26*(2), 83–91. doi:10.1016/j.intmar.2012.01.003

Dutta, S. (2011). Let the revolution begin! Enterprise 2.0. *IESE Insight*, (9), 13–20. doi:10.15581/002.ART-1966

Dutta, S. (2018). *The Importance of Following Marketing Trends*. Business2Community. Retrieved from https://www.business2community.com/marketing/the-importance-of-following-marketing-trends-02074695

Dwivedi, Y. K., Ismagilova, E., Rana, N. P., & Raman, R. (2021). *Social Media Adoption, Usage And Impact In Business-To-Business (B2B) Context: A State-Of-The-Art*. Academic Press.

El Samad, M., Nasserddine, G., & Kheir, A. (2023). *Introduction to Artificial Intelligence. In Artificial Intelligence and Knowledge Processing*. CRC Press. doi:10.1201/9781003328414-1

Ezeife, L. (2017). *Social media strategies for increasing sales* [Doctoral dissertation]. Walden University.

Fosfuri, A., & Tribó, J. A. (2008). Exploring the antecedents of potential absorptive capacity and its impact on innovation performance. *Omega, 36*(2), 173–187. doi:10.1016/j.omega.2006.06.012 PMID:18680889

Freudenreich, B., Lüdeke-Freund, F., & Schaltegger, S. (2020). A stakeholder theory perspective on business models: Value creation for sustainability. *Journal of Business Ethics, 166*(1), 3–18. doi:10.1007/s10551-019-04112-z

Fundin, A. P., & Bergman, B. L. (2003). Exploring the customer feedback process. *Measuring Business Excellence, 7*(2), 55–65. doi:10.1108/13683040310477995

Geurin, A. N., & Burch, L. M. (2017). User-generated branding via social media: An examination of six running brands. *Sport Management Review*, *20*(3), 273–284. doi:10.1016/j.smr.2016.09.001

Grönroos, C. (1989). Defining marketing: A market-oriented approach. *European Journal of Marketing*, *23*(1), 52–60. doi:10.1108/EUM0000000000541

Grundy, T. (2006). Rethinking and reinventing Michael Porter's five forces model. *Strategic Change*, *15*(5), 213–229. doi:10.1002/jsc.764

Gu, B., & Ye, Q. (2014). First step in social media: Measuring the influence of online management responses on customer satisfaction. *Production and Operations Management*, *23*(4), 570–582. doi:10.1111/poms.12043

Gummerus, J., Liljander, V., Weman, E., & Pihlström, M. (2012). Customer engagement in a Facebook brand community. *Management Research Review*, *35*(9), 857–877. doi:10.1108/01409171211256578

Gupta, S., & Chopra, C. (2020). *Impact of Social Media on Consumer Behavior*. Research Gate.

Gurl, E. (2017). *SWOT analysis: A theoretical review*. Academic Press.

Hako, B. (1972). Strategies for diversification. *Long Range Planning*, *5*(2), 65–69. doi:10.1016/0024-6301(72)90048-9

Hartemo, M. (2016). Email marketing in the era of the empowered consumer. *Journal of Research in Interactive Marketing*, *10*(3), 212–230. doi:10.1108/JRIM-06-2015-0040

He, W., Wu, H., Yan, G., Akula, V., & Shen, J. (2015). A novel social media competitive analytics framework with sentiment benchmarks. *Information & Management*, *52*(7), 801–812. doi:10.1016/j.im.2015.04.006

Herppich, S., Praetorius, A. K., Förster, N., Glogger-Frey, I., Karst, K., Leutner, D., & Südkamp, A. (2018). Teachers' assessment competence: Integrating knowledge-, process-, and product-oriented approaches into a competence-oriented conceptual model. *Teaching and Teacher Education*, *76*, 181–193. doi:10.1016/j.tate.2017.12.001

Homburg, C., Jozić, D., & Kuehnl, C. (2017). Customer experience management: Toward implementing an evolving marketing concept. *Journal of the Academy of Marketing Science*, *45*(3), 377–401. doi:10.1007/s11747-015-0460-7

Hull, C. E. (2022). Competitive sustainability: The intersection of sustainability and business success. *Sustainability (Basel)*, *14*(24), 16420. doi:10.3390/su142416420

Hunt, K. G. (2010). Finders keepers: Social media strategies help find top talent. *Journal of Property Management, 75*(6), 36. https://go.exlibris.link/HR5JcHY8

Ibáñez-Sánchez, S., Orus, C., & Flavian, C. (2022). Augmented reality filters on social media. Analyzing the drivers of playability based on uses and gratifications theory. *Psychology and Marketing*, *39*(3), 559–578. doi:10.1002/mar.21639

Ind, N. (1997). *The Corporate Brand*. Macmillan Press Ltd. doi:10.1057/9780230375888

Infante, A., & Mardikaningsih, R. (2022). The Potential of Social Media as a Means of Online Business Promotion. *Journal of Social Science Studies, 2*(2), 45–49. doi:10.56348/jos3.v2i2.26

Invespcro. (2021). *The Importance of Online Customer Reviews*. https://www.invespcro.com/blog/theimportance-of-online-custo mer-reviews-infograp

Jenkins, S. (2008). *The truth about email marketing*. FT Press.

K v, S., Kp, N., & Kamath, G. B. (2021). Social media advertisements and their influence on consumer purchase intention. *Cogent Business & Management*, *8*(1), 2000697. doi:10.1080/23311975.2021.2000697

Kahaner, L. (1997). *Competitive intelligence: how to gather analyze and use information to move your business to the top*. Simon and Schuster.

Kapitan, S., Kennedy, A., & Berth, N. (2019). Sustainably superior versus greenwasher: A scale measure of B2B sustainability positioning. *Industrial Marketing Management*, *76*, 84–97. doi:10.1016/j.indmarman.2018.08.003

Kaplan, A., & Haenlein, M. (2010). Users of the World, Unite! The Challenges and Opportunities of Social Media. *Business Horizons*, *53*(1), 59–68. doi:10.1016/j.bushor.2009.09.003

Kaplan, A. M., & Haenlein, M. (2019). *Siri, Siri, in my hand: Who's the fairest in the land?* Academic Press.

Kasavana, M. L. (2008). *The unintended consequences of social media and the hospitality industry*. Hospitality Upgrade. https://www.hospitalityupgrade.com/Hospitalityupgrade.com-00 93-2016Redesign/media/hospitalityupgrade.com-0093/File_Artic les/HUFall08_Kasavana_SocialMediaandHospitality.pdf

Kasavana, M. L., Nusair, K., & Teodosic, K. (2010). Online social networking: Redefining the human web. *Journal of Hospitality and Tourism Technology*, *1*(1), 68–82. doi:10.1108/17579881011023025

Kazmaier, J., & van Vuuren, J. H. (2020). Sentiment analysis of unstructured customer feedback for a retail bank. *ORiON*, *36*(1), 35–71. doi:10.5784/36-1-668

Keller, K. L., & Kotler, P. (2022). Branding in B2B firms. In *Handbook of business-to-business marketing* (pp. 205–224). Edward Elgar Publishing. doi:10.4337/9781800376878.00021

Khamis, S., Ang, L., & Welling, R. (2017). Self-branding,'micro-celebrity'and the rise of social media influencers. *Celebrity Studies*, *8*(2), 191–208. doi:10.1080/19392397.2016.1218292

Khan, M. A., & Iqbal, S. (2015). The effectiveness of sales incentives on sales force performance: An empirical study of pharmaceutical companies in Pakistan. *Journal of Marketing Management*, *6*(2), 1–21. doi:10.12785/jmm.060101

Kim, A. J., & Ko, E. (2012). Do social media marketing activities enhance customer equity? An empirical study of luxury fashion brand. *Journal of Business Research*, *65*(10), 1480–1486. doi:10.1016/j.jbusres.2011.10.014

Kotler, P., & Armstrong, G. (2021). *Principles of marketing*. Pearson Education Limited.

Kotorov, R. (2003). Customer relationship management: Strategic lessons and future directions. *Business Process Management Journal*, *9*(5), 566–571. doi:10.1108/14637150310496686

KPMG International. (2011). *Going Social. How businesses are making the most of social media.* KPMG International. http://www.grazersoft.com/media/pdf/Going-Social.pdf

Kumar, A. (2016). An empirical study of sales incentives in the Indian retail sector. *Journal of Marketing and Consumer Research*, *21*, 73–80.

Kumar, A., Bezawada, R., Rishika, R., Janakiraman, R., & Kannan, P. K. (2016). From Social to Sale: The Effects of Firm-Generated Content in Social Media on Customer Behavior. *Journal of Marketing*, *80*(1), 7–25. doi:10.1509/jm.14.0249

Kumar, V. (2018). *The Benefits of Following Marketing Trends*. Entrepreneur. Retrieved from https://www.entrepreneur.com/article/309031

Kurdi, B. A., Alshurideh, M., Akour, I., Tariq, E., AlHamad, A. Q. M., & Alzoubi, H. M. (2022b). The effect of social media influencers' characteristics on consumer intention and attitude toward Keto products purchase intention. *International Journal of Data and Network Science*, *6*(4), 1135–1146. doi:10.5267/j.ijdns.2022.7.006

Lanz, L., Fischhof, B., & Lee, R. (2010). *How are Hotels Embracing Social Media in 2010? Examples of How to Start Engaging*. HVS Sales and Marketing Services. https://www.hvs.com/staticcontent/library/nyu2010/journal/articles/socialmediain2010.pdf

Lee, J. Y., Lee, M. S., & Feick, L. (2017). The effect of personalized recommendations and consumer innovativeness on purchase intention in a social commerce setting. *Journal of Interactive Marketing*, *38*, 29–41.

Leung, F. F., Gu, F. F., Li, Y., Zhang, J. Z., & Palmatier, R. W. (2022). Influencer Marketing Effectiveness. *Journal of Marketing*, *86*(6), 93–115. doi:10.1177/00222429221102889

Li, F., Larimo, J., & Leonidou, L. C. (2021). Social media marketing strategy: Definition, conceptualization, taxonomy, validation, and future agenda. *Journal of the Academy of Marketing Science*, *49*(1), 51–70. doi:10.1007/s11747-020-00733-3

Li, X., Chen, W., & Li, D. (2019). Personalized recommendation algorithms and consumer purchase behavior: An empirical study. *Electronic Commerce Research and Applications*, *36*, 100843.

Lin, W. L., Yip, N., Ho, J. A., & Sambasivan, M. (2020). The adoption of technological innovations in a B2B context and its impact on firm performance: An ethical leadership perspective. *Industrial Marketing Management*, *89*, 61–71. doi:10.1016/j.indmarman.2019.12.009

Linqia. (2019). *The state of influencer marketing*. Retrieved April 1, 2023 from https://linqia.com/wp-content/uploads/2019/04/Linqia-State-of-Influencer-Marketing-2019-Report.pdf

Liu, B. (2012). Sentiment analysis and opinion mining. *Synthesis Lectures on Human Language Technologies*, *1*(5), 1–168.

Lou, C., & Yuan, S. (2019). Influencer marketing: How message value and credibility affect consumer trust of branded content on social media. *Journal of Interactive Advertising*, *19*(1), 58–73. doi:10.1080/15252019.2018.1533501

Lu, H., & Hsiao, K. (2010). The influence of extro/introversion on the intention to pay for social networking sites. *Information & Management*, *47*(3), 150–157. doi:10.1016/j.im.2010.01.003

Luchs, Swan, & Creusen. (2015, July 27). *Perspective: A review of Marketing Research on*. Wiley Online Library.

Malhotra, N. K., Birks, D. F., & Wills, P. (2020). *Marketing research: An applied approach*. Pearson.

Manninen, K., & Huiskonen, J. (2022). Factors influencing the implementation of an integrated corporate sustainability and business strategy. *Journal of Cleaner Production*, *343*, 131036. doi:10.1016/j.jclepro.2022.131036

Mooi, E. A., & Sarstedt, M. (2011). *A concise guide to market research: the process, data, and methods using IBM SPSS Statistics*. Springer. doi:10.1007/978-3-642-12541-6

Nelson, O., & Deborah, A. (2017). Celebrity endorsement influence on brand credibility: A critical review of previous studies. *Online Journal of Communication and Media Technologies*, *7*(1), 15–32. doi:10.29333/ojcmt/2577

Panda, A. (2017). Sales promotion and its effectiveness in the Indian retail industry. International Journal of Sales. *Retailing and Marketing*, *6*(1), 1–9. doi:10.14303/ijsrm.2017.002

Paramita, W., Nhu, H. B. C., Ngo, L. V., Tran, Q. H. M., & Gregory, G. (2021). Brand experience and consumers' social interactive engagement with brand page: An integrated-marketing perspective. *Journal of Retailing and Consumer Services*, *62*, 102611. doi:10.1016/j.jretconser.2021.102611

Pires, G. D., & Stanton, J. (2018). Marketing trends: A review and future directions. *Journal of Business Research*, *89*, 198–207. doi:10.1016/j.jbusres.2018.02.014

Popovič, A., Hackney, R., Coelho, P. S., & Jaklič, J. (2012). Towards business intelligence systems success: Effects of maturity and culture on analytical decision making. *Decision Support Systems*, *54*(1), 729–739. doi:10.1016/j.dss.2012.08.017

Pourkhani, A., Abdipour, K., Baher, B., & Moslehpour, M. (2019). The impact of social media in business growth and performance: A scientometrics analysis. *International Journal of Data and Network Science (Print)*, *3*(3), 223–244. doi:10.5267/j.ijdns.2019.2.003

Pulizzi, J., & Barrett, N. (2009). Get content get customers-Turn Prospects into buyers with content marketing. *Saxena NSB Management Review*, *2*(2), 98–100.

Putri, A. M. A., & Sanica, I. G. (2022). Digital Marketing Strategy to Survive during Covid-19 Pandemic. *International Journal of Economics Business and Accounting Research, 6*(1), 27–33.

Ramanathan, U., Subramanian, N., & Parrott, G. (2017). Role of social media in retail network operations and marketing to enhance customer satisfaction. *International Journal of Operations & Production Management, 37*(1), 105–123. doi:10.1108/IJOPM-03-2015-0153

Russo, S., Schimperna, F., Lombardi, R., & Ruggiero, P. (2022). Sustainability performance and social media: An explorative analysis. *Meditari Accountancy Research, 30*(4), 1118–1140. doi:10.1108/MEDAR-03-2021-1227

Sadeq, N., Nassreddine, G., & Younis, J. (2023). Impact of Artificial Intelligence on E-marketing. *International Journal of Trend in Scientific Research and Development, 7*(1), 1318-1331. https://www.ijtsrd.com/papers/ijtsrd53850.pdf

Safko, L. (2015). *Why sharing valuable content is the key to successful marketing*. Social Media Today. Retrieved from https://www.socialmediatoday.com/marketing/why-sharing-valuable-content-key-successful-marketing

Sahni, N. S., Wheeler, S. C., & Chintagunta, P. (2018). Personalization in email marketing: The role of noninformative advertising content. *Marketing Science, 37*(2), 236–258. doi:10.1287/mksc.2017.1066

Saini, A., & Saini, R. (2017). Sales incentives: A review of literature. International Journal of Research in Management. *Economics and Commerce, 7*(3), 26–31. doi:10.20431/2454-9437.0703003

Saini, R., & Saini, R. (2017). Sales force incentive schemes: A review of the literature. *Journal of Applied Economics and Business Research, 7*(3), 180–187.

Samad, M. E., El-Chaarani, H., Nemar, S. E., & Raimi, L. (2022). Digital corporate entrepreneurship in the workplace. In Routledge eBooks (pp. 126–136). doi:10.4324/9781003283386-13

Samuel Craig, C., & Douglas, S. P. (2001). Conducting international marketing research in the twenty-first century. *International Marketing Review, 18*(1), 80–90. doi:10.1108/02651330110398413

Selden, L., & MacMillan, I. C. (2006). Manage customer-centric innovation-systematically. *Harvard Business Review, 84*(4), 108. PMID:16579418

Seth, G. (2012). *Analyzing the Effects of Social Media on the Hospitality Industry*. UNLV Theses/Dissertations/ Professional Papers/Capstones. Paper 1346. https://digitalscholarship.unlv.edu/thesesdissertations/1346 /

Setyani, V., Zhu, L., Hidayanto, A. N., Sandhyaduhita, P. I., & Hsiao, B. (2019). Exploring the psychological mechanisms from personalized advertisements to urge to buy impulsively on social media. *International Journal of Information Management*, *48*, 96–107. doi:10.1016/j.ijinfomgt.2019.01.007

Sher, P. J., & Lee, S. (2009). Consumer skepticism and online reviews: An elaboration likelihood model perspective. *Social Behavior and Personality*, *37*(1), 137–143. doi:10.2224/sbp.2009.37.1.137

Singh, T. P., & Sinha, R. (2017). The Impact of Social Media on Business Growth and Performance in India. *International Journal of Research in Management & Business Studies*, *4*(1), 2348–6503. http:// s3.amazonaws.com/arena-attachments/2329377/43839f512f 38d032594f26fb03b4ee5b.pdf?1529398740

Sivarajah, U., Irani, Z., Gupta, S., & Mahroof, K. (2020). Role of big data and social media analytics for business to business sustainability: A participatory web context. *Industrial Marketing Management*, *86*, 163–179. doi:10.1016/j. indmarman.2019.04.005

Slater, S. F., & Narver, J. C. (1999). Market-oriented is more than being customer-led. *Strategic Management Journal*, *20*(12), 1165–1168. doi:10.1002/(SICI)1097-0266(199912)20:12<1165::AID-SMJ73>3.0.CO;2-#

Starkov, M., & Mechoso, M. (2008). *Best Practices on Monitoring Hotel Review Sites, Hospitality eBusiness Strategies*. https://www.hospitalitynet.org/opinion/4037310. html

Sussman, S. W., & Siegal, W. S. (2003). Informational influence in organizations: An integrated approach to knowledge adoption. *Information Systems Research*, *14*(1), 47–65. doi:10.1287/isre.14.1.47.14767

Swani, K., Milne, G., & Brown, P., B. (. (2013). Spreading the word through likes on Facebook: Evaluating the message strategy effectiveness of Fortune 500 companies. *Journal of Research in Interactive Marketing*, *7*(4), 269–294. doi:10.1108/JRIM-05-2013-0026

Trachuk, T., Vdovichena, O., Andriushchenko, M., Semenda, O., & Pashkevych, M. (2021). Branding and advertising on social networks: Current trends. *International Journal of Computer Science & Network Security*, *21*(4), 178–185.

Veltri, G. A., Lupiáñez-Villanueva, F., Folkvord, F., Theben, A., & Gaskell, G. (2023). The impact of online platform transparency of information on consumers' choices. *Behavioural Public Policy*, *7*(1), 55–82. doi:10.1017/bpp.2020.11

Verhoef, P. C., Kannan, P. K., & Inman, J. J. (2015). From multi-channel retailing to omni-channel retailing: Introduction to the special issue on multi-channel retailing. *Journal of Retailing*, *91*(2), 174–181. doi:10.1016/j.jretai.2015.02.005

Voorveld, H. A., Van Noort, G., Muntinga, D. G., & Bronner, F. (2018). Engagement with social media and social media advertising: The differentiating role of platform type. *Journal of Advertising*, *47*(1), 38–54. doi:10.1080/00913367.2017.1405754

Voramontri, D., & Klieb, L. (2019). Impact of social media on consumer behaviour. *International Journal of Information and Decision Sciences*, *11*(3), 209. doi:10.1504/IJIDS.2019.101994

Wang, R. Y., & Strong, D. M. (1996). Beyond Accuracy: What Data Quality Means to Data Consumers. *Journal of Management Information Systems*, *12*(4), 4, 5–33. doi:10.1080/07421222.1996.11518099

Wilson, S., & Abel, I. (2001, December 12). So you want to get involved in e-commerce. *Industrial Marketing Management*.

Winnard, J., Adcroft, A., Lee, J., & Skipp, D. (2014). Surviving or flourishing? integrating business resilience and sustainability. *Journal of Strategy and Management*, *7*(3), 303–315. doi:10.1108/JSMA-11-2012-0059

Yang, M., Evans, S., Vladimirova, D., & Rana, P. (2017). Value uncaptured perspective for sustainable business model innovation. *Journal of Cleaner Production*, *140*, 1794–1804. doi:10.1016/j.jclepro.2016.07.102

# Chapter 11
# Transforming Human Resources With AI:
## Empowering Talent Management and Workforce Productivity

**Mazen Fawaz Massoud**
https://orcid.org/0000-0002-9018-0687
*Jinan University, Lebanon*

**Bassel Maaliky**
*Luna Space Holding Company, Saudi Arabia*

**Abir Fawal**
*Beirut Arab University, Lebanon*

**Allam Mawllawi**
*Jinan University, Lebanon*

**Fadlallah Yahkni**
*Jinan University, Lebanon*

## ABSTRACT

*AI is an irreplaceable human resources technological tool in the era of new technologies. AI allows recruiters to face tense talent shortages and resignation peril. AI benefits include talent identification, working time optimization, productivity elevation, and empowerment. Machine learning and profound learning advances imply faster processing speeds for applications and efficient solutions endorsed by human-artificial intelligence collaboration. Artificial intelligence experts in artificial intelligence concluded that AI will never replace employees but will act*

DOI: 10.4018/979-8-3693-1046-5.ch011

*as an intelligent assistant supporting them to attain the organization's mission. Therefore, the biggest challenge for AI adoption is not technical but human. Innovative technologies depend on experts to train employees to use these intelligent machinery and systems intelligently. AI and talented workforces are partners in supporting the human resources transformation. Ultimately, employees gain in productivity and use their expertise for strategic decisions.*

## INTRODUCTION

The technology landscape has become increasingly dynamic in recent years (Akanksha Saxena, 2020). Over the past decade, AI has synthetically evolved to assimilate sophisticated solutions in human resources technologies. Artificial intelligence grounded on technology is still in its infancy. However, the future of HR is going through increased AI capabilities. AI is a positive Human resource force (Alnamrouti et al., 2022). This chapter aims to provide a better understanding of how artificial intelligence is changing the world of human resources. It highlights changes and benefits leading to improving talent management. The correlation between human potential and technical intelligence has been at the heart of Human Resources management since its conception.

Artificial Intelligence (AI) has emerged as a decisive tool within Human resource (HR) management due to its potential to increase productivity and work process effectiveness (Alnamrouti et al., 2022; Votto et al., 2021). The development of big data and other AI technologies, notably natural language processing and deep learning, has caused an astounding technological revolution in human resources. AI technologies are being utilized to automate the hiring process, starting with reviewing and screening resumes, conducting job interviews, and choosing the most suitable candidate for a position (Tambe et al., 2019; Nawaz, 2020).

Artificial Intelligence (AI) affects the workplace, potentially impacting jobs, productivity, and employee well-being (Saxena, 2020; Nguyen et al., 2022). In the Human Resources sphere, artificial Intelligence benefits recruitment and talent management. Modern organizations are adopting Artificial Intelligence as a time-saving tool with robust strengths, allowing recruiters and talent managers to work efficiently with algorithm-driven suggestions (Samad et al., 2023). Artificial intelligence's main objectives in the context of talents are to optimize recruitment and talent management results, improve the user experience and strengthen process efficiency through machine learning and reasoning mechanisms (Kaushal et al., 2023). Various AI-powered tools, such as semantic search and candidate screening, meet these objectives. The job quality improvements associated with artificial Intelligence embrace reduced boredom and increased commitment. The latter may be its strongest endorsement from the employee's perspective. Artificial Intelligence is incorporated into the performance appraisal procedure. Intelligent systems are used to appraise employees' performance regularly to eliminate biases relating to the subjectivity of supervisors (Rožman et al., 2022). AI keeps track of employees' progress and determines employees' needs in terms of training or coaching. Organizations use big data on employees to develop valuable predictions for managing jobs and changing skills (Nair et al., 2020; Sivathanu & Pillai, 2018).

However, critical interrogations are posed regarding adjusting organizations and the workforce to artificial intelligence applications (El Samad, El-Chaarani, et al., 2022). Critical challenges facing AI implementation include a shortage of specialized AI skills and the need for higher skill requirements (Tambe et al., 2019).

Artificial Intelligence (AI) is transforming labor markets. The influence of Artificial Intelligence on human resources is the subject of never-ending debate. Suseno et al. (2020) and Pillai & Sivathanu (2020) suggested that AI led to a labor market disruption and a limited role for humans. Rožman et al. (2022), Nair et al. (2020), and Liu et al. (2021) argue that AI increases productivity, progresses talents and enhances employees' well-being. Artificial Intelligence is considered automated help and support to humans, but it was not created to replace them (Aksoy & Gurol, 2021).

AI reduces the stress of information overload, giving the chance to focus on the core business. Therefore, Human Resource professionals should take advantage of these technologies while being aware of their possible abuses (Gélinas et al., 2022). HR must ensure that algorithms do not cause ethical problems. To successfully implement AI in the human resources department, managers must meet the challenge of technology reconciliation in a profession where humans are central to maximizing performance effectiveness (Gethe, 2022; Grover, 2022).

This chapter examines the transformation in human resources due to artificial intelligence. It highlights significant alterations in HR functions resulting from artificial intelligence applications. Hence, this chapter is divided into ten sections. The first section presented a revaluation of work in the era of artificial intelligence. The second section underlines the definition of AI in the human resources field. The third section emphasizes significant applications and transformations in HR functions. The fourth section discovers AI benefits in human resource management. The fifth section summarizes critical challenges. The sixth section explains the role of AI in enhancing skills detection, transfer and acquisition. The seventh section will determine the role of Artificial Intelligence in the talent management framework. The eighth and ninth sections emphasize AI's influence on talent management and employee productivity.

## REDEFINING WORK IN THE ERA OF ARTIFICIAL INTELLIGENCE

The development and advancement of the Internet of Things within organizations is notable progress in revolutionizing the human resources domain (Kremer, 2022). The Internet of Things (IoT) has become a routine in modern sectors. IoT technologies have upsurged numerous flagship applications in diverse sectors (Alshehri & Muhammad, 2021).

The artificial intelligence revolution's success is due to innovation speed. AI has accelerated considerably due to a clear improvement in its learning capabilities, also known as machine learning, more specifically as domains of (reinforcement learning, deep learning and machine learning). For instance, facial recognition has improved significantly in the last two years. The facial recognition algorithm possesses a reduced error rate of just 0.05%, according to a recent test by Mishra and Sarkar (2022), Kumar et al. (2022) and Aikyn et al. (2023).

AI developments are attributable to enhanced access to big data from reliable sources such as international banks, e-commerce, reputable journals, social media, and governments (Haghi Kashani et al., 2021). Accessibility to this genuine data has developed influential algorithms and machine learning systems. Deep learning constructed on human brain capabilities is proficient in inducing learning from unstructured data in an unsupervised manner. AI processes vast sources of data Using deep learning. AI can process massive amounts of data in minutes, while it would take humans decades to understand and extract relevant information (Strohmeier, 2022). Deep learning encompasses innovative interpretation skills in object detection, speech recognition, and language interpretation to take decisions at unprecedented speeds (El Samad et al., 2022). Organizations realize the potential of untangling this information capital and are increasingly adopting deep learning-driven AI systems to gain a competitive advantage through data and automation. Priya et al. (2021), Gao & Wu (2021) and Madhavi et al. (2020) argued that deep learning and self-learning abilities will eventually replace human experts. The influence of artificial intelligence on workforce layouts is highly debatable (El Samad, El-Chaarani, et al., 2022). The reality-augmentation vision goes beyond AI-driven automation and the resulting workforce downsizing to establishing mutual capacity building and sustainable competitive advantage to work nature (Samad et al., 2023). Augmentation allows organizations to use automation to free employees from repetitive and error-prone tasks. Artificial intelligence allows employees to fully utilize their skills, enhance interpretation capabilities and leverage their empathy to make complex decisions (El Samad et al., 2022). Consequently, AI helps to unleash employees' competencies to generate innovative value sources (Gethe, 2022; Grover, 2022; Pillai & Sivathanu, 2020).

AI and the efficient implementation of its domains are contingent on human collaboration. The workforce and intelligent machine collaboration accomplish organizational objectives. Collaboration possibilities between skilled workers and AI seem almost endless. However, it requires a prior analysis of employees' respective human skills and machines to attain the most effective combination (Palos-Sánchez et al., 2022). The workforce will, therefore, need to be trained to take full advantage of these new human-machine alliances. AI training on intelligent machines is vital for international consulting and technology organizations, as is creating a pool of qualified workers dedicated to intelligent machines. Consequently, the training department choosing to increase this partnership and cooperation will have to support workforces in their professional development and train them on human-machine applications and domains (Abdeldayem & Aldulaimi, 2020; Kambur & Akar, 2022).

The coronavirus pandemic has propelled AI progress by accelerating the adoption of three major trends (Sallam et al., 2023). First is the significant use of teleworking, followed by increased e-commerce and virtual transactions. Third, the optimization of automation has accelerated its implementation. These transformations were implemented urgently to deal with the health crisis; however, experts agree that these technological changes will affect organizational culture permanently and induce alterations in employee behavior (Sulaiman & Mustafa, 2021) (Gaur, Bashir, & Sanghvi, 2021; Gaur et al., 2021; Lainjo, 2021).

## ARTIFICIAL INTELLIGENCE SOLUTIONS

As with human intelligence, AI embraces generic definitions. Kambur & Akar (2022), Sallam et al. (2023), and Sulaiman & Mustafa (2021) definition is generic and describes AI as "conventional of theories and instigated techniques to create machines capable of simulating human intelligence." Artificial intelligence groups together under the term "Artificial Intelligence," a set of notions "inspired by human cognition or the biological brain to assist or supplement organizations in processing massive information." (El Samad et al., 2023). Information refers to data and forms a critical characteristic of AI effectiveness. It is imperative to distinguish between narrow and general artificial intelligence (Chevalier, 2022; Islam & Tamzid, 2023). Narrow AI is concerned with developing machines that can perform a specific or at least relatively specific task. General AI is about developing machines to accomplish human tasks and developing super artificial intelligence (Verma, 2020).

AI uses rational procedures to achieve targeted objectives and performance based on prearranged information. For example, a purchasing process is a rational procedure. Customers are aware of their needs. They search for information to find solutions, evaluate them, and make purchasing decisions. AI combines different elements: computer techniques (storage processes, programs), mathematical techniques (creation of algorithms, use of statistical models) and cognitive techniques (language interpretation) (I. Kumar et al., 2021). It uses these techniques to resolve a problem (recruiting a person to evaluate an employee's skills). Thus, it appears less complex than human intelligence, combining fewer tangible elements such as intuition and observation. AI, therefore, simulates human development (Gong et al., 2022). The most popular solutions are machine learning and language processing.

## Machine Learning

Artificial learning is defined as a set of methods constructing a model of "reality" from available "data" (data being defined as objective activities) by improving a system partly describing this reality and, therefore, by completing it or by creating models such as the ex-nihilo model. The construction of these models is customarily carried out with a combination of deductive and inductive approaches (Milojević & Redzepagic, 2021).

The deductive approach allows knowledge deduction and transformation from specifications or examples. Learning occurs on an explanation basis. Technically, methods are founded on particularization, mathematical inductions or "modus ponens" type (Sadeq et al., 2023). The latter uses methods of generalization, abstraction, abduction, inversion of the resolution or induction based on a finite number of cases. The induction approach induces knowledge from identified cases or by similarity (Anastasi et al., 2021). These approaches are accessible in diverse methods and modalities depending on the existing "materials" offered to generate learning, data and operating rules. Modalities include procedural, explicit and implicit knowledge. First, procedural knowledge is simplified as declarative and algorithmic. Second, explicit knowledge of the problem is attained based on "behavior traces," for instance, traces left on the internet (Mhlanga, 2022).

The results of samples can be positive, leading to "generalization," or either positive or negative samples related to "inductive logic programming." Third, implicit knowledge is completed by excluding explicit knowledge (Olugbade et al., 2022). It is based on the use of classified samples. Techniques used are mainly neural networks, decision trees and statistical learning. Unclassified samples require either classification - creating classes that allow symbolic, neural statistical methods - or discovering associations (Aydın & Turan, 2023).

## Language Processing

Semantics examines the meaning of words in the sentence and its context (El Samad et al., 2023). Semantic analysis is, therefore, a relatively complex technique

*Figure 1. Semantic analysis*
*Source: Majumder & Mondal, 2021; Selvapandian et al., 2020; Mah et al., 2022*

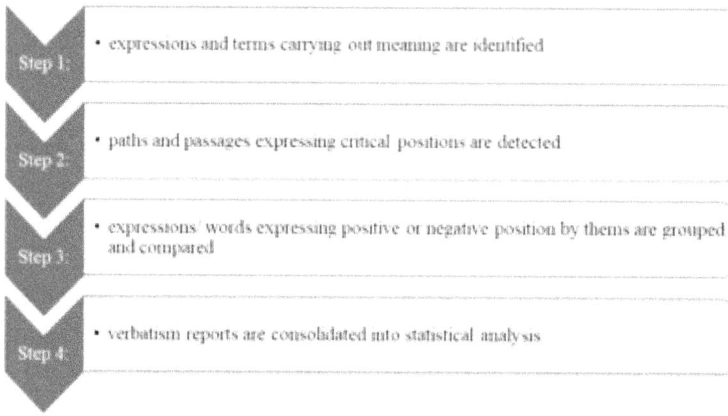


that exceeds in technicality and interest lexical analysis techniques (mainly using dictionaries) or grammatical analysis techniques (mainly using formalized grammar) (van Erp et al., 2021).

Semantic analysis is at the heart of applications of automatic human language processing, opening up a wide field of applications such as translations, spelling corrections, or, more recently, searching for similarities or relationships between different texts. Semantic analysis techniques are mainly based on linguistic and statistical approaches (Jing, 2020). First, the linguistic approach establishes rules a priori. Second, the statistical approach analyzes a large volume of text, from which the machine will automatically extract rules using language processing (artificial learning). Semantic analysis in language processing goes through four steps (T. Alqahtani et al., 2023):

## THE ROLE OF AI SOLUTIONS IN THE HR DEPARTMENT

AI in the HR management context is delineated as software algorithms induced by computer systems to perform HR management activities requiring human cognition and intervention. Talent is based on AI solutions to advance HR procedures. Patheja et al. (2023) and Vasantham (2021) defined AI as "a combination of algorithms and techniques which is located at the frontier of mathematics, computer and cognitive sciences. AI compiles areas of expertise and consequently aims to "reproduce as best as possible, using machines, mental activities, following a logic of reasoning, perception, and decision." The term "intelligence" in the context of Artificial

Intelligence calls upon the notion of adaptation. It comprises "modeling the resolution of a problem." (Delecraz et al., 2022; Qamar et al., 2021).

AI tasks in HR departments are multiple. They consist of selecting and hiring personnel, establishing a job classification and remuneration system, scheduling employee training activities, and planning workforce needs (El Samad, El-Chaarani et al., 2022). AI programs study employee satisfaction program activities relating to the quality of life at work. Advanced programs participate in collective bargaining and the settlement of grievances. AI activities embrace performance evaluation and form daily support for employees. AI is presented as an opportunity to reduce costs associated with the HR department, increase the efficiency of HR management and foster the strategic role of HR professionals (Patheja et al., 2023; Delecraz et al., 2022).

Vasantham (2021), Qamar et al. (2021), and Gaur et al. (2021) show that implementing AI for HR transforms professions and the organization's relationship with its employees. This technology also presents several challenges relating to the design of tools and their reliability, data security and respect for ethical principles. Artificial intelligence adopts a large number of techniques and technologies. Artificial intelligence in the human resources sphere is particularly limited to technologies regarding software solutions offered on the market:

- Systems experts and robotics
- Language processing (with machine translation, classification, text generation, context extraction),
- Machine Learning techniques (with supervised and unsupervised learning and Deep Learning techniques),
- Images and shapes recognition, and speech processing,
- Planning and organizing techniques

Algorithmic human resources management (AHRM) is increasingly discussed within organizations about the growing use of digital data to support human resources (HR) decision-making. This algorithm-based decision-making shapes organizations' work management and HR practices (Soleimani et al., 2022).

Indeed, the information generated by AI systems distinguishes solutions among different courses of action and predicts the future impacts of the organization's HR decisions. AI can provide HR leaders and managers insights into problems by merging historical data with predictive analytics (Lauriola et al., 2022).

HR decisions are taken without human intervention due to AI advances and the sophistication of algorithms. This fully automated decision-making is widespread, particularly with online work platforms. Automated recruitment platform specialized for self-employed employees; the algorithm acts to select members. It grants or denies workers access to the platform fully automatedly (Guo, 2022). Similarly, the algorithm takes remuneration decisions. It adjusts salaries according to the dynamics of labor supply and demand. Algorithms distribute tasks between workers automatically. Its predictive approach to logistics flows makes it possible to anticipate employee availability. The development of the system required integrating a large amount of data, including task preparation times and employee availability (Ammer et al., 2023).

Automating HR management decision-making is an integral part of the digital business strategy of these online labor platforms, where labor supply and demand meet electronically. Given the size of the workforce operating on these platforms, which are symbolic of the merger between technology and the world of work, it would take a lot of time for human managers to execute HR activities. It would limit the ability of these organizations to operate effectively and evolve efficiently (Sallam et al., 2023; Sulaiman & Mustafa, 2021).

Successful applications encountered in the world of HR are still relatively rare. Human resources experts increasingly encounter techniques relating to artificial (or machine) learning, expert systems and semantic analysis (Lauriola et al., 2022; Guo, 2022).

Machine learning techniques are deployed to progress Human Resources analytics policy. Consequently, machine learning techniques identify operating "patterns" and new management rules (Ardichvili, 2022). Scrutinizing data from machine learning helps to understand poorly understood or identified operations or results. The instrumentality of machine learning techniques is beneficial to identifying career management and paths correlated with detained skills or analyzing the causes of absenteeism (Laumer & Morana, 2022). Semantic analysis usage in HR is promising due to the significant quantity of texts, reports and qualitative data. For instance, feedback from performance appraisal interviews is automatically analyzed to inform employees about their professional progress or stipulate training needs. These fascinating tools are systematic and do not permit imagination or sidetracking. These tools only reflect existing learning conditions and are used mainly to detect correlations (Alqahtani, 2023).

## ARTIFICIAL INTELLIGENCE AND HUMAN RESOURCES TRANSFORMATION

Artificial Intelligence (AI) is transforming and revolutionizing all industries, including their human resources practices. Artificial Intelligence has affected human resources management, mainly selection and recruitment after task automation (Tiwari et al., 2021). Recruitment agencies use chatbots to facilitate initial candidate screening, saving top recruiters time and resources. AI also enables companies to increase transparency and diminish bias in the hiring process by automating manual tasks like screening resumes, scheduling interviews, and gathering candidate information (Bhatt & Shah, 2023).

Artificial intelligence capabilities improve employees' skills in an efficient and personalized method. Well-integrated artificial intelligence AI in the Human Resources departments creates new job opportunities. Positions such as HR AI specialists or digital transformation managers have emerged (Sindu, 2018). These positions offer new career prospects. Artificial intelligence promises to dramatically change human resources by introducing automation, advanced analytics, and process optimization. HR professionals are repositioning themselves by developing new skills focused on using and managing AI tools (Biliavska et al., 2022).

Artificial intelligence AI has significantly improved the efficiency of human resources departments by automating administrative tasks. Administrative tasks such as scheduling, managing leave, generating reports and data updating are accomplished swiftly and accurately with AI (M. Islam et al., 2022). The latter helps eliminate the monotonous and time-consuming workload, freeing time for HR professionals. Delegating administrative tasks to AI technology helps optimize departmental efficiency and improve employee and employer experience. Task automation helps HR professionals save valuable time, allowing them to focus on strategic and valuable activities (Kambur & Akar, 2022).

Growing organizations' needs for efficiency, cost reduction, and informed decision-making have supported the adoption of AI. AI significantly impacts HR professions by redefining roles and requiring skills adapted to this new technological era. Artificial intelligence will fundamentally reposition the Human Resources functions at two levels (Kremer, 2022).

First, task automation procedures leverage human value. Predictable and repetitive human tasks are automated as a part of HR digitalization processes. The HR manager has complete control of tasks robotization and the needed level of artificial intelligence efficiency. Work automation in artificial intelligence usually correlates with the potential for jobs and the disappearance of human labor. However, to focus on this perspective is to miss other massive and factual consequences (Priya et al., 2021; Gao & Wu, 2021).

On the contrary, automation will profoundly increase the human contribution to work. Indeed, as counter-intuitive, Artificial Intelligence (AI) will highlight the role of humans at work. Thanks to an impact at three levels. First, most human activities will be replaced by machines, but only part of the most predictive and repetitive tasks. The human being, freed by the machine from the most "alienating" tasks, can refocus on added-value tasks (Tiwari et al., 2021; Bhatt & Shah, 2023).

Job losses caused by automation will be largely offset in the long term by new jobs created by innovative AI technologies. Jaiswal et al. (2022) and Ernst et al. (2019) did not foresee large-scale technological unemployment due to automation.

AI is expected to increasingly automate repetitive and sometimes dangerous tasks like assembly line manufacturing. These jobs, newly improved by AI technologies, are beneficial for individuals to demonstrate creativity, strategy and initiative, and organizations notice gains in productivity. However, these newly created jobs will require new skills and significant investments in continuing training and requalification (Hunt et al., 2022).

Second, intelligent data boosts human intervention. HR receives notifications from data created and analyzed by artificial intelligence (Basu et al., 2022). Managers detect where, when and how to intervene to provide added value to the organization and employees. AI deciphers data generated by employees resulting from interactions with digital tools. Data interpretation alerts the HR manager about problems his teams encounter in real-time. AI could notify the HR manager about motivation drops, workloads, employee stress and revenue losses (Pandey, 2020).

The HR manager's functions will fundamentally change (Geisel, 2018). Upstream, managers are responsible for artificial intelligence configuration according to organizational vision, values and culture. Managers decide the employees-services level of interaction. HR is the moment of truth experience designer. HR can act in the right place and time to unlock individual and collective human dynamics. The HR manager, informed by AI, is a human expert, tailors employees' coaching and teams, and supports their development. Data access by AI will give humans superpowers of analysis and decision-making. AI analyzes complex situations and precisely identifies human intervention needs (Shoss & Ciarlante, 2022).

Artificial intelligence traced noteworthy progress in human resources management (HRM). Organizations are gradually adopting diverse AI functionalities to modernize their HR practices for efficient employee engagement, involvement and collaboration. However, potential advantages and benefits depend primarily on implementing innovative technology in the workplace (Shubhabrata Basu et al., 2023).

HR professionals are assisted by robotic technologies advancing the management of employees' daily relationships. Chatbots are available to instantly respond to various employee queries previously handled by HR staff, such as requests for changes in leave requests or even absence notices (Rahmani & Kamberaj, 2021). Employees who are unable to attend work due to health issues can message HR through chatbots. These bots relay the information to their supervisors and managers, then automatically adjust the team's work schedules to compensate for their absence. Chatbots respond to employee inquiries related to leave and company policies, respond to requests for technical assistance, and evaluate employee performance at all levels of the company hierarchy (Mehr, 2017). The tool also specializes in predicting the jobs that will be created in the future and the talents and skills required. Chatbot employee data is collected and analyzed for AI tools to generate talent predictions. AI multi-faceted technology tools are transforming human resources. The following types of artificial intelligence improve organizational ROI, save time and money, progress IOT culture, and manage employee productivity (Sheikh, 2019; Mohan, 2019).

- Workforce Analytics – AI tools help HR professionals access unparalleled depth of data. Data analytics possibilities range from in-depth analysis of assessment metrics to transforming learning and development programs. It improves trust in HR reports.
- Augmented Content – VR-based content is more engaging for learners but also improves the internalization and application of learned skills and behaviors.
- Enhanced Access – AI-powered learning management systems (LMS) make training and development programs accessible on demand. Employees access the content conveniently, track their progress with career-tracking tools, map their career paths, and forecast their learning and development needs (Berşe et al., 2023).
- Personalization – AI transforms training beyond traditional one-size-fits-all programs. Language, learning style, and communication preferences are customizable, putting learners in control.

## AI BENEFITS IN HUMAN RESOURCE MANAGEMENT

Artificial intelligence adoption levels in HRM practices are still modest within organizations. Nevertheless, reliable data demonstrated potential for growth in the future. (Conn, 2017) P maintains that HR functions in international organizations are currently using AI applications at various scales, primarily for recruitment processes. Artificial intelligence real-time learning has great potential for different HRM practices. AI collects data regularly, allowing managers to gather regular feedback and helping them take corrective actions to meet employees' needs. It reduces manual data collection time and eliminates waiting time for annual employee satisfaction survey results. AI has proven very useful in managerial decision-making, whether in recruitment or monitoring employee productivity. It enhances and progresses communication due to Humanized devices. Solutions like IBM's Attrition Prediction Program boosted workforce retention (Sanyaolu & Atsaboghena, 2022).

AI is creating new opportunities for professional development. The influence of artificial intelligence on human resources management is not limited to the following (Saranya, 2022).

- **Personalized Training.** AI is offering personalized training programs adapted to individuals' specific needs. AI can recommend targeted training modules to fill skills gaps by analyzing current skills and gaps in performance appraisal.

- **Organized Information**. Artificial intelligence facilitates access to large amounts of human resources data and knowledge. Due to advances in semantic search and natural language processing, AI is sorting, organizing and offering relevant and up-to-date information, allowing employees to deepen their knowledge in their area of expertise.
- **Simulation and Virtual Reality.** Artificial intelligence creates simulations and virtual reality environments, providing immersive learning experiences. Simulation and virtual reality allow employees to practice in realistic situations and develop their practical skills in a safe and controlled environment (Sakka & El Hadi El Maknouzi, 2022).
- **Employees Turnover.** AI helps human resources managers to estimate employee turnover. Machine learning algorithms predict which employees will stay or leave a company. Machine learning techniques are applied to analyze responses to employee surveys regarding factors that influence job satisfaction, such as work environment, leadership and other hygiene factors. Managers use this data to decide recruitment, training and retention strategies.
- **Tasks Automation.** AI helps automate repetitive tasks. Artificial intelligence allows employers to save time by automating some of their administrative tasks or mundane functions such as payroll processing. By doing so, they can give their employees more freedom and flexibility when making decisions about their working hours or other aspects of their work that may require autonomy so that they can focus on more important matters, such as recruiting talented people for roles within the company (Chowdhury et al., 2023).
- **Selection and Recruitment.** AI helps find the best candidates based on the skills and experience an organization needs, rather than just those who meet specific criteria, like having the right degree from a prestigious university or a high score on standardized tests taken during the college years (which do not necessarily indicate the level of aptitude). Organizations integrating AI tools into their hiring process have an advantage over competitors who do not use technology. They can find better-qualified candidates with less effort.
- **Shortlisting.** AI speeds up work by allowing recruiters to spend quality time interviewing qualified people and less time sifting through giant pools of unqualified candidates. Additionally, AI allows recruiters to eliminate duplicitous applications, saving organizations' resources. AI is used to filter candidates based on specific criteria and schedule interviews. AI is improving the quality of work by providing insights into candidate data without human intervention. For instance, an algorithm can recommend candidates based on selected performance criteria and traits.

AI has decreased human resources overhead expenses associated with recruitment staffing functions, such as administration and interview scheduling. It also improves job fitting accuracy because machines have a controlled margin of error. Machines have higher reading and feedback interpretation accuracy than humans (Garg et al., 2018).

## AI CHALLENGES IN HRM

Artificial intelligence can analyze and progress swiftly in colossal amounts of data. However, AI can yield errors, particularly in emotional interpretation associated with complex human situations. The absence of human elements such as empathy, emotional intelligence and understanding of context can lead to inappropriate or insensitive decisions in HR functions, especially in conflict management, disciplinary decision-making or human interactions. Besides, data protection is one of the main challenges that human resources HR faces when integrating artificial intelligence into Human Resource Management HRM. Challenges surface for several reasons (Hossin et al., 2021). HR professionals should consider some drawbacks of AI, including (Mohamad et al., 2022):

### Data Security and Privacy

First, AI requires massive collection and use of personal employee data, raising security and privacy concerns. Organizations must ensure the data collected is secure and complies with data protection regulations. Additionally, HR experts need to be transparent concerning data usage. Therefore, experts must ensure that only the required data is collected for legitimate purposes. Proactive privacy and data protection management are vital to building employee trust. Protective measures guarantee the respect of individual rights (Kemendi et al., 2022).

### AI Complexity and Biases

Second, there is an inability to understand the reasoning behind an AI decision. It can be challenging to recognize the AI system choice factors of a selected candidate with ambiguous previous experience. There is also no guarantee of AI consistency with organizational values in hiring decisions or other HR management functions (Prikshat et al., 2023).

Biased algorithms may not be apparent until they are put into practice. Algorithms can reflect biases in their design and implementation. For instance, algorithm biases entail using gender stereotypes in promotions or performance reviews. The latter results in discrimination against some work groups (Chilunjika et al., 2022).

## High Costs Associated With Technologies Implementation

Fourth, artificial intelligence encounters impediments in its implementation and maintenance. It necessitates high initial investment and ongoing maintenance costs. Sophisticated artificial intelligence technologies may require additional staff, especially for mandatory training before deployment. Therefore, machine purchasing, training and operating software costs hinder implementation. Workplace transformation and adaptation costs are added to the equation, restraining access to automation (El Samad, El-Chaarani et al., 2022). Organizations may not have the means to invest in introducing an innovative technology, even if it sustains financial profitability. Researchers found that AI application developments in HRM represent a small share of total business investment compared to other departments, such as robotics, marketing, sales and customer relations (Sadeq et al., 2023; Verma & Bandi, 2020).

## Excessive Monitoring

Excessive monitoring tools are associated with high turnover and absenteeism rates, low morale, low managerial trust and a deterioration of the relationship between employers and employees. The advent of innovative technologies in professional environments led to legislation and regulation updates regarding labor standards. This update aims to regulate the power of control and the growing managerial prerogatives of employers. The challenge is reconciling conflicting interests between the employer's need for information and respect for confidentiality (Giermindl et al., 2022).

## Integration Challenges

Technical difficulties pose a barrier to the rapid integration of technology and automation. Indeed, AI technology should be specifically adapted to the intended tasks. Machines are invented and trained to meet specific needs and demonstrate their effectiveness in real situations, laboratories or by modeling. Technological development can only be gradual according to industry-specific needs. Needs variation inevitably influences AI integration into the organization (Hossin et al., 2021).

Technical difficulties and the application of technologies linked to AI could slow down the automation procedures and employee replacement by AI systems. For example, artificial intelligence systems should ensure reliability in making adoption decisions. AI system's ability to perform many tasks with precision is impressive. Nevertheless, if this system produces errors, it could limit its adoption in the workplace (Prikshat et al., 2023).

## Talent Shortage

Organizations are facing challenges in talent shortage. Talented labor scarcity possessing crucial qualifications to assist in AI systems implementation is a noncompliance defiance. The deficiency and shortage of talented and competent employees restrict AI deployment. The second major challenge of data intelligence lies in creating future teams, joining the dynamics of agility and combining the right skills. Internalizing AI tools requires skills because it is rare to identify needed skills and talents that meet organizational needs (C. Liu et al., 2019).

## Profitability

The return on investment is a financial concern when management considers investing in artificial intelligence machines as a human labor alternative that would ultimately replace one or more employees. AI requires an initial investment cost represented in purchasing applications and machines and an ongoing investment in maintenance, software updates and occasional adjustment. Hence, profitability calculation is not a simple task. It comprises an overhead investment derived from employees' salaries and training (Giermindl et al., 2022).

## Social Acceptability

Social acceptability contributes to accelerating AI automation and implementation speed. Service organizations depend on employees for the first impression as organizational value and prefer to embrace automation partially. Therefore, management should consider modifying employees' behavior for an effective AI integration rather than eliminating jobs and increasing investment costs. Besides, introducing robots to provide different services requires social adaptation that will inevitably take time (Hossin et al., 2021).

## Human Resistance to AI

AI circulation and appropriation in HR management vary according to organizational characteristics, employees and the workplace. Longoni et al. (2019) and Cadario et al. (2021) reported that HR managers cannot always assimilate these new tools and develop data analysis skills. Therefore, adopting and using the technologies may face resistance from HR and team members. Hence, HR experts are not always ready to use AI technologies.

HR recruiters and candidates do not seem to favor complete digital recruitment methods. Even if technology is appreciated in the preliminary stages of the search, HR managers prefer to establish personal links with candidates once they have refined their choices. The latter is decisive in the final selection. For candidates, digital recruiting involves taking a myriad of online tests. These assessments are time-consuming, and without human intervention, candidates may not get any return on their efforts from human resources. In addition, the authors indicate that not all candidates are equal in the hiring process of organizations (Chilunjika et al., 2022; Verma & Bandi, 2020). Talented employees are hunted in the job market. A talented workforce can push for a personalized experience, forcing employers to accept their demands. For some, this observation constitutes an example of discrimination, with a two-speed hiring process – personalized for specific candidates and standardized for the majority. Furthermore, studies show that individuals react differently to decisions depending on whether they are made by technology or humans. However, sometimes, decisions are more accessible to accept when derived from an algorithm than when made by a colleague, primarily when those decisions result in negative consequences for the person (Chowdhury et al., 2023).

AI is adapted as an employee evaluation and control tool. Algorithmic HR management has the effect of transforming the relationship between the organization and the workforce. These practices affect the feeling of justice employees perceive and their trust level in employment. Innovative work processes induced by AI tools must merge with organizational strategy and culture. Organizations are called upon to prepare for these transformations affecting management methods and organizational culture (Berşe et al., 2023; Sanyaolu & Atsaboghena, 2022; Saranya, 2022).

## INNOVATIVE COMPETENCIES PREREQUISITES TO ARTIFICIAL INTELLIGENCE

A demand for experienced laborers with interpersonal and management skills convoys the adoption of advanced technologies. Those intelligent machines do not master these competencies. The meta-analysis of Rott et al. (2022) and Akyazi et al. (2020) associating skills competencies to occupations has exemplified skills such as creativity, conceptualization, managing complex strategic planning and emotional intelligence as significant to career progress. The OECD encourages employees to develop inimitable skills through artificial intelligence, such as creativity, innovation, the capacity to sustain complex social interactions and challenging coping strategies derived from ambiguity. Leadership and personnel management are prerequisites to artificial intelligence. The latter is advanced by cognitive skills, decision-making, developing complex information, and critical thinking (Marquez et al., 2023).

The competition era of artificial intelligence is technology-driven. Implementing innovative organizational structures hinges on technology implementation and employees' innovative competencies. Machines and humans are integrated to complement each other. Machines perform repetitive and automated tasks precisely. Human creativity, intuition, adaptability, and innovation skills are increasingly essential to artificial intelligence. Despite their intelligence level, these human skills cannot be outsourced to robots (Kandlhofer et al., 2021).

AI attested to be a powerful assistant and supporter of talent management. AI implications in skilled professions have led to developing associations between talented employees and intelligent machines. Accordingly, talent management strategies and artificial intelligence amalgamate their strengths and skills to achieve an augmented talented workforce. Artificial intelligence incorporated in strategic HRD lays the foundation of an innovative skills model (Mehr, 2017; Sheikh, 2019).

## ARTIFICIAL INTELLIGENCE AND RECRUITMENT

AI is a powerful transformation tool in recruitment and skill acquisition. AI can help recruiters be more efficient. AI can help find candidates in various ways, including keyword research, contextual matching and filtering, and social media monitoring. Recruiters no longer worry about their biases or preferences interfering with candidate selection; machine learning algorithms are objective when finding the most qualified candidates (Ernst et al., 2019). AI eases candidates' engagement. HR recruitment officers don't have to waste time contacting each candidate individually after compiling an initial list of potential candidates. The system automates follow-up steps (Hunt et al., 2022; Geisel, 2018).

A conversational agent helps recruiters describe the ideal candidate profile according to the position to be filled, the missions, required skills, and planned objectives. Using the recorded conversations, AI can offer suggestions on the qualities, motivations, and soft skills. These recommendations are required for efficient shortlisting. AI is an automated technology assisting in job descriptions and writing dynamic job offers aligned with the organization's mission and vision by re-structuring job descriptions. Consequently, potential candidates can quickly project themselves, identify their strengths and weaknesses, and determine whether the company meets their professional expectations (Tiwari et al., 2021; Bhatt & Shah, 2023; Sindu, 2018).

Artificial intelligence saves time and helps select the most efficient websites to publish job ads, hence receiving relevant CVs according to the required skill level for the position. AI can prepare interview questions. The latter is adapted to the candidate profile and position. It summarizes the interview. The possibilities for artificial intelligence are endless in human resources processes and digitalization automation (Soleimani et al., 2022).

AI is equipping HRM with advanced tools leveraging employee autonomy. AI allows them to plan training, take talent stock, advance their careers, implement coaching, and provide direct feedback. AI is providing the power to steer career paths. AI functionalities assess employees in terms of performance, skills, training, coaching, and mobility. AI capacitates employee empowerment (Qamar et al., 2021).

AI is a vital asset for organizational transformation. Advanced algorithm learning models can analyze employee skills and performance data to identify gaps and training needs. In-depth analysis is developing personalized training programs adapted to the employees' needs. Training programs are becoming more practical, designed to meet individual needs and promote faster and more accurate learning. AI recommends relevant training content, online courses, or additional resources to improve employee skills. Additionally, AI tracks each employee's progress and adjusts recommendations in real-time, ensuring continuous and scalable training (Vasantham, 2021; Delecraz et al., 2022).

## ARTIFICIAL INTELLIGENCE FUNCTIONS IN TALENT MANAGEMENT FRAMEWORK

Human resources have been significantly improved due to the effective integration of artificial intelligence (AI) in this department. Technological tools and recruitment processes have become more efficient and precise. Advanced algorithms like GPT quickly scan thousands of resumes, identifying the most qualified candidates for a given position. These tools accelerate talent management by detecting high-potential employees and offering personalized development plans. AI-powered chatbots provide instant assistance to employees. They answer their common questions and guide them to the appropriate resources (Gurusinghe et al., 2021).

AI implementation is radically transforming talent management frameworks. It combines advanced techniques such as facial recognition, natural language processing, voice analysis, and "micro-expression" reading to determine traits closely matching high-performing employees. Technology promotes green HR management by reducing the environmental impact of the travel required for face-to-face job interviews. Therefore, the results provided by these tools outweigh the human involvement advantages in selecting talented candidates (Takhi et al., 2020).

AI is renovating talent management as an HR function. This framework is perceived as more favorable to the organization than to employees, even if it's

*Figure 2. Artificial intelligence in talent management framework*
*Source: Rajesh et al., 2018; Faqihi & Miah, 2023; Vinichenko et al., 2019; Zhang, 2022*

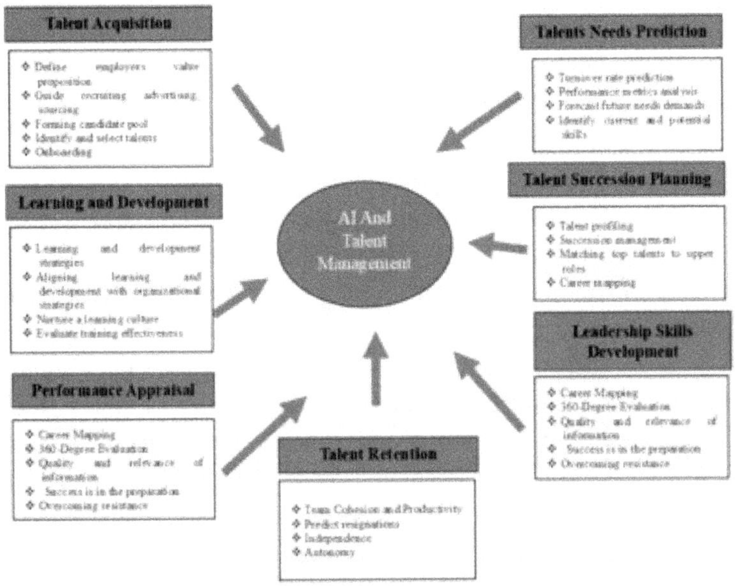


function-oriented towards employees, offering them a transparent workplace without biased decisions. Experts pointed out that the most complicated talent management task with data science techniques is talent identification recruiting due to legal and fairness problems that should be addressed in the hiring process (Sollini et al., 2020).

## Talent Acquisition

AI technologies accelerate talent acquisition by automating the recruitment process. This procedure is initiated by reviewing and screening curriculum vitae (CVs), conducting job interviews, and selecting the most talented candidate. AI software executes monotonous tasks of reviewing CVs from a large applicant pool. CVs are scrutinized and filtered following job description, skills and recruitment criteria. Therefore, AI automates talent exploration, identification and screening processes (Vedapradha et al., 2023).

CV examination foresees crucial criteria, including candidates' skills, previous experience, and employment references. It creates correlations with job offers by using optical character recognition technology. Beyond the applications received, AI-equipped recruitment software recognizes candidates by collecting and analyzing data from several sources, such as job sites. This software is "trained" to recognize job descriptions and comprehend critical job skills and knowledge (Yadav et al., 2023). This training is based on historical data, and then learnings integrated by the software are correlated with thousands of anonymous CVs plus scores indicating whether candidates were shortlisted, interviewed and hired. AI learns candidates' successful qualifications and applies that knowledge to screen potential candidates and evaluate their records (Shen, 2022).

Countless variables are combined to generate algorithms using machine learning technology and a score evaluating and ranking applications. Recruitment software automatically contacts talented candidates to complete their application files or conduct digital job interviews. Video interviews are scheduled, recorded, and then analyzed by AI tools. These intelligent tools recommend the most talented candidates who match organizational needs (de la Torre et al., 2021).

According to studies, automating the recruitment process offers organizational benefits. It allows for a significant reduction in the costs and time of recruitment processes and a three-fold increase in efficiency. AI implementation empowers and streamlines application assessment and reduces biases associated with human judgment (Tiwari et al., 2022). AI promotes fairness between candidates and increases diversity among hired employees. Well-designed algorithms contribute to selecting talented candidates without prejudice or discrimination based on age, gender or race. Algorithms standardize evaluation criteria and remove information irrelevant to an application review, influencing hiring managers' decisions (Xin et al., 2022).

## Learning and Development

AI ensures employees' access to ongoing learning and development, significantly enhancing productivity, performance and talent. improving healthcare and improving access to education. AI, through machine learning software, assimilates significant amounts of information. This information dispenses knowledge, developing training programs for effective learning (P. Bhatt & Muduli, 2022). Learning and development specialists are aware of AI's rapid evolution and maneuver this evolution as a force to improve learning processes. Learning and development explore and implement artificial intelligence progress, consenting human resources to develop new training strategies and techniques (Volkmar et al., 2022).

The training and development experts build skills by relying on Conversational AI. The latter collects facets from learners, allowing them to individualize training content and methods. The AI can emphasize these aspects by considering a prior analysis of mastered skills. Depending on learners ' preferences, it builds an educational path combining synchronous and asynchronous, remote and face-to-face (Al Ka'bi, 2023).

AI transformation is correlated with learning and development. Both depend on optimized and effective training techniques (Sircar et al., 2021). AI allows training programs to adapt to employees. The benefits of adopting AI include personalized learning, time-saving, increased involvement, and commitment. Employees achieve learning goals swiftly because they obtain accurate information based on preferences and goals (Wang & Wang, 2022). AI-powered learning system analyzes each learner and then suggests a learning program based on past performance and goals. AI modifies human behavior and components. It helps employees move between jobs (job rotation), prepares for job enrichment and enlargement and ensures continued efforts in learning, training and skills development. Human Resources experts develop work planning by improving learning and development programs. AI advances employee performance and productivity, enabling those experts to attract and retain talent and boost adaptation and innovation capacities (Koromina et al., 2019).

## Performance Appraisal

Employee activity evaluation and monitoring existed in traditional work environments. However, the arrival of digital technology and AI has accentuated this procedure and encouraged excessive control. AI is implemented for continuous monitoring objectives. The data collected comes from various sources such as surveillance cameras, innovative equipment, wearable devices, and customer reviews shared online (Alrashedi & Abbod, 2021). These practices increase the level of pressure and stress at work. AI system establishes task baseline models to compare to and sends a warning when employees deviate from norms. Alerts are sent to HR when an organizational policy is violated. AI determines employees' time spent at their desks with the same objective of controlling employee behavior. Therefore, applying AI data to HR raises concerns of hyper surveillance where individuals are controlled without their consent. The use of AI for control and surveillance comes with concerns about the security and protection of workers' data (Sinniah et al., 2022).

AI technologies facilitate employee Performance Appraisal. AI functions marked the transition from direct and physical control by the employer towards a remote-control model based on data collection (M & Elangovan, 2021). HR is adopting an eclectic range of advanced control and assessment, such as sensors embedded in smart devices, GPS tracking, and sociometric badges to collect employee data. This data concerns employee behavior, colleague relationships, and customer satisfaction (Verma & Bandi, 2019).

Intelligent systems combine metrics on individual employee performance goals, records and traces in applications used for daily task execution, and scores assigned by managers, their colleagues and clients (Tabassum, 2018). These systems evaluate performance in real-time and daily. Automated and continuous evaluation offers the advantage of reducing bias relating to the work environment and evaluator prejudices. Data analysis determines employees' training or coaching needs and offers personalized programs. It evaluates training results and verifies their effects on performance. Data analysis highlights decisive factors in employee productivity. AI analyzes this information to evaluate their performance and productivity at work (Singh & Shaurya, 2021).

## Talents Needs Prediction

Organizations use big data on employees to develop job management and skills development predictions. AI HR management software predicts a candidate's future performance. It detects employees experiencing work difficulties by cross-referencing data on employee performance, commitment level, job satisfaction, and historical data on turnover causes (Sinniah et al., 2022; M & Elangovan, 2021).

These analyses predict employee-specific needs and identify employees who adapt less to their professional environment or are disappointed by work-life balance. AI detects employees at risk of leaving the organization (Koromina et al., 2019; Wang & Wang, 2022). AI tools measure the effects and weight of different elements, creating predictive formulas based on the relative weighting of each factor. Results accuracy provided by these tools helps talented employees and leaders to make appropriate hiring decisions, promote proactive employee retention and boost their motivation, involvement and performance (Tabassum, 2018).

## Talent Succession Planning

Beyond talent predictions, AI helps manage succession planning for talented employees. AI data analysis identifies employee training and growth needs and detects skills gaps and career advancement opportunities (Barboza, 2019). Succession planning is reviewing key roles and determining the readiness levels of potential internal talents to fill these roles. It is a necessary process that provides a critical link between talent development and talent acquisition (Meister, 2019). Artificial intelligence functions facilitate talent development activities and processes but rely heavily on human resources input and support. Talent succession planning development processes require durable involvement and feedback. Succession planning is a process controlled and facilitated by artificial intelligence algorithms. It is a factual human resources method that fundamentally impacts organizational performance. In the era of the "war for talent," organizations should plan to retain and develop core talents. Advancing talents through artificial intelligence improves competitive advantage (Wan Ibrahim & Hassan, 2019).

Artificial intelligence creates plans to retain high-potential leaders, generates talent pools to grow the organization, and avoids interruptions due to unanticipated turnover (Yun et al., 2020). It allows human resources to systematically evaluate talent internally and externally for crucial roles. Furthermore, AI supports performance management by tracking and analyzing employee performance, allowing managers to provide accurate and constructive feedback. Consequently, AI systems manage succession planning, identify employees with leadership potential, and propose suitable development plans. Therefore, AI contributes to strategic and future-oriented human resources management (Aditia Putra Hamid et al., 2023).

## Leadership Skills Development

Due to the proliferation of AI machinery, the HR training department must develop employees' leadership skills. Adopting AI requires significant organizational changes, such as re-structuring teams, training employees and adapting corporate processes. Leadership necessitates managing these changes and convincing employees to adopt AI. Deploying AI requires specific skills in IT, data analysis and project management (Moldenhauer & Londt, 2018). Leadership skills are categorized as "Soft Skills". Its indicators include planning, adaptability and critical reasoning skills. Development workshops should reinforce workforce creativity, interpersonal skills, and problem-solving skills, differentiating humans from machines. Cooperation and teamwork are also highly valued as complementary Leadership skills (Setiawan et al., 2021).

Leadership skills are imperative in digital work environments due to the need to interpret large amounts of data. Planning, problem-solving, communication and teamwork are among the most in-demand leadership Skills for positions with high recruitment demand and expected turnover (Giraud et al., 2022). Managers need to improve their leadership skills to sustain long-term success in a world progressively dominated by AI. Leadership skills serve as a mediator variable between people and machines. It requires effective communication, organizational skills, and a faultless work ethic (Titareva, 2021).

Leadership skills development contributes significantly to the human resources department. Specialists are developing AI strategies to improve productivity, employee satisfaction and organizational performance. AI detects potential areas for improvement. Nonetheless, leadership skills such as communication and collaboration are required to implement these strategies (Peifer et al., 2022).

Leaders must develop and retain the right talent to successfully implement AI projects. Organizations encourage an AI culture of innovation and continuous learning, encouraging employees to experiment, share their ideas and train in new technologies. Leaders lead by example by investing in their development and supporting the learning initiatives of their teams. Employees perform better on the job and better accept AI-generated feedback from managers with transformational leadership styles (Effendi & Pribadi, 2021). The latter focuses on transforming employees' technological skills to provide a bridge between the workforce and artificial intelligence technologies. It allies inclusion and innovation. Relying on transformational leaders ensures that technological advancements are integrated to improve employee productivity. As more teams begin to work with and rely on AI, Leaders will need to deepen their understanding of core collaboration skills (Quaquebeke & Gerpott, 2023).

## Talent Retention

Candidates lacking technological talents constitute undoubtedly one of the significant organizational challenges. This talent shortage leads human resources to rethink recruitment, retention and talent management strategies. The latter pushes HR recruiters to headhunt talents. Turnover negatively impacts team cohesion and productivity (Saranya, 2022; Sakka & El Hadi El Maknouzi, 2022).

Understanding high turnover motives allows HR to consider corrective actions. Artificial intelligence provides realistic information to identify the causes of past and future resignations and anticipate recruitment decision-making (Ernst et al., 2019). AI digital solutions are simple. It aims to improve understanding and anticipation of resignations to perpetuate and retain talented teams. In other words, its innovative features revolve around two facets. First, turnover anticipation depends on data processing and collection by artificial intelligence (Paigude et al., 2023). These solutions will alert HR in the event of a potential resignation by identifying risk factors. The second embraces employment sustainability. AI solutions ponder the evolution of salary offers in the market (Sadeq et al., 2023). It proposes and analyzes corrective actions on these various resignation risk factors. Artificial intelligence is an innovative solution for taking long-term, in-depth action on talent retention (Chitrao et al., 2022).

Consequently, advanced artificial intelligence solutions can predict employee turnover. AI possesses numerous prominent indices to predict employee turnover, including job tenure, compensation history, performance reviews, number of sick and vacation days used, and promotions. However, advanced algorithms rely on elusive and informative indicators. Two critical approaches can leverage artificial intelligence to predict and prevent employee turnover and overcome talent retention challenges (Ruby Merlin, 2018).

The first approach is "responsibility evaluation". Employees who are aware of their work responsibilities and values are committed to going the extra mile in their job responsibilities and achieving organizational missions without SMART goals, responsibility drops, and turnover increases. AI is a simple tool to assess employees' responsibilities. Human resources managers use AI statistics to understand employee participation, involvement and engagement fully. The HR labels and follows up on empowerment by adopting AI, determining which indicators most predict significant empowerment levels. Therefore, clarifying employees' responsibilities is crucial to employee retention. Normative commitment and social obligation arise when employees feel indebted to the organization. Responsibility and accountability are vital because they inspire commitment and leverage productivity and performance (Saxena et al., 2023).

The second approach is grounded on assessing the manager-employee relationship. Management/employee relationship is a powerful turnover indicator. Employees rating their supervisor's performance low have higher intentions to apply to competitive organizations than their counterparts who rate them high. Executives assess the quality of communications between employees and leaders. Using opinion mining and conversational analytics, they evaluate if employees are passionate, motivated, committed, engaged, or frustrated and disengaged. It assesses the extent to which managers make employees feel valued at work. Turnover increases due to a lack of appreciation as the main factor for leaving (Sinniah et al., 2022; M & Elangovan, 2021; Verma & Bandi, 2019).

Furthermore, AI assesses the quantity of managerial feedback to team members. Employee engagement declines when employees do not receive constructive feedback. Equally important is assessing whether employees are giving positive feedback to managers. Employees uncomfortable giving positive feedback are less likely to stay with their company (Faqihi & Miah, 2023; Vinichenko et al., 2019; Zhang, 2022).

Managers can closely monitor their employees' workload through artificial intelligence applications, preventing professional burnout. Managers follow AI to understand employees' workload accurately. AI provides managers with an accurate understanding of this workload and helps anticipate turnover, especially when algorithms are integrated into work management solutions. Ultimately, accurate workload quantity assessment gives managers essential insights to boost organizational commitment and productivity (Saxena et al., 2023).

## THE CONTRIBUTION OF AI TO TALENT MANAGEMENT

AI has an imperative role in talent and skills management policies. It allows organizations to gain considerable capacity for anticipation, reaction and agility (Odugbesan et al., 2023). More than ever, in today's agile organization, the machine and the human are intended to complement each other - the first being, without ambiguity, at the service of the second. Digitalization in general and AI in particular considerably leveraged the potential of HR functions in talent management. The

HR team uses AI applications to personalize the monitoring of the workforce career management and development to an outstanding degree while remaining consistent with organizational objectives. The human resources department can process complex and constantly changing data such as skill levels or job descriptions. Recruitment specialists can identify vacant positions due to a lack of existing skills and, at the same time, potential candidates for internal promotions and mobility (Gupta et al., 2018).

Organizations use intelligent tools based on artificial intelligence for talent management strategies to personalize career management and promote the match between demand and skills, offering career support individualization. Human Resources trust data reliability from AI intelligent tools to make decisions (S. Basu et al., 2022; Pandey, 2020).

Using talent management tools requires technical and managerial support as a practice integrated into HR systems. Undoubtedly, artificial intelligence is overflowing with innovations incorporated into talent management solutions. Talent management solutions are available according to the organization's classification, size, and operation field. AI's primary concern is to improve talent management strategies such as talent acquisition, training, leadership skills development and performance management (Shanthi & Sam, 2021).

Nevertheless, implementing AI in talent management requires managers' and employees' commitment, change management, and ongoing training for HR users to exploit fully. The training department is in charge of conducting training workshops during and after its implementation. AI offers a range of training and coaching methods, which the human resource manager chooses the most effective, sustaining the best fit (Hangal, 2019). Appropriate equipment for talent management solutions is a prerequisite for artificial intelligence to be convenient. Talent management AI evolves on three aspects: its ability to deliver fast training and learning, comprehend unstructured language, and model skills transferability. Artificial intelligence can multiply a human task, such as tagging skills on training courses and building a succession plan. It adapts training programs and thus accelerates employee skills adaptation (Cascio, 2020).

Using HR technology and performance management software to conduct performance reviews and track poor performance within a team allows HR managers and professionals to find performance gaps in knowledge and skills and remedy them rather than providing generalized training. Benefits are twofold: costs are reduced by only providing essential training, and employees' individual needs are being addressed (Spina & Spina, 2021).

Knowledge gaps for new hires are anticipated, allowing HR to be active rather than reactive in their succession planning. AI-powered learning and development tools leverage adaptive machine learning and AI capabilities to collect and analyze data on learner preferences and continuously adapt training to their needs. Personalization enabled by AI integration allows learners to take ownership of their skill development, defining their goals, pace, and learning style, which drives employee engagement and improves productivity. Its advanced implications for employees embrace those with difficulties with traditional learning methods, particularly retaining written information (Kelly et al., 2019).

## AI INFLUENCE ON EMPLOYEE PRODUCTIVITY

The impact of innovative artificial intelligence on employee productivity is impressive. Studies cited in OECD reports present artificial intelligence as a revolutionary and transformative force (Rock, 2019). It stimulates economic production and productivity and boosts organizational innovation and creativity. Investment in implementing AI systems is an undeniable advantage to ensure productivity in periods of full employment when organizations struggle to recruit talented employees. Using AI systems sustains and upsurges productivity in a labor shortage where talented employees are rare (Arora et al., 2021).

Conversely, when jobs are scarce, the number of people available to fill them is more remarkable when candidates compete for the same position. Therefore, employers can offer lower wages and working conditions while still having the certainty of being able to fill the positions offered at a lower cost than artificial intelligence. Under these conditions, the incentive to invest in automation is less. However, this cost-saving does not secure needed productivity (Galagan, Hirt, & Vital, 2020).

The productivity of low-skilled employees has been significantly boosted due to algorithmic applications. After the ChatGPT outbreak (Budhwar et al., 2023), researchers have figured out the impact of generative AI on productivity for the first time. Artificial intelligence (AI) is an essential tool and a practical solution that potentially improves the efficiency of employee productivity and work procedures (Ahmad et al., 2022).

Employees fear that AI will be a replacement for routine tasks. However, it is essential to emphasize that AI is not intended to replace employees entirely but rather to assist and empower them. By collaborating with AI systems, employees can accomplish their tasks efficiently and focus on areas that require unique human skills, such as creativity, complex problem-solving, and strategic decision-making. Therefore, rather than eliminating jobs, AI has the potential to transform existing jobs and create new professional opportunities. Organizations can take full advantage of AI's positive impact on employee productivity by taking a proactive approach and training employees to develop skills that complement AI (Chima, 2022).

Artificial intelligence tools particularly benefited the lowest-skilled and newly hired staff. AI has assisted agents with a few months of experience to increase their productivity. AI systems allow intrusive employee surveillance. AI applications track and measure employee productivity. Employee surveillance is dedicated to jobs requiring tasks outside the organizations. For example, artificial intelligence measures the productivity of medical representatives according to GPS location and travel distance to doctors as tasks in their job analysis. AI can significantly increase surveillance and control (Jatobá et al., 2019). Therefore, AI enables systematic and intrusive productivity observation by tracking and analyzing task accomplishments metrics. However, it is not all doom and gloom because AI improves employee monitoring to identify employee's improvement needs adequately. AI algorithm endows internal promotions, reduces turnover and increases retention rates. AI increases productivity (Barboza, 2019; Wan Ibrahim & Hassan, 2019; Meister, 2019).

## CONCLUSION

HR is undergoing an impressive technological shift thanks to the growth of big data and AI technologies, notably deep learning and natural language processing. Technologies of the fourth industrial revolution driven by AI are poised to fundamentally redefine employees' talents and productivity. AI technologies are expected to create more jobs than replaced in this redefinition of talent management. Therefore, workforce obsolescence is not planned as AI benefits. According to experts, AI automation frees humans from repetitive and tedious errands to focus on more complex and intellectually stimulating projects. The artificial intelligence of the future will not replace humans but will be cognitively functional alongside them to help them have a better quality of work and life. Human faculty for compassion and empathy will be a valuable asset in the workforce, and jobs centered around creativity and education are vital to the organization.

Artificial intelligence implications are multidimensional and profound. AI is paving the way to radically transform talent management. However, AI remains a tool and not a magical solution. Successful implementation necessitates strategic thinking, a good understanding of its capabilities and limitations, and constant attention to ethics and reliability. Successful organizations navigate this rapidly changing environment by leveraging AI to create value while preserving their core principles. AI contributes to human resources transformation businesses through innovative technologies and process automation.

Privacy considerations are paramount when leveraging AI and evaluating manager/employee relationships. Organizations must ensure that employees acknowledge the importance of conversations via artificial intelligence platforms. Ideally, leaders and employees will take the opportunity to strengthen their relationships. Staff retention is a priority for organizations. Traditional methods of forecasting employee turnover, such as pulse surveys, are no longer sufficient to arm human resources with a clear understanding of employee turnover forecasting. By leveraging AI, businesses can proactively prevent employee turnover and, for the first time, have the power to act and the chance to retain their best talent.

Innovative technologies have disruptive effects during their development and integration stage. AI revolution will require readjustments and financial sacrifice. Therefore, this AI epoch necessitates organizational adoption of technological approaches. Workforce-machine collaboration is vital. Humans and artificial intelligence bring diverse capabilities and strengths.

Artificial intelligence vision is futuristic as organizations adapt to changes brought about by the pandemic. AI represents an unprecedented lever of transformation for humans who will be able to exploit their capabilities and their potential for innovation and creativity. Artificial intelligence in HR functions involves collecting, storing and analyzing large amounts of sensitive employee data, such as personal information, payroll data, and performance reviews. Protecting confidentiality and security is essential to avoid data breaches, privacy breaches and the resulting legal and financial consequences. Automation saves time, improves efficiency, makes informed decisions and safeguards a reliable and fair approach to recruitment processes. It frees HR professionals from tedious administrative tasks to emphasize higher value-added activities, such as strategic talent management and the development of innovative HR policies. Automating HR procedures helps modernize recruiting and talent management practices and provides a competitive advantage to companies seeking to attract, recruit and retain the best talent in today's job market.

## REFERENCES

Abdeldayem, M. M., & Aldulaimi, S. H. (2020). Trends and opportunities of artificial intelligence in human resource management: Aspirations for public sector in Bahrain. *International Journal of Scientific and Technology Research.*

Ahmad, M. F., Husin, N. A. A., Ahmad, A. N. A., Abdullah, H., Wei, C. S., & Nawi, M. N. M. (2022). Digital Transformation: An Exploring Barriers and Challenges Practice of Artificial Intelligence in Manufacturing Firms in Malaysia. *Journal of Advanced Research in Applied Sciences and Engineering Technology*. doi:10.37934/araset.29.1.110117

Aikyn, N., Zhanegizov, A., Aidarov, T., Bui, D. M., & Tu, N. A. (2023). Efficient facial expression recognition framework based on edge computing. *The Journal of Supercomputing*. Advance online publication. doi:10.1007/s11227-023-05548-x

Aksoy, T., & Gurol, B. (2021). Artificial Intelligence in Computer-Aided Auditing Techniques and Technologies (CAATTs) and an Application Proposal for Auditors. In Contributions to Finance and Accounting. doi:10.1007/978-3-030-72628-7_17

Akyazi, T., Goti, A., Oyarbide, A., Alberdi, E., & Bayon, F. (2020). A guide for the food industry to meet the future skills requirements emerging with industry 4.0. *Foods*, *9*(4), 492. Advance online publication. doi:10.3390/foods9040492 PMID:32295238

Al Ka'bi, A. (2023). Proposed artificial intelligence algorithm and deep learning techniques for development of higher education. *International Journal of Intelligent Networks*. doi:10.1016/j.ijin.2023.03.002

Alnamrouti, A., Rjoub, H., & Ozgit, H. (2022). *Do Strategic Human Resources and Artificial Intelligence Help to Make Organisations More Sustainable? Evidence from Non-Governmental Organisations*. Sustainability. doi:10.3390/su14127327

Alqahtani, M. M. (2023). Artificial intelligence and entrepreneurship education: A paradigm in Qatari higher education institutions after covid-19 pandemic. *International Journal of Data and Network Science*. doi:10.5267/j.ijdns.2023.3.002

Alqahtani, T., Badreldin, H. A., Alrashed, M., Alshaya, A. I., Alghamdi, S. S., bin Saleh, K., Alowais, S. A., Alshaya, O. A., Rahman, I., Al Yami, M. S., & Albekairy, A. M. (2023, August). The emergent role of artificial intelligence, natural learning processing, and large language models in higher education and research. *Research in Social & Administrative Pharmacy*, *19*(8), 1236–1242. Advance online publication. doi:10.1016/j.sapharm.2023.05.016 PMID:37321925

Alrashedi, A., & Abbod, M. (2021). The Effect of Using Artificial Intelligence on Performance of Appraisal System: A Case Study for University of Jeddah Staff in Saudi Arabia. In Advances in Intelligent Systems and Computing. doi:10.1007/978-3-030-55180-3_11

Alshehri, F., & Muhammad, G. (2021). *A Comprehensive Survey of the Internet of Things (IoT) and AI-Based Smart Healthcare*. IEEE. doi:10.1109/ACCESS.2020.3047960

Ammer, M. A., Ahmed, Z. A. T., Alsubari, S. N., Aldhyani, T. H. H., & Almaaytah, S. A. (2023). Application of Artificial Intelligence for Better Investment in Human Capital. *Mathematics*, *11*(3), 612. Advance online publication. doi:10.3390/math11030612

Anastasi, S., Madonna, M., & Monica, L. (2021). Implications of embedded artificial intelligence - Machine learning on safety of machinery. Procedia Computer Science. doi:10.1016/j.procs.2021.01.171

Ardichvili, A. (2022). The Impact of Artificial Intelligence on Expertise Development: Implications for HRD. *Advances in Developing Human Resources, 24*(2), 78–98. Advance online publication. doi:10.1177/15234223221077304

Arora, M., Prakash, A., Mittal, A., & Singh, S. (2021). HR Analytics and Artificial Intelligence-Transforming Human Resource Management. *2021 International Conference on Decision Aid Sciences and Application, DASA 2021*. 10.1109/DASA53625.2021.9682325

Aydın, E., & Turan, M. (2023). *An AI-Based Shortlisting Model for Sustainability of Human Resource Management*. Sustainability. doi:10.3390/su15032737

Barboza, C. (2019). Artificial Intelligence and HR: The New Wave of Technology - Converge. *Journal of Advances in Social Science and Humanities*.

Basu, S., Majumdar, B., Mukherjee, K., Munjal, S., & Palaksha, C. (2022). The role of artificial intelligence in HRM: A systematic review and future research direction. *Human Resource Management Review*. Advance online publication. doi:10.1016/j.hrmr.2022.100893

Basu, S., Majumdar, B., Mukherjee, K., Munjal, S., & Palaksha, C. (2023, March). Majumdar, B., Mukherjee, K., Munjal, S., & Palaksha, C. (2023). Artificial Intelligence–HRM Interactions and Outcomes: A Systematic Review and Causal Configurational Explanation. *Human Resource Management Review, 33*(1), 100893. Advance online publication. doi:10.1016/j.hrmr.2022.100893

Berşe, S., Akça, K., Dirgar, E., & Kaplan Serin, E. (2023). The Role and Potential Contributions of the Artificial Intelligence Language Model ChatGPT. *Annals of Biomedical Engineering*. Advance online publication. doi:10.1007/s10439-023-03296-w PMID:37378876

Bhatt, M., & Shah, P. (2023). Acceptance of Artificial Intelligence in Human Resource Practices by Employees. In *The Adoption and Effect of Artificial Intelligence on Human Resources Management*. Part B. doi:10.1108/978-1-80455-662-720230002

Bhatt, P., & Muduli, A. (2022). Artificial intelligence in learning and development: A systematic literature review. *European Journal of Training and Development*. Advance online publication. doi:10.1108/EJTD-09-2021-0143

Biliavska, V., Castanho, R. A., & Vulevic, A. (2022). Analysis of the Impact of Artificial Intelligence in Enhancing the Human Resource Practices. *Journal of Intelligent Management Decision*. doi:10.56578/jimd010206

Budhwar, P., Chowdhury, S., Wood, G., Aguinis, H., Bamber, G. J., Beltran, J. R., Boselie, P., Lee Cooke, F., Decker, S., DeNisi, A., Dey, P. K., Guest, D., Knoblich, A. J., Malik, A., Paauwe, J., Papagiannidis, S., Patel, C., Pereira, V., Ren, S., ... Varma, A. (2023). Human resource management in the age of generative artificial intelligence: Perspectives and research directions on ChatGPT. *Human Resource Management Journal, 33*(3), 606–659. Advance online publication. doi:10.1111/1748-8583.12524

Cadario, R., Longoni, C., & Morewedge, C. K. (2021). Understanding, explaining, and utilizing medical artificial intelligence. *Nature Human Behaviour, 5*(12), 1636–1642. Advance online publication. doi:10.1038/s41562-021-01146-0 PMID:34183800

Cascio, W. F. (2020). Implications of the Changing Nature of Work for Recruitment and Retention. In The Cambridge Handbook of the Changing Nature of Work. doi:10.1017/9781108278034.015

Chevalier, F. (2022). Artificial Intelligence and Human Resources. *Proceedings - Academy of Management, 2022*(1), 16478. Advance online publication. doi:10.5465/AMBPP.2022.16478abstract

Chilunjika, A., Intauno, K., & Chilunjika, S. R. (2022). Artificial intelligence and public sector human resource management in South Africa: Opportunities, challenges and prospects. *SA Journal of Human Resource Management, 20.* Advance online publication. doi:10.4102/sajhrm.v20i0.1972

Chima, C. C. (2022). *Artificial Intelligence in Human Resources Management and Human Resource Accounting in Nigerian Public Sector.* Management and Human Resource Research Journal.

Chitrao, P., Bhoyar, P. K., Divekar, R., & Bhatt, P. (2022). Study on Use of Artificial Intelligence in Talent Acquisition. *2022 International Conference on Interdisciplinary Research in Technology and Management, IRTM 2022 - Proceedings.* 10.1109/IRTM54583.2022.9791659

Chowdhury, S., Dey, P., Joel-Edgar, S., Bhattacharya, S., Rodriguez-Espindola, O., Abadie, A., & Truong, L. (2023). Unlocking the value of artificial intelligence in human resource management through AI capability framework. *Human Resource Management Review, 33*(1), 100899. Advance online publication. doi:10.1016/j.hrmr.2022.100899

Conn, S. (2017). *Gartner Says By 2020.* Artificial Intelligence Will Create More Jobs Than It Eliminates.

de la Torre, R., Calvet, L. O., Lopez-Lopez, D., Juan, A. A., & Hatami, S. (2021). Business Analytics in Sport Talent Acquisition. *International Journal of Business Analytics*, *9*(1), 1–20. Advance online publication. doi:10.4018/IJBAN.290406

Delecraz, S., Eltarr, L., Becuwe, M., Bouxin, H., Boutin, N., & Oullier, O. (2022). Responsible Artificial Intelligence in Human Resources Technology: An innovative inclusive and fair by design matching algorithm for job recruitment purposes. *Journal of Responsible Technology*, *11*, 100041. Advance online publication. doi:10.1016/j.jrt.2022.100041

Effendi, G. N., & Pribadi, U. (2021). The Effect of Leadership Style on the Implementation of Artificial Intelligence in Government Services. *IOP Conference Series: Earth and Environmental Science*. 10.1088/1755-1315/717/1/012018

El Samad, M., Dennaoui, H., & El Nemar, S. (2023). Machine Learning and Big Data in Finance Services. Artificial Intelligence for Capital Markets. doi:10.1201/9781003327745-2

El Samad, M., El-Chaarani, H., El Nemar, S., & Raimi, L. (2022). Digital corporate entrepreneurship in the workplace. Managing the Digital Workplace in the Post-Pandemic. doi:10.4324/9781003283386-13

El Samad, M., El Nemar, S., Sakka, G., & El-Chaarani, H. (2022). An innovative big data framework for exploring the impact on decision-making in the European Mediterranean healthcare sector. *EuroMed Journal of Business*, *17*(3), 312–332. Advance online publication. doi:10.1108/EMJB-11-2021-0168

El Samad, M., Nasserddine, G., & Kheir, A. (2023). Introduction to Artificial Intelligence. In *Artificial Intelligence and Knowledge Processing*. Improved Decision-Making and Prediction. doi:10.1201/9781003328414-1

Ernst, E., Merola, R., & Samaan, D. (2019). Economics of Artificial Intelligence: Implications for the Future of Work. *IZA Journal of Labor Policy*, *9*(1), 20190004. Advance online publication. doi:10.2478/izajolp-2019-0004

Faqihi, A., & Miah, S. J. (2023). Artificial Intelligence-Driven Talent Management System: Exploring the Risks and Options for Constructing a Theoretical Foundation. *Journal of Risk and Financial Management*, *16*(1), 31. Advance online publication. doi:10.3390/jrfm16010031

Galagan, P., Hirt, M., & Vital, C. (2020). *Capabilities for Talent Development Shaping the Future of the Profession*. ATD Press.

Gao, Y., & Wu, L. (2021). *Efficiently mastering the game of nogo with deep reinforcement learning supported by domain knowledge*. Electronics. doi:10.3390/electronics10131533

Garg, V., Srivastav, S., & Gupta, A. (2018). Application of Artificial Intelligence for Sustaining Green Human Resource Management. *2018 International Conference on Automation and Computational Engineering, ICACE 2018*. 10.1109/ICACE.2018.8686988

Gaur, B., Bashir, R., & Sanghvi, B. (2021). An AI based training framework for Telecommuting Employees to combat perennial skill shortages post pandemic. *Proceedings of 2021 2nd International Conference on Intelligent Engineering and Management, ICIEM 2021*. 10.1109/ICIEM51511.2021.9445329

Geisel, A. (2018). The current and future impact of artificial intelligence on business. *International Journal of Scientific and Technology Research*.

Gélinas, D., Sadreddin, A., & Vahidov, R. (2022). *Artificial intelligence in human resources management: A review and research agenda*. Pacific Asia Journal of the Association for Information Systems. doi:10.17705/1pais.14601

Gethe, R. K. (2022). Extrapolation of talent acquisition in AI aided professional environment. *International Journal of Business Innovation and Research*. doi:10.1504/IJBIR.2022.122510

Giermindl, L. M., Strich, F., Christ, O., Leicht-Deobald, U., & Redzepi, A. (2022). The dark sides of people analytics: Reviewing the perils for organisations and employees. *European Journal of Information Systems*, *31*(3), 410–435. Advance online publication. doi:10.1080/0960085X.2021.1927213

Giraud, L., Zaher, A., Hernandez, S., & Akram, A. A. (2022). The impacts of artificial intelligence on managerial skills. *Journal of Decision Systems*. Advance online publication. doi:10.1080/12460125.2022.2069537

Gong, Y., Zhao, M., Wang, Q., & Lv, Z. (2022). Design and interactive performance of human resource management system based on artificial intelligence. *PLoS One*, *17*(1), e0262398. Advance online publication. doi:10.1371/journal.pone.0262398 PMID:35089946

Grover, K. L. (2022). Artificial Intelligence: A Tool for Optimizing Talent Acquisition. *International Journal of Law Management & Humanities*.

Guo, Q. (2022). A Fuzzy Comprehensive Dynamic Evaluation Algorithm for Human Resource Quality Growth Based on Artificial Intelligence. *Mobile Information Systems, 2022*, 1–14. Advance online publication. doi:10.1155/2022/8402975

Gupta, P., Fernandes, S. F., & Jain, M. (2018). Automation in recruitment: a new frontier. *Journal of Information Technology Teaching Cases*. doi:10.1057/s41266-018-0042-x

Gurusinghe, R. N., Arachchige, B. J. H., & Dayarathna, D. (2021). Predictive HR analytics and talent management: a conceptual framework. *Journal of Management Analytics*. doi:10.1080/23270012.2021.1899857

Haghi Kashani, M., Madanipour, M., Nikravan, M., Asghari, P., & Mahdipour, E. (2021). A systematic review of IoT in healthcare: Applications, techniques, and trends. *Journal of Network and Computer Applications, 192*, 103164. Advance online publication. doi:10.1016/j.jnca.2021.103164

Hamid, Al-Hakim, Arief, Dionova, & Alrahman. (2023). Recent Updates on Intelligent System for Talent Management: Does That Become a Helpful System? *SATESI: Jurnal Sains Teknologi Dan Sistem Informasi*. doi:10.54259/satesi.v3i1.1590

Hangal, A. (2019). *Role of HR Analytics on Employees Performance Improvement*. Gavesana Journal of Management.

Hossin, S., Arije Ulfy, M., Ali, I., Karim, W., & Karim, M. W. (2021). *Challenges in Adopting Artificial Intelligence (AI) in HRM Practices: A study on Bangladesh Perspective*. International Fellowship Journal of Interdisciplinary Research.

Hunt, W., Sarkar, S., & Warhurst, C. (2022). Measuring the impact of AI on jobs at the organization level: Lessons from a survey of UK business leaders. *Research Policy, 51*(2), 104425. Advance online publication. doi:10.1016/j.respol.2021.104425

Islam, M., Mamun, A. Al, Afrin, S., Ali Quaosar, G. M. A., & Uddin, M. A. (2022). Technology Adoption and Human Resource Management Practices: The Use of Artificial Intelligence for Recruitment in Bangladesh. *South Asian Journal of Human Resources Management*. doi:10.1177/23220937221122329

Islam, M. T., & Tamzid, M. (2023). Artificial Intelligence in Human Resource Management. In Management Education for Achieving Sustainable Development Goals in the Context of Bangladesh. doi:10.57240/DUJMBK04

Jaiswal, A., Arun, C. J., & Varma, A. (2022). Rebooting employees: Upskilling for artificial intelligence in multinational corporations. *International Journal of Human Resource Management, 33*(6), 1179–1208. Advance online publication. doi:10.1080/09585192.2021.1891114

Jatobá, M., Santos, J., Gutierriz, I., Moscon, D., Fernandes, P. O., & Teixeira, J. P. (2019). Evolution of Artificial Intelligence Research in Human Resources. Procedia Computer Science. doi:10.1016/j.procs.2019.12.165

Jing, Y. (2020). Research on the Application of Artificial Intelligence Natural Language Processing Technology in Japanese Teaching. In *Journal of Physics.* Conference Series. doi:10.1088/1742-6596/1682/1/012081

Kambur, E., & Akar, C. (2022). Human resource developments with the touch of artificial intelligence: A scale development study. *International Journal of Manpower, 43*(1), 168–205. Advance online publication. doi:10.1108/IJM-04-2021-0216

Kandlhofer, M., Steinbauer, G., Lassnig, J., Menzinger, M., Baumann, W., Ehardt-Schmiederer, M., Bieber, R., Winkler, T., Plomer, S., Strobl-Zuchtriegl, I., Miglbauer, M., Ballagi, A., Pozna, C., Miltenyi, G., Alfoldi, I., & Szalay, I. (2021). EDLRIS: A European Driving License for Robots and Intelligent Systems. *KI -. Kunstliche Intelligenz, 35*(2), 221–232. Advance online publication. doi:10.1007/s13218-021-00716-8

Kaushal, N., Kaurav, R. P. S., Sivathanu, B., & Kaushik, N. (2023). *Artificial intelligence and HRM: identifying future research Agenda using systematic literature review and bibliometric analysis.* Management Review Quarterly. doi:10.1007/s11301-021-00249-2

Kelly, O. W., Armstrong, M., Taylor, S., Teo, T. C., Low, K. C. P., Bradley, S., ... Sundiman, D. (2019). Human Resources and Management in Projects. *Human Resource Management Journal.*

Kemendi, Á., Michelberger, P., & Mesjasz-Lech, A. (2022). Industry 4.0 and 5.0 – Organizational and competency challenges of enterprises. *Polish Journal of Management Studies.* doi:10.17512/pjms.2022.26.2.13

Koromina, M., Pandi, M. T., & Patrinos, G. P. (2019). Rethinking Drug Repositioning and Development with Artificial Intelligence, Machine Learning, and Omics. *OMICS: A Journal of Integrative Biology, 23*(11), 539–548. Advance online publication. doi:10.1089/omi.2019.0151 PMID:31651216

Kremer, K. (2022). *HR practices in the context of the Internet of Things.* Strategic Management. doi:10.5937/StraMan2110002K

Kumar, A., Rahmath, M., Raju, Y., Reddy Vulapula, S., Prathap, B. R., Hassan, M. M., Mohamed, M. A., & Asakipaam, S. A. (2022). Enhanced Secure Technique for Detecting Cyber Attacks Using Artificial Intelligence and Optimal IoT. *Security and Communication Networks*, *2022*, 1–13. Advance online publication. doi:10.1155/2022/8024518

Kumar, I., Rawat, J., Mohd, N., & Husain, S. (2021). Opportunities of Artificial Intelligence and Machine Learning in the Food Industry. *Journal of Food Quality*, *2021*, 1–10. Advance online publication. doi:10.1155/2021/4535567

Lainjo, B. (2021). *COVID-19: The Dynamics of Quality of Life (QOL) and Artificial Intelligence (AI)*. African Journal of Inter/Multidisciplinary Studies. doi:10.51415/ajims.v3i1.908

Laumer, S., & Morana, S. (2022). HR natural language processing - conceptual overview and state of the art on conversational agents in human resources management. Handbook of Research on Artificial Intelligence in Human Resource Management.

Lauriola, I., Lavelli, A., & Aiolli, F. (2022). An introduction to Deep Learning in Natural Language Processing: Models, techniques, and tools. *Neurocomputing*, *470*, 443–456. Advance online publication. doi:10.1016/j.neucom.2021.05.103

Liu, C., Li, Z., Zhou, D., & Shi, Y. (2019). Organizational innovation of sci-tech societies in the era of intelligence: A case study in China. *PICMET 2019 - Portland International Conference on Management of Engineering and Technology: Technology Management in the World of Intelligent Systems, Proceedings*. 10.23919/PICMET.2019.8893783

Liu, S., Li, G., & Xia, H. (2021). Analysis of Talent Management in the Artificial Intelligence Era. *Proceedings of the 5th Asia-Pacific Conference on Economic Research and Management Innovation (ERMI 2021)*. 10.2991/aebmr.k.210218.007

Longoni, C., Bonezzi, A., & Morewedge, C. K. (2019). Resistance to Medical Artificial Intelligence. *The Journal of Consumer Research*, *46*(4), 629–650. Advance online publication. doi:10.1093/jcr/ucz013

M, K. K., & Elangovan, R. (2021). To Study Impact of Artificial Intelligence on HR Practices. *ComFin Research*. doi:10.34293/commerce.v9i4.4134

Madhavi, I., Chamishka, S., Nawaratne, R., Nanayakkara, V., Alahakoon, D., & De Silva, D. (2020). A Deep Learning Approach for Work Related Stress Detection from Audio Streams in Cyber Physical Environments. *IEEE International Conference on Emerging Technologies and Factory Automation, ETFA*. 10.1109/ETFA46521.2020.9212098

Mah, P. M., Skalna, I., & Muzam, J. (2022). *Natural Language Processing and Artificial Intelligence for Enterprise Management in the Era of Industry 4.0*. Applied Sciences. doi:10.3390/app12189207

Majumder, S., & Mondal, A. (2021). Are chatbots really useful for human resource management? *International Journal of Speech Technology*, *24*(4), 969–977. Advance online publication. doi:10.1007/s10772-021-09834-y

Marquez, R., Barrios, N., Vera, R. E., Mendez, M. E., Tolosa, L., Zambrano, F., & Li, Y. (2023). A perspective on the synergistic potential of artificial intelligence and product-based learning strategies in biobased materials education. *Education for Chemical Engineers*, *44*, 164–180. Advance online publication. doi:10.1016/j.ece.2023.05.005

Mehr, H. (2017). *Artificial Intelligence for Citizen Services and Government*. Harvard Ash Center Technology & Democracy.

Meister, J. (2019). Ten HR Trends In The Age Of Artificial Intelligence. *Forbes*.

Merlin, Ruby.P, J. (2018). Artificial Intelligence in Human Resource Management International Journal of Pure and Applied Mathematics. *International Journal of Pure and Applied Mathematics*.

Mhlanga, D. (2022). The Role of Artificial Intelligence and Machine Learning Amid the COVID 19 Pandemic: What Lessons Are We Learning on 4IR and the Sustainable Development Goals. *International Journal of Environmental Research and Public Health*, *19*(3), 1879. Advance online publication. doi:10.3390/ijerph19031879 PMID:35162901

Milojević, N., & Redzepagic, S. (2021). Prospects of Artificial Intelligence and Machine Learning Application in Banking Risk Management. *Journal of Central Banking Theory and Practice*. doi:10.2478/jcbtp-2021-0023

Mishra, S. K., & Sarkar, A. (2022). Service-oriented architecture for Internet of Things: A semantic approach. *Journal of King Saud University. Computer and Information Sciences*, *34*(10), 8765–8776. Advance online publication. doi:10.1016/j.jksuci.2021.09.024

Mohamad, Z., Chaudhary, R., Iyer, S., Sutarto, & Khan, S. (2022). A Probing: How Artificial Intelligence is Beneficial in Different Fields of Human Resource Management. *Pacific Business Review International*.

Mohan, R. (2019). The Chatbot revolution and the Indian HR professionals. *International Journal of Information and Computing Science*.

Moldenhauer, L., & Londt, C. (2018). Leadership, artificial intelligence and the need to redefine future skills development. *Proceedings of the 14th European Conference on Management, Leadership and Governance, ECMLG 2018*. 10.33423/jlae.v16i1.1363

Nair, V. C., Suresh, P., & Vijaya. (2020). Artificial Intelligence Interventions and Human Resources in the New Millennium. *International Journal of Advanced Science and Technology*.

Nawaz, N. (2020). Exploring Artificial Intelligence Applications in Human Resource Management. *Journal of Management Information and Decision Sciences*.

Nguyen, D. P., Phan, L. T., Ho, H. X., & Le, A. N. H. (2022). Human resource management practices in higher education: A literature review using co-word analysis. *International Journal of Management Education, 16*(1), 40. Advance online publication. doi:10.1504/IJMIE.2022.119682

Odugbesan, J. A., Aghazadeh, S., Al Qaralleh, R. E., & Sogeke, O. S. (2023). Green talent management and employees' innovative work behavior: The roles of artificial intelligence and transformational leadership. *Journal of Knowledge Management, 27*(3), 696–716. Advance online publication. doi:10.1108/JKM-08-2021-0601

Olugbade, S., Ojo, S., Imoize, A. L., Isabona, J., & Alaba, M. O. (2022). A Review of Artificial Intelligence and Machine Learning for Incident Detectors in Road Transport Systems. *Mathematical & Computational Applications, 27*(5), 77. Advance online publication. doi:10.3390/mca27050077

Paigude, S., Pangarkar, S. C., Hundekari, S., Mali, M., Wanjale, K., & Dongre, Y. (2023). Potential of Artificial Intelligence in Boosting Employee Retention in the Human Resource Industry. *International Journal on Recent and Innovation Trends in Computing and Communication, 11*(3s), 01–10. Advance online publication. doi:10.17762/ijritcc.v11i3s.6149

Palos-Sánchez, P. R., Baena-Luna, P., Badicu, A., & Infante-Moro, J. C. (2022). Artificial Intelligence and Human Resources Management: A Bibliometric Analysis. *Applied Artificial Intelligence, 36*(1), 2145631. Advance online publication. doi:10.1080/08839514.2022.2145631

Pandey, S. (2020). Exploring the role of Artificial Intelligence (AI) in transforming HR functions: An Empirical Study in the Indian Context. *International Journal of Scientific Research and Engineering Development*.

Patheja, S., Kumar, D., & Singh, S. (2023). *Role of Artificial Intelligence in Human Resource*. Effulgence-A Management Journal. doi:10.33601/effulgence.rdias/v21/i1/2023/1-5

Peifer, Y., Jeske, T., & Hille, S. (2022). Artificial Intelligence and its Impact on Leaders and Leadership. Procedia Computer Science. doi:10.1016/j.procs.2022.01.301

Pillai, R., & Sivathanu, B. (2020). Adoption of artificial intelligence (AI) for talent acquisition in IT/ITeS organizations. *Benchmarking*, *27*(9), 2599–2629. Advance online publication. doi:10.1108/BIJ-04-2020-0186

Prikshat, V., Malik, A., & Budhwar, P. (2023). AI-augmented HRM: Antecedents, assimilation and multilevel consequences. *Human Resource Management Review*, *33*(1), 100860. Advance online publication. doi:10.1016/j.hrmr.2021.100860

Priya, B., Kumar, J. A., Khushboo, A., Neha, G., Vanshika, B., & Abhishek, K. (2021). AI revolutionizing health care: A descriptive review. *International Journal of Advances in Scientific Research.*

Qamar, Y., Agrawal, R. K., Samad, T. A., & Chiappetta Jabbour, C. J. (2021). When technology meets people: The interplay of artificial intelligence and human resource management. *Journal of Enterprise Information Management*, *34*(5), 1339–1370. Advance online publication. doi:10.1108/JEIM-11-2020-0436

Rahmani, D., & Kamberaj, H. (2021). Implementation and Usage of Artificial Intelligence Powered Chatbots in Human Resources Management Systems. ICSAS.

Rajesh, S., Kandaswamy, M. U., & Rakesh, M. A. (2018). The Impact of Artificial Intelligence in Talent Acquisition Lifecycle of organizations A Global Perspective. *International Journal of Engineering Development and Research.*

Rock, D. (2019). Engineering Value: The Returns to Technological Talent and Investments in Artificial Intelligence. SSRN *Electronic Journal*. doi:10.2139/ssrn.3427412

Rott, K. J., Lao, L., Petridou, E., & Schmidt-Hertha, B. (2022). Needs and requirements for an additional AI qualification during dual vocational training: Results from studies of apprentices and teachers. *Computers and Education: Artificial Intelligence*. doi:10.1016/j.caeai.2022.100102

Rožman, M., Oreški, D., & Tominc, P. (2022). Integrating artificial intelligence into a talent management model to increase the work engagement and performance of enterprises. *Frontiers in Psychology*, *13*, 1014434. Advance online publication. doi:10.3389/fpsyg.2022.1014434 PMID:36506984

Sadeq, N. (2023). The impact of Blockchain technique on trustworthy healthcare sector. *Mesopotamian Journal of Cyber Security*, (May), 105–115. doi:10.58496/MJCS/2023/015

Sadeq, N., Nassreddine, G., & Younis, J. (2023). Impact of Artificial Intelligence on E-marketing. *International Journal of Trend in Scientific Research and Development, 7*(1), 1318–1331. www.ijtsrd.com/papers/ijtsrd53850.pdf

Sakka, F., & El Hadi El Maknouzi, M. (2022). Human Resource Management in the Era of Artificial Intelligence: Future Hr Work Practices, Anticipated Skill Set, Financial and Legal Implications. *Academy of Strategic Management Journal.*

Sallam, M., Salim, N. A., Al-Tammemi, A. B., Barakat, M., Fayyad, D., Hallit, S., Harapan, H., Hallit, R., & Mahafzah, A. (2023). ChatGPT Output Regarding Compulsory Vaccination and COVID-19 Vaccine Conspiracy: A Descriptive Study at the Outset of a Paradigm Shift in Online Search for Information. *Cureus*. Advance online publication. doi:10.7759/cureus.35029 PMID:36819954

Sanyaolu, E., & Atsaboghena, R. (2022). *Role of Artificial Intelligence in Human Resource Management: Overview of its benefits and challenges*. ResearchGate.

Saranya, A. (2022). *The Impact of Artificial Intelligence (AI) in Human Resource Management (HRM)*. Shanlax International Journal of Arts, Science and Humanities. doi:10.34293/sijash.v9i4.4758

Saxena, A. (2020). *The growing role of artificial intelligence in human resource. EPRA International Journal of Multidisciplinary Research.* doi:10.36713/epra4924

Saxena, P., Sharma, S., & Jora, R. B. (2023). Impact of Emotional Intelligence and Artificial Intelligence on Employee Retention: A Review of the Service Industry. *2023 9th International Conference on Advanced Computing and Communication Systems, ICACCS 2023*. 10.1109/ICACCS57279.2023.10113017

Selvapandian, D., Mary, R. U. N., & Karthikeyan, C. (2020). Artificial intelligence in online shopping using natural language processing (NLP). *Journal of Critical Reviews*. doi:10.31838/jcr.07.04.165

Setiawan, R., Pio Leonardo Cavaliere, L., Koti, K., Ayodeji Ogunmola, G., Abdul Jalil, N., Kalyan Chakravarthi, M., ... Singh, S. (2021). *The Artificial Intelligence and Inventory Effect on Banking Industrial Performance. Turkish Online Journal of Qualitative Inquiry.*

Shanthi, V., & Sam, A. (2021). Impact of Artificial Intelligence Techniques on Employee Well-being for Employee Retention. *International Journal of Engineering Research & Technology (Ahmedabad).*

Sheikh, S. A. (2019). Artificial Intelligence based Chatbot for Human Resource:A Survey View project. *Journal of Emerging Technologies and Innovative Research.*

Shen, G. (2022). AI-enabled talent training for the cross-cultural news communication talent. *Technological Forecasting and Social Change, 185*, 122031. Advance online publication. doi:10.1016/j.techfore.2022.122031

Shoss, M. K., & Ciarlante, K. (2022). Supplemental Material for Are robots/AI viewed as more of a workforce threat in unequal societies? Evidence from the Eurobarometer survey. *Technology, Mind, and Behavior, 3*(2). Advance online publication. doi:10.1037/tmb0000078.supp

Sindu, M. (2018). Artificial intelligence vs human resource practices in Banking sector. *International Journal of Social Science and Economic Research.*

Singh, A., & Shaurya, A. (2021). Impact of Artificial Intelligence on HR practices in the UAE. *Humanities & Social Sciences Communications, 8*(1), 312. Advance online publication. doi:10.1057/s41599-021-00995-4

Sinniah, S., Al Mamun, A., Md Salleh, M. F., Makhbul, Z. K. M., & Hayat, N. (2022). Modeling the Significance of Motivation on Job Satisfaction and Performance Among the Academicians: The Use of Hybrid Structural Equation Modeling-Artificial Neural Network Analysis. *Frontiers in Psychology, 13*, 935822. Advance online publication. doi:10.3389/fpsyg.2022.935822 PMID:35795432

Sircar, A., Yadav, K., Rayavarapu, K., Bist, N., & Oza, H. (2021). *Application of machine learning and artificial intelligence in oil and gas industry*. Petroleum Research. doi:10.1016/j.ptlrs.2021.05.009

Sivathanu, B., & Pillai, R. (2018). Smart HR 4.0 – how industry 4.0 is disrupting HR. *Human Resource Management International Digest, 26*(4), 7–11. Advance online publication. doi:10.1108/HRMID-04-2018-0059

Soleimani, M., Intezari, A., & Pauleen, D. J. (2022). Mitigating cognitive biases in developing ai-assisted recruitment systems: A knowledge-sharing approach. *International Journal of Knowledge Management.* Advance online publication. doi:10.4018/IJKM.290022

Sollini, M., Bartoli, F., Marciano, A., Zanca, R., Slart, R. H. J. A., & Erba, P. A. (2020). Artificial intelligence and hybrid imaging: The best match for personalized medicine in oncology. *European Journal of Hybrid Imaging*, *4*(1), 24. Advance online publication. doi:10.1186/s41824-020-00094-8 PMID:34191197

Spina, J. D., & Spina, L. J. (2021). Looking Ahead: Artificial Intelligence and Developing Talent. In Beyond Succession Planning: New Ways to Develop Talent. doi:10.1108/978-1-83982-078-620211011

Strohmeier, S. (2022). 1. Artificial intelligence in human resources – an introduction. Handbook of Research on Artificial Intelligence in Human Resource Management.

Sulaiman, Y. H., & Mustafa, A. S. (2021). COVID-19: Toward Artificial Intelligence Algorithms. *HORA 2021 - 3rd International Congress on Human-Computer Interaction, Optimization and Robotic Applications, Proceedings*. 10.1109/HORA52670.2021.9461323

Suseno, Y., Hudik, M., Fang, E. S., & Guo, Z. (2020). Employee Attitudes, Technological Anxiety, and Change Readiness for Artificial Intelligence Adoption. *Proceedings - Academy of Management*, *2020*(1), 20045. Advance online publication. doi:10.5465/AMBPP.2020.20045abstract

Tabassum, F. (2018). *Future of Performance Management in Artificial Intelligence ERA*. Shanlax International Journal of Arts.

Takhi, S., Gosain, M., & Singh, V. (2020). *Reinforce The Talent Acquisition Using Kaizen and Artificial Intelligence. International Journal of Scientific and Research Publications*. doi:10.29322/IJSRP.10.05.2020.p10127

Tambe, P., Cappelli, P., & Yakubovich, V. (2019). Artificial intelligence in human resources management: Challenges and A path forward. *California Management Review*, *61*(4), 15–42. Advance online publication. doi:10.1177/0008125619867910

Titareva, T. (2021). Leadership in an Artificial Intelligence Era. *#LEADCC: Leading Change Conference*.

Tiwari, P., Pandey, R., Garg, V., & Singhal, A. (2021). Application of artificial intelligence in human resource management practices. *Proceedings of the Confluence 2021: 11th International Conference on Cloud Computing, Data Science and Engineering*. 10.1109/Confluence51648.2021.9377160

Tiwari, P., Rajput, N., & Garg, V. (2022). Artificial Intelligence and Talent Acquisition-Role of HR leaders in Adoption. *Proceedings of 3rd International Conference on Intelligent Engineering and Management, ICIEM 2022.* 10.1109/ICIEM54221.2022.9853104

van Erp, M., Reynolds, C., Maynard, D., Starke, A., Ibáñez Martín, R., Andres, F., Leite, M. C. A., Alvarez de Toledo, D., Schmidt Rivera, X., Trattner, C., Brewer, S., Adriano Martins, C., Kluczkovski, A., Frankowska, A., Bridle, S., Levy, R. B., Rauber, F., Tereza da Silva, J., & Bosma, U. (2021). Using Natural Language Processing and Artificial Intelligence to Explore the Nutrition and Sustainability of Recipes and Food. *Frontiers in Artificial Intelligence*, *3*, 621577. Advance online publication. doi:10.3389/frai.2020.621577 PMID:33733227

Van Quaquebeke, N., & Gerpott, F. H. (2023). The Now, New, and Next of Digital Leadership: How Artificial Intelligence (AI) Will Take Over and Change Leadership as We Know It. *Journal of Leadership & Organizational Studies*, *30*(3), 265–275. Advance online publication. doi:10.1177/15480518231181731

Vasantham, D. S. T. (2021). *The Role of Artificial Intelligence in Human Resource Management.* Engineering and Scientific International Journal. doi:10.30726/esij/v8.i2.2021.82013

Vedapradha, R., Hariharan, R., David Winster Praveenraj, D., Sudha, E., & Ashok, J. (2023). Talent acquisition-artificial intelligence to manage recruitment. E3S Web of Conferences. doi:10.1051/e3sconf/202337605001

Verma, R. (2020). Challenges of Artificial Intelligence in Human Resource. *XXI Annual International Conference Proceedings.* Http://Www.Internationalconference.in/XXI_AIC/INDEX.HTM

Verma, R., & Bandi, S. (2019). Artificial Intelligence & Human Resource Management in Indian IT Sector. SSRN *Electronic Journal.* doi:10.2139/ssrn.3319897

Verma, R., & Bandi, S. (2020). Challenges of Artificial Intelligence in Human Resource Management in Indian IT Sector richa. *XXI Annual International Conference Proceedings.* Http://Www.Internationalconference.in/XXI_AIC/INDEX.HTM

Vinichenko, M. V., Rybakova, M. V., Chulanova, O. L., Kuznetsova, I. V., Makushkin, S. A., & Lobacheva, A. S. (2019). Using natural and artificial intelligence in the talent management system. *International Journal of Recent Technology and Engineering.* doi:10.35940/ijrte.C6152.098319

Volkmar, G., Fischer, P. M., & Reinecke, S. (2022). Artificial Intelligence and Machine Learning: Exploring drivers, barriers, and future developments in marketing management. *Journal of Business Research*, *149*, 599–614. Advance online publication. doi:10.1016/j.jbusres.2022.04.007

Votto, A. M., Valecha, R., Najafirad, P., & Rao, H. R. (2021). Artificial Intelligence in Tactical Human Resource Management: A Systematic Literature Review. *International Journal of Information Management Data Insights*. doi:10.1016/j.jjimei.2021.100047

Wan Ibrahim, W. M. R., & Hassan, R. (2019). Recruitment Trends in the Era of Industry 4.0 Using Artificial Intelligence: Pro and Cons. *Asian Journal of Research in Business and Management*.

Wang, Y. Y., & Wang, Y. S. (2022). Development and validation of an artificial intelligence anxiety scale: An initial application in predicting motivated learning behavior. *Interactive Learning Environments*, *30*(4), 619–634. Advance online publication. doi:10.1080/10494820.2019.1674887

Xin, O. K., Wider, W., & Ling, L. K. (2022). *Human Resource Artificial Intelligence Implementation and Organizational Performance in Malaysia*. Asia-Pacific Social Science Review.

Yadav, P. V., Kollimath, U. S., Chavan, T. V., Pisal, D. T., Giramkar, S. A., & Swamy, S. M. (2023). Impact of Artificial Intelligence (AI) in Talent Acquisition Process: A study with reference to IT Industry. *Proceedings of the International Conference on Intelligent and Innovative Technologies in Computing, Electrical and Electronics, ICIITCEE 2023*. 10.1109/IITCEE57236.2023.10090973

Yun, D., Xiang, Y., Liu, Z., Lin, D., Zhao, L., Guo, C., Xie, P., Lin, H., Liu, Y., Zou, Y., & Wu, X. (2020). Attitudes towards medical artificial intelligence talent cultivation: An online survey study. *Annals of Translational Medicine*, *8*(11), 708. Advance online publication. doi:10.21037/atm.2019.12.149 PMID:32617328

Zhang, F. (2022). Design and Application of Artificial Intelligence Technology-Driven Education and Teaching System in Universities. *Computational and Mathematical Methods in Medicine*, *2022*, 1–10. Advance online publication. doi:10.1155/2022/8503239 PMID:36124170

# Compilation of References

Abdeldayem, M. M., & Aldulaimi, S. H. (2020). Trends and opportunities of artificial intelligence in human resource management: Aspirations for public sector in Bahrain. *International Journal of Scientific and Technology Research.*

Adiyono, N. G., Rahmat, T. Y., & Anindita, R. (2021). Digital Marketing Strategies to Increase Online Business Sales through Social Media. *Journal of Humanities, Social Science Public Administration and Management, 1*(2), 31–37.

Adom, A. Y., Nyarko, I. K., & Som, G. N. K. (2016). Competitor analysis in strategic management: Is it a worthwhile managerial practice in contemporary times. *Journal of Resources Development and Management, 24*(1), 116–127.

Agbehadji, I. E., Awuzie, B. O., Ngowi, A. B., & Millham, R. C. (2020). Review of big data analytics, artificial intelligence, and nature-inspired computing models towards accurate detection of COVID-19 pandemic cases and contact tracing. *International Journal of Environmental Research and Public Health, 17*(15), 5330. doi:10.3390/ijerph17155330 PMID:32722154

Agbo, C. C., Mahmoud, Q. H., & Eklund, J. M. (2019). Blockchain technology in healthcare: A systematic review. *Health Care, 7*(2), 56. PMID:30987333

Agnihotri, Kothandaraman, Kashyap, & Singh. (2012). Bringing "Social" Into Sales: The Impact of Salespeople's Social Media Use on Service Behaviors and Value Creation. *The Journal of Personal Selling and Sales Management, 32*, 333-348. https://www.researchgate.net/publication/260178184_Bringing_Social_Into_Sales_The_Impact_of_Salespeople'S_Social_Media_Use_on_Service_Behaviors_and_Value_Creation

Ahmad, M. F., Husin, N. A. A., Ahmad, A. N. A., Abdullah, H., Wei, C. S., & Nawi, M. N. M. (2022). Digital Transformation: An Exploring Barriers and Challenges Practice of Artificial Intelligence in Manufacturing Firms in Malaysia. *Journal of Advanced Research in Applied Sciences and Engineering Technology*. doi:10.37934/araset.29.1.110117

Aikyn, N., Zhanegizov, A., Aidarov, T., Bui, D. M., & Tu, N. A. (2023). Efficient facial expression recognition framework based on edge computing. *The Journal of Supercomputing*. Advance online publication. doi:10.1007/s11227-023-05548-x

Aji, P., Nadhila, V., & Sanny, L. (2020). Effect of social media marketing on Instagram towards purchase intention: Evidence from Indonesia's ready-to-drink tea industry. *International Journal of Data and Network Science*, *4*(2), 91–104. doi:10.5267/j.ijdns.2020.3.002

Aksoy, T., & Gurol, B. (2021). Artificial Intelligence in Computer-Aided Auditing Techniques and Technologies (CAATTs) and an Application Proposal for Auditors. In Contributions to Finance and Accounting. doi:10.1007/978-3-030-72628-7_17

Akyazi, T., Goti, A., Oyarbide, A., Alberdi, E., & Bayon, F. (2020). A guide for the food industry to meet the future skills requirements emerging with industry 4.0. *Foods*, *9*(4), 492. Advance online publication. doi:10.3390/foods9040492 PMID:32295238

Al Ka'bi, A. (2023). Proposed artificial intelligence algorithm and deep learning techniques for development of higher education. *International Journal of Intelligent Networks*. doi:10.1016/j.ijin.2023.03.002

AlharbyM.MoorselA. V. (2017). *Blockchain-based smart contracts: A systematic mapping study*. doi:10.5121/csit.2017.71011

AL-Khatib, A., & Shuhaiber, A. (2022). Green intellectual capital and green supply chain performance: Does big data analytics capabilities matter? *Sustainability (Basel)*, *14*(16), 10054. doi:10.3390/su141610054

Almutairi, A. F., Sarfraz, Z., & Basalamah, A. (2022). Blockchain in Healthcare: A Survey on Day-To-Day Applications and Challenges Ahead. *Applied Sciences (Basel, Switzerland)*, *12*(2), 679.

Alnamrouti, A., Rjoub, H., & Ozgit, H. (2022). *Do Strategic Human Resources and Artificial Intelligence Help to Make Organisations More Sustainable? Evidence from Non-Governmental Organisations*. Sustainability. doi:10.3390/su14127327

Alphand, O. (2023). *IoTChain: A Blockchain Security Architecture for the Internet of Things. In 2018 IEEE Wireless Communications and Networking Conference (WCNC)*. IEEE.

Alqahtani, M. M. (2023). Artificial intelligence and entrepreneurship education: A paradigm in Qatari higher education institutions after covid-19 pandemic. *International Journal of Data and Network Science*. doi:10.5267/j.ijdns.2023.3.002

Alqahtani, T., Badreldin, H. A., Alrashed, M., Alshaya, A. I., Alghamdi, S. S., bin Saleh, K., Alowais, S. A., Alshaya, O. A., Rahman, I., Al Yami, M. S., & Albekairy, A. M. (2023, August). The emergent role of artificial intelligence, natural learning processing, and large language models in higher education and research. *Research in Social & Administrative Pharmacy*, *19*(8), 1236–1242. Advance online publication. doi:10.1016/j.sapharm.2023.05.016 PMID:37321925

Alrashedi, A., & Abbod, M. (2021). The Effect of Using Artificial Intelligence on Performance of Appraisal System: A Case Study for University of Jeddah Staff in Saudi Arabia. In Advances in Intelligent Systems and Computing. doi:10.1007/978-3-030-55180-3_11

Alshehri, F., & Muhammad, G. (2021). *A Comprehensive Survey of the Internet of Things (IoT) and AI-Based Smart Healthcare*. IEEE. doi:10.1109/ACCESS.2020.3047960

Ammer, M. A., Ahmed, Z. A. T., Alsubari, S. N., Aldhyani, T. H. H., & Almaaytah, S. A. (2023). Application of Artificial Intelligence for Better Investment in Human Capital. *Mathematics, 11*(3), 612. Advance online publication. doi:10.3390/math11030612

Anastasi, S., Madonna, M., & Monica, L. (2021). Implications of embedded artificial intelligence - Machine learning on safety of machinery. Procedia Computer Science. doi:10.1016/j.procs.2021.01.171

Ang, K.-M., Seow, E.-K., Fam, P.-S., & Cheng, L.-H. (2022). Classification of edible bird's nest samples using a logistic regression model through the mineral ratio approach. *Food Control, 137*, 108921. doi:10.1016/j.foodcont.2022.108921

Angraal, S., Krumholz, H. M., & Schulz, W. L. (2017). Blockchain technology: Applications in health care. *Circulation: Cardiovascular Quality and Outcomes, 10*(9), e003800. doi:10.1161/CIRCOUTCOMES.117.003800 PMID:28912202

Anshari, M., Almunawar, M. N., Lim, S. A., & Al-Mudimigh, A. (2019). Customer relationship management and Big Data enabled: Personalization & Customization Of Services. *Applied Computing and Informatics, 15*(2), 94–101. doi:10.1016/j.aci.2018.05.004

Ardichvili, A. (2022). The Impact of Artificial Intelligence on Expertise Development: Implications for HRD. *Advances in Developing Human Resources, 24*(2), 78–98. Advance online publication. doi:10.1177/15234223221077304

Arner, D. W., Narbel, P. A., & Buckley, R. P. (2020). *FinTech for financial inclusion: A framework for digital financial transformation.* World Bank.

Arora, M., Prakash, A., Mittal, A., & Singh, S. (2021). HR Analytics and Artificial Intelligence-Transforming Human Resource Management. *2021 International Conference on Decision Aid Sciences and Application, DASA 2021.* 10.1109/DASA53625.2021.9682325

Ashley, C., & Tuten, T. (2015). Creative strategies in social media marketing: An exploratory study of branded social content and consumer engagement. *Psychology and Marketing, 32*(1), 15–27. doi:10.1002/mar.20761

Atzei, N. (2018). SoK: Unraveling Bitcoin Smart Contracts. In L. Bauer & R. Küsters (Eds.), Lecture Notes in Computer Science: Vol. 10804. *Principles of Security and Trust. POST 2018.* Springer.

Aula, P. (2010). Social media, reputation risk and ambient publicity management. *Strategy and Leadership, 38*(6), 43–49. doi:10.1108/10878571011088069

Aydın, E., & Turan, M. (2023). *An AI-Based Shortlisting Model for Sustainability of Human Resource Management.* Sustainability. doi:10.3390/su15032737

Azaria, A., Ekblaw, A., Vieira, T., & Lippman, A. (2016). Medrec: Using blockchain for medical data access and permission management. *2016 2nd International Conference on Open and Big Data (OBD),* 25-30.

Bahrammirzaee, A. (2010). A comparative survey of artificial intelligence applications in finance: Artificial neural networks, expert system, and hybrid intelligent systems. *Neural Computing & Applications*, *19*(8), 1165–1195. doi:10.1007/s00521-010-0362-z

Barboza, C. (2019). Artificial Intelligence and HR: The New Wave of Technology - Converge. *Journal of Advances in Social Science and Humanities.*

Barney, J. (1991). Firm resources and sustained competitive advantage. *Journal of Management*, *17*(1), 99–120. doi:10.1177/014920639101700108

Barone, R., & Masciandaro, D. (2011). Organized crime, money laundering and legal economy: Theory and simulations. *European Journal of Law and Economics*, *32*(1), 115–142. doi:10.1007/s10657-010-9203-x

Bartoletti, M., & Pompianu, L. (2017). An empirical analysis of smart contracts: platforms, applications, and design patterns. In *International conference on financial cryptography and data security*. Springer. 10.1007/978-3-319-70278-0_31

Ba, S., Jin, Y., Li, X., & Lu, X. (2020). One size fits all? The differential impact of online reviews and coupons. *Production and Operations Management*, *29*(10), 2403–2424. doi:10.1111/poms.13233

Basu, S., Majumdar, B., Mukherjee, K., Munjal, S., & Palaksha, C. (2022). The role of artificial intelligence in HRM: A systematic review and future research direction. *Human Resource Management Review*. Advance online publication. doi:10.1016/j.hrmr.2022.100893

Batra, S., & Kazmi, S. H. H. (2018). Sales incentives and employee performance: A review of the literature. *Journal of Management Development*, *37*(3), 219–231. doi:10.1108/JMD-08-2016-0159

Behera, R. K., Gunasekaran, A., Gupta, S., Kamboj, S., & Bala, P. K. (2020). Personalized digital marketing recommender engine. *Journal of Retailing and Consumer Services*, *53*, 101799. doi:10.1016/j.jretconser.2019.03.026

Benchoufi, M., Porcher, R., & Ravaud, P. (2022). Blockchain protocols in clinical research: Transparency and traceability of consent through distributed ledgers. *F1000 Research*, 10.

Benchoufi, M., & Ravaud, P. (2017). Blockchain technology for improving clinical research quality. *Trials*, *18*(1), 1–5. doi:10.1186/s13063-017-2035-z PMID:28724395

Benzidia, S., Makaoui, N., & Bentahar, O. (2021). The impact of big data analytics and artificial intelligence on green supply chain process integration and hospital environmental performance. *Technological Forecasting and Social Change*, *165*, 120557. doi:10.1016/j.techfore.2020.120557

Berşe, S., Akça, K., Dirgar, E., & Kaplan Serin, E. (2023). The Role and Potential Contributions of the Artificial Intelligence Language Model ChatGPT. *Annals of Biomedical Engineering*. Advance online publication. doi:10.1007/s10439-023-03296-w PMID:37378876

Bhattacharya, S., Maddikunta, P. K. R., Pham, Q.-V., Gadekallu, T. R., Krishnan, S. S. R., Chowdhary, C. L., Alazab, M., & Piran, M. (2021). Deep learning and medical image processing for coronavirus (COVID-19) pandemic: A survey. *Sustainable Cities and Society*, *65*, 102589. Advance online publication. doi:10.1016/j.scs.2020.102589 PMID:33169099

Bhatt, M., & Shah, P. (2023). Acceptance of Artificial Intelligence in Human Resource Practices by Employees. In *The Adoption and Effect of Artificial Intelligence on Human Resources Management*. Part B. doi:10.1108/978-1-80455-662-720230002

Bhatt, P., & Muduli, A. (2022). Artificial intelligence in learning and development: A systematic literature review. *European Journal of Training and Development*. Advance online publication. doi:10.1108/EJTD-09-2021-0143

Bhosale Jayashree. (2022, September 19). *Cotton production: India's cotton production to increase by 15% in 2022-23 - The Economic Times*. https://economictimes.indiatimes.com/news/economy/agriculture/indias-cotton-production-to-increase-by-15-in-2022-23/articleshow/94288018.cms

Biliavska, V., Castanho, R. A., & Vulevic, A. (2022). Analysis of the Impact of Artificial Intelligence in Enhancing the Human Resource Practices. *Journal of Intelligent Management Decision*. doi:10.56578/jimd010206

Blinder, A. S. (2010). How central should the central bank be? *Journal of Economic Literature*, *48*(1), 123–133. doi:10.1257/jel.48.1.123

Boell, S. K., & Cecez-Kecmanovic, D. (2015). On being 'systematic'in literature reviews. *Formulating Research Methods for Information Systems*, *2*, 48–78. doi:10.1057/9781137509888_3

Bogner, A., Chanson, M., & Meeuw, A. (2016). A Decentralised Sharing App Running a Smart Contract on the Ethereum Blockchain. In *Proceedings of the 6th International Conference on the Internet of Things*. ACM. 10.1145/2991561.2998465

Bolton, R. N., Parasuraman, A., Hoefnagels, A., Migchels, N., Kabadayi, S., Gruber, T., & Solnet, D. (2013). Understanding Generation Y and their use of social media: A review and research agenda. *Journal of Service Management*, *24*(3), 245–267. doi:10.1108/09564231311326987

Bonabeau, E. (2004). The Perils of the Imitation Age. *Harvard Business Review*, *82*(6), 45–54. PMID:15202286

Bowen, M. D., Lai-Bennejean, C. J., Haas, A., & Rangarajan, D. (2021). Social media in B2B sales: Why and when does salesperson social media usage affect salesperson performance? *Industrial Marketing Management*, *96*, 166–182. doi:10.1016/j.indmarman.2021.05.007

Bravi, L., Santos, G., Pagano, A., & Murmura, F. (2020). Environmental management system according to ISO 14001: 2015 as a driver to sustainable development. *Corporate Social Responsibility and Environmental Management*, *27*(6), 2599–2614. doi:10.1002/csr.1985

Breiman, L., Friedman, J., Stone, C. J., & Olshen, R. A. (1984). *Classification and Regression Trees*. CRC Press.

Brock, J. J. (1984). Competitor analysis: Some practical approaches. *Industrial Marketing Management, 13*(4), 225–231. doi:10.1016/0019-8501(84)90017-8

Bryman, A., & Bell, E. (2019). *Business research methods*. Oxford University Press.

Bterin, V. (2018). *A next-generation smart contract and de-centralized application platform.* Available online at: https://github.com/ethereum/wiki/wiki/White-Paper/

Buchanan, B. (2019). Artificial intelligence in finance. A Report by the Alan Turing Institute.

Budhwar, P., Chowdhury, S., Wood, G., Aguinis, H., Bamber, G. J., Beltran, J. R., Boselie, P., Lee Cooke, F., Decker, S., DeNisi, A., Dey, P. K., Guest, D., Knoblich, A. J., Malik, A., Paauwe, J., Papagiannidis, S., Patel, C., Pereira, V., Ren, S., ... Varma, A. (2023). Human resource management in the age of generative artificial intelligence: Perspectives and research directions on ChatGPT. *Human Resource Management Journal, 33*(3), 606–659. Advance online publication. doi:10.1111/1748-8583.12524

Buterin, V. (2014). *A Next-generation Smart Contract and Decentralized Application Platform.* White paper 3: 37.

Cadario, R., Longoni, C., & Morewedge, C. K. (2021). Understanding, explaining, and utilizing medical artificial intelligence. *Nature Human Behaviour, 5*(12), 1636–1642. Advance online publication. doi:10.1038/s41562-021-01146-0 PMID:34183800

Cai, G. (2020). Impact of media use on consumer product knowledge. *Social Behavior and Personality, 48*(2), 11–24. Advance online publication. doi:10.2224/sbp.8558

Cambria, E., Schuller, B., Xia, Y., & Havasi, C. (2013). New avenues in opinion mining and sentiment analysis. *IEEE Intelligent Systems, 28*(2), 15–21. doi:10.1109/MIS.2013.30

Cascio, W. F. (2020). Implications of the Changing Nature of Work for Recruitment and Retention. In The Cambridge Handbook of the Changing Nature of Work. doi:10.1017/9781108278034.015

Casey, D., & Sieber, S. (2016). Employees, sustainability, and motivation: Increasing employee engagement by addressing sustainability and corporate social responsibility. *Research in Hospitality Management, 6*(1), 69–76. doi:10.2989/RHM.2016.6.1.9.1297

Chaffey, D., & Ellis-Chadwick, F. (2019). *Digital marketing*. Pearson UK.

Chaffey, D., & Smith, P. R. (2022). *Digital marketing excellence: planning, optimizing and integrating online marketing*. Taylor & Francis. doi:10.4324/9781003009498

Chaker, N. N., Nowlin, E. L., Pivonka, M. T., Itani, O. S., & Agnihotri, R. (2022). Inside sales social media use and its strategic implications for salesperson-customer digital engagement and performance. *Industrial Marketing Management, 100*, 127–144. doi:10.1016/j.indmarman.2021.10.006

Chandra, S., Bhat, R., Singh, H., & Chauhan, D. S. (n.d.). Detection of brain tumors from MRI using gaussian RBF kernel-based support vector machine. *IJACT, 1*(1), 46–51.

Chapman, P., Clinton, J., Kerber, R., Khabaza, T., Reinartz, T., Shearer, C., & Wirth, R. (2000). *CRISP-DM 1.0 step-by-step data mining guide*. Academic Press.

Chatterjee, S., Chaudhuri, R., Sakka, G., Grandhi, B., Galati, A., Siachou, E., & Vrontis, D. (2021). Adoption of social media marketing for sustainable business growth of SMEs in emerging economies: The moderating role of leadership support. *Sustainability (Basel)*, *13*(21), 12134. doi:10.3390/su132112134

Chen, Y., Fay, S., & Wang, Q. (2011). The role of marketing in social media: How online consumer reviews evolve. *Journal of Interactive Marketing, 25*(2), 85-94. doi:10.1016/j.intmar.2011.01.003

Chen, D. Q., Preston, D. S., & Swink, M. (2021). How big data analytics affects supply chain decision-making: An empirical analysis. *Journal of the Association for Information Systems*, *22*(5), 1224–1244. doi:10.17705/1jais.00713

Chen, L. (2017). Decentralized Execution of Smart Contracts: Agent Model Perspective and its Implications. In *International Conference on Financial Cryptography and Data Security*. Springer. 10.1007/978-3-319-70278-0_29

Chen, M. J. (1996). Competitor analysis and interfirm rivalry: Toward a theoretical integration. *Academy of Management Review*, *21*(1), 100–134. doi:10.2307/258631

ChenT.TerziE. (2019). Problems and solutions in developments of AI in anti-money laundering: A survey. ArXiv. https://arxiv.org/abs/1910.07450

Cheung, C. M. K., Xiao, B. S., & Liu, I. L. B. (2014). Do actions speak louder than voices? The signaling role of social information cues in influencing consumer purchase decisions. *Decision Support Systems*, *65*, 50–58. doi:10.1016/j.dss.2014.05.002

Chevalier, F. (2022). Artificial Intelligence and Human Resources. *Proceedings - Academy of Management*, *2022*(1), 16478. Advance online publication. doi:10.5465/AMBPP.2022.16478abstract

Chilunjika, A., Intauno, K., & Chilunjika, S. R. (2022). Artificial intelligence and public sector human resource management in South Africa: Opportunities, challenges and prospects. *SA Journal of Human Resource Management*, *20*. Advance online publication. doi:10.4102/sajhrm.v20i0.1972

Chima, C. C. (2022). *Artificial Intelligence in Human Resources Management and Human Resource Accounting in Nigerian Public Sector*. Management and Human Resource Research Journal.

Chitrao, P., Bhoyar, P. K., Divekar, R., & Bhatt, P. (2022). Study on Use of Artificial Intelligence in Talent Acquisition. *2022 International Conference on Interdisciplinary Research in Technology and Management, IRTM 2022 - Proceedings*. 10.1109/IRTM54583.2022.9791659

Choi, S. M., & Rifon, N. J. (2012). It is a match: The impact of congruence between celebrity image and consumer ideal self on endorsement effectiveness. *Psychology and Marketing*, *29*(9), 639–650. doi:10.1002/mar.20550

Chowdhury, S., Dey, P., Joel-Edgar, S., Bhattacharya, S., Rodriguez-Espindola, O., Abadie, A., & Truong, L. (2023). Unlocking the value of artificial intelligence in human resource management through AI capability framework. *Human Resource Management Review*, *33*(1), 100899. Advance online publication. doi:10.1016/j.hrmr.2022.100899

Christensen, L.B., Johnson, B., Turner, L.A., & Christensen, L.B. (2011). *Research methods, design, and analysis*. Academic Press.

Chua, A. Y. K., Banerjee, S., & Kim, Y. (2019). Understanding consumers' responses to personalized advertising: A privacy calculus perspective. *Journal of Interactive Marketing*, *46*, 86–98.

Chung, Y. J., & Koo, C. (2016). The effects of social media marketing on brand loyalty: A case study of online fashion brand. *Journal of Global Fashion Marketing*, *7*(3), 204–213. doi:10.1080/20932685.2016.1193386

Clack, C. D., Bakshi, V. A., & Braine, L. (2016). Smart Contract Templates: Essential Requirements and Design Options. *arXiv preprint arXiv:1612.04496*

Cong, L. W., & Wang, L. (2019). *Tokenomics and Blockchain-Enabled Transformation of the Healthcare Research Ecosystem*. Blockchain Research Institute. https://blockchainresearchinstitute.io/tokenomics-and-blockchain-enabled-transformation-of-the-healthcare-research-ecosystem/

Conn, S. (2017). *Gartner Says By 2020*. Artificial Intelligence Will Create More Jobs Than It Eliminates.

Constantinescu, M., Orindaru, A., Pachitanu, A., Rosca, L., Caescu, S.-C., & Orzan, M. C. (2019). Attitude evaluation on using the neuromarketing approach in social media: Matching company's purposes and consumer's benefits for sustainable business growth. *Sustainability (Basel)*, *11*(24), 7094. doi:10.3390/su11247094

Cotton Corporation India Ltd. (2022). *National Cotton Scenario*. https://cotcorp.org.in/national_cotton.aspx

*Cotton Manufacturing Companies, Cotton Manufacturers and Exporters in India*. (2022). India Brand Equity Foundation. https://www.ibef.org/exports/cotton-industry-india

*Cotton update*. (2022). International Cotton Advisory Committee; International cotton advisory committee. https://icac.org/Content/PublicationsPdf Files/35f65863_c1fa_48c6_8570_cb3ca9225152/CU_2022_05_19.pdf.pdf

Cover, T., & Hart, P. (1967). Nearest neighbor pattern classification. *IEEE Transactions on Information Theory*, *13*(1), 21–27. doi:10.1109/TIT.1967.1053964

Cozzolino, A., Corbo, L., & Aversa, P. (2021). Digital platform-based ecosystems: The evolution of collaboration and competition between incumbent producers and entrant platforms. *Journal of Business Research*, *126*, 385–400. doi:10.1016/j.jbusres.2020.12.058

CramerJ. S. (2002). *The Origins of Logistic Regression*. doi:10.2139/ssrn.360300

Crawford, M. (2017). The Insurance Implications of Blockchain. *Risk Management*, *64*, 24.

Das, G., Li, S., Tunio, R. A., Jamali, R. H., Ullah, I., & Fernando, K. W. T. M. (2023). The implementation of green supply chain management (GSCM) and environmental management system (EMS) practices and its impact on market competitiveness during COVID-19. *Environmental Science and Pollution Research International*, *30*(26), 1–16. doi:10.1007/s11356-023-27077-z PMID:37121948

Dash, R., McMurtrey, M., Rebman, C., & Kar, U. K. (2019). Application of artificial intelligence in automation of supply chain management. *Journal of Strategic Innovation and Sustainability*, *14*(3), 43–53.

De Bellis, E., Lassar, W. M., & Carr, C. T. (2019). The impact of personalization on email marketing metrics: Evidence from a field experiment. *Journal of Business Research*, *98*, 214–223.

de la Torre, R., Calvet, L. O., Lopez-Lopez, D., Juan, A. A., & Hatami, S. (2021). Business Analytics in Sport Talent Acquisition. *International Journal of Business Analytics*, *9*(1), 1–20. Advance online publication. doi:10.4018/IJBAN.290406

de Vries, L., Gensler, S., & Leeflang, P. S. H. (2012). Popularity of brand posts on brand fan pages: An investigation of the effects of social media marketing. *Journal of Interactive Marketing*, *26*(2), 83–91. doi:10.1016/j.intmar.2012.01.003

Delecraz, S., Eltarr, L., Becuwe, M., Bouxin, H., Boutin, N., & Oullier, O. (2022). Responsible Artificial Intelligence in Human Resources Technology: An innovative inclusive and fair by design matching algorithm for job recruitment purposes. *Journal of Responsible Technology*, *11*, 100041. Advance online publication. doi:10.1016/j.jrt.2022.100041

Dignum, V. (2019). *Responsible artificial intelligence: how to develop and use AI in a responsible way* (Vol. 2156). Springer. doi:10.1007/978-3-030-30371-6

Ding, J., Cheng, H. D., Xian, M., Zhang, Y., & Xu, F. (2015). Local-weighted Citation-kNN algorithm for breast ultrasound image classification. *Optik (Stuttgart)*, *126*(24), 5188–5193. doi:10.1016/j.ijleo.2015.09.231

Doss, A. N., Maurya, N., Guru, K., Masood, G., Jaiswal, S., & Naved, M. 2022, June. The Impact of Data Mining and Artificial Intelligence on Supply Chain Management and Environmental Performance. In *Proceedings of Second International Conference in Mechanical and Energy Technology: ICMET 2021, India* (pp. 503-511). Singapore: Springer Nature Singapore.

Dow, S. (2019). Monetary reform, central banks, and digital currencies. *International Journal of Political Economy*, *48*(2), 153–173. doi:10.1080/08911916.2019.1624317

Dubey, R., Gunasekaran, A., Childe, S. J., Bryde, D. J., Giannakis, M., Foropon, C., Roubaud, D., & Hazen, B. T. (2020). Big data analytics and artificial intelligence pathway to operational performance under the effects of entrepreneurial orientation and environmental dynamism: A study of manufacturing organisations. *International Journal of Production Economics*, *226*, 107599. doi:10.1016/j.ijpe.2019.107599

Dutta, S. (2018). *The Importance of Following Marketing Trends.* Business 2 Community. Retrieved from https://www.business2community.com/marketing/the-importance-of-following-marketing-trends-02074695

Dutta, P., Jaikumar, B., & Arora, M. S. (2021). Applications of data envelopment analysis in supplier selection between 2000 and 2020: A literature review. *Annals of Operations Research*, 1–56.

Dutta, S. (2011). Let the revolution begin! Enterprise 2.0. *IESE Insight*, (9), 13–20. doi:10.15581/002.ART-1966

Dwivedi, Y. K., Ismagilova, E., Rana, N. P., & Raman, R. (2021). *Social Media Adoption, Usage And Impact In Business-To-Business (B2B) Context: A State-Of-The-Art.* Academic Press.

Dwivedi, A. D., Srivastava, G., Dhar, S., & Singh, R. (2019). A decentralized privacy-preserving healthcare blockchain for IoT. *Sensors (Basel)*, *19*(2), 326. doi:10.3390/s19020326 PMID:30650612

Effendi, G. N., & Pribadi, U. (2021). The Effect of Leadership Style on the Implementation of Artificial Intelligence in Government Services. *IOP Conference Series: Earth and Environmental Science.* 10.1088/1755-1315/717/1/012018

Ekblaw, A., Azaria, A., Halamka, J. D., & Lippman, A. (2016). A case study for blockchain in healthcare: "MedRec" prototype for electronic health records and medical research data. *Proceedings of IEEE Open & Big Data Conference.*

Ekblaw, A., Azaria, A., Halamka, J. D., & Lippman, A. (2016). A Case Study for Blockchain in Healthcare: "MedRec" prototype for electronic health records and medical research data. *Proceedings of IEEE Open & Big Data Conference.* https://doi.org/10.13140/RG.2.2.30823.39849

el al Aggarwal, S. (2019). Blockchain for Smart Communities: Applications, Challenges and Opportunities. *Journal of Network and Computer Applications*, *144*, 13–48. doi:10.1016/j.jnca.2019.06.018

El Amraoui, K., Ezzaki, A., Masmoudi, L., Hadri, M., El Belrhiti, H., El Ansari, M., & Amari, A. (2022). Machine learning algorithm for Avocado image segmentation based on quantum enhancement and Random Forest. In B. Benhala, K. Mansouri, A. Raihani, & M. Qbadou (Eds.), *2022 2nd international conference on innovative research in applied science, engineering and technology (iraset'2022)* (pp. 149–155). 10.1109/IRASET52964.2022.9738360

El Samad, M., Dennaoui, H., & El Nemar, S. (2023). Machine Learning and Big Data in Finance Services. Artificial Intelligence for Capital Markets. doi:10.1201/9781003327745-2

El Samad, M., El Nemar, S., Sakka, G., & El-Chaarani, H. (2022). An innovative big data framework for exploring the impact on decision-making in the European Mediterranean healthcare sector. *EuroMed Journal of Business*, *17*(3), 312–332. Advance online publication. doi:10.1108/EMJB-11-2021-0168

El Samad, M., Nasserddine, G., & Kheir, A. (2023). *Introduction to Artificial Intelligence. In Artificial Intelligence and Knowledge Processing.* CRC Press. doi:10.1201/9781003328414-1

Elgendy, N., Elragal, A., & Päivärinta, T. (2022). DECAS: A modern data-driven decision theory for big data and analytics. *Journal of Decision Systems*, *31*(4), 337–373. doi:10.1080/12460125.2021.1894674

Eriksen, M. B., & Frandsen, T. F. (2018). The impact of patient, intervention, comparison, outcome (PICO) as a search strategy tool on literature search quality: A systematic review. *Journal of the Medical Library Association: JMLA*, *106*(4), 420. doi:10.5195/jmla.2018.345 PMID:30271283

Ernst, E., Merola, R., & Samaan, D. (2019). Economics of Artificial Intelligence: Implications for the Future of Work. *IZA Journal of Labor Policy*, *9*(1), 20190004. Advance online publication. doi:10.2478/izajolp-2019-0004

ETMarkets. (2022, September 24). *Kharif production: Origo Commodities' estimate suggests a drop in kharif production - The Economic Times*. https://economictimes.indiatimes.com/markets/commodities/news/origo-commodities-estimate-suggests-a-drop-in-kharif-production/articleshow/94413715.cms

Ezeife, L. (2017). *Social media strategies for increasing sales* [Doctoral dissertation]. Walden University.

Fakhari, A., & Moghadam, A. M. E. (2013). Combination of classification and regression in decision tree for multi-labeling image annotation and retrieval. *Applied Soft Computing*, *13*(2), 1292–1302. doi:10.1016/j.asoc.2012.10.019

FAO in India. (n.d.). *India at a Glance | FAO in India | Food and Agriculture Organization of the United Nations*. Food and Agriculture Organization of the United Nations.

Faqihi, A., & Miah, S. J. (2023). Artificial Intelligence-Driven Talent Management System: Exploring the Risks and Options for Constructing a Theoretical Foundation. *Journal of Risk and Financial Management*, *16*(1), 31. Advance online publication. doi:10.3390/jrfm16010031

Feedzai. (2018). *Feedzai helps FTC capital reduce false positives by over 95 percent*. https://feedzai.com/cases/ftc/

Feng, Q., He, D., Zeadally, S., Khan, M. K., & Kumar, N. (2019). A Survey on Privacy Protection in Blockchain System. *Journal of Network and Computer Applications*, *126*, 45–58. doi:10.1016/j.jnca.2018.10.020

Fernández, A. (2019). Artificial intelligence in financial services. *Banco de Espana Article*, *3*, 19.

Ferwerda, J. (2013). The effects of money laundering. In M. D. Jesilow & S. S. Simpson (Eds.), *International handbook of financial crimes*. Edward Elgar Publishing.

Financial Action Task Force (FATF). (2019). *Guidance for a risk-based approach to virtual assets and virtual asset service providers*. https://www.fatf-gafi.org/media/fatf/documents/recommendations/RBA-VA-VASPs.pdf

Flinn, L., Braham, L., & das Nair, R. (2015). How reliable are case formulations? A systematic literature review. *British Journal of Clinical Psychology*, *54*(3), 266–290. doi:10.1111/bjc.12073 PMID:25515566

Fogarty, E. S., Swain, D. L., Cronin, G., & Trotter, M. (2018). Autonomous on-animal sensors in sheep research: A systematic review. *Computers and Electronics in Agriculture*, *150*, 245–256. doi:10.1016/j.compag.2018.04.017

Foley, S., Karlsen, J. R., & Putniņš, T. J. (2019). Sex, drugs, and bitcoin: How much illegal activity is financed through cryptocurrencies? *Review of Financial Studies*, *32*(5), 1798–1853. doi:10.1093/rfs/hhz015

Fosfuri, A., & Tribó, J. A. (2008). Exploring the antecedents of potential absorptive capacity and its impact on innovation performance. *Omega*, *36*(2), 173–187. doi:10.1016/j.omega.2006.06.012 PMID:18680889

Freudenreich, B., Lüdeke-Freund, F., & Schaltegger, S. (2020). A stakeholder theory perspective on business models: Value creation for sustainability. *Journal of Business Ethics*, *166*(1), 3–18. doi:10.1007/s10551-019-04112-z

Fundin, A. P., & Bergman, B. L. (2003). Exploring the customer feedback process. *Measuring Business Excellence*, *7*(2), 55–65. doi:10.1108/13683040310477995

Galagan, P., Hirt, M., & Vital, C. (2020). *Capabilities for Talent Development Shaping the Future of the Profession*. ATD Press.

Gallo, H., Khadem, A., & Alzubi, A. (2023). The Relationship between Big Data AnalyticArtificial Intelligence and Environmental Performance: A Moderated Mediated Model of Green Supply Chain Collaboration (GSCC) and Top Management Commitment (TMC). *Discrete Dynamics in Nature and Society*.

Gao, Y., & Wu, L. (2021). *Efficiently mastering the game of nogo with deep reinforcement learning supported by domain knowledge*. Electronics. doi:10.3390/electronics10131533

Garg, V., Srivastav, S., & Gupta, A. (2018). Application of Artificial Intelligence for Sustaining Green Human Resource Management. *2018 International Conference on Automation and Computational Engineering, ICACE 2018*. 10.1109/ICACE.2018.8686988

Gaur, B., Bashir, R., & Sanghvi, B. (2021). An AI based training framework for Telecommuting Employees to combat perennial skill shortages post pandemic. *Proceedings of 2021 2nd International Conference on Intelligent Engineering and Management, ICIEM 2021*. 10.1109/ICIEM51511.2021.9445329

Geisel, A. (2018). The current and future impact of artificial intelligence on business. *International Journal of Scientific and Technology Research*.

Gélinas, D., Sadreddin, A., & Vahidov, R. (2022). *Artificial intelligence in human resources management: A review and research agenda*. Pacific Asia Journal of the Association for Information Systems. doi:10.17705/1pais.14601

Gethe, R. K. (2022). Extrapolation of talent acquisition in AI aided professional environment. *International Journal of Business Innovation and Research*. doi:10.1504/IJBIR.2022.122510

Geurin, A. N., & Burch, L. M. (2017). User-generated branding via social media: An examination of six running brands. *Sport Management Review*, *20*(3), 273–284. doi:10.1016/j.smr.2016.09.001

Ghafoor, S., Hussain, O. K., Muhammad, Y., Al-Turjman, F., & Bakar, A. H. A. (2021). A framework for secure and decentralized sharing of electronic health records using blockchain technology. *Computer Communications*, *174*, 64–72.

Giermindl, L. M., Strich, F., Christ, O., Leicht-Deobald, U., & Redzepi, A. (2022). The dark sides of people analytics: Reviewing the perils for organisations and employees. *European Journal of Information Systems*, *31*(3), 410–435. Advance online publication. doi:10.1080/0960085X.2021.1927213

Giraud, L., Zaher, A., Hernandez, S., & Akram, A. A. (2022). The impacts of artificial intelligence on managerial skills. *Journal of Decision Systems*. Advance online publication. doi:10.1080/12460125.2022.2069537

Gong, Y., Zhao, M., Wang, Q., & Lv, Z. (2022). Design and interactive performance of human resource management system based on artificial intelligence. *PLoS One*, *17*(1), e0262398. Advance online publication. doi:10.1371/journal.pone.0262398 PMID:35089946

Goodell, J. W., Kumar, S., Lim, W. M., & Pattnaik, D. (2021). Artificial intelligence and machine learning in finance: Identifying foundations, themes, and research clusters from bibliometric analysis. *Journal of Behavioral and Experimental Finance*, *32*, 100577. doi:10.1016/j.jbef.2021.100577

Goodhart, C. (1995). *The central bank and the financial system*. Springer. doi:10.1057/9780230379152

Goodhart, C. A. E. (2011). The changing role of central banks. *Financial History Review*, *18*(2), 135–154. doi:10.1017/S0968565011000096

Gordon, W. J., & Catalini, C. (2018). Blockchain technology for healthcare: Facilitating the transition to patient-driven interoperability. *Computational and Structural Biotechnology Journal*, *16*, 224–230. doi:10.1016/j.csbj.2018.06.003 PMID:30069284

Grönroos, C. (1989). Defining marketing: A market-oriented approach. *European Journal of Marketing*, *23*(1), 52–60. doi:10.1108/EUM0000000000541

Group, E. T. C. (2016). *Software vs. hardware vs. nowhere*. ETCGroup.org. https://www.etcgroup.org/sites/www.etcgroup.org/files/files/software_vs._hardware_vs._nowhere_-_briefing_dec_2016.pdf

Grover, K. L. (2022). Artificial Intelligence: A Tool for Optimizing Talent Acquisition. *International Journal of Law Management & Humanities*.

Grover, V., Chiang, R. H., Liang, T. P., & Zhang, D. (2018). Creating strategic business value from big data analytics: A research framework. *Journal of Management Information Systems, 35*(2), 388–423. doi:10.1080/07421222.2018.1451951

Grundy, T. (2006). Rethinking and reinventing Michael Porter's five forces model. *Strategic Change, 15*(5), 213–229. doi:10.1002/jsc.764

Guan, Y., Huang, Y., & Qin, H. (2022). Inventory management optimization of green supply chain using ipso-bpnn algorithm under the artificial intelligence. *Wireless Communications and Mobile Computing, 2022*, 2022. doi:10.1155/2022/8428964

Gu, B., & Ye, Q. (2014). First step in social media: Measuring the influence of online management responses on customer satisfaction. *Production and Operations Management, 23*(4), 570–582. doi:10.1111/poms.12043

Gummerus, J., Liljander, V., Weman, E., & Pihlström, M. (2012). Customer engagement in a Facebook brand community. *Management Research Review, 35*(9), 857–877. doi:10.1108/01409171211256578

Guo, Y. (2018). WISChain: An Online Insurance System based on Blockchain and DengLu1 for Web Identity Security. *2018 1st IEEE International Conference on Hot Information-Centric Networking (HotICN),* 242–243.

Guo, Q. (2022). A Fuzzy Comprehensive Dynamic Evaluation Algorithm for Human Resource Quality Growth Based on Artificial Intelligence. *Mobile Information Systems, 2022*, 1–14. Advance online publication. doi:10.1155/2022/8402975

Guo, Y., & Liang, C. (2016). Blockchain application and outlook in the banking industry. *Financial Innovation, 2*(1), 24. doi:10.1186/s40854-016-0034-9

Gupta, P., Fernandes, S. F., & Jain, M. (2018). Automation in recruitment: a new frontier. *Journal of Information Technology Teaching Cases.* doi:10.1057/s41266-018-0042-x

Gupta, S., & Chopra, C. (2020). *Impact of Social Media on Consumer Behavior.* Research Gate.

Gurl, E. (2017). *SWOT analysis: A theoretical review.* Academic Press.

Gurusinghe, R. N., Arachchige, B. J. H., & Dayarathna, D. (2021). Predictive HR analytics and talent management: a conceptual framework. *Journal of Management Analytics.* doi:10.1080/23270012.2021.1899857

Haghi Kashani, M., Madanipour, M., Nikravan, M., Asghari, P., & Mahdipour, E. (2021). A systematic review of IoT in healthcare: Applications, techniques, and trends. *Journal of Network and Computer Applications, 192*, 103164. Advance online publication. doi:10.1016/j.jnca.2021.103164

Hako, B. (1972). Strategies for diversification. *Long Range Planning, 5*(2), 65–69. doi:10.1016/0024-6301(72)90048-9

Halachmi, I., Guarino, M., Bewley, J., & Pastell, M. (2019). Smart animal agriculture: Application of real-time sensors to improve animal well-being and production. *Annual Review of Animal Biosciences*, *7*(1), 403–425. doi:10.1146/annurev-animal-020518-114851 PMID:30485756

HallidayT. C.LeviM.ReuterP. (2020). Global surveillance of dirty money: Assessing assessments of regimes to control money-laundering and combat the financing of terrorism. American Bar Foundation. https://doi.org/ doi:10.2139/ssrn.3528830

Hamid, Al-Hakim, Arief, Dionova, & Alrahman. (2023). Recent Updates on Intelligent System for Talent Management: Does That Become a Helpful System? *SATESI: Jurnal Sains Teknologi Dan Sistem Informasi*. doi:10.54259/satesi.v3i1.1590

Hangal, A. (2019). *Role of HR Analytics on Employees Performance Improvement*. Gavesana Journal of Management.

Hans, R., Zuber, H., Rizk, A., & Steinmetz, R. (2017). Blockchain and Smart Contracts: Disruptive Technologies for the Insurance Market. *2017 Americas Conference on Information Systems*, 1-10.

Hartemo, M. (2016). Email marketing in the era of the empowered consumer. *Journal of Research in Interactive Marketing*, *10*(3), 212–230. doi:10.1108/JRIM-06-2015-0040

Hasan, R., Kamal, M. M., Daowd, A., Eldabi, T., Koliousis, I., & Papadopoulos, T. (2022). Critical analysis of the impact of big data analytics on supply chain operations. *Production Planning and Control*, 1–25.

Hayes, B. (1999). Computing Science Seeing Between the Pixels. *American Scientist*, *87*(3), 202–207. doi:10.1511/1999.24.202

Helo, P., & Hao, Y. (2022). Artificial intelligence in operations management and supply chain management: An exploratory case study. *Production Planning and Control*, *33*(16), 1573–1590. doi:10.1080/09537287.2021.1882690

He, P. (2017). Survey on Blockchain Technology and its Application Prospect. *Computer Science*, *44*, 1–7.

Herppich, S., Praetorius, A. K., Förster, N., Glogger-Frey, I., Karst, K., Leutner, D., & Südkamp, A. (2018). Teachers' assessment competence: Integrating knowledge-, process-, and product-oriented approaches into a competence-oriented conceptual model. *Teaching and Teacher Education*, *76*, 181–193. doi:10.1016/j.tate.2017.12.001

He, W., Wu, H., Yan, G., Akula, V., & Shen, J. (2015). A novel social media competitive analytics framework with sentiment benchmarks. *Information & Management*, *52*(7), 801–812. doi:10.1016/j.im.2015.04.006

Homburg, C., Jozić, D., & Kuehnl, C. (2017). Customer experience management: Toward implementing an evolving marketing concept. *Journal of the Academy of Marketing Science*, *45*(3), 377–401. doi:10.1007/s11747-015-0460-7

Hopwood, D., Bowe, S., Hornby, T., & Wilcox, N. (2016). *Zcash Protocol Specification*, Tech. rep. 2016–1.10. Zerocoin Electric Coin Company.

Hornberger, B., & Rangu, S. (2020). *Designing inclusion and exclusion criteria*. Academic Press.

Hossin, S., Arije Ulfy, M., Ali, I., Karim, W., & Karim, M. W. (2021). *Challenges in Adopting Artificial Intelligence (AI) in HRM Practices: A study on Bangladesh Perspective*. International Fellowship Journal of Interdisciplinary Research.

Hull, C. E. (2022). Competitive sustainability: The intersection of sustainability and business success. *Sustainability (Basel), 14*(24), 16420. doi:10.3390/su142416420

Hum Y. (2018). *A Delay-Tolerant Payment Scheme Based on the Ethereum Blockchain.* CoRR abs/1801.10295

Hunt, K. G. (2010). Finders keepers: Social media strategies help find top talent. *Journal of Property Management, 75*(6), 36. https://go.exlibris.link/HR5JcHY8

Hunt, W., Sarkar, S., & Warhurst, C. (2022). Measuring the impact of AI on jobs at the organization level: Lessons from a survey of UK business leaders. *Research Policy, 51*(2), 104425. Advance online publication. doi:10.1016/j.respol.2021.104425

Husu, H., Jussila, J., & Vuori, V. (2021). Blockchain in healthcare: A systematic literature review, synthesis, and future research agenda. *International Journal of Information Management, 57*, 102297.

Hu, T., Wu, W., & Liu, L. (2014). Combination of hard and soft classification method based on adaptive threshold. *2014 IEEE Geoscience and Remote Sensing Symposium*, 4180–4183. 10.1109/IGARSS.2014.6947409

Hu, W. C., Wu, H. T., Cho, H. H., & Tseng, F. H. (2020). Optimal route planning system for logistics vehicles based on artificial intelligence. *Journal of Internet Technology, 21*(3), 757–764.

Hu, W., & Chen, Y. (2022, July). Application of Artificial Intelligence in Financial Risk Management. In *International Conference on Adaptive and Intelligent Systems* (pp. 180-188). Cham: Springer International Publishing. 10.1007/978-3-031-06794-5_15

Ibáñez-Sánchez, S., Orus, C., & Flavian, C. (2022). Augmented reality filters on social media. Analyzing the drivers of playability based on uses and gratifications theory. *Psychology and Marketing, 39*(3), 559–578. doi:10.1002/mar.21639

Ikram, M., Zhang, Q., & Sroufe, R. (2021). Future of quality management system (ISO 9001) certification: Novel grey forecasting approach. *Total Quality Management & Business Excellence, 32*(15-16), 1666–1693. doi:10.1080/14783363.2020.1768062

Ind, N. (1997). *The Corporate Brand.* Macmillan Press Ltd. doi:10.1057/9780230375888

Infante, A., & Mardikaningsih, R. (2022). The Potential of Social Media as a Means of Online Business Promotion. *Journal of Social Science Studies, 2*(2), 45–49. doi:10.56348/jos3.v2i2.26

Invespcro. (2021). *The Importance of Online Customer Reviews.* https://www.invespcro.com/blog/theimportance-of-online-customer-reviews-infograp

Islam, M. T., & Tamzid, M. (2023). Artificial Intelligence in Human Resource Management. In Management Education for Achieving Sustainable Development Goals in the Context of Bangladesh. doi:10.57240/DUJMBK04

Islam, M., Mamun, A. Al, Afrin, S., Ali Quaosar, G. M. A., & Uddin, M. A. (2022). Technology Adoption and Human Resource Management Practices: The Use of Artificial Intelligence for Recruitment in Bangladesh. *South Asian Journal of Human Resources Management.* doi:10.1177/23220937221122329

Jackson, J. P., & Manning, M. J. (2007). Central bank intraday collateral policy and implications for tiering in RTGS payment systems. *The future of payment systems*, 138.

Jackson, T., Thomas, S., Stabile, V., Shotwell, M., Han, X., & McQueen, K. (2016). A systematic review and metaanalysis of the global burden of chronic pain without clear etiology in low-and middle-income countries: Trends in heterogeneous data and a proposal for new assessment methods. *Anesthesia and Analgesia, 123*(3), 739–748. doi:10.1213/ANE.0000000000001389 PMID:27537761

Jaiswal, A., Arun, C. J., & Varma, A. (2022). Rebooting employees: Upskilling for artificial intelligence in multinational corporations. *International Journal of Human Resource Management, 33*(6), 1179–1208. Advance online publication. doi:10.1080/09585192.2021.1891114

Jajodia, A., Amrith, B., Madhukar, A., Chaturvedi, A., Mehta, A., Kapur, R., Dewan, A., Agarwal, M., Mahwar, V., Yadav, V., Pasricha, S., & Koyyala, V. P. B. (2020). 286P Improved diagnostic accuracy on MR imaging in post-surgical recurrent head and neck SCC lesions using decision tree classification system. *Annals of Oncology : Official Journal of the European Society for Medical Oncology, 31*, S1353. doi:10.1016/j.annonc.2020.10.280

Jatobá, M., Santos, J., Gutierriz, I., Moscon, D., Fernandes, P. O., & Teixeira, J. P. (2019). Evolution of Artificial Intelligence Research in Human Resources. Procedia Computer Science. doi:10.1016/j.procs.2019.12.165

Jemai, J., Do Chung, B., & Sarkar, B. (2020). Environmental effect for a complex green supplychain management to control waste: A sustainable approach. *Journal of Cleaner Production, 277*, 122919. doi:10.1016/j.jclepro.2020.122919

Jenifa, A., Ramalakshmi, R., & Ramachandran, V. (2019, April 1). Classification of Cotton Leaf Disease Using Multi-Support Vector Machine. *IEEE International Conference on Intelligent Techniques in Control, Optimization and Signal Processing, INCOS 2019.* 10.1109/INCOS45849.2019.8951356

Jenkins, S. (2008). *The truth about email marketing.* FT Press.

Jing, Y. (2020). Research on the Application of Artificial Intelligence Natural Language Processing Technology in Japanese Teaching. In *Journal of Physics*. Conference Series. doi:10.1088/1742-6596/1682/1/012081

Johnson, K., Pasquale, F., & Chapman, J. (2019). Artificial intelligence, machine learning, and bias in finance: Toward responsible innovation. *Fordham Law Review*, *88*, 499.

K v, S., Kp, N., & Kamath, G. B. (2021). Social media advertisements and their influence on consumer purchase intention. *Cogent Business & Management*, *8*(1), 2000697. doi:10.1080/23311975.2021.2000697

Kahaner, L. (1997). *Competitive intelligence: how to gather analyze and use information to move your business to the top*. Simon and Schuster.

Kahyaoglu, H. (2021). The Impact of Artificial Intelligence on Central Banking and Monetary Policies. *The Impact of Artificial Intelligence on Governance, Economics and Finance*, *I*, 83–98.

Kalra, K., Kumar Goswami, A., & Gupta, R. (2013). A Comparative Study of Supervised Image Classification Algorithms for Satellite Images. *International Journal of Electronics*, *1*(10), 2320–2084.

Kambur, E., & Akar, C. (2022). Human resource developments with the touch of artificial intelligence: A scale development study. *International Journal of Manpower*, *43*(1), 168–205. Advance online publication. doi:10.1108/IJM-04-2021-0216

Kandel, B. (2020). Qualitative Versus Quantitative Research. *Journal of Product Innovation Management*, *32*(5), 658.

Kandlhofer, M., Steinbauer, G., Lassnig, J., Menzinger, M., Baumann, W., Ehardt-Schmiederer, M., Bieber, R., Winkler, T., Plomer, S., Strobl-Zuchtriegl, I., Miglbauer, M., Ballagi, A., Pozna, C., Miltenyi, G., Alfoldi, I., & Szalay, I. (2021). EDLRIS: A European Driving License for Robots and Intelligent Systems. *KI -. Kunstliche Intelligenz*, *35*(2), 221–232. Advance online publication. doi:10.1007/s13218-021-00716-8

Kapitan, S., Kennedy, A., & Berth, N. (2019). Sustainably superior versus greenwasher: A scale measure of B2B sustainability positioning. *Industrial Marketing Management*, *76*, 84–97. doi:10.1016/j.indmarman.2018.08.003

Kaplan, A. M., & Haenlein, M. (2019). *Siri, Siri, in my hand: Who's the fairest in the land?* Academic Press.

Kaplan, A., & Haenlein, M. (2010). Users of the World, Unite! The Challenges and Opportunities of Social Media. *Business Horizons*, *53*(1), 59–68. doi:10.1016/j.bushor.2009.09.003

Kasavana, M. L. (2008). *The unintended consequences of social media and the hospitality industry*. Hospitality Upgrade. https://www.hospitalityupgrade.com/Hospitalityupgrade.com-0093-2016Redesign/media/hospitalityupgrade.com-0093/File_Articles/HUFall08_Kasavana_SocialMediaandHospitality.pdf

Kasavana, M. L., Nusair, K., & Teodosic, K. (2010). Online social networking: Redefining the human web. *Journal of Hospitality and Tourism Technology*, *1*(1), 68–82. doi:10.1108/17579881011023025

Kaur, H., Alam, M. A., Javed, A., Anjum, A., & Alrasheedi, M. (2020). A blockchain-based communication infrastructure for future healthcare cybersecurity enhancement. *Electronics (Basel)*, *9*(12), 2133.

Kaushal, N., Kaurav, R. P. S., Sivathanu, B., & Kaushik, N. (2023). *Artificial intelligence and HRM: identifying future research Agenda using systematic literature review and bibliometric analysis*. Management Review Quarterly. doi:10.1007/s11301-021-00249-2

Kazancoglu, Y., Kazancoglu, I., & Sagnak, M. (2018). A new holistic conceptual framework for green supply chain management performance assessment based on circular economy. *Journal of Cleaner Production*, *195*, 1282–1299. doi:10.1016/j.jclepro.2018.06.015

Kazmaier, J., & van Vuuren, J. H. (2020). Sentiment analysis of unstructured customer feedback for a retail bank. *ORiON*, *36*(1), 35–71. doi:10.5784/36-1-668

Keister, T., & Sanches, D. (2023). Should central banks issue digital currency? *The Review of Economic Studies*, *b90*(1), 404-431.

Keller, K. L., & Kotler, P. (2022). Branding in B2B firms. In *Handbook of business-to-business marketing* (pp. 205–224). Edward Elgar Publishing. doi:10.4337/9781800376878.00021

Kelly, O. W., Armstrong, M., Taylor, S., Teo, T. C., Low, K. C. P., Bradley, S., ... Sundiman, D. (2019). Human Resources and Management in Projects. *Human Resource Management Journal*.

Kemendi, Á., Michelberger, P., & Mesjasz-Lech, A. (2022). Industry 4.0 and 5.0 – Organizational and competency challenges of enterprises. *Polish Journal of Management Studies*. doi:10.17512/pjms.2022.26.2.13

Khamis, S., Ang, L., & Welling, R. (2017). Self-branding, 'micro-celebrity' and the rise of social media influencers. *Celebrity Studies*, *8*(2), 191–208. doi:10.1080/19392397.2016.1218292

Khan, M. A., & Iqbal, S. (2015). The effectiveness of sales incentives on sales force performance: An empirical study of pharmaceutical companies in Pakistan. *Journal of Marketing Management*, *6*(2), 1–21. doi:10.12785/jmm.060101

Khan, S. N., Loukil, F., Ghedira-Guegan, C., Benkhelifa, E., & Bani-Hani, A. (2021). Blockchain smart contracts: Applications, challenges, and future trends. *Peer-to-Peer Networking and Applications*, *14*(5), 2901–2925. doi:10.1007/s12083-021-01127-0 PMID:33897937

Khare, S., Khan, B., & Agnihotri, G. (2015). A Shapley value approach for transmission usage cost allocation under contingent restructured market. *2015 1st International Conference on Futuristic Trends in Computational Analysis and Knowledge Management, ABLAZE 2015*, 170–173. 10.1109/ABLAZE.2015.7154987

Kim, A. J., & Ko, E. (2012). Do social media marketing activities enhance customer equity? An empirical study of luxury fashion brand. *Journal of Business Research*, *65*(10), 1480–1486. doi:10.1016/j.jbusres.2011.10.014

Knecht, A. C., Campbell, M. T., Caprez, A., Swanson, D. R., & Walia, H. (2016). Image Harvest: An open-source platform for high-throughput plant image processing and analysis. *Journal of Experimental Botany*, *67*(11), 3587–3599. doi:10.1093/jxb/erw176 PMID:27141917

Končar, J., Vučenović, S., & Marić, R. (2020). Green supply chain management in retailing based on Internet of things. *Integration of Information Flow for Greening Supply Chain Management*, 181-202.

Königstorfer, F., & Thalmann, S. (2020). Applications of Artificial Intelligence in commercial banks–A research agenda for behavioral finance. *Journal of Behavioral and Experimental Finance*, *27*, 100352. doi:10.1016/j.jbef.2020.100352

Koromina, M., Pandi, M. T., & Patrinos, G. P. (2019). Rethinking Drug Repositioning and Development with Artificial Intelligence, Machine Learning, and Omics. *OMICS: A Journal of Integrative Biology*, *23*(11), 539–548. Advance online publication. doi:10.1089/omi.2019.0151 PMID:31651216

Kotler, P., & Armstrong, G. (2021). *Principles of marketing*. Pearson Education Limited.

Kotorov, R. (2003). Customer relationship management: Strategic lessons and future directions. *Business Process Management Journal*, *9*(5), 566–571. doi:10.1108/14637150310496686

Kou, Y., Chou, C., & Lou, J. (2020). Artificial intelligence and money laundering. *Asian Journal of Law and Economics*, *11*(2), 375–391.

KPMG International. (2011). *Going Social. How businesses are making the most of social media.* KPMG International. http://www.grazersoft.com/media/pdf/Going-Social.pdf

Kremer, K. (2022). *HR practices in the context of the Internet of Things*. Strategic Management. doi:10.5937/StraMan2110002K

Kuhn, M. (2021). *CARET: Classification and Regression Training*. https://cran.r-project.org/package=caret

Kumar, V. (2018). *The Benefits of Following Marketing Trends*. Entrepreneur. Retrieved from https://www.entrepreneur.com/article/309031

Kumar, A. (2016). An empirical study of sales incentives in the Indian retail sector. *Journal of Marketing and Consumer Research*, *21*, 73–80.

Kumar, A., Bandopadhyay, S., Das, P. K., Alazab, M., & Irish, Q. Y. (2021). Blockchain-Based Preservation of Archival Medical Images. *IEEE Journal of Biomedical and Health Informatics*, *26*(2), 519–530.

Kumar, A., Bezawada, R., Rishika, R., Janakiraman, R., & Kannan, P. K. (2016). From Social to Sale: The Effects of Firm-Generated Content in Social Media on Customer Behavior. *Journal of Marketing*, *80*(1), 7–25. doi:10.1509/jm.14.0249

Kumar, A., Rahmath, M., Raju, Y., Reddy Vulapula, S., Prathap, B. R., Hassan, M. M., Mohamed, M. A., & Asakipaam, S. A. (2022). Enhanced Secure Technique for Detecting Cyber Attacks Using Artificial Intelligence and Optimal IoT. *Security and Communication Networks*, *2022*, 1–13. Advance online publication. doi:10.1155/2022/8024518

Kumar, I., Rawat, J., Mohd, N., & Husain, S. (2021). Opportunities of Artificial Intelligence and Machine Learning in the Food Industry. *Journal of Food Quality*, *2021*, 1–10. Advance online publication. doi:10.1155/2021/4535567

Kuo, T. T., Kim, H. E., & Ohno-Machado, L. (2017). Blockchain distributed ledger technologies for biomedical and health care applications. *Journal of the American Medical Informatics Association : JAMIA*, *24*(6), 1211–1220. doi:10.1093/jamia/ocx068 PMID:29016974

Kurdi, B. A., Alshurideh, M., Akour, I., Tariq, E., AlHamad, A. Q. M., & Alzoubi, H. M. (2022b). The effect of social media influencers' characteristics on consumer intention and attitude toward Keto products purchase intention. *International Journal of Data and Network Science*, *6*(4), 1135–1146. doi:10.5267/j.ijdns.2022.7.006

Laari, S., Töyli, J., & Ojala, L. (2018). The effect of a competitive strategy and green supply chain management on the financial and environmental performance of logistics service providers. *Business Strategy and the Environment*, *27*(7), 872–883. doi:10.1002/bse.2038

Lainjo, B. (2021). *COVID-19: The Dynamics of Quality of Life (QOL) and Artificial Intelligence (AI)*. African Journal of Inter/Multidisciplinary Studies. doi:10.51415/ajims.v3i1.908

Lanz, L., Fischhof, B., & Lee, R. (2010). *How are Hotels Embracing Social Media in 2010? Examples of How to Start Engaging*. HVS Sales and Marketing Services. https://www.hvs.com/staticcontent/library/nyu2010/journal/articles/socialmediain2010.pdf

Larsen, W., Nielsen, G., & Tyler, D. (1994). Precision navigation with GPS. *Computers and Electronics in Agriculture*, *11*(1), 85–95. doi:10.1016/0168-1699(94)90054-X

Laumer, S., & Morana, S. (2022). HR natural language processing - conceptual overview and state of the art on conversational agents in human resources management. Handbook of Research on Artificial Intelligence in Human Resource Management.

Lauriola, I., Lavelli, A., & Aiolli, F. (2022). An introduction to Deep Learning in Natural Language Processing: Models, techniques, and tools. *Neurocomputing*, *470*, 443–456. Advance online publication. doi:10.1016/j.neucom.2021.05.103

Lee, I., & Mangalaraj, G. (2022). Big data analytics in supply chain management: A systematic literature review and research directions. *Big Data and Cognitive Computing*, *6*(1), 17.

Lee, I., & Lee, K. (2021). The Internet of Things (IoT) healthcare: Issues and challenges. *Cluster Computing*, *24*(1), 353–360.

Lee, J. Y., Lee, M. S., & Feick, L. (2017). The effect of personalized recommendations and consumer innovativeness on purchase intention in a social commerce setting. *Journal of Interactive Marketing*, *38*, 29–41.

Lehman, C. D., Wellman, R. D., Buist, D. S. M., Kerlikowske, K., Tosteson, A. N. A., Miglioretti, D. L., & Surveillance, B. C. (2015). Diagnostic Accuracy of Digital Screening Mammography with and Without Computer-Aided Detection. *JAMA Internal Medicine*, *175*(11), 1828–1837. doi:10.1001/jamainternmed.2015.5231 PMID:26414882

Leisch, D. M. (2021). *e1071: Misc Functions of the Department of Statistics, Probability Theory Group (Formerly: E1071)*. TU Wien.

Lerman, L. V., Benitez, G. B., Müller, J. M., de Sousa, P. R., & Frank, A. G. (2022). Smart green supply chain management: A configurational approach to enhance green performance through digital transformation. *Supply Chain Management*, *27*(7), 147–176. doi:10.1108/SCM-02-2022-0059

Leung, F. F., Gu, F. F., Li, Y., Zhang, J. Z., & Palmatier, R. W. (2022). Influencer Marketing Effectiveness. *Journal of Marketing*, *86*(6), 93–115. doi:10.1177/00222429221102889

Levi, M. (2022). Money for crime and money from crime: Financing crime and laundering crime proceeds. *Annual Review of Criminology*, *5*, 241–261. doi:10.1146/annurev-criminol-011419-041508

Levi, M., Reuter, P., & Halliday, T. (2018). Can the AML system be evaluated without better data? *Crime, Law, and Social Change*, *69*(2), 307–328. doi:10.1007/s10611-017-9757-4

Li, F., Larimo, J., & Leonidou, L. C. (2021). Social media marketing strategy: Definition, conceptualization, taxonomy, validation, and future agenda. *Journal of the Academy of Marketing Science*, *49*(1), 51–70. doi:10.1007/s11747-020-00733-3

Linqia. (2019). *The state of influencer marketing*. Retrieved April 1, 2023 from https://linqia.com/wp-content/uploads/2019/04/Linqia-State-of-Influencer-Marketing-2019-Report.pdf

Lin, T. C. (2019). Artificial intelligence, finance, and the law. *Fordham Law Review*, *88*, 531.

Lin, W. L., Yip, N., Ho, J. A., & Sambasivan, M. (2020). The adoption of technological innovations in a B2B context and its impact on firm performance: An ethical leadership perspective. *Industrial Marketing Management*, *89*, 61–71. doi:10.1016/j.indmarman.2019.12.009

Liu, C., Li, Z., Zhou, D., & Shi, Y. (2019). Organizational innovation of sci-tech societies in the era of intelligence: A case study in China. *PICMET 2019 - Portland International Conference on Management of Engineering and Technology: Technology Management in the World of Intelligent Systems, Proceedings*. 10.23919/PICMET.2019.8893783

Liu, B. (2012). Sentiment analysis and opinion mining. *Synthesis Lectures on Human Language Technologies*, *1*(5), 1–168.

Liu, S., Li, G., & Xia, H. (2021). Analysis of Talent Management in the Artificial Intelligence Era. *Proceedings of the 5th Asia-Pacific Conference on Economic Research and Management Innovation (ERMI 2021)*. 10.2991/aebmr.k.210218.007

Li, X., Chen, W., & Li, D. (2019). Personalized recommendation algorithms and consumer purchase behavior: An empirical study. *Electronic Commerce Research and Applications*, *36*, 100843.

Lo, C.-S., & Wang, C.-M. (2012). Support vector machine for breast MR image classification. *Computers & Mathematics with Applications (Oxford, England)*, *64*(5), 1153–1162. doi:10.1016/j.camwa.2012.03.033

Longoni, C., Bonezzi, A., & Morewedge, C. K. (2019). Resistance to Medical Artificial Intelligence. *The Journal of Consumer Research*, *46*(4), 629–650. Advance online publication. doi:10.1093/jcr/ucz013

Lopez-Corleone, M., Begum, S., & Sixuan Li, G. (2022). Artificial intelligence (AI) from a regulator's perspective: The future of AI in central banking and financial services. *Journal of AI. Robotics & Workplace Automation*, *2*(1), 7–16.

Lou, C., & Yuan, S. (2019). Influencer marketing: How message value and credibility affect consumer trust of branded content on social media. *Journal of Interactive Advertising*, *19*(1), 58–73. doi:10.1080/15252019.2018.1533501

Luchs, Swan, & Creusen. (2015, July 27). *Perspective: A review of Marketing Research on*. Wiley Online Library.

Lu, H., & Hsiao, K. (2010). The influence of extro/introversion on the intention to pay for social networking sites. *Information & Management*, *47*(3), 150–157. doi:10.1016/j.im.2010.01.003

Luu, L. (2017). Practical Decentralized Pooled Mining. *26th fUSENIXg Security Symposium (fUSENIXg Security 17),* 1409–1426.

M, K. K., & Elangovan, R. (2021). To Study Impact of Artificial Intelligence on HR Practices. *ComFin Research*. doi:10.34293/commerce.v9i4.4134

Mackey, T. K., Nayyar, G., & Hocquard, J. (2019). Applying blockchain technology to improve healthcare supply chain management. In *Transforming healthcare with blockchain* (pp. 97–117). Apress.

Macrinici, D., Cartofeanu, C., & Gao, S. (2018). Smart Contract Applications within Blockchain Technology: A Systematic Mapping Study. *Telematics and Informatics*, *35*(8), 2337–2354. doi:10.1016/j.tele.2018.10.004

Madhavi, I., Chamishka, S., Nawaratne, R., Nanayakkara, V., Alahakoon, D., & De Silva, D. (2020). A Deep Learning Approach for Work Related Stress Detection from Audio Streams in Cyber Physical Environments. *IEEE International Conference on Emerging Technologies and Factory Automation, ETFA*. 10.1109/ETFA46521.2020.9212098

Mah, P. M., Skalna, I., & Muzam, J. (2022). *Natural Language Processing and Artificial Intelligence for Enterprise Management in the Era of Industry 4.0*. Applied Sciences. doi:10.3390/app12189207

Majumder, S., & Mondal, A. (2021). Are chatbots really useful for human resource management? *International Journal of Speech Technology*, *24*(4), 969–977. Advance online publication. doi:10.1007/s10772-021-09834-y

Maldonado, S., & Weber, R. (2009). A Wrapper Method for Feature Selection Using Support Vector Machines. *Information Sciences*, *179*(13), 2208–2217. doi:10.1016/j.ins.2009.02.014

Malhotra, N. K., Birks, D. F., & Wills, P. (2020). *Marketing research: An applied approach*. Pearson.

Manninen, K., & Huiskonen, J. (2022). Factors influencing the implementation of an integrated corporate sustainability and business strategy. *Journal of Cleaner Production*, *343*, 131036. doi:10.1016/j.jclepro.2022.131036

Manzoor, Y. (2018). A Delay-Tolerant Payment Scheme on the Ethereum Blockchain. *2018 IEEE 19th International Symposium on A World of Wireless, Mobile and Multimedia Networks (WoWMoM)*, 14–16.

Marino, B., & Juels, A. (2016). Setting Standards for Altering and Undoing Smart Contracts. *International Symposium on Rules and Rule Markup Languages for the Semantic Web*, 151–166. 10.1007/978-3-319-42019-6_10

Marquez, R., Barrios, N., Vera, R. E., Mendez, M. E., Tolosa, L., Zambrano, F., & Li, Y. (2023). A perspective on the synergistic potential of artificial intelligence and product-based learning strategies in biobased materials education. *Education for Chemical Engineers*, *44*, 164–180. Advance online publication. doi:10.1016/j.ece.2023.05.005

Martínez-Plumed, F., Contreras-Ochando, L., Ferri, C., Hernández-Orallo, J., Kull, M., Lachiche, N., Ramírez-Quintana, M. J., & Flach, P. (2021). CRISP-DM Twenty Years Later: From Data Mining Processes to Data Science Trajectories. *IEEE Transactions on Knowledge and Data Engineering*, *33*(8), 3048–3061. doi:10.1109/TKDE.2019.2962680

Masciandaro, D., & Takats, E. (2007). The dark side of global finance: The black hole of illegal money laundering. *Economic Notes*, *36*(1), 1–37.

McCarthy, J. (2007). *What is artificial intelligence*. Academic Press.

Mehr, H. (2017). *Artificial Intelligence for Citizen Services and Government*. Harvard Ash Center Technology & Democracy.

Meister, J. (2019). Ten HR Trends In The Age Of Artificial Intelligence. *Forbes*.

Merlin, Ruby.P, J. (2018). Artificial Intelligence in Human Resource Management International Journal of Pure and Applied Mathematics. *International Journal of Pure and Applied Mathematics*.

Mettler, M. (2016). Blockchain technology in healthcare: The revolution starts here. In *2016 IEEE 18th International Conference on e-Health Networking, Applications and Services (Healthcom)* (pp. 1-3). IEEE.

Mhlanga, D. (2022). The Role of Artificial Intelligence and Machine Learning Amid the COVID 19 Pandemic: What Lessons Are We Learning on 4IR and the Sustainable Development Goals. *International Journal of Environmental Research and Public Health*, *19*(3), 1879. Advance online publication. doi:10.3390/ijerph19031879 PMID:35162901

Milana, C., & Ashta, A. (2021). Artificial intelligence techniques in finance and financial markets: A survey of the literature. *Strategic Change*, *30*(3), 189–209. doi:10.1002/jsc.2403

Milojević, N., & Redzepagic, S. (2021). Prospects of Artificial Intelligence and Machine Learning Application in Banking Risk Management. *Journal of Central Banking Theory and Practice*. doi:10.2478/jcbtp-2021-0023

Mishra, S. K., & Sarkar, A. (2022). Service-oriented architecture for Internet of Things: A semantic approach. *Journal of King Saud University. Computer and Information Sciences*, *34*(10), 8765–8776. Advance online publication. doi:10.1016/j.jksuci.2021.09.024

Mohamad, Z., Chaudhary, R., Iyer, S., Sutarto, & Khan, S. (2022). A Probing: How Artificial Intelligence is Beneficial in Different Fields of Human Resource Management. *Pacific Business Review International*.

Mohan, R. (2019). The Chatbot revolution and the Indian HR professionals. *International Journal of Information and Computing Science*.

Moldenhauer, L., & Londt, C. (2018). Leadership, artificial intelligence and the need to redefine future skills development. *Proceedings of the 14th European Conference on Management, Leadership and Governance, ECMLG 2018*. 10.33423/jlae.v16i1.1363

Mollaee, M., Mobli, A., Mutti, N. K., Manalil, S., & Chauhan, B. S. (2019). Challenges and Opportunities in Cotton Production. In *Cotton Production* (pp. 371–390). John Wiley & Sons, Ltd. doi:10.1002/9781119385523.ch18

Mooi, E. A., & Sarstedt, M. (2011). *A concise guide to market research: the process, data, and methods using IBM SPSS Statistics*. Springer. doi:10.1007/978-3-642-12541-6

Moyano, J. P., & Ross, O. (2017). KYC Optimization Using Distributed Ledger Technology. *Business & Information Systems Engineering*, *59*(6), 411–423. doi:10.1007/s12599-017-0504-2

Nabilou, H., & Prum, A. (2019). Central banks and regulation of cryptocurrencies. *Banking and Financial Law*, *39*, 1003.

Nagothu, D. (2023). A Microservice-enabled Architecture for Smart Surveillance using Blockchain Technology. *2018 IEEE International Smart Cities Conference (ISC2)*, 1–4.

Nair, V. C., Suresh, P., & Vijaya. (2020). Artificial Intelligence Interventions and Human Resources in the New Millennium. *International Journal of Advanced Science and Technology*.

Nakamoto, S. (2009). *Bitcoin: A Peer-to-peer Electronic Cash System.* http://www:bitcoin:org/bitcoin:pdf

Nakashima, E. (2018, April 2). The algorithms that detect hate speech online are biased against blacks. *The Washington Post.* https://wapo.st/3OpYM7f

Nawaz, N. (2020). Exploring Artificial Intelligence Applications in Human Resource Management. *Journal of Management Information and Decision Sciences.*

Naz, F., Agrawal, R., Kumar, A., Gunasekaran, A., Majumdar, A., & Luthra, S. (2022). Reviewing the applications of artificial intelligence in sustainable supply chains: Exploring research propositions for future directions. *Business Strategy and the Environment, 31*(5), 24002423. doi:10.1002/bse.3034

Nekmahmud, M. D., Rahman, S., Sobhani, F. A., Olejniczak-Szuster, K., & Fekete-Farkas, M. (2020). A systematic literature review on development of green supply chain management. *Polish Journal of Management Studies, 22*(1), 351–370. doi:10.17512/pjms.2020.22.1.23

Nelson, O., & Deborah, A. (2017). Celebrity endorsement influence on brand credibility: A critical review of previous studies. *Online Journal of Communication and Media Technologies, 7*(1), 15–32. doi:10.29333/ojcmt/2577

Nesteruk, S., Shadrin, D., Pukalchik, M., Somov, A., Zeidler, C., Zabel, P., & Schubert, D. (2021). Image Compression and Plants Classification Using Machine Learning in Controlled-Environment Agriculture: Antarctic Station Use Case. *IEEE Sensors Journal, 21*(16), 17564–17572. doi:10.1109/JSEN.2021.3050084

Neyapti, B. (2003). Budget deficits and inflation: The roles of central bank independence and financial market development. *Contemporary Economic Policy, 21*(4), 458–475. doi:10.1093/cep/byg025

NFSM: National Food Security Mission. (n.d.). *Brief Note on Cotton.* Retrieved September 28, 2022, from https://www.nfsm.gov.in/

Ngai, V. (2011). Financial institutions and the anti-money laundering regulations: Cost-benefit study from anti-money laundering regulation perspective in the UK. *Journal of Money Laundering Control, 14*(3), 217–234.

Nguyen, D. P., Phan, L. T., Ho, H. X., & Le, A. N. H. (2022). Human resource management practices in higher education: A literature review using co-word analysis. *International Journal of Management Education, 16*(1), 40. Advance online publication. doi:10.1504/IJMIE.2022.119682

Nightingale, A. (2009). A guide to systematic literature reviews. *Surgery (Oxford), 27*(9), 381384. doi:10.1016/j.mpsur.2009.07.005

Nikam, T. A., Latpate, C. B., Ramesh, K. B., & Thakare, V. S. (2017). Efficacy of conventional and newer insecticides against leafhopper, Amarasca biguttula biguttula (Ishada) in Bt cotton under high density planting system. *Bull Environ Pharmacol Life Sci, 6*(2), 274–281.

Norta, A. (2016). Designing a Smart-contract Application Layer for Transacting Decentralized Autonomous Organizations. *International Conference on Advances in Computing and Data Sciences*, 595–604.

Nozari, H., Fallah, M., & Szmelter-Jarosz, A. (2021). A conceptual framework of green smart IoTbased supply chain management. *International Journal of Research in Industrial Engineering, 10*(1), 22-34.

Nugent, T., Upton, D., & Cimpoesu, M. (2016). Improving data transparency in clinical trials using blockchain smart contracts. *F1000 Research, 5*, 5. doi:10.12688/f1000research.9756.1 PMID:28357041

O'Fallon, J. R., Cormack, R. M., & Bithell, J. F. (1983). Obituaries. *Biometrics, 39*(4), 1107–1111.

Odugbesan, J. A., Aghazadeh, S., Al Qaralleh, R. E., & Sogeke, O. S. (2023). Green talent management and employees' innovative work behavior: The roles of artificial intelligence and transformational leadership. *Journal of Knowledge Management, 27*(3), 696–716. Advance online publication. doi:10.1108/JKM-08-2021-0601

Oesterreich, T. D., Anton, E., & Teuteberg, F. (2022). What translates big data into business value? A metaanalysis of the impacts of business analytics on firm performance. *Information & Management, 59*(6), 103685. doi:10.1016/j.im.2022.103685

Okwuashi, O., & Ndehedehe, C. E. (2020). Deep support vector machine for hyperspectral image classification. *Pattern Recognition, 103*, 107298. doi:10.1016/j.patcog.2020.107298

Olugbade, S., Ojo, S., Imoize, A. L., Isabona, J., & Alaba, M. O. (2022). A Review of Artificial Intelligence and Machine Learning for Incident Detectors in Road Transport Systems. *Mathematical & Computational Applications, 27*(5), 77. Advance online publication. doi:10.3390/mca27050077

Önder, I., Malinauskas, V., & Berniūnas, E. (2020). Blockchain-based decentralized management of cross-border healthcare data exchange: Methodology and framework. *BMC Medical Informatics and Decision Making, 20*(1), 1–17. PMID:31906929

Opportunities and Challenges of New Technologies for AML/CFT. (n.d.). https://www.fatf-gafi.org/content/dam/fatf-gafi/guidance/Opportunities-Challenges-of-New-Technologies-for-AML-CFT.pdf

Ozili, P. K. (2020). Does competence of central bank governors influence financial stability? *Future Business Journal, 6*(1), 24. doi:10.1186/s43093-020-00031-y

Ozili, P. K. (2023a). *Big data and artificial intelligence for financial inclusion: benefits and issues*. Artificial Intelligence Fintech, and Financial Inclusion. doi:10.1201/9781003125204-1

Ozili, P. K. (2023b). Central bank digital currency research around the World: A review of literature. *Journal of Money Laundering Control, 26*(2), 215–226. doi:10.1108/JMLC-11-2021-0126

Page, M. J., McKenzie, J. E., Bossuyt, P. M., Boutron, I., Hoffmann, T. C., Mulrow, C. D., Shamseer, L., Tetzlaff, J. M., Akl, E. A., Brennan, S. E., Chou, R., Glanville, J., Grimshaw, J. M., Hróbjartsson, A., Lalu, M. M., Li, T., Loder, E. W., Mayo-Wilson, E., McDonald, S., ... Moher, D. (2021). The PRISMA 2020 statement: An updated guideline for reporting systematic reviews. *International Journal of Surgery*, *88*, 105906. doi:10.1016/j.ijsu.2021.105906 PMID:33789826

Paigude, S., Pangarkar, S. C., Hundekari, S., Mali, M., Wanjale, K., & Dongre, Y. (2023). Potential of Artificial Intelligence in Boosting Employee Retention in the Human Resource Industry. *International Journal on Recent and Innovation Trends in Computing and Communication*, *11*(3s), 01–10. Advance online publication. doi:10.17762/ijritcc.v11i3s.6149

Palos-Sánchez, P. R., Baena-Luna, P., Badicu, A., & Infante-Moro, J. C. (2022). Artificial Intelligence and Human Resources Management: A Bibliometric Analysis. *Applied Artificial Intelligence*, *36*(1), 2145631. Advance online publication. doi:10.1080/08839514.2022.2145631

Panda, A. (2017). Sales promotion and its effectiveness in the Indian retail industry. International Journal of Sales. *Retailing and Marketing*, *6*(1), 1–9. doi:10.14303/ijsrm.2017.002

Pandey, S. (2020). Exploring the role of Artificial Intelligence (AI) in transforming HR functions: An Empirical Study in the Indian Context. *International Journal of Scientific Research and Engineering Development*.

Paramita, W., Nhu, H. B. C., Ngo, L. V., Tran, Q. H. M., & Gregory, G. (2021). Brand experience and consumers' social interactive engagement with brand page: An integrated-marketing perspective. *Journal of Retailing and Consumer Services*, *62*, 102611. doi:10.1016/j.jretconser.2021.102611

Patheja, S., Kumar, D., & Singh, S. (2023). *Role of Artificial Intelligence in Human Resource*. Effulgence-A Management Journal. doi:10.33601/effulgence.rdias/v21/i1/2023/1-5

Patil, S. P., & SZambre, R. (2014). Classification of Cotton Leaf Spot Disease Using Support Vector Machine. In *Journal of Engineering Research and Applications* (Vol. 4, Issue 5). www.ijera.com

Peifer, Y., Jeske, T., & Hille, S. (2022). Artificial Intelligence and its Impact on Leaders and Leadership. Procedia Computer Science. doi:10.1016/j.procs.2022.01.301

Perez-Careta, E., Guzman-Sepulveda, J.-R., Lozano-Garcia, J.-M., Torres-Cisneros, M., & Guzman-Cabrera, R. (2022). Classification of medical images using machine learning. *Dyna (Bilbao)*, *97*(1), 35–38. doi:10.6036/10117

Petersen, K., Feldt, R., Mujtaba, S., & Mattsson, M. (2008). Systematic mapping studies in software engineering. *EASE*, *8*, 68–77.

Peters, G. W., & Panayi, E. (2016). *Understanding modern banking ledgers through blockchain technologies: Future of transaction processing and smart contracts on the internet of money. In Banking beyond banks and money*. Springer.

Peterson, K., Deeduvanu, R., Kanjamala, P., & Boles, K. (2016). A blockchain-based approach to health information exchange networks. *Proceedings of the NIST workshop blockchain healthcare*, 1-10.

Pillai, R., & Sivathanu, B. (2020). Adoption of artificial intelligence (AI) for talent acquisition in IT/ITeS organizations. *Benchmarking*, *27*(9), 2599–2629. Advance online publication. doi:10.1108/BIJ-04-2020-0186

Pires, G. D., & Stanton, J. (2018). Marketing trends: A review and future directions. *Journal of Business Research*, *89*, 198–207. doi:10.1016/j.jbusres.2018.02.014

Polyzos, G. C., & Fotiou, N. (2022). Blockchain-Assisted Information Distribution for the Internet of Things. *2017 IEEE International Conference on Information Reuse and Integration (IRI)*, 75–78.

Popovič, A., Hackney, R., Coelho, P. S., & Jaklič, J. (2012). Towards business intelligence systems success: Effects of maturity and culture on analytical decision making. *Decision Support Systems*, *54*(1), 729–739. doi:10.1016/j.dss.2012.08.017

Pourkhani, A., Abdipour, K., Baher, B., & Moslehpour, M. (2019). The impact of social media in business growth and performance: A scientometrics analysis. *International Journal of Data and Network Science (Print)*, *3*(3), 223–244. doi:10.5267/j.ijdns.2019.2.003

Pournader, M., Ghaderi, H., Hassanzadegan, A., & Fahimnia, B. (2021). Artificial intelligence applications in supply chain management. *International Journal of Production Economics*, *241*, 108250. doi:10.1016/j.ijpe.2021.108250

Prikshat, V., Malik, A., & Budhwar, P. (2023). AI-augmented HRM: Antecedents, assimilation and multilevel consequences. *Human Resource Management Review*, *33*(1), 100860. Advance online publication. doi:10.1016/j.hrmr.2021.100860

Priya, B., Kumar, J. A., Khushboo, A., Neha, G., Vanshika, B., & Abhishek, K. (2021). AI revolutionizing health care: A descriptive review. *International Journal of Advances in Scientific Research*.

Pulizzi, J., & Barrett, N. (2009). Get content get customers-Turn Prospects into buyers with content marketing. *Saxena NSB Management Review*, *2*(2), 98–100.

Putri, A. M. A., & Sanica, I. G. (2022). Digital Marketing Strategy to Survive during Covid-19 Pandemic. *International Journal of Economics Business and Accounting Research*, *6*(1), 27–33.

Qader, G., Junaid, M., Abbas, Q., & Mubarik, M. S. (2022). Industry 4.0 enables supply chain resilience and supply chain performance. *Technological Forecasting and Social Change*, *185*, 122026. doi:10.1016/j.techfore.2022.122026

Qamar, Y., Agrawal, R. K., Samad, T. A., & Chiappetta Jabbour, C. J. (2021). When technology meets people: The interplay of artificial intelligence and human resource management. *Journal of Enterprise Information Management*, *34*(5), 1339–1370. Advance online publication. doi:10.1108/JEIM-11-2020-0436

Qian, Y. (2019). Central Bank Digital Currency: Optimization of the currency system and its issuance design. *China Economic Journal, 12*(1), 1–15. doi:10.1080/17538963.2018.1560526

Queirós, A., Faria, D., & Almeida, F. (2017). Strengths and limitations of qualitative and quantitative research methods. *European Journal of Education Studies.*

Quinlan, J. R. (1986). Induction of Decision Trees. *Machine Learning, 1*(1), 81–106. doi:10.1007/BF00116251

Qu, Z., Feng, H., Zeng, Z., Zhuge, J., & Jin, S. (2010). A SVM-based pipeline leakage detection and pre-warning system. *Measurement, 43*(4), 513–519. doi:10.1016/j.measurement.2009.12.022

Rahman, M.S. (2020). *The advantages and disadvantages of using qualitative and quantitative approaches and methods in language "testing and assessment" research: A literature review.* Academic Press.

Rahman, A. (2022). Anti-money laundering: The promise and limitations of AI. *Journal of Investment Compliance, 23*(1), 20–26.

Rahmani, D., & Kamberaj, H. (2021). Implementation and Usage of Artificial Intelligence Powered Chatbots in Human Resources Management Systems. ICSAS.

Rajesh, S., Kandaswamy, M. U., & Rakesh, M. A. (2018). The Impact of Artificial Intelligence in Talent Acquisition Lifecycle of organizations A Global Perspective. *International Journal of Engineering Development and Research.*

Raj, M. V., & Murugan, S. S. (2019). Underwater Image Classification using Machine Learning Technique. In P. R. S. Pillai, M. H. Supriya, & A. A. Balakrishnan (Eds.), *Proceedings of the 2019 international symposium on ocean technology (sympol 2019)* (pp. 166–173). IEEE. doi:10.1109/SYMPOL48207.2019.9005299

Ramanathan, U., Subramanian, N., & Parrott, G. (2017). Role of social media in retail network operations and marketing to enhance customer satisfaction. *International Journal of Operations & Production Management, 37*(1), 105–123. doi:10.1108/IJOPM-03-2015-0153

Raman, S., Patwa, N., Niranjan, I., Ranjan, U., Moorthy, K., & Mehta, A. (2018). Impact of big data on supply chain management. *International Journal of Logistics, 21*(6), 579–596. doi:10.1080/13675567.2018.1459523

Ramesh Kumar, P., & Vijaya, A. (2022). Naïve Bayes machine learning model for image classification to assess the level of deformation of thin components. *Materials Today: Proceedings.* https://doi.org/https://doi.org/10.1016/j.matpr.2022.08.489

Raskin, M., & Yermack, D. (2016). *Digital currencies, decentralized ledgers, and the future of central banking (No. w22238).* National Bureau of Economic Research. doi:10.3386/w22238

Rathore, S., Kwon, B. W., & Park, J. H. (2022). Blockseciotnet: Blockchain-based decentralized security architecture for iot network. *Journal of Network and Computer Applications, 143*, 167–177. doi:10.1016/j.jnca.2019.06.019

Reuter, P. (2013). Are estimates of the volume of money laundering either feasible or useful? In B. Unger & D. van der Linde (Eds.), *Research handbook on money laundering* (pp. 224–233). Edward Elgar Publishing. doi:10.4337/9780857934000.00028

Rock, D. (2019). Engineering Value: The Returns to Technological Talent and Investments in Artificial Intelligence. SSRN *Electronic Journal*. doi:10.2139/ssrn.3427412

Roehrs, A., da Costa, C. A., da Rosa Righi, R., da Silva, V. F., Goldim, J. R., & Schmidt, D. C. (2017). Analyzing the performance of a blockchain-based personal health record implementation. *JBI*, *78*, 169–178. doi:10.1016/j.jbi.2017.08.018

Roever, L. (2015). Critical appraisal of a questionnaire study. *Evid Based Med Pract*, *1*(2), 1–2.

Rosner, M. T., & Kang, A. (2015). Understanding and Regulating Twenty-first Century Payment Systems: The Ripple Case Study. *Michigan Law Review*, *114*, 649.

Rother, E. T. (2007). Systematic literature review X narrative review. *Acta Paulista de Enfermagem*, *20*, v–vi. doi:10.1590/S0103-21002007000200001

Rott, K. J., Lao, L., Petridou, E., & Schmidt-Hertha, B. (2022). Needs and requirements for an additional AI qualification during dual vocational training: Results from studies of apprentices and teachers. *Computers and Education: Artificial Intelligence*. doi:10.1016/j.caeai.2022.100102

Rožman, M., Oreški, D., & Tominc, P. (2022). Integrating artificial intelligence into a talent management model to increase the work engagement and performance of enterprises. *Frontiers in Psychology*, *13*, 1014434. Advance online publication. doi:10.3389/fpsyg.2022.1014434 PMID:36506984

Russ, J. C. (1990). Image Processing. In Computer-Assisted Microscopy: The Measurement and Analysis of Images (pp. 33–69). Springer US. doi:10.1007/978-1-4613-0563-7_3

Russo, S., Schimperna, F., Lombardi, R., & Ruggiero, P. (2022). Sustainability performance and social media: An explorative analysis. *Meditari Accountancy Research*, *30*(4), 1118–1140. doi:10.1108/MEDAR-03-2021-1227

Saad, S. M., & Khamkham, M. (2022). The Applications of AI in GSCM–A Systematic Literature Review. *Advances in Manufacturing Technology*, *35*, 348–353. doi:10.3233/ATDE220615

Sadeq, N., Nassreddine, G., & Younis, J. (2023). Impact of Artificial Intelligence on E-marketing. *International Journal of Trend in Scientific Research and Development*, *7*(1), 1318-1331. https://www.ijtsrd.com/papers/ijtsrd53850.pdf

Sadeq, N., Nassreddine, G., & Younis, J. (2023). Impact of Artificial Intelligence on E-marketing. *International Journal of Trend in Scientific Research and Development*, *7*(1), 1318–1331. www.ijtsrd.com/papers/ijtsrd53850.pdf

Sadeq, N. (2023). The impact of Blockchain technique on trustworthy healthcare sector. *Mesopotamian Journal of Cyber Security*, (May), 105–115. doi:10.58496/MJCS/2023/015

Safko, L. (2015). *Why sharing valuable content is the key to successful marketing*. Social Media Today. Retrieved from https://www.socialmediatoday.com/marketing/why-sharing-valuable-content-key-successful-marketing

Sahni, N. S., Wheeler, S. C., & Chintagunta, P. (2018). Personalization in email marketing: The role of noninformative advertising content. *Marketing Science*, *37*(2), 236–258. doi:10.1287/mksc.2017.1066

Saini, A., & Saini, R. (2017). Sales incentives: A review of literature. International Journal of Research in Management. *Economics and Commerce*, *7*(3), 26–31. doi:10.20431/2454-9437.0703003

Saini, R., & Saini, R. (2017). Sales force incentive schemes: A review of the literature. *Journal of Applied Economics and Business Research*, *7*(3), 180–187.

Sakka, F., & El Hadi El Maknouzi, M. (2022). Human Resource Management in the Era of Artificial Intelligence: Future Hr Work Practices, Anticipated Skill Set, Financial and Legal Implications. *Academy of Strategic Management Journal*.

Sallam, M., Salim, N. A., Al-Tammemi, A. B., Barakat, M., Fayyad, D., Hallit, S., Harapan, H., Hallit, R., & Mahafzah, A. (2023). ChatGPT Output Regarding Compulsory Vaccination and COVID-19 Vaccine Conspiracy: A Descriptive Study at the Outset of a Paradigm Shift in Online Search for Information. *Cureus*. Advance online publication. doi:10.7759/cureus.35029 PMID:36819954

Samad, M. E., El-Chaarani, H., Nemar, S. E., & Raimi, L. (2022). Digital corporate entrepreneurship in the workplace. In Routledge eBooks (pp. 126–136). doi:10.4324/9781003283386-13

Samuel Craig, C., & Douglas, S. P. (2001). Conducting international marketing research in the twenty-first century. *International Marketing Review*, *18*(1), 80–90. doi:10.1108/02651330110398413

Sankar, L. S., Sindhu, M., & Sethumadhavan, M. (2017) Survey of Consensus Protocols on Blockchain Applications. *2017 4th International Conference on Advanced Computing and Communication Systems (ICACCS)*, 1–5.

Sanyaolu, E., & Atsaboghena, R. (2022). *Role of Artificial Intelligence in Human Resource Management: Overview of its benefits and challenges*. ResearchGate.

Saranya, A. (2022). *The Impact of Artificial Intelligence (AI) in Human Resource Management (HRM)*. Shanlax International Journal of Arts, Science and Humanities. doi:10.34293/sijash.v9i4.4758

SAS. (2021). *AI-driven AML gives Nordea 50% detection boost*. https://www.sas.com/en_gb/customers/nordea.html

Saxena, P., Sharma, S., & Jora, R. B. (2023). Impact of Emotional Intelligence and Artificial Intelligence on Employee Retention: A Review of the Service Industry. *2023 9th International Conference on Advanced Computing and Communication Systems, ICACCS 2023*. 10.1109/ICACCS57279.2023.10113017

Saxena, A. (2020). *The growing role of artificial intelligence in human resource. EPRA International Journal of Multidisciplinary Research.* doi:10.36713/epra4924

Schneider, F. (2010). Turnover of organized crime and money laundering: Some preliminary empirical findings. *Public Choice*, *144*(3), 473–486. doi:10.1007/s11127-010-9676-8

Schröer, C., Kruse, F., & Gómez, J. M. (2021). A Systematic Literature Review on Applying CRISP-DM Process Model. *Procedia Computer Science*, *181*, 526–534. doi:10.1016/j.procs.2021.01.199

Seijas, Thompson, & McAdams. (2016). Scripting smart contracts for distributed ledger technology. *IACR Cryptology ePrint*, 1156.

Selden, L., & MacMillan, I. C. (2006). Manage customer-centric innovation-systematically. *Harvard Business Review*, *84*(4), 108. PMID:16579418

Selvapandian, D., Mary, R. U. N., & Karthikeyan, C. (2020). Artificial intelligence in online shopping using natural language processing (NLP). *Journal of Critical Reviews.* doi:10.31838/jcr.07.04.165

Seman, N. A. A., Zakuan, N., Jusoh, A., Arif, M. S. M., & Saman, M. Z. M. (2012). Green supply chain management: A review and research direction. *International Journal of Managing Value and Supply Chains*, *3*(1), 1–18. doi:10.5121/ijmvsc.2012.3101

Sengupta, J., Ruj, S., & Bit, S. D. (2020). A Comprehensive Survey on Attacks, Security Issues and Blockchain Solutions for IoT and IIoT. *Journal of Network and Computer Applications*, *149*, 102481. doi:10.1016/j.jnca.2019.102481

Seth, G. (2012). *Analyzing the Effects of Social Media on the Hospitality Industry.* UNLV Theses/Dissertations/ Professional Papers/Capstones. Paper 1346. https://digitalscholarship.unlv.edu/thesesdissertations/1346/

Setiawan, R., Pio Leonardo Cavaliere, L., Koti, K., Ayodeji Ogunmola, G., Abdul Jalil, N., Kalyan Chakravarthi, M., ... Singh, S. (2021). *The Artificial Intelligence and Inventory Effect on Banking Industrial Performance. Turkish Online Journal of Qualitative Inquiry.*

Setyani, V., Zhu, L., Hidayanto, A. N., Sandhyaduhita, P. I., & Hsiao, B. (2019). Exploring the psychological mechanisms from personalized advertisements to urge to buy impulsively on social media. *International Journal of Information Management*, *48*, 96–107. doi:10.1016/j.ijinfomgt.2019.01.007

Shabsigh, G., & Boukherouaa, E. B. (2023). Generative Artificial Intelligence in Finance. *FinTech Notes*, *2023*(6).

Shahzad, F., Du, J., Khan, I., & Wang, J. (2022). Decoupling institutional pressure on green supply chain management efforts to boost organizational performance: Moderating impact of big data analytics capabilities. *Frontiers in Environmental Science*, *10*, 911392. doi:10.3389/fenvs.2022.911392

Shanthi, V., & Sam, A. (2021). Impact of Artificial Intelligence Techniques on Employee Well-being for Employee Retention. *International Journal of Engineering Research & Technology (Ahmedabad).*

Sharman, J. C. (2010). Anti-money laundering systems in international banking. *New Political Economy, 15*(3), 317–330.

Sheikh, S. A. (2019). Artificial Intelligence based Chatbot for Human Resource:A Survey View project. *Journal of Emerging Technologies and Innovative Research.*

Shen, G. (2022). AI-enabled talent training for the cross-cultural news communication talent. *Technological Forecasting and Social Change, 185*, 122031. Advance online publication. doi:10.1016/j.techfore.2022.122031

Sher, P. J., & Lee, S. (2009). Consumer skepticism and online reviews: An elaboration likelihood model perspective. *Social Behavior and Personality, 37*(1), 137–143. doi:10.2224/sbp.2009.37.1.137

Shokouhyar, S., Seddigh, M. R., & Panahifar, F. (2020). Impact of big data analytics capabilities on supply chain sustainability. *Development, 17*(1), 33–57.

Shoss, M. K., & Ciarlante, K. (2022). Supplemental Material for Are robots/AI viewed as more of a workforce threat in unequal societies? Evidence from the Eurobarometer survey. *Technology, Mind, and Behavior, 3*(2). Advance online publication. doi:10.1037/tmb0000078.supp

Shrank, W. H., Rogstad, T. L., & Parekh, N. (2019). Waste in the US Health Care System: Estimated Costs and Potential for Savings. *Journal of the American Medical Association, 322*(15), 1501–1509. doi:10.1001/jama.2019.13978 PMID:31589283

Sinclair, P. J. (2000). *Central banks and financial stability.* Bank of England Quarterly Bulletin.

Sindu, M. (2018). Artificial intelligence vs human resource practices in Banking sector. *International Journal of Social Science and Economic Research.*

Singh, A., Click, K., Parizi, R. M., Zhang, Q., Dehghantanha, A., & Choo, K.-K. R. (2020). Sidechain Technologies in Blockchain Networks: An Examination and State-of-the-art Review. *Journal of Network and Computer Applications, 149*, 102471. doi:10.1016/j.jnca.2019.102471

Singh, A., & Shaurya, A. (2021). Impact of Artificial Intelligence on HR practices in the UAE. *Humanities & Social Sciences Communications, 8*(1), 312. Advance online publication. doi:10.1057/s41599-021-00995-4

Singh, T. P., & Sinha, R. (2017). The Impact of Social Media on Business Growth and Performance in India. *International Journal of Research in Management & Business Studies, 4*(1), 2348–6503. http://s3.amazonaws.com/arena-attachments/2329377/43839f512f38d032594f26fb03b4ee5b.pdf?1529398740

Sinniah, S., Al Mamun, A., Md Salleh, M. F., Makhbul, Z. K. M., & Hayat, N. (2022). Modeling the Significance of Motivation on Job Satisfaction and Performance Among the Academicians: The Use of Hybrid Structural Equation Modeling-Artificial Neural Network Analysis. *Frontiers in Psychology*, *13*, 935822. Advance online publication. doi:10.3389/fpsyg.2022.935822 PMID:35795432

Sircar, A., Yadav, K., Rayavarapu, K., Bist, N., & Oza, H. (2021). *Application of machine learning and artificial intelligence in oil and gas industry*. Petroleum Research. doi:10.1016/j.ptlrs.2021.05.009

Sivarajah, U., Irani, Z., Gupta, S., & Mahroof, K. (2020). Role of big data and social media analytics for business to business sustainability: A participatory web context. *Industrial Marketing Management*, *86*, 163–179. doi:10.1016/j.indmarman.2019.04.005

Sivathanu, B., & Pillai, R. (2018). Smart HR 4.0 – how industry 4.0 is disrupting HR. *Human Resource Management International Digest*, *26*(4), 7–11. Advance online publication. doi:10.1108/HRMID-04-2018-0059

Slater, S. F., & Narver, J. C. (1999). Market-oriented is more than being customer-led. *Strategic Management Journal*, *20*(12), 1165–1168. doi:10.1002/(SICI)1097-0266(199912)20:12<1165::AID-SMJ73>3.0.CO;2-#

Soleimani, M., Intezari, A., & Pauleen, D. J. (2022). Mitigating cognitive biases in developing ai-assisted recruitment systems: A knowledge-sharing approach. *International Journal of Knowledge Management*. Advance online publication. doi:10.4018/IJKM.290022

Sollini, M., Bartoli, F., Marciano, A., Zanca, R., Slart, R. H. J. A., & Erba, P. A. (2020). Artificial intelligence and hybrid imaging: The best match for personalized medicine in oncology. *European Journal of Hybrid Imaging*, *4*(1), 24. Advance online publication. doi:10.1186/s41824-020-00094-8 PMID:34191197

Sood, A., Sharma, R. K., & Bhardwaj, A. K. (2021). Artificial intelligence research in agriculture: a review. *Online Information Review*. doi:10.1108/OIR-10-2020-0448

Sousa, J., Bessani, A., & Vukolic, M. (2018). A Byzantine Fault-tolerant Ordering Service for the Hyperledger Fabric Blockchain Platform. *2018 48th annual IEEE/IFIP international conference on dependable systems and networks (DSN),* 51–58.

Spina, J. D., & Spina, L. J. (2021). Looking Ahead: Artificial Intelligence and Developing Talent. In Beyond Succession Planning: New Ways to Develop Talent. doi:10.1108/978-1-83982-078-620211011

Stadtler, H. (2014). Supply chain management: An overview. *Supply chain management and advanced planning: Concepts, models, software, and case studies*, 3-28.

Starkov, M., & Mechoso, M. (2008). *Best Practices on Monitoring Hotel Review Sites, Hospitality eBusiness Strategies*. https://www.hospitalitynet.org/opinion/4037310.html

Strohmeier, S. (2022). 1. Artificial intelligence in human resources – an introduction. Handbook of Research on Artificial Intelligence in Human Resource Management.

Sulaiman, Y. H., & Mustafa, A. S. (2021). COVID-19: Toward Artificial Intelligence Algorithms. *HORA 2021 - 3rd International Congress on Human-Computer Interaction, Optimization and Robotic Applications, Proceedings*. 10.1109/HORA52670.2021.9461323

Sun, J., Xiao, Q., Wen, J., & Wang, F. (2014). Natural gas pipeline small leakage feature extraction and recognition based on LMD envelope spectrum entropy and SVM. *Measurement, 55*, 434–443. doi:10.1016/j.measurement.2014.05.012

Suseno, Y., Hudik, M., Fang, E. S., & Guo, Z. (2020). Employee Attitudes, Technological Anxiety, and Change Readiness for Artificial Intelligence Adoption. *Proceedings - Academy of Management, 2020*(1), 20045. Advance online publication. doi:10.5465/AMBPP.2020.20045abstract

Sussman, S. W., & Siegal, W. S. (2003). Informational influence in organizations: An integrated approach to knowledge adoption. *Information Systems Research, 14*(1), 47–65. doi:10.1287/isre.14.1.47.14767

Swani, K., Milne, G., & Brown, P., B. (. (2013). Spreading the word through likes on Facebook: Evaluating the message strategy effectiveness of Fortune 500 companies. *Journal of Research in Interactive Marketing, 7*(4), 269–294. doi:10.1108/JRIM-05-2013-0026

Swinburne, M. (1991). 25 Central Bank Independence and Central Bank Functions. In *The evolving role of central banks*. International Monetary Fund.

Tabassum, F. (2018). *Future of Performance Management in Artificial Intelligence ERA*. Shanlax International Journal of Arts.

Tadapaneni, N. R. (2019). Artificial intelligence in finance and investments. *International Journal of Innovative Research in Science, Engineering and Technology, 9*(5).

Taherdoost, H. (2021). Smart Contracts in Blockchain Technology: A Critical Review. *Information (Basel), 14*(2), 117. doi:10.3390/info14020117

Takhi, S., Gosain, M., & Singh, V. (2020). *Reinforce The Talent Acquisition Using Kaizen and Artificial Intelligence. International Journal of Scientific and Research Publications*. doi:10.29322/IJSRP.10.05.2020.p10127

Tambe, P., Cappelli, P., & Yakubovich, V. (2019). Artificial intelligence in human resources management: Challenges and A path forward. *California Management Review, 61*(4), 15–42. Advance online publication. doi:10.1177/0008125619867910

Teixeira, C. R. B., Assumpção, A. L., Correa, A. L., Savi, A. F., & Prates, G. A. (2018). The contribution of green logistics and sustainable purchasing for green supply chain management. *Independent Journal of Management & Production, 9*(3), 1002–1026. doi:10.14807/ijmp.v9i3.789

Titareva, T. (2021). Leadership in an Artificial Intelligence Era. *#LEADCC: Leading Change Conference*.

Tiwari, P., Pandey, R., Garg, V., & Singhal, A. (2021). Application of artificial intelligence in human resource management practices. *Proceedings of the Confluence 2021: 11th International Conference on Cloud Computing, Data Science and Engineering*. 10.1109/Confluence51648.2021.9377160

Tiwari, P., Rajput, N., & Garg, V. (2022). Artificial Intelligence and Talent Acquisition-Role of HR leaders in Adoption. *Proceedings of 3rd International Conference on Intelligent Engineering and Management, ICIEM 2022*. 10.1109/ICIEM54221.2022.9853104

Toorajipour, R., Sohrabpour, V., Nazarpour, A., Oghazi, P., & Fischl, M. (2021). Artificial intelligence in supply chain management: A systematic literature review. *Journal of Business Research*, *122*, 502–517. doi:10.1016/j.jbusres.2020.09.009

Trachuk, T., Vdovichena, O., Andriushchenko, M., Semenda, O., & Pashkevych, M. (2021). Branding and advertising on social networks: Current trends. *International Journal of Computer Science & Network Security*, *21*(4), 178–185.

*Training Manual on "Cultivation of Long Staple Cotton (ELS) ."* (2007). Central Institute for Cotton Research, Regional Station, Coimbatore.

Tseng, M. L., Islam, M. S., Karia, N., Fauzi, F. A., & Afrin, S. (2019). A literature review on green supply chain management: Trends and future challenges. *Resources, Conservation and Recycling*, *141*, 145–162. doi:10.1016/j.resconrec.2018.10.009

Tucker, P., & Council, S. R. (2014). The political economy of central banking in the digital age. *Bank of England Quarterly Bulletin*, Q1.

Udokwu, C. (2018). *An Exploration of Blockchain Enabled Smart-contracts Application in the Enterprise.* Technical Report 2.2:36464.97287

Unger, B., Ferwerda, J., van den Broek, M., & Deleanu, I. (2006). *The economic and legal effectiveness of the European Union's anti-money laundering policy.* Edward Elgar Publishing. https://www.napier.ai/post/ai-aml-challenges

Usha Kumari, C., Arun Vignesh, N., Panigrahy, A. K., Ramya, L., & Padma, T. (2019). Fungal disease in cotton leaf detection and classification using neural networks and support vector machine. *International Journal of Innovative Technology and Exploring Engineering*, *8*(10), 3664–3667. doi:10.35940/ijitee.J9648.0881019

van Dinter, R., Tekinerdogan, B., & Catal, C. (2021). Automation of systematic literature reviews: A systematic literature review. *Information and Software Technology*, *136*, 106589. doi:10.1016/j.infsof.2021.106589

van Erp, M., Reynolds, C., Maynard, D., Starke, A., Ibáñez Martín, R., Andres, F., Leite, M. C. A., Alvarez de Toledo, D., Schmidt Rivera, X., Trattner, C., Brewer, S., Adriano Martins, C., Kluczkovski, A., Frankowska, A., Bridle, S., Levy, R. B., Rauber, F., Tereza da Silva, J., & Bosma, U. (2021). Using Natural Language Processing and Artificial Intelligence to Explore the Nutrition and Sustainability of Recipes and Food. *Frontiers in Artificial Intelligence*, *3*, 621577. Advance online publication. doi:10.3389/frai.2020.621577 PMID:33733227

Van Quaquebeke, N., & Gerpott, F. H. (2023). The Now, New, and Next of Digital Leadership: How Artificial Intelligence (AI) Will Take Over and Change Leadership as We Know It. *Journal of Leadership & Organizational Studies*, *30*(3), 265–275. Advance online publication. doi:10.1177/15480518231181731

Vasantham, D. S. T. (2021). *The Role of Artificial Intelligence in Human Resource Management.* Engineering and Scientific International Journal. doi:10.30726/esij/v8.i2.2021.82013

Vedapradha, R., Hariharan, R., David Winster Praveenraj, D., Sudha, E., & Ashok, J. (2023). Talent acquisition-artificial intelligence to manage recruitment. E3S Web of Conferences. doi:10.1051/e3sconf/202337605001

Veloso, M., Balch, T., Borrajo, D., Reddy, P., & Shah, S. (2021). Artificial intelligence research in finance: Discussion and examples. *Oxford Review of Economic Policy*, *37*(3), 564–584. doi:10.1093/oxrep/grab019

Veltri, G. A., Lupiáñez-Villanueva, F., Folkvord, F., Theben, A., & Gaskell, G. (2023). The impact of online platform transparency of information on consumers' choices. *Behavioural Public Policy*, *7*(1), 55–82. doi:10.1017/bpp.2020.11

Verhoef, P. C., Kannan, P. K., & Inman, J. J. (2015). From multi-channel retailing to omni-channel retailing: Introduction to the special issue on multi-channel retailing. *Journal of Retailing*, *91*(2), 174–181. doi:10.1016/j.jretai.2015.02.005

Verma, R. (2020). Challenges of Artificial Intelligence in Human Resource. *XXI Annual International Conference Proceedings.* Http://Www.Internationalconference.in/XXI_AIC/INDEX.HTM

Verma, R., & Bandi, S. (2019). Artificial Intelligence & Human Resource Management in Indian IT Sector. SSRN *Electronic Journal.* doi:10.2139/ssrn.3319897

Verma, R., & Bandi, S. (2020). Challenges of Artificial Intelligence in Human Resource Management in Indian IT Sector richa. *XXI Annual International Conference Proceedings.* Http://Www.Internationalconference.in/XXI_AIC/INDEX.HTM

Verma, R., Bhardwaj, N., Singh, P. D., Bhavsar, A., & Sharma, V. (2021). Estimation of sex through morphometric landmark indices in facial images with strength of evidence in logistic regression analysis. *Forensic Science International. Reports*, *4*, 100226. doi:10.1016/j.fsir.2021.100226

Vinichenko, M. V., Rybakova, M. V., Chulanova, O. L., Kuznetsova, I. V., Makushkin, S. A., & Lobacheva, A. S. (2019). Using natural and artificial intelligence in the talent management system. *International Journal of Recent Technology and Engineering*. doi:10.35940/ijrte.C6152.098319

Volkmar, G., Fischer, P. M., & Reinecke, S. (2022). Artificial Intelligence and Machine Learning: Exploring drivers, barriers, and future developments in marketing management. *Journal of Business Research*, *149*, 599–614. Advance online publication. doi:10.1016/j.jbusres.2022.04.007

Voorveld, H. A., Van Noort, G., Muntinga, D. G., & Bronner, F. (2018). Engagement with social media and social media advertising: The differentiating role of platform type. *Journal of Advertising*, *47*(1), 38–54. doi:10.1080/00913367.2017.1405754

Voramontri, D., & Klieb, L. (2019). Impact of social media on consumer behaviour. *International Journal of Information and Decision Sciences*, *11*(3), 209. doi:10.1504/IJIDS.2019.101994

Votto, A. M., Valecha, R., Najafirad, P., & Rao, H. R. (2021). Artificial Intelligence in Tactical Human Resource Management: A Systematic Literature Review. *International Journal of Information Management Data Insights*. doi:10.1016/j.jjimei.2021.100047

Wan Ibrahim, W. M. R., & Hassan, R. (2019). Recruitment Trends in the Era of Industry 4.0 Using Artificial Intelligence: Pro and Cons. *Asian Journal of Research in Business and Management*.

Wang, R. Y., & Strong, D. M. (1996). Beyond Accuracy: What Data Quality Means to Data Consumers. *Journal of Management Information Systems*, *12*(4), 4, 5–33. doi:10.1080/07421222.1996.11518099

Wang, S. (2018). An Overview of Smart Contract: Architecture, Applications, and Future Trends. *2018 IEEE Intelligent Vehicles Symposium (IV),* 108–113. 10.1109/IVS.2018.8500488

Wang, W., Chen, Y., Chen, T., & Terzi, E. (2022). Financial transaction graph analysis for anti-money laundering using deep learning. *Applied Network Science*, *7*(1).

Wang, Y. Y., & Wang, Y. S. (2022). Development and validation of an artificial intelligence anxiety scale: An initial application in predicting motivated learning behavior. *Interactive Learning Environments*, *30*(4), 619–634. Advance online publication. doi:10.1080/10494820.2019.1674887

Wang, Y., Yang, Y., Qin, Z., Yang, Y., & Li, J. (2023). A Literature Review on the Application of Digital Technology in Achieving Green Supply Chain Management. *Sustainability (Basel)*, *15*(11), 8564. doi:10.3390/su15118564

Weber, V. (2019). The data science approaches used in anti-money laundering. *Journal of Tax Administration*, *5*(2), 120–133.

Wickham, H., & Girlich, M. (n.d.). *TIDYR: Tidy Messy Data. R package version 1.2.0.* Academic Press.

Wickham, H., François, R., Henry, L., & Müller, K. (2018). *DPLYR: A Grammar of Data Manipulation*. Academic Press.

Wilson, S., & Abel, I. (2001, December 12). So you want to get involved in e-commerce. *Industrial Marketing Management*.

Winnard, J., Adcroft, A., Lee, J., & Skipp, D. (2014). Surviving or flourishing? integrating business resilience and sustainability. *Journal of Strategy and Management*, *7*(3), 303–315. doi:10.1108/JSMA-11-2012-0059

WrightA.FilippiP. D. (2015). Decentralized Blockchain Technology and the Rise of Lex Cryptographia. doi:10.2139/ssrn.2580664

Wust, K., & Gervais, A. (2018). Do You Need a Blockchain? *2018 Crypto Valley Conference on Blockchain Technology (CVCBT)*, 45–54. 10.1109/CVCBT.2018.00011

Xia. (2017). *BBDS: Blockchain-Based Data Sharing for Electronic Medical Records*. Academic Press.

Xin, O. K., Wider, W., & Ling, L. K. (2022). *Human Resource Artificial Intelligence Implementation and Organizational Performance in Malaysia*. Asia-Pacific Social Science Review.

Xu, X. (2017). A taxonomy of Blockchain-based Systems for Architecture Design. *2017 IEEE International Conference on Software Architecture (ICSA)*, 243–252. 10.1109/ICSA.2017.33

Yadav, R. D., & Goel, R. (2019). Problems of Cotton Farmers in Haryana. *Int. J. Curr. Microbiol. App. Sci* (Vol. 8, Issue 03, pp. 2139–2142). https://doi.org/https://doi.org/10.1016/S0308-521X(02)00051-3

Yadav, P. V., Kollimath, U. S., Chavan, T. V., Pisal, D. T., Giramkar, S. A., & Swamy, S. M. (2023). Impact of Artificial Intelligence (AI) in Talent Acquisition Process: A study with reference to IT Industry. *Proceedings of the International Conference on Intelligent and Innovative Technologies in Computing, Electrical and Electronics, ICIITCEE 2023*. 10.1109/IITCEE57236.2023.10090973

Yang, M., Evans, S., Vladimirova, D., & Rana, P. (2017). Value uncaptured perspective for sustainable business model innovation. *Journal of Cleaner Production*, *140*, 1794–1804. doi:10.1016/j.jclepro.2016.07.102

Yang, Y., Chen, J., Lee, P. K., & Cheng, T. C. E. (2023). How to enhance the effects of the green supply chain management strategy in the organization: A diffusion process perspective. *Transportation Research Part E, Logistics and Transportation Review*, *175*, 103148. doi:10.1016/j.tre.2023.103148

Yun, D., Xiang, Y., Liu, Z., Lin, D., Zhao, L., Guo, C., Xie, P., Lin, H., Liu, Y., Zou, Y., & Wu, X. (2020). Attitudes towards medical artificial intelligence talent cultivation: An online survey study. *Annals of Translational Medicine*, *8*(11), 708. Advance online publication. doi:10.21037/atm.2019.12.149 PMID:32617328

Yusup, M., Naufal, R. S., & Hardini, M. (2018). Management of utilizing data analysis and hypothesis testing in improving the quality of research reports. *Aptisi Transactions on Management*, *2*(2), 159–167.

Zhang. (2018). *FHIRChain: Applying Blockchain to Securely and Scalably Share Clinical Data*. Academic Press.

Zhang, F. (2022). Design and Application of Artificial Intelligence Technology-Driven Education and Teaching System in Universities. *Computational and Mathematical Methods in Medicine*, *2022*, 1–10. Advance online publication. doi:10.1155/2022/8503239 PMID:36124170

Zhang, J., Blaschke, T., Chen, Y., Chen, T., & Terzi, E. (2022). AI for anti-money laundering: A framework for representation learning. *Applied Sciences (Basel, Switzerland)*, *12*(2), 728.

Zhang, Q., Gao, B., & Luqman, A. (2022). Linking green supply chain management practices with competitiveness during covid 19: The role of big data analytics. *Technology in Society*, *70*, 102021. doi:10.1016/j.techsoc.2022.102021 PMID:36090699

Zhang, X., Hao, S., Xu, C., Qian, X., Wang, M., & Jiang, J. (2015). Image classification based on low-rank matrix recovery and Naive Bayes collaborative representation. *Neurocomputing*, *169*, 110–118. doi:10.1016/j.neucom.2015.01.085

Zheng, Z., Xie, S., Dai, H. N., Chen, X., & Wang, H. (2018). Blockchain Challenges and Opportunities: A Survey. *International Journal of Web and Grid Services*, *14*(4), 352–375. doi:10.1504/IJWGS.2018.095647

Zhou, S. S., Zhou, A. J., Feng, J., & Jiang, S. (2019). Dynamic capabilities and organizational performance: The mediating role of innovation. *Journal of Management & Organization*, *25*(5), 731–747. doi:10.1017/jmo.2017.20

# About the Contributors

**Mahmoud El Samad** received his B.S., M.S. and PhD degree in Computer Science from Paul Sabatier University, Toulouse, France. He is currently an Associate Professor at the Lebanese International University (LIU), Tripoli. He is occupying the position of the campus coordinator (Tripoli) for the department of computer science and information technology. His main research interests include blockchain, big data, mobiles agents and query optimization for large-scale distributed systems.

**Hani El-Chaarani** is a full professor of finance. He is a financial consultant in many public and private institutions. He holds a Ph.D in Business Administration from the University of Bordeaux-IV (France), MSc in Business Administration from the IAE-Bordeaux (France) and MSc in Finance and Accounting from the Lebanese University. In addition, he holds a Rural and Economic Development diploma from Illinois University, Excellence in Teaching diploma from Illinois University-USA and Crisis Economic Leadership Diploma from London Business School. He is a charted accountant and visiting professor at various universities, research centers and international organizations. He is the head of Business School at Beirut Arab University - Lebanon. He acted as the keynote speaker and delivered professional talks on various international forums. He is leading the IBERA (International Business and Economic Research Academy). He published close to 50 scientific works in high ranked journals and international conferences. He is a reviewer in several ranked journals. His research interests include financial behavior, corporate governance, SMEs performance, and big data management.

* * *

**Amal El Arid** is a lab engineer and instructor in the electrical and computer engineering department at Rafik Hariri University in Lebanon. She is currently doing a lot of research on information technology in education. She did her Master's Degree in Electrical and Computer Engineering at the American University of Beirut in Lebanon.

**Abir Mounir El Fawal** is a PhD holder in Management from the Lebanese University since January 2018. Born and raised in Tripoli Lebanon. She started her university level education in 2002; she obtained her BS degree in Business Administration from the USJ University in 2005.She completed her Masters degree (DEA) in Management from the USJ University in 2007.She achieved her PhD studies in Management from the Lebanese University in 2018. She has worked for over 13 years at university level in different academic and administrative positions. She is fluent in French and English and experienced in teaching Business Ethics, Human Resource Management and International Business. She is an active researcher and has published many articles in the Marketing, Management and Banking fields. She is engaged in supervising MBA graduate students' projects in Management and Marketing.

**Majida Jrad** has a PhD in Financial Economics- Entrepreneurship, University of Lorraine, France. Master Finance and Financial Institution. Master of Management and Business Administration. Bachelor's degree Accounting and Finance.

**Manohar Kapse** is presently associated with Symbiosis International University, SCMHRD Pune as Assistant Professor in Business Analytics. He had been awarded PhD in Management from Institute of Management Studies, Devi Ahilya Vishwavidyalaya Indore in 2013. He had also done Master Degree in Statistics and M. Phil in Statistics. He teaches Machine Learning, Statistics, Multivariate Analysis, R, SPSS, Research Methodology and Quantitative Techniques. He had been part of many workshops on Machine Learning, SPSS and R as Resource Person in many renowned Institutes, Such as AIIMS Bhopal, Medi-caps University, Jagran Lakecity University, SVIM Indore, APEX Institute of Management, etc. Other than Teaching he is also involved in statistical consultancy to researchers working in different Sciences. He had published more than 20 research papers, many cases and one books.

**Nour Khalil** has a Master of Business Administration, Concentration Marketing, in addition to a Bachelor of Business Administration, Concentration Management. Nour aspires to use her knowledge and expertise to solve challenging business problems, inspire innovation, and have a major influence on the corporate world, while fostering her pursuit of lifelong learning and creative thinking.

**Kasturi Laturkar** is currently working as a Validation Engineer for Validation Associates LLC. She graduated with a M.S. in Chemical Engineering from Syracuse University and a B.Tech in Chemical Engineering from Guru Gobind Singh Indraprastha University, Delhi, India. She has more than 4 years of experience working in commissioning, qualification and validation of upstream and downstream bioprocessing equipment and critical utilities.

**Bassel Maaliky** is the Group Chief Financial Officer (CFO) and Certified Management Accountant (CMA) of Luna Space Holding Company-KSA. He has over 20 years of experience in the finance industry, and he is passionate about helping businesses achieve their financial goals. Having a PhD degree in Business Administration is a valuable asset for Bassel as a Group Chief Financial Officer. It helped him a lot in developing the skills and the knowledge necessary to be successful in his role, especially in developing financial strategies that align with the group's overall business goals. As a CMA, he believes that this certification demonstrates his commitment to the highest standards of professional excellence. CMAs are trained in all aspects of financial management, and they are uniquely qualified to help businesses make informed financial decisions.

**Elangovan N.** is currently Associate Professor in the Institute of Management and PhD –Coordinator for Management programme at CHRIST (Deemed to be University). Before that he served as the Campus Director of National Institute of Fashion Technology, Kannur, Kerala. His educational background spans Engineering, Science and Management with Bachelor degrees with a BE in Mechanical Engineering and BA in Psychology, Post Graduate degrees of MBA Marketing and MSc Psychology, and a MPhil in Psychology. He holds a Doctorate in Management Science specialising in Information systems from Anna University, Chennai. His interest of research is in Strategic Information System Area. Before moving to academics, his experience spans in the textile area where he managed his family business of screen printing for almost 16 years. He has completed a research project funded by Indo-Korean Science and Technology centre (IKST) established by Korea Institute of Science and Technology (KIST), South Korea focused on Social Network Services and Social Medial Platform/ Technology. He has published in Scopus indexed Journals.

**Rita Nasr** holds a Bachelor in Business Administration, well as a Master of Business Administration, both with a Marketing concentration. Rita aims to leverage her education and experience to drive innovation, solve complex business challenges, and make a significant impact in the corporate world, all while nurturing a passion for continuous learning and creativity.

**Ghalia Nassreddine** is an Associate Professor at the Rafik Hariri University, Lebanon. She is a Ph.D holder in information technology and systems from University of Technology of Compiegne, France since 2009. Currently, she is doing a lot of research in Machine Learning and its application in education, Healthcare sector, and renewable systems.

**Jeanne Poulose** is an Associate Professor of Management with School of Business and Management, CHRIST (Deemed to be University), Delhi NCR, India. She is PhD and M. Phil. in Management, and MBA with the specialization in Finance and Human Resources from Osmania University, Hyderabad. She has around 22 years of Industry-Academic experience in the Retail, Banking and Educational sectors through leadership and teaching roles in organizations like ICICI Bank, Global Nxt University, St. Joseph's Degree & PG College etc. She teaches Workforce Planning and Employee Selection, Performance Management and Employee Counselling, Compensation Management, International Human Resource Management, Labour Economics, Managerial Economics and Financial Systems and Services.

**Najib Saab** received his Bachelor of Science degree (BSc.) in Computer Science with the highest distinction from Lebanese International University (LIU), Lebanon. Throughout his undergraduate studies, he ranked first on the Dean's honor list in the Computer Science and IT department for three years. Currently, He is pursuing his Master's degree (MSc.) in Computer Science at Lebanese International University (LIU), where he continues to excel in his academic endeavors. His primary research focus revolves around the dynamic and transformative realm of blockchain technology, and how it can evolve nowadays through its contemporary applications, such as Bitcoin and Ethereum.

**Vinod Sharma** has around 22 years of experience including both academia and industry, at different levels of management, prepare him to be an effective researcher and instructor. He is specialized in Marketing Strategy, Marketing Research & Analytics, and Consumer Behaviour. He has authored over 65 papers in national and international journals and completed in 3 International projects with Yale University, USA on Climate Change and Business Strategy. He has been involved in various consultation research projects, conducted various research workshops and also conducted training program in association with MSME and FIEO on various subjects of management. He is MBA from University of Wales, UK and PhD in Management from University of Indore, India.

# Index


## A

AI 1-3, 5-6, 9-11, 14-19, 24, 26, 28-29, 35-43, 45-71, 73-81, 118, 120, 125, 133, 173-174, 177-179, 205, 224-229, 232, 235-236, 254-262, 264-278, 282-283, 286, 288-289, 291, 293-296, 298-299
Anonymity 130-131, 145, 159-160
Artificial Intelligence 1-2, 5, 9, 14, 19-24, 26, 28-29, 35-62, 64, 66, 68, 70-82, 118-120, 125-127, 133, 173-174, 177, 179, 219, 224, 235, 245, 251, 254-258, 260-274, 276-299
Auditability 89, 107, 131-132, 149, 188

## B

BDA 3-6, 9-11, 14-19
Big Data 1-5, 9, 14, 19-25, 49, 82, 94-95, 123-124, 126, 133, 173-174, 177, 180, 226, 228, 239, 242, 252, 255-257, 276, 282, 287
Blockchain 17-18, 72, 83-98, 101-150, 152-153, 155-162, 164, 166-192, 194, 196-203, 295

## C

Central Bank 70-82
Compliance 59, 66-67, 69, 76, 84, 90, 93, 102-104, 109, 112, 114-115, 117-120, 122, 127-128, 132

## D

Data Analysis 4, 25, 46, 63, 209, 228, 269, 276-277
Data Management 84, 92, 107, 115, 120
Decentralization 130-131, 133, 145, 160, 166, 168, 174, 177, 184, 188, 197
Decentralized Apps (dApps) 146, 158
Deep Learning 42-45, 51-52, 54, 56, 61-62, 69, 204-205, 214, 255, 257, 261, 282, 284, 291
Defect Detection 26, 43, 57
Digital Presence 220, 222

## E

Exploration 2-3, 47, 97, 99, 101, 104-105, 110, 112-113, 116, 118-119, 122, 124, 126, 129, 202, 273

## F

Financial Stability 70-71, 74, 77, 79, 82
Frontiers 1, 7, 24, 122-123, 294, 296, 298
Future Directions 22, 123-124, 248, 250

## G

Geothermal Energy Plant 57

Google Scholar 1, 7, 191

## H

Healthcare 54, 83-96, 125, 128, 274, 284, 287, 289, 295
Human Resources 254-257, 261-267, 270, 272, 274-280, 282-291, 293-294, 297

## I

Image Classification 204, 206-208, 212-213, 215-219
Information 4-5, 11, 16-17, 20-24, 39-40, 52, 55, 60, 66, 70, 74-76, 79, 84, 86, 88-89, 95-99, 101-105, 107-114, 116, 121, 128, 131, 140, 146-147, 155, 159-160, 164, 170, 174, 176, 178, 189, 192, 200-202, 215, 217, 219, 221, 224-226, 228, 232-233, 235, 237-238, 241-242, 244, 246-247, 250, 252-253, 256-258, 261, 263-264, 266, 268, 271, 274-276, 278, 281, 283, 288-289, 292-295, 299
Interoperability 83-86, 91, 95, 112, 189-190, 197
IoT 1, 5, 18, 43-44, 54, 95-96, 103, 106-108, 113, 115, 118, 120, 123, 127, 132-133, 163, 173, 175-177, 202, 205, 257, 265, 284, 289, 291

## M

Machine Learning 1, 17, 26, 37-38, 46-47, 50-51, 53-54, 56-58, 60-63, 66, 73, 80-81, 116, 118-119, 127, 133, 173, 175, 177, 198, 204-206, 210-211, 213, 215, 217-218, 224, 254-255, 257, 259, 261-262, 266, 271, 274, 280, 284, 287, 290-293, 296, 299
Marketing Strategies 220-222, 226, 228-229, 231-232, 236-239, 241-242
Money Laundering 58-64, 66-69, 82

## O

Oil and Gas 97-113, 115-116, 118-129, 296

## P

Persistency 130-131
Power Prediction 26, 44, 46-47, 55-57
Privacy 64-65, 67, 70, 73, 75-76, 79, 84, 86, 88-89, 91-93, 105, 110-112, 114, 116, 131-132, 160, 180, 184-185, 189, 191-192, 195, 197-198, 200, 237, 244, 267, 282-283
Proof of Stake (PoS) 130, 132-133, 153, 161, 165, 168, 172, 177, 181
Proof of Work (PoW) 130, 133, 139, 141, 153, 161, 165-166, 168, 176

## Q

Quantitative Method 11

## R

Renewable Power System 57

## S

Science Direct 1, 7
Security 29, 43, 64, 67, 73, 76, 79, 83-87, 90-93, 101-102, 104, 107, 109-110, 112, 115-116, 119-120, 123, 126-127, 131-132, 136-138, 140, 142, 145, 147-148, 151, 155, 157-158, 160, 162, 166, 169-174, 176, 179-181, 184-185, 190-192, 194, 197-202, 206, 218, 253, 261, 267, 275, 283, 291, 295
Smart Contract 83, 109, 122-123, 146, 148-160, 170, 173, 178, 180, 184-187, 190-192, 194, 197, 199-202
Smart Contracts 86, 88-90, 92, 96-97, 103, 105, 107-109, 113-114, 116-117, 122-123, 126, 130, 132-133, 145-147, 150, 154-158, 160, 167-171, 173, 175-177, 179-181, 183-194, 196-202
Solar Photovoltaic Systems 26, 30, 41-42
Supply Chain 1-6, 9, 11, 14-25, 83-84, 89, 91, 94, 96, 108-109, 116, 120, 122, 126, 131, 156, 175-176, 196-197, 245
Support Vector Machine 44-45, 205, 207, 209-214, 217-219

Sustainability 2-3, 5, 16, 19-20, 24-25, 51, 97, 101, 115-116, 118-119, 167-168, 174, 179, 223, 244-247, 250-253, 278, 284-285, 298
Sustainable Business Growth 220-221, 237-240, 244
Systematic Review 11, 14, 21-22, 55, 87, 94, 125, 128, 216, 285, 289

# T

Talent Management 254-256, 271-273, 278-280, 282-283, 287, 289, 291, 293-294, 298
Taxonomy 55, 85, 133-134, 138, 183, 188, 192-193, 199, 203, 249
Technologies 3, 5, 9, 11, 14-19, 29, 39, 43-44, 48, 50-52, 56, 58, 64, 66, 69, 72, 95, 97, 99, 106-107, 111, 113, 118-121, 125, 127, 129, 131, 133, 155, 160, 166-167, 173, 175, 177, 180, 188, 200-202, 225, 227, 232, 249-250, 254-257, 261, 263-264, 268-270, 273, 275, 277-278, 282-284, 291, 296, 299
Technology 4-5, 16, 18, 20-21, 24-28, 35, 41, 43, 50, 53-55, 60-61, 63-64, 67, 70, 74, 79, 82-85, 87-98, 101, 103, 105-110, 112-127, 129-133, 135-136, 139, 143-145, 155-156, 158, 160, 166, 171-177, 180-181, 184-185, 187-189, 192, 196-202, 205, 213, 215, 218-226, 228, 232, 235-236, 248, 255-256, 258, 261-264, 266, 268, 270-275, 280, 283, 285-294, 296, 298
Transparency 14, 58-59, 64-67, 79, 83-90, 92-94, 96, 101, 104, 107, 119-120, 132, 141, 149, 158, 175-177, 190, 197, 235, 253, 262

# U

Upstream 97-101, 106-107, 110-122, 124-125, 264

# W

Wind Turbine 26, 32-33, 44-47, 50-51, 53, 57
Wind Turbine Plant 26
Workforce Productivity 254

# Recommended Reference Books

IGI Global's reference books are available in three unique pricing formats:
Print Only, E-Book Only, or Print + E-Book.

Order direct through IGI Global's Online Bookstore at **www.igi-global.com** or through your preferred provider.

ISBN: 9781799884552
EISBN: 9781799884576
© 2022; 394 pp.
List Price: US$ **270**

ISBN: 9781799897101
EISBN: 9781799897125
© 2022; 335 pp.
List Price: US$ **250**

ISBN: 9781668441398
EISBN: 9781668441411
© 2022; 291 pp.
List Price: US$ **270**

ISBN: 9781668441534
EISBN: 9781668441558
© 2023; 335 pp.
List Price: US$ **270**

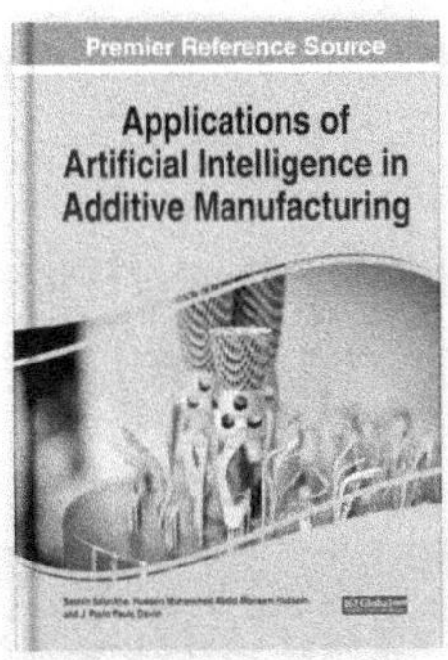


ISBN: 9781799885160
EISBN: 9781799885184
© 2022; 240 pp.
List Price: US$ **270**

ISBN: 9781799887638
EISBN: 9781799887652
© 2022; 306 pp.
List Price: US$ **270**

**Do you want to stay current on the latest research trends, product announcements, news, and special offers?**
Join IGI Global's mailing list to receive customized recommendations, exclusive discounts, and more.
Sign up at: **www.igi-global.com/newsletters.**

Publisher of Timely, Peer-Reviewed Inclusive Research Since 1988

IGI Global
PUBLISHER of TIMELY KNOWLEDGE

**www.igi-global.com** Sign up at www.igi-global.com/newsletters facebook.com/igiglobal twitter.com/igiglobal

www.ingramcontent.com/pod-product-compliance
Lightning Source LLC
LaVergne TN
LVHW081345300926
849161LV00008B/2074